The Edinburgh Companion to Scots

The Edinburgh Companion to Scots

Edited by
John Corbett, J. Derrick McClure and Jane Stuart-Smith

Edinburgh University Press

© in this edition Edinburgh University Press, 2003
© in the individual contributions is retained by the authors

Edinburgh University Press Ltd
22 George Square, Edinburgh

Transferred to digital print 2006

Typeset in 11 on 13pt Ehrhardt
by Hewer Text Ltd, Edinburgh, and
printed and bound in Great Britain by
CPI Antony Rowe. Eastbourne. East Sussex

A CIP record for this book is available from the British Library

ISBN 10: 0 7486 1596 2   (paperback)
ISBN 13: 978 0 7486 1596 4 (paperback)

The right of the contributors
to be identified as authors of this work
has been asserted in accordance with
the Copyright, Designs and Patents Act 1988.

Recipient of a University of Edinburgh
Award for Distinguished Scottish Scholarship

Contents

Acknowledgements

The editors would like to acknowledge the advice and support given by the members of the Language Committee of the Association for Scottish Literary Studies throughout the development of this volume. We are grateful to the International Phonetics Association for permission to reproduce the International Phonetics Alphabet. Thanks are also due to Sarah Edwards of Edinburgh University Press for her guidance, patience and tact. While the editors are grateful to all the contributors for their professionalism and promptness in sharing their expertise, we feel that particular thanks are due to Dr Caroline Macafee for generously making available to us some of her unpublished work on the history of Scots, and for general guidance that has been highly influential in shaping the present volume. Whatever errors remain are, of course, our responsibility.

Notes on Contributors

Dr John Corbett is a Senior Lecturer in English Language at the University of Glasgow. He is the author of *Language and Scottish Literature, Written in the Language of the Scottish Nation: A History of Literary Translation into Scots* and *An Intercultural Approach to English Language Teaching*. He chairs the Language Committee of the Association for Scottish Literary Studies.

Dr Carole Hough is a Lecturer in English Language at the University of Glasgow. She has published extensively on onomastic and other topics, and is editor of the journal *Nomina*. She is a founder member of the Scottish Place-Name Society, a member of the Council of the English Place-Name Society, and a member of the committee of the Society for Name Studies in Britain and Ireland.

Dr Caroline Macafee is a freelance writer and lexicographer, and former reader in English at the University of Aberdeen. She is a leading expert on the Scots language, on which she has written extensively.

J. Derrick McClure is a Senior Lecturer in the School of English and Film Studies at the University of Aberdeen, and author of *Why Scots Matters, Scots and its Literature, Scotland o Gael an Lawlander* (a volume of Scots translations from contemporary Gaelic poetry), *Language, Poetry and Nationhood* and numerous articles and papers. He is Chairman of the Forum for Research in the Languages of Scotland and Ulster, and editor of *Scottish Language*.

Dr Anneli Meurman-Solin is a Lecturer in English Philology at the University of Helsinki. She has published widely in the fields of sociohistorical linguistics, historical stylistics and corpus linguistics. She has compiled the *Helsinki Corpus of Older Scots, 1450–1700*. An outline of the historical development of different non-literary genres is given in her book, *Variation and Change in Early Scottish Prose*.

Jim Miller is Professor of Linguistics and Spoken Language at the University of Edinburgh. He began working on the syntax of Scots and Scottish English in the mid-seventies and has since extended his research to clause syntax and discourse organisation in spontaneous spoken language and in written genres. Other interests are case, aspect and voice and Russian.

Michael B. Montgomery is Distinguished Professor Emeritus of English and Linguistics at the University of South Carolina. He has published extensively on varieties of English in the American South, and has a particular interest in the influence of Scottish and Irish emigrants on North American English. His dictionary of English spoken in the southern Appalachian mountains in the USA is due to be published in 2003.

Margaret Scott is an Assistant Etymology Editor for the *Oxford English Dictionary*, and a member of the committee of the society for Name Studies in Britain and Ireland. Her forthcoming PhD thesis at the University of Glasgow is entitled 'The Germanic Toponymicon of Southern Scotland: Place-Name Elements and their Contribution to the Lexicon and Onomasticon'.

Jeremy J. Smith is Professor of English Philology at the University of Glasgow. Recent publications include *An Historical Study of English, Essentials of Early English* and (with S. Horobin) *An Introduction to Middle English*. He is currently working, with S. Horobin and M. Stenroos, on a new grammar of Middle English.

Dr Jane Stuart-Smith is a Lecturer in English Language at the University of Glasgow. She has been working on the phonetics and phonology of Glaswegian since 1997. Her main research interests are: phonetics; the causes and mechanisms of sound change (historical, sociolinguistic, and phonetic); and British Asian languages, especially Panjabi.

List of Figures and Tables

TABLES

THE INTERNATIONAL PHONETIC ALPHABET (revised to 1993, updated 1996)

CONSONANTS (PULMONIC)

© 1996 IPA

	Bilabial	Labiodental	Dental	Alveolar	Postalveolar	Retroflex	Palatal	Velar	Uvular	Pharyngeal	Glottal
Plosive	p b			t d		ʈ ɖ	c ɟ	k ɡ	q ɢ		ʔ
Nasal	m	ɱ		n		ɳ	ɲ	ŋ	N		
Trill	B			r					R		
Tap or Flap				ɾ		ɽ					
Fricative	ɸ β	f v	θ ð	s z	ʃ ʒ	ʂ ʐ	ç ʝ	x ɣ	χ ʁ	ħ ʕ	h ɦ
Lateral fricative				ɬ ɮ							
Approximant		ʋ		ɹ		ɻ	j	ɰ			
Lateral approximant				l		ɭ	ʎ	L			

Where symbols appear in pairs, the one to the right represents a voiced consonant. Shaded areas denote articulations judged impossible.

CONSONANTS (NON-PULMONIC)

Clicks		Voiced implosives		Ejectives	
ʘ	Bilabial	ɓ	Bilabial	'	Examples:
ǀ	Dental	ɗ	Dental/alveolar	p'	Bilabial
ǃ	(Post)alveolar	ʄ	Palatal	t'	Dental/alveolar
ǂ	Palatoalveolar	ɠ	Velar	k'	Velar
ǁ	Alveolar lateral	ʛ	Uvular	s'	Alveolar fricative

OTHER SYMBOLS

ʍ Voiceless labial-velar fricative	ɕ ʑ Alveolo-palatal fricatives
w Voiced labial-velar approximant	ɺ Voiced alveolar lateral flap
ɥ Voiced labial-palatal approximant	ɧ Simultaneous ʃ and x
ʜ Voiceless epiglottal fricative	
ʢ Voiced epiglottal fricative	Affricates and double articulations can be represented by two symbols joined by a tie bar if necessary. k͡p t͡s
ʡ Epiglottal plosive	

VOWELS

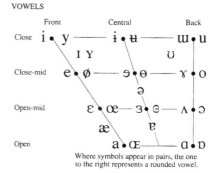

Where symbols appear in pairs, the one to the right represents a rounded vowel.

SUPRASEGMENTALS

ˈ	Primary stress
ˌ	Secondary stress ˌfoʊnəˈtɪʃən
ː	Long eː
ˑ	Half-long eˑ
˘	Extra-short ĕ
|	Minor (foot) group
‖	Major (intonation) group
.	Syllable break ɹi.ækt
‿	Linking (absence of a break)

DIACRITICS

Diacritics may be placed above a symbol with a descender, e.g. ŋ̊

̥	Voiceless	n̥ d̥	̤ Breathy voiced	b̤ a̤	̪ Dental	t̪ d̪
̬	Voiced	s̬ t̬	̰ Creaky voiced	b̰ a̰	̺ Apical	t̺ d̺
ʰ	Aspirated	tʰ dʰ	̼ Linguolabial	t̼ d̼	̻ Laminal	t̻ d̻
̹	More rounded	ɔ̹	ʷ Labialized	tʷ dʷ	̃ Nasalized	ẽ
̜	Less rounded	ɔ̜	ʲ Palatalized	tʲ dʲ	ⁿ Nasal release	dⁿ
̟	Advanced	u̟	ˠ Velarized	tˠ dˠ	ˡ Lateral release	dˡ
̠	Retracted	e̠	ˤ Pharyngealized	tˤ dˤ	̚ No audible release	d̚
̈	Centralized	ë	̴ Velarized or pharyngealized	ɫ		
̽	Mid-centralized	e̽	̝ Raised	e̝ (ɹ̝ = voiced alveolar fricative)		
̩	Syllabic	n̩	̞ Lowered	e̞ (β̞ = voiced bilabial approximant)		
̯	Non-syllabic	e̯	̘ Advanced Tongue Root	e̘		
˞	Rhoticity	ɚ a˞	̙ Retracted Tongue Root	e̙		

TONES AND WORD ACCENTS

LEVEL		CONTOUR	
e̋ or ꜒	Extra high	ě or ꜓	Rising
é ꜓	High	ê ꜔	Falling
ē ꜔	Mid	e᷄ ꜓	High rising
è ꜕	Low	e᷅ ꜕	Low rising
ȅ ꜖	Extra low	e᷈ ꜖	Rising-falling
ꜜ	Downstep	↗	Global rise
ꜛ	Upstep	↘	Global fall

Reproduced with the permission of the International Phonetic Association:
http://www.arts.gla.ac.uk/IPA/ipa.html

CHAPTER I

A Brief History of Scots

John Corbett, J. Derrick McClure and Jane Stuart-Smith

This volume has a specific purpose. It attempts to help younger or less experienced scholars to identify key topics of research into historical and present-day language use in Scotland with respect to 'Scots', here conceived of as a language continuum that ranges from 'Broad' Scots to 'Scottish Standard English'. In addition, the chapters in the volume outline some of the methods that have been or might be used to explore these research topics. Thus, the editors and contributors hope to stimulate further exploration of language use in Scotland, whether in the form of undergraduate essays and dissertations, or larger-scale post-graduate and post-doctoral research.

As Charles Jones observes in his preface to *The Edinburgh History of the Scots Language* (1997), Scots has suffered from relative scholarly neglect in comparison to English. Jones' anthology goes a long way towards remedying this neglect by providing 'the first full-scale, detailed and comprehensive attempt to provide a history of the Scots language from the time of its earliest records to the modern period' (Jones ed. 1997: vii). The present volume is not a 'condensed' version of *The Edinburgh History of the Scots Language*, nor does it pretend to be full-scale, detailed and comprehensive. Rather, while the various chapters of this book do indeed sketch out some of the main areas of our understanding of Scots, they are also concerned with indicating the remaining gaps in our understanding, and they invite succeeding generations to begin to fill them. In this sense, the present volume is intended as a companion to those students who are interested not only in learning the known facts about Scots but also in *creating* knowledge through further exploration.

For those readers newly embarking on this scholarly adventure, some orientation is necessary, and so this introductory chapter offers a working definition of 'Scots' and a brief summary of its historical development. The more pessimistic chapters in this book speak of Scots being in the last stages of 'language death'. Even if this is so, the speech of earlier generations in lowland Scotland still profoundly influences everyday language use today, and an understanding of that speech is necessary for us to comprehend fully current and future use. In linguistic terms, *synchronic* studies (that is, studies of contemporary language) require a *diachronic* (or historical) perspective.

WHAT IS 'SCOTS'?

'Scots' is described above as 'a language continuum ranging from Broad Scots to Scottish Standard English'. All Scots speakers are instantly recognisable by their accent, and even Scottish Standard English speakers are distinguished from the speakers of other standard varieties of English at the phonological level, not just the phonetic. In other words, the system of pronunciation of Scots and its prosody are distinctive. However, while written Broad Scots is easily identifiable by its distinctive vocabulary and grammar, written Scottish Standard English differs less obviously from other standard varieties of English around the world. At the written level, only certain idioms, vocabulary items, grammatical uses and possibly distribution of such linguistic features as modal auxiliary verb uses, distinguish written Scottish Standard English from the written forms of Standard English south of the border or across the Atlantic. Some therefore prefer to exclude 'Scottish Standard English' from their definition of Scots, and focus on the more distinctive 'Broad Scots' end of the continuum. When the term 'Scots' is used without qualification in this book, it is a variety of Broad Scots that is usually meant. However, since this book seeks to encourage exploration of all aspects of language usage in lowland Scotland, an inclusive definition is here preferred (cf. the entries on 'Scots' and 'Scottish English' in McArthur ed. 1992: 893–9; 903–5).

The concept of a linguistic 'continuum' from 'Broad Scots' to 'Scottish Standard English' also requires some refinement. A continuum suggests that there is a shading and overlap of language uses from 'Broad Scots', with its highly distinctive vocabulary, pronunciation and grammar, to 'Scottish Standard English', whose vocabulary and grammar are largely shared with other standard varieties of English around the globe. However, the image of a continuum as a simple line running from 'Broad Scots' to 'Scottish Standard English' ignores substantial complexities. First of all, 'Broad Scots' refers not to a single linguistic entity, but to overlapping regional and social language varieties, most of which are declining or transforming, generation on generation. 'Broad Scots' is now largely spoken, although it was once written, and even today it continues to be used in poetry, fiction and drama, whether in regional, social or in 'synthesised' literary varieties, and there have been efforts to broaden its written uses to non-literary genres (cf. McClure and Corbett this volume). The term 'Broad Scots' today covers the regional varieties of Shetland and Orkney; the North East around Aberdeen; the Central Belt from Edinburgh and the Lothians, down through

Stirlingshire, Glasgow, Ayrshire and Galloway; the Borders; and the 'Ulster Scots' regions of Northern Ireland. Within these regional varieties there is, of course, further local variation. In particular, the major cities of Aberdeen, Dundee, Edinburgh and Glasgow also have a wide range of social varieties.

By no means have all of these regional and social varieties been equally studied. One of the most ambitious attempts to provide an overview of regional variation was the Linguistic Survey of Scotland, undertaken by the University of Edinburgh in 1949 after earlier preparatory work. It focused on Gaelic and regional Scots, but neglected urban social varieties. Its findings were published in the *Linguistic Atlas of Scotland* (Mather and Spietel eds 1975, 1977, 1986). The work of the LSS complements the other major linguistic projects of the twentieth century, the *Scottish National Dictionary* (SND) and the *Dictionary of the Older Scottish Tongue* (DOST). SND attempted to provide a record of the distinctive vocabulary of regional Scots (omitting those lexical items shared with southern English) from 1700 to the twentieth century, while DOST took on the more ambitious task of providing a record of the whole vocabulary of Scots (including items shared with southern English) from 1375 to 1700. These ambitious, independent lexicographical projects each took several generations to complete. The publication of the final volume of DOST in 2002 coincides with the formation of a single new body, Scottish Language Dictionaries (www.sldl.org.uk), whose aim is to continue the distinguished lexicographical tradition of its predecessors. There is indeed much more lexicographical work to be done, specifically the updating of SND, whose final volume was edited in 1976, the expansion of the early and less comprehensive volumes of DOST and the revision of the *Concise Scots Dictionary* (1985), a single-volume selection from the two multi-volume parent dictionaries. If dialect studies and lexicography stand out as the most sustained and distinguished forms of linguistic research in the twentieth century, both fall into the trap of having favoured regional forms of Broad Scots and neglected urban Scots. This omission was conditioned by negative linguistic attitudes towards urban Scots, particularly Glaswegian, in the first half of the twentieth century, when the two dictionary projects were initiated. One of the tasks of the new dictionaries body must be to make good this gap.

In recent years, sociolinguistic studies have turned to urban Scots (e.g. Macaulay and Trevelyan 1977; Macafee 1983, 1994; cf. Stuart Smith this volume) and it has been the turn of regional varieties to be relatively neglected (though see Macaulay 1991). Ideally, neither regional nor social varieties of Scots should suffer neglect, but linguistic research is labour-intensive and time-consuming. We badly need a framework for funding and training so that individuals and teams can work systematically to ensure that our understanding of language use in Scotland is comprehensive and up-to-date.

In contrast with the wide variety of usages found in Broad Scots, it is in the nature of a standard language variety to be relatively fixed, to suppress variation at least in vocabulary and grammar. At the Scottish Standard English end of the language continuum we find those usages that are most influenced by the mass education system and the mass media, both of which are crucial in instilling the belief that a fixed set of linguistic usages is 'normal' and 'correct'. Nevertheless, Scottish Standard English differs in some features of grammar and idiom from those standard varieties of English found south of the border, in North America, in Australasia and now elsewhere. For example, it is widely believed that the Scottish Standard English system of modal auxiliary verbs is influenced by Broad Scots, although more extensive study is needed to determine exactly how (cf. Miller this volume). The vocabulary of Scottish Standard English also includes distinctive items such as *firth* 'estuary', *uplift* 'collect' and *outwith* 'outside of'. Partly because it falls somewhere between Broad Scots and southern Standard English, Scottish Standard English is also under-researched, again with sporadic exceptions (e.g. Douglas 2000). The occasional and labour-intensive nature of research into language use in Scotland has contributed to the patchiness of its coverage. However, with the institution of the SCOTS corpus project by Glasgow and Edinburgh Universities (www.scottishcorpus.ac.uk), the opportunity exists for collecting and analysing data on the whole range of the Broad Scots–SSE continuum, as well as on the other languages of Scotland, although this project is currently in its very early days. As this volume goes to press, there is also a glimmer of hope that a proposed Institute for the Languages of Scotland will help co-ordinate future research efforts into language use in Scotland.

A BRIEF HISTORY OF SCOTS

The early history of Scots was outlined by Murison (1979) and Aitken (1985), and further details have been filled in by, for example, the contributors to Jones ed. (1997). Macafee and Aitken's introduction to the final volume of DOST (2002) offers a detailed description of current knowledge based on lexicographical, archaeological and place-name evidence (see also Scott this volume). Meurman-Solin (this volume) demonstrates the potential for linguistic study of computerised corpora of Older Scots. This summary draws largely on these sources. A fuller treatment can be found in McClure (1994).

Old English to Pre-literary Scots (before 1375)

What makes Scots similar to present-day English is a shared origin in the related, or 'cognate', Germanic language varieties introduced to the British Isles by Angle and Saxon invaders and settlers, from the fifth to the seventh centuries. What makes Scots different from present-day English is partly that it owes more to the Anglian than the Saxon variety of Old English, and partly that, over the generations, the different kinds of contact that Scots and English have engaged in with other languages (and with each other) have given them distinctive linguistic characteristics.

There are two separate strands of the Old English legacy to Scots. The earliest appearance of a language derived from Old English into what is now Scotland is that of Anglian invaders, who established the Kingdom of Bernicia in 547. By the first half of the seventh century, this kingdom had probably expanded to include part of the present-day Lothians. Present-day Broad Scots still has traces of its Old English foundations, for example in the terms *oxter* ('armpit' < OE *ōhsta* or *ōxta*) and in the term *quean* or *quine* ('young girl' < OE *cwene*). The Scots pronunciations of words like 'mouse' and 'house' as [mus] and [hus] (from OE *mūs*, and *hūs*) are also closer than most current southern English pronunciations to the Anglo-Saxon sound system introduced into the Lothians a millennium ago.

The rest of Scotland at this time spoke several Celtic languages. North of the Anglian settlements, people spoke Q-Celtic, the ancestor of today's Gaelic. This language had come over from Ireland with the Scoti tribe in the late fifth century, and it largely replaced P-Celtic, or 'Cumbric', an earlier variety that, south of the border, developed into present-day Welsh. The names 'P' and 'Q' Celtic refer to one variety having the sound 'p' where the other has 'q' (pronounced [kw] and usually spelled <c>). The older variety, P-Celtic, was spoken from Galloway through Cumbria to northern Yorkshire (Spietel and Mather 1968: 522ff). Place-name studies trace the fortunes of these different language communities (see Scott, this volume).

The Anglian language that was established by the early settlers was supplemented by further waves of settlers speaking cognate Germanic language varieties. In the eighth century, Vikings began raiding the northern and western isles of Scotland, establishing themselves particularly in the northern isles and Caithness. The Earls of Orkney held dual allegiance to the Kings of Norway and Scotland from the eleventh century until the fifteenth century, when Orkney and Shetland fell forfeit to Scotland as a consequence of an unpaid dowry. The language that the Vikings bequeathed Orkney and Shetland was a Norwegian variety, 'Norn', which survived in Orkney until the eighteenth century, and in Shetland until the beginning of the nineteenth. When, in the fourteenth century, the Scots language belatedly arrived in the northern isles, it assumed the status of the prestige variety, until this role was taken by English from the sixteenth century onwards. Old Norse and Norn, however, impacted powerfully on the place-names of the northern isles and on the everyday vocabulary of the Insular variety of Scots. Many Insular Scots terms have Old Norse origins or contemporary Norwegian cognates; for example *kyauve* ('struggle', 'tumble' < ON *kafa*, 'to plunge or dive'), *kemp* ('contend' < ON *kempa*, 'contender'), and *knap* ('munch', 'eat greedily'; compare Norwegian *knappa*, 'to eat noisily and greedily').

As well as settling in the northern islands, Vikings, even more significantly, attacked and finally settled in the central part of what is now England, leaving Wessex in the south, and part of Northumbria in the north, under Anglo-Saxon rule. There are different theories about the process of the Scandinavian settlement of England, but what cannot be disputed is that the settlers who lived under the Danelaw in the 'Great Scandinavian Belt' in central England left their indelible mark on the place-names and language. The speech of the Vikings and that of the Anglo-Saxons were related, and possibly, to some extent, mutually intelligible, and a mixed language, sometimes called 'Anglo-Scandinavian', was the result of contact between the various speech communities. It is possible that the area of Scandinavian influence extended north of the border into the earlier Anglian territory in Lothian. Certainly, from 1066 onwards, the historical influence of the mixture of Old Norse and Old English was to be much greater than the earlier influence of Anglian on its own. Of all the contact languages that have contributed to the vocabulary of Scots, it is the Scandinavian ones that most distinguish it from southern English. The Anglo-Scandinavian tongue introduced into Scotland terms like *gowk* ('cuckoo', 'fool', 'trick' < ON *gaukr*), *gype* ('to stare foolishly', 'to play the fool' or 'a foolish person' < ON *geip* 'nonsense', or *geipa* 'to talk nonsense') and *lachter* or *louchter* ('lock of hair', 'tuft of grass', or 'handful of hay' < ON *lagð*, 'tuft of wool or hair'). It is important to remember, however, that Old Norse and Old English were cognate languages, and so it is sometimes difficult to tell if a Scots word has its origin in one or the other. A case in point is *handsel* 'a gift intended to bring good luck', which might derive from OE *handselen* 'giving into the hands' or ON *handsal* 'giving of the hands'. Certainly, however, Old Norse profoundly affects not simply the vocabulary but also the pronunciation of Scots. Murison (1979: 4) points out that ON had velar plosive consonants, /k/ and /g/, before front vowels, where OE had affricates, /tʃ/ and /dʒ/:

> This phonological correspondence explains many of the distinctions between the Northern and Scots forms and the Southern and Standard English: *kirk, church; kirn, churn; muckle, much; breeks, breeches; dike, ditch; sic, such; ilk, each; brig, bridge; rig, ridge; sing, singe;* similarly with *sk* and *sh* as in *skirl, shrill; skriech, shriek; mask, mash.*
>
> There are also differences arising from variations in vowel development, as in *lowp, leap; cowp* (to bargain), *cheap; nowt, neat; ain, own; strae, straw; hing, hang; trig; true,* and somewhat similarly *blae, blue; brae, brow.*

More detail can be found on the reconstruction of the sounds of Older Scots in Macafee (Chapter 7 of this volume).

The spread of Anglo-Scandinavian throughout lowland Scotland, eventually replacing Q-Celtic in the north-east and P-Celtic in the south-west, was indirectly furthered by the Norman Conquest of England in 1066. At this period, the language of the King of Scots and his courtiers was Q-Celtic, the ancestor of present-day Gaelic. When Norman French rule was established in England, the English princess, Margaret, fled to Scotland to marry the widower, King Malcom III. Margaret, who was later canonised, and whose chapel still stands in Edinburgh Castle, brought with her an entourage of English-speaking courtiers. She also exerted an anglicising influence on the personnel of the Scottish church and a romanising influence on its doctrines and practices. After Malcolm's death, the kingdom passed first into the hands of his brother, then of four of his sons. His youngest son, David I, who had spent many of his formative years in the Normanised English court, did most to spread the use of Anglo-Scandinavian through lowland Scotland. During his reign, from 1124–53, he granted land to Norman French-speaking barons, feudal tenants, who brought with them considerable numbers of Anglo-Scandinavian-speaking retainers from the 'Great Scandinavian Belt'. On the Norman model, David I and his successors established burghs, towns with special trading privileges, conferred by royal charter. These privileged trading towns became magnets for immigrants from 'Flanders, the Rhineland, northern France, and England, especially eastern England' (Barrow 1981: 92). Finally, David I established abbeys and monasteries, such as that at Jedburgh, and put in place a parochial administration that probably also spoke Anglo-Scandinavian.

In short, what we now call Scots developed from an extended and complicated period of immigration and language contact. There is some evidence of the interaction between Celtic and Anglo-Scandinavian speech communities in the relatively few loan-words from Gaelic into Scots, words such as *gow* (a literary term for a blacksmith, surviving now as a personal name < Gael. *gobha*), *golach* ('insect', 'ground beetle' < Gael. *gobhlag*, 'earwig', or 'fork-shaped stick') and *fallachan* ('concealed store' < Gael. *falachan* 'hidden treasure'). Other language groups were added to the linguistic mix; for example, a colony of skilled Dutch- or Flemish-speaking settlers was established by the feudal kings to encourage the indigenous weaving industry, bequeathing us the Scottish surname *Fleming* (cf. Hough this volume) and various other Dutch or Flemish borrowings, such as *growgrane* (the fabric, 'grogram' < MFl *grouvegrain*). Murison (1979: 5) writes:

> The practical result of all this mixing of populations can be seen in the attestations to charters, where the several signatories may have Welsh, Gaelic, Norse, Anglo-Saxon and French names. Gaelic families tended to choose English or French names for their children; Celtic officials are followed by ones with non-Celtic names. The population must have become even more polyglot in the twelfth and thirteenth centuries, and we must suppose that the *lingua franca* of them all was the one that ultimately prevailed, the new, highly Frenchified English.

Large-scale immigration from the Anglo-Scandinavian areas of England in the eleventh and twelfth centuries, as suggested by Barrow (1980), helps explain various mysteries about the early development of Scots, namely, the relatively low amount of lexical borrowing from the Celtic languages, and the relatively high influence of Scandinavian on Scots (Macafee and Aitken 2002). However, as Murison observes, the Anglo-Scandinavian speech that operated as the *lingua franca* of the traders in the burghs, the administrators of feudal law and the clerics in the church was itself continuing to change. For some period of time, at least, the Norman aristocracy spoke a Scandinavian-influenced French (the Normans, too, came from Viking stock). The church clerics might have spoken Anglo-Scandinavian, but they wrote in medieval Latin, the European language of scholarship, religion and law. The Anglo-Scandinavian ancestor of Scots would originally have been restricted to certain contexts of use, mainly speech, and possibly (in some cases) for trading purposes between native speakers of other languages, like Gaelic, French and Dutch. However, in a classic case of 'language shift' (cf. Corbett this volume) it began gradually to spread into a broader range of communicative functions, written as well as spoken. It became the everyday language of the aristocracy as well as the bourgeoisie and peasantry. It continued to spread north and west. Over time, it also gained a name, *Inglis*, a term used initially by Scots to refer to Scots and English, in contrast, say, to *Erse* 'Irish', that is, 'Gaelic'. Not until the late fifteenth and early sixteenth centuries did lowland Scots begin to distinguish their own language as 'Scottis' (McClure 1981a).

Early Scots (1375–1450)

Literary Scots is marked by the appearance of John Barbour's *Brus* in 1375. The late fourteenth and early fifteenth centuries saw Inglis beginning to encroach into other communicative functions that had previously been the sole preserve of French and Latin. Inglis superseded French in leisure and instructional reading, with the *Brus* joined, for example, by a translation of a romance about Alexander the Great, and versions of French chivalric manuals in the first half of the fifteenth century. Inglis also superseded Latin in administrative prose; crucially, the Acts of the Parliament of Scotland began to be recorded in the vernacular in 1390, and the earlier Latin Acts were also translated in 1425. Scots clearly had attained pre-eminent status in lowland Scotland by this time, though activity in the other languages of Scotland continued (cf. Jack 1997; Jack and Rozendaal 1997).

As Scots moved from speech into the written domains formerly associated with French and Latin, its vocabulary necessarily changed, particularly to incorporate technical and learned vocabulary from these languages, and the 'aureate' latinate terms used by both Scottish and English poets in the Early and Middle Scots period to elevate their literary style (see Smith this volume). Whereas the Old

English, Old Norse, Gaelic and Dutch vocabulary items that came into Scots have the everyday flavour of natural features of landscape and weather, or agricultural and small-town occupations such as farming and weaving, the Latin and French borrowings into the written language speak of law, religion, philosophy and power, as well as other, more mundane activities. So we have, for example, *exerce* ('make use of', 'discharge the duties of an office' < OF *exercer* < L *exercēre*), *justiciary* ('the office or jurisdiction of a justice' < MedL *justitiarius*) and *pallalls* or *pallies* ('hopscotch', or 'the counter with which it is played' < F. *palet*, 'a stone thown at a target in various games'). Up until the fourteenth century, borrowings into Scots from French tended to come from the Norman variety that was used by the feudal aristocracy. Later borrowings come from central French, the language of the court in Paris. These two streams of borrowing result in Norman/Parisian 'doublets' in Scots and southern English (Murison 1979: 7). That is, most often the Scots form derives from Norman French while today's southern English cognate term derives from central French, as in *spulyie/spulzie* 'spoil', *failyie/failzie* 'fail', and *campioun* 'champion'. Occasionally, it is the Scots term that derives from central French, while the southern English term is from Norman French, as in *chanoun*, 'the religious office of canon', and *leal* 'loyal'. The relatively greater impact of French loanwords into Scots than into southern English between the fourteenth and the sixteenth centuries can partly be explained by the 'Auld Alliance'. This expression of cultural and political affinity between Scotland and France goes back to antiquity, at least according to tradition, and was expressed in a formal pact made by John Balliol and Philip the Fair in 1295. It lasted through to the Reformation in 1560.

Middle Scots (1450–1700)

If the Early Scots period saw a rise in status and a shift towards Scots in Scotland, the Middle Scots period saw its consolidation, before another language shift towards English prompted its gradual decline from the mid-sixteenth century onwards. Murison (1979: 8–9) writes:

> The years 1460–1560 can be considered the heyday of the Scots tongue as a full national language showing all the signs of a rapidly developing, all-purpose speech, as distinct from English as Portuguese from Spanish, Dutch from German or Swedish from Danish. The Spanish ambassador at the court of James IV described the distinction as like that between Castilian and Aragonese.

This 'full national language' was, however, in speech and writing, far from a single homogenous language variety. The Early Scots period is usually considered a time in which Scots was closest in vocabulary, grammar and orthography to the

Northern English dialect of Middle English. As we have seen, both varieties were largely the products of Anglo-Scandinavian speakers, influenced over time by contact with other speech communities. As the Middle Scots period continues, there is first divergence from and then convergence with the forms used south of the border. Meurman-Solin (1997a: 7) notes some of the orthographic features that English and Scots share at this time, and those spellings and lexical variants that tend to differentiate them:

'Scots' forms	'English' forms
guid, gude	*gude, good*
adoir	*adore*
eis	*ese/ease*
cais	*case*
buik	*buke/boke*
quh-	*wh-*
thai	*thay*
knaw	*know*
sa	*so*
richt	*right*
scho, sche	*she*
spoilze, distrenze	*spoil, distrain*

By tracing the preferred use of such forms across a range of Scots texts over the Early and Middle Scots periods, scholars such as Devitt (1989) and Meurman-Solin (1993a, 1997a) have attempted to gauge the degree of differentiation between Scots and English, and the progress of Scots towards a standard written variety. While Meurman-Solin (1997a: 21) acknowledges that 'continued variation characterises the history of Scots', she confirms Murison's claim that divergence of Scots from Northern English is clear from the mid-fifteenth century. By the middle of the following century there is increased variation that results from a tension between further divergence and the tendency towards convergence with English forms, as the two nations moved closer politically and, in some respects, culturally.

The forces driving anglicisation in Scotland from the mid-sixteenth century are well-known. The marriage in 1503 of James IV to Margaret Tudor of England ('The Thistle and the Rose') signalled an early attempt at rapprochement with the 'auld enemie', albeit that this was to be shattered by renewed hostilities culminating in a disastrous Scottish defeat at Flodden Field in 1513. James V's reign saw the impact in Scotland of a cultural revolution that was sweeping through Europe: the Reformation. The rise of the reformed church in Scotland proved to be a significant anglicising force for a variety of reasons. First, its preachers used the power of the printing press to reach readerships in both

Scotland and England. Secondly, the reformers championed a vernacular 'plain style' of writing that rejected the long complex sentences, modelled on Latin 'periods', and the aureate diction that characterised 'baroque' (and, by association, Catholic) Scottish prose. Most importantly, however, the reformers also championed access to holy writ in the vernacular, and the biblical translation they adopted was produced in Geneva in 1560 by Protestants exiled from England. It was conveniently sized, printed in legible Roman type, clearly laid out, and, until the appearance of the Authorised Version in 1611, the most popular version of the Bible in Scotland, forging a close association between the communicative domain of religion and written English.

The proliferation of printed books, and the productivity of English printers compared to their Scottish-based counterparts, led to further anglicisation of written texts in the late 1500s. There were home-based printers who published in Scots, but there were also Scottish-based printers who shifted significantly towards English. In short, the process of language shift had begun, with English encroaching into several key domains, and this process accelerated after the Union of Crowns in 1603. A century after the marriage of the Thistle and the Rose, James V's grandson successfully negotiated his claim to the English crown, left vacant by the death of Elizabeth I, and the United Kingdom was born. James VI had been a considerable patron of the arts in Scotland, and his patronage continued in England (for example, Shakespeare wrote *Macbeth* to celebrate his ancestry and to flatter his interest in witchcraft). The king's own published writing, and that of the courtiers he took with him to London, quickly adapted to the norms governing Early Modern English. Even those Scots who chose to remain in Scotland, like William Drummond of Hawthornden, were careful to follow the 'polite' conventions of courtly language in their anglicised poems. Non-literary texts, private letters and public documents, followed the same pattern. By the end of the 1600s, most texts in Scotland were written after the English fashion.

It is difficult to determine the extent of anglicising forces on speech towards the end of the Middle Scots period. The anglicising of written texts is so overwhelming that it is sometimes assumed that Broad Scots died out in the late 1600s. However, as Macafee and Aitken (forthcoming; original emphasis) points out, 'The history of the development of *Scots* from the late 16th century to the 18th is still to be written'. Certainly, there is evidence that Broad Scots was being spoken across a wide range of communicative domains until the late seventeenth century. Not least of these was law, which became, with the Church of Scotland, one of the key Scottish civic institutions after the departure south of the Scottish court. George Mackenzie, Lord Advocate between 1677 and 1689, and an author whose written vernacular prose is in elegant Augustan English, is still able to claim in *What Eloquence is Fit for the Bar* that, of French, English and Scots, the best language for pleading a case in law is Scots. Even so, as Aitken (1979: 91–3) notes, after the restoration of Charles II in 1660, upper-class and ambitious Scots were more likely than before to frequent southern England, seeking opportunities for advancement, and giving rise to the stereotype of the 'Scotchman on the make'. In their private letters, which are more likely than public documents to reflect spoken norms, there is some evidence of a mixing of Broad Scots and English options. However, in Archibald Pitcairne's play, *The Assembly*, written in 1692, the speech of all but the oldest of the upper classes is presented as southern English.

Modern Scots (1700 onwards)

The Treaty of Union of 1707, whereby the Scottish parliament was absorbed into the Westminster assembly, giving birth to Great Britain as a single political and economic entity, is sometimes presented as the final nail in the coffin of Broad Scots. Murison (1979: 9) writes:

> The Union of 1707 was the last act in the story. When the legislature removed to London, English became in effect the official language of the whole country for law, administration, education and church usage, spoken as well as written. Scots became more restricted in use and scope, having lost spiritual status at the Reformation, social status at the Union of the Crowns, and political status with the Parliamentary Union.

Despite the Treaty, however, there was a revival of written Broad Scots, although largely confined to the sphere of literature. The very unpopularity of political union prompted a cultural backlash, involving the updating and republishing of older Scottish literature, and new poems and songs, often based on the ballads and songs of the oral tradition. The *literateurs* were no longer courtiers but members of the middle classes: people like Allan Ramsay, a wigmaker, bookseller and publisher, Robert Fergusson, a university-educated clerk, and Robert Burns, whose immediate ancestors were 'substantial tenant farmers' (Sprott 1996: 12). These writers and their imitators drew upon the still ubiquitous Broad Scots speech to craft sophisticated popular verse. However, they were writing for a readership largely schooled in written English, and written Scots from 1700 on shows ample evidence of this new state of affairs. The spelling practices of Ramsay, for example, introduced elements of English orthography to represent Scottish pronunciation, for example, < oo > rather than < ou > to signify /u/ in words like *aboot*, *hoose*. Ramsay also introduced the practice of using apostrophes to indicate where letters would be missing, were the word spelled in the English fashion, thus *fu'* for *full*. While these strategies no doubt increased the accessibility of Broad Scots for an English-reading market, they also had the unfortunate effect of suggesting that Broad Scots was not a separate language system, but rather a divergent and inferior form of English.

Meanwhile, others in the middle and upper classes sought to eradicate traces of Broad Scots, first from their writing and then, up to a point, from their speech. For example, the philosopher and historian David Hume compiled a list of 'scotticisms' to be banished from his writings, while the lawyer and writer James Boswell wished to avoid the broadest features of Scottish pronunciation without necessarily aping a southern English accent. In his biography of Samuel Johnson, Boswell (1952: 192; original emphasis) recalls:

> Upon another occasion I talked to him [Johnson] on this subject, having taken some pains to improve my pronunciation, by the aid of the late Mr. Love, of Drury-lane theatre, when he was a player at Edinburgh, and also of old Mr. Sheridan. Johnson said to me, 'Sir, your pronunciation is not offensive.' With this concession I was well satisfied; and let me give my countrymen of North Britain an advice not to aim at absolute perfection in this respect; not to speak *High English*, as we are apt to call what is far removed from the *Scotch*, but which is by no means *good English*, and makes, 'the fools who use it,' truly ridiculous. Good English is plain, easy and smooth in the mouth of an unaffected English Gentleman. A studied and factitious pronunciation, which requires perpetual attention and imposes perpetual constraint, is exceedingly disgusting. A small intermixture of provincial peculiarities may, perhaps, have an agreeable effect, as the notes of different birds concur in the harmony of the grove, and please more than if they were exactly alike.

Hume and Boswell's like-minded contemporaries were aided in their quest for a more refined Scottish pronunciation by the growing industry of language gurus such as William Scott, who in the 1780s taught classes and gave lectures in elocution to gentlemen and ladies, old and young, and who published guides to grammar, spelling, pronunciation and reading (Jones 1997: 272). Jones (1996, 1997: 279) painstakingly reconstructs eighteenth-and nineteenth-century Scottish pronunciation from hitherto neglected evidence in the form of surviving catalogues of pronunciation characteristics, special spelling systems (sometimes written by would-be reformers), spelling books (often aimed at schoolchildren or 'ladies'), pronouncing dictionaries, grammar books and general essays on the language. What he charts is the development of a new 'refined' Scottish pronunciation amongst the rising middle classes, influenced by but not identical to the prestige accent adopted by polite society in southern England. The 'Scottish Standard English' end of the language continuum in Scotland was thus born in the eighteenth century, and continues to exert its influence today.

However, broader accents of Scots also survive, from the eighteenth century restricted largely to the rural peasantry and the increasing numbers of the urban working class.

Since the Union of the Crowns in 1603, the Scottish aristocracy had sent their sons, and then their daughters, to be educated in the English public schools, changing their mode of speech until it was practically indistinguishable from southern Standard English. Middle-class Scots and their working-class compatriots, however, lived in close enough proximity for there to be a considerable fund of knowledge about Broad Scots amongst the middle classes throughout the nineteenth and early twentieth centuries. Often middle-class Scots would themselves only be a generation or two away from working-class, Broad Scots speakers. Curiosity about, affection for, and a philological interest in Broad Scots is evident from the general essays of the eighteenth and nineteenth centuries, mentioned in Jones (1997), from John Jamieson's *An Etymological Dictionary of the Scottish Language* (1808), to James Murray's *The Dialect of the Southern Counties of Scotland* (1873). No doubt this familiarity and affection continued to support the writing, publication and reception of literature in Scots, often by middle-class writers, both in book form and in the periodical press (cf. Donaldson 1989). Philological interest continued into the twentieth century, as is seen in the establishment of the *Scottish National Dictionary* and the *Dictionary of the Older Scottish Tongue*, mentioned earlier, and in the occasional publication of scholarly monographs such as Wilson's *Lowland Scotch, As Spoken in the Lower Strathearn District of Perthshire* (1915), *The Dialect of Robert Burns as Spoken in Central Ayrshire* (1923) and *The Dialects of Central Scotland* (1926). This philological interest sparked a new branch of literature in Scots. Inspired particularly by Jamieson's dictionary, and Wilson's dialect study of the lower Strathearn district of Perthshire, the poet Hugh MacDiarmid attempted to create a literature in 'reintegrated' Scots that would be capable of tackling the range of topics and genres that had been available to Scottish poets in the Middle Scots period. MacDiarmid's example was followed most enthusiastically by a group of poets who wrote after the Second World War, among them Robert Garioch, Alexander Scott, Tom Scott, Sydney Goodsir Smith, William Soutar and Douglas Young. Their achievements influenced the work of younger poets, who enjoy the freedom to write in a form of Scots that owes as much to dictionaries and dialect surveys as to the spoken word. Others rejected the reintegrated Scots as 'artificial' and continued to model their written Scots on the speech of their regional and social communities (see McClure this volume).

As the twentieth century proceeded, Broad Scots came under greater pressures from education and from new threats from the communications media that established English as the first truly global language. Mass education in the first half of the twentieth century stigmatised Broad Scots as 'uneducated', although in the latter half of the century a more liberal attitude began to prevail (see Corbett this volume). A greater threat to traditional Broad Scots, however, came in the changing nature of material culture and the pervasive influence of radio, cinema, television and the Internet. Broad Scots had originally grown to serve the communicative needs of a largely rural society, and clearly it had to develop further in order to meet the needs of a largely urban population whose knowledge of the world was increasingly mediated by print and electronic communications in English. The title of Macafee's case study of Glasgow vernacular, *Traditional Dialect in the Modern World* (1994), indicates the pressures on language use, particularly in the cities, although the spread of mass media has exponentially increased the potential for language contact in all areas of Scotland. If the potential of the media to change language behaviour remains a controversial issue, old-fashioned immigration and emigration has continued, with the linguistic influence of waves of, for example, Italian, Polish, Chinese and Pakistani immigrants so far going largely uncharted, even in the Scottish cities, although the consequences are evident in the fiction of writers such as Suhayl Saadi (2001). Since the major dictionaries of contemporary Scots have not been updated for almost two decades, developments in Scots lexical borrowings and changes in pronunciation over the last two decades have gone largely unpublished. The recent establishment of Scottish Language Dictionaries and the SCOTS corpus, as well as the proposed Institute for the Languages of Scotland, have the potential to rectify the relative scholarly neglect from which language studies in Scotland has suffered. But these projects and their successors will require a new generation of scholars willing to commit their energies to exploring them.

ABOUT THIS BOOK

In one sense the story of Scots is a seamless narrative of continual transformation, as the shifting political fortunes of dominant speech communities shape and reshape the language behaviour of subordinate ones. Broad Scots was born of a fusion of Anglo-Scandinavian, French, Latin, Gaelic and Dutch. It gradually replaced Gaelic in lowland Scotland, and then, in turn, was influenced and constrained by the encroaching power and prestige of English. The various chapters of this book trace the many factors that contribute to our understanding of these processes of linguistic change. The contributions cover both the study of Older Scots (pre-1700) and Modern Scots (1700–today).

The evidence for the early history of Scots is found in onomastics, the study of names. The contributions of Maggie Scott (Chapter 2) and Carole Hough (Chapter 3) illuminate this aspect of scholarly research. Anneli Meurman-Solin is a pioneer in the use of twenty-first-century technology to elucidate Older Scots, and in Chapter 8 she surveys of the use of computerised corpora to shed light on the patterns of vocabulary and grammar of this period. Jeremy Smith's contribution, Chapter 9, is a reminder that Older Scots literature is an aesthetic as well as a linguistic resource, and he considers the literary craft of the early makars. The reconstruction of Older Scots pronunciation is discussed by Caroline Macafee in Chapter 7, drawing on published and still unpublished work by the late A. J. Aitken.

Caroline Macafee also draws upon her considerable sociolinguistic and lexicographical experience to provide a guide to the study of Scots vocabulary (Chapter 4). This is complemented by Jim Miller's detailed introduction to modern Scots syntax and discourse (Chapter 5) and Jane Stuart-Smith's discussion of present-day urban Scots phonology (Chapter 6). A variety of language, whether written or spoken, is defined by its vocabulary and grammar, rather than the accent or accents associated with it. However, the pronunciation of Scots is a central area of research in its own right, and Stuart-Smith draws upon current investigations into changes in accent across generations of Scots in Glasgow. Together, Chapters 6 and 7 give a chronological overview of the study of Scottish pronunciation, past and present.

Written Scots since 1700 has largely been confined to the domain of literature, and J. Derrick McClure offers a survey of the diverse traditions that constitute the remarkable range of contemporary poetry in Scots (Chapter 10). In Chapter 11, Michael Montgomery reminds us that Scots exists as a historical and current language variety furth of, or beyond, Scotland itself, in his exploration of Ulster Scots and Appalachian English. Finally, given the impact of political events on the development of a language, it is unsurprising that pressure groups attempt to 'manage' linguistic change, and in Chapter 12, John Corbett surveys the mixed fortunes of language planning in Scotland.

As stated at the beginning of this chapter, the contributions to this volume are not meant to be comprehensive, and they are far from the last word on the history, development and current state of Scots in lowland Scotland and beyond. They are offered here to help you find some starting points in your own investigations of a complex and fascinating subject that still suffers from undeserved neglect. We wish you well in your own explorations.

CHAPTER 2

Scottish Place-names

Margaret Scott

INTRODUCTION

Place-name studies can be approached through a variety of different disciplines. Geography, history, archaeology, sociology and cultural studies have all contributed to our understanding of how names are formed and changed, and conversely, place-names have had an illuminating effect on many aspects of these subjects. This chapter aims to illustrate some of the linguistic approaches to place-names, and to provide a general background to the place-names of Scotland.

Scotland has been influenced by many different languages throughout its history, and any attempt to unravel the complexities of its place-names is not without its challenges. The current map of names can be likened to a palimpsest; earlier sketches have been partly erased, but new layers still allow a glimpse of the past. 'Language' is used in this chapter to refer to any identifiable linguistic layer represented in Scotland's place-names, and each of the major strata is considered in chronological order below. It has often been said that there is no linguistic means of determining what constitutes a 'language', and the application of the term is largely dependent on historical, political and cultural factors. There are at present many different public and academic opinions regarding the precise applications of the labels Scots, English and Scottish Standard English, and so a modern Scottish place-name element such as *hill* may acquire any of the above labels in accordance with the subjective views of the individual commentator.

PLACE-NAME STRUCTURE

A place-name is most commonly composed of two elements, one which is a generic term identifying the type of place described (farm, estate, hill, valley, and so on), and one which is a specific term, qualifying the generic by providing additional information. With the exception of a small number of folk-names, generics are either habitative or topographical. The order in which the elements are arranged differs depending on the linguistic influences underpinning the compound. In Germanic languages like English and Scots, this order is commonly expressed as 'specific + generic'. For example, the habitative name Fishwick BWK 'dwelling where fish were sold or cured' is composed of the Old English elements *fisc* 'fish' and *wīc* 'dwelling'.[1] In Celtic languages from about the ninth century onwards, however, this order is reversed, so that the qualifying element is preceded by the generic term.[2] Gaelic place-names which typically demonstrate this Celtic structure include the topographical name Auchenbegg LAN, a compound of an anglicised form of *achadh* 'field' and *beag* 'small'. It would be an over-simplification, however, to say that the distinction between Germanic and Celtic word-order is always rigidly maintained.

Name formations may include a number of different components, but many names are also simplex, consisting of one element, such as Dale SHE from Old Norse *dalr* 'valley'. Tautologous compounds are sometimes formed as a result of one language replacing another, as in Knockhill FIF, where *Knock* is an anglicised form of Gaelic *cnoc* 'hill', with the same meaning as *hill*, derived from Old English *hyll*.[3] This type of name can also be formed as a result of speakers of one language moving into new territory and re-naming, or partially re-naming, the settlements there. Such constructions help to illustrate the semantic opacity which a place-name can acquire over time, and this developmental feature often allows place-name evidence to contribute to the study of sound-change, as discussed below.

Place-names can also reveal the interaction of different languages over time. Contact between Scandinavian, Anglian and Gaelic in the south-west of Scotland is illustrated by place-names which have been affected by all three influences. In Kirkcudbright KCB, Old Norse *kirkja* 'church' has been combined with 'Cuthbert', the name of an English saint, following the pattern expected for Celtic word-order.[4] This type of construction is sometimes referred to as an 'inversion compound', because the elements are Germanic although the morphology is not.

Place-names can arise from surnames which are historically associated with a particular area. Hamilton LAN and Melville MLO derive from personal names, and are discussed in the following chapter. In both of these cases there is sufficient evidence to trace the development of the anthroponymic form to the toponymic form, but there are many other instances in which it is very difficult to know which was the original usage.

The reinterpretation of place-names by folk-etymology, or 'analogical reformation', is another common development, reflected in the historical spellings of Cassock Hill DMF.[5] This name is recorded as *Cowsowgill* (c.1481), *Coschogill* (1526, 1538, 1590, 1619), *Cashogill* (1654) and *Cowshogill* (1646), and Williamson establishes that the original sequence of Middle Scots elements was *cow* 'cow', *schaw* 'small woodland, thicket', *gill* 'ravine, gully' (Williamson 1941: 301). When these elements were combined to form a place-name, their individual semantic significance became obscured. The name may have been reinterpreted first as *Coshog hill*, and then later as *Cassockhill*, with a more descriptive 'meaning' providing an erroneous but plausible explanation. This folk-etymology is very different from the historical derivation, and so provides a valuable illustration of some of the changes which can fundamentally affect a name's structure.

Analysis of historical spellings is key to the unravelling of any place-name's etymology. This is illustrated by the example of the lost name *Wheatacre(s)* WLO (Macdonald 1941: 105).[6] The first element is *wet*, derived from Anglian *wēt*, and later spellings in *Wheat-* appear to have been introduced by folk-etymology. However, in order to establish this interpretation, it is necessary to examine the history of the name in some detail.

The earliest recorded forms of the name date from the Early Middle Scots period: *Weytakre* and *Weyt Akyr* (both 1426), in which the vowel is represented as < ey >. In the Later Middle Scots period, we find the spellings *Weitacre* (1567), *Weitaker* (1573 and 1667), *Weitaiker* (1687), *(Lie) Weitaikeris* (1588), and *Weitacres* (1644), in which the vowel is consistently represented as < ei > (Macdonald 1941: 105). The Older Scots spellings < ey >, < ei > and < ee > represented Middle Scots [i:] which derived from Early Scots [e:] and [ɛ:] (Aitken 1977: 3; cf. Chapter 7 this volume). In the Anglian dialect of Old English, *æ* is often changed to *ē* when it is followed by a dental consonant, as exemplified by *hwēte* for *hwæte* 'wheat', in the Mercian Rushworth Gospels (Campbell 1959: 124). The use of < ei >, where < i > functions to indicate that the preceding vowel is long, is thought to have been introduced to the British Isles through the influence of Norman French orthographic practices, and there are many examples of < ei > for Old English *æ* and *ē* in the Domesday Book (Knieza 1989: 443). Thus it is possible to trace the development of Old English *æ* and *ē* to Middle Scots < ey > and < ei >. The commonest orthographic form for Middle Scots 'wet' was *weet* [wit] (Robinson 1985: s.v. WEET[1]). In the Middle Scots period, the reflexes of *hwēte* and *wēt* would have differed only in the pronunciation of the initial consonant. Old English *hw* would have become *quh* in Middle Scots, at which time the Scots word for 'wheat' is recorded as *quhete*, *qwet* and *quhite*, most commonly representing [hwit] (Robinson 1985: s.v. WHITE[3]). Contemporary historical spellings for the place-name show an initial *w-* preceding the vowel, demonstrating that the first element of *Wheatacre(s)* WLO cannot be derived from OE *hwēte*.

Detailed analysis is an essential part of the study of place-names, but that can only begin after all possible linguistic influences have been identified. A brief discussion of each of the languages which has had a significant impact on the place-names of Scotland is therefore outlined below.

'OLD EUROPEAN' HYDRONYMY

The earliest identifiable linguistic layer in the place-names of Scotland is found in a number of river-names, or hydronyms. The names of major rivers are often very old, particularly when the river in question has been significant for travel or trade. Hans Krahe published a number of influential papers on the subject of European hydronymy during the 1950s. He developed the theory of 'Old European' hydronymy, identifying these names as belonging to an extinct Indo-European language. Over the years, his work has been supported and embellished by the efforts of subsequent scholars, notably W. F. H. Nicolaisen.[7] Alternative interpretations, however, have also been suggested. One of the most recent challenges to the 'Old European' construct was put forward by Theo Venneman in 1994, who argued that this stratum of river-names represents a non-Indo-European language with many similarities to Basque (Venneman 1994). Nevertheless, the prevailing opinion of the scholarly community favours the Indo-European stance taken by Krahe and his followers (Kitson 1996; Trask 1997: 365–7).

Several of the river-names in Scotland and other parts of Britain have parallel formations which can be found across continental Europe. The river Ayr AYR is one possible member of this ancient linguistic layer, and Nicolaisen has argued that it is phonologically plausible for the early spellings to indicate an original short *a*, suggesting a pre-Celtic Indo-European origin for the name. If so, it would be possible to consider this name together with the Oare Water SOM, recorded as *Ar* in 1279, the Ahr and the *Ahre* in Germany, the *Aar* in Belgium and the *Ara* in Spain. The reconstructed form *$Ar\bar{a}$* 'water-course' can then be assumed to be derived from *$or\bar{a}$* 'flowing movement', from the Indo-European root *er-/*or- 'to cause to move, to stimulate' (Nicolaisen 2001: 241). The speakers of this pre-Celtic Indo-European language therefore appear to have left a linguistic imprint in the river-names of Europe which can still be observed to this day.

PICTISH

Pictish evidence survives largely in the form of images, symbols and ogham inscriptions carved on stones which have been found in the north-east and far north of Scotland, and in the records of non-Pictish commentators. The Picts are thought to have been active from approximately AD 200 until the unification of the eastern kingdom of Pictland and the western kingdom of Dalriada under Kenneth mac Alpin in the mid-ninth century (Nicolaisen 1996: 4–5; Duncan 1975). However, scholars are divided as to whether the Pictish period ended suddenly or gradually (Lynch 1991: 21; Barrow 1998; Duncan 1975: 101–16).

The language spoken by the Picts is thought to have been P-Celtic, although other suggestions have been made, including the idea that they spoke two different languages, only one of which was Celtic (Jackson 1955: 152). Many questions remain unanswered regarding these people, and the puzzling inscriptions on a number of 'Pictish' ogham stones continue to inspire controversial explanations.[8] However, current scholarly opinion holds that Pictish was a P-Celtic language (Nicolaisen 1996: 32; Forsyth 1998), and therefore related to Cumbric, Cornish, Welsh and Breton.[9]

There is a striking correspondence between the location of place-names in *Pit-* and Pictish archaeological evidence (Nicolaisen 2001: 197–9). The element *Pit-* is recorded in the majority of the oldest available spellings of the relevant place-names as *Pet-*, from which it is possible to postulate a P-Celtic **pett*, cognate with similar P-Celtic terms with the meaning 'thing', as in Welsh *peth* and Cornish *peth*, or 'piece' as in Breton *pez*. As a name-forming element *Pit-* has been translated as the more literal 'portion, share, piece of land' (Nicolaisen 1996: 6–7), although a more recent interpretation as 'holding' has also been proposed (Taylor 1997: 10). This word is associated specifically with the Picts because it is not found outside the known 'Pictish' region. A large number of names in *Pit-* contain Gaelic elements, and this is thought to indicate either that Gaelic speakers borrowed the term and used it to coin new names after the unification of the eastern and western kingdoms of Scotland in the mid-ninth century, or that there was contact between the Picts and Scots prior to this time.

Jackson identified a group of place-name elements which he regarded as Pictish: *carden* 'thicket', *pert* 'wood', *lanerc* 'glade', *pevr* 'radiant' and *aber* 'river-mouth' (Jackson 1955: 149). *Carden-* names have a largely similar distribution to those in *Pit-*, with Cardenden and Kincardine in Fife and Cardno and Cairney in Aberdeenshire. *Pert* is found in *Perth* PER, *lanerc* in Lanrick ANG, *pevr* in Strathpaffer ROS and *aber* in Aberdeen ABD. However, the geographical distribution of these elements is not limited to the areas of Scotland which historical and archaeological evidence has identified as subject to Pictish influence. P-Celtic cognates may easily be confused with these 'Pictish' elements in areas south of the Forth-Clyde line, and therefore some commentators have chosen to follow Jackson's suggestion by labelling the southern P-Celtic forms 'Cumbric', and the people who used this language 'Cumbrians'.

CUMBRIC

Having identified Cumbric in the previous section as a P-Celtic language found south of the Forth-Clyde line, it may be useful to consider a number of examples which fall into this category of place-nomenclature. The distribution of the element *cair* 'fort, stockaded farm' has been used to delineate the territory of speakers of the Cumbric language, which includes parts of northern England as well as southern Scotland.[10] These people are thought to have lived in this area from before the beginning of the first millennium until about the year 1100 (Nicolaisen 2001: 206). *Cair* is found in the name Cramond MLO, 'fort on the river Almond' where the second element is the river-name, and in *Caerlanrig* ROX, where it is combined with *lanerc* to form a habitative name. As stated above, Jackson included *lanerc* 'glade' in his group of Pictish place-name elements, but this element is found in a small number of names in central and southern Scotland, as well as in areas of the north-east. Lanark LAN shows the use of this word in a simplex name.

In the south of Scotland P-Celtic *penn* 'end, head' is found in Pennygant Hill ROX, Penvalla PEB, Penicuik MLO and Penpont DMF, and is thought to have been used to refer to a prominent natural feature. *Pren* 'tree' is found in the lost simplex name *Pirn* PEB, showing metathesis, and in the compounds Primside ROX and *Pirny Braes* ELO.[11] Another element in this group is *tref* 'homestead, village', which is found in southern names including Traprain ELO and *Traquair* PEB, but there are also a significant number of names in *tref* north of the Forth.[12]

GAELIC

Gaelic speakers are thought to have begun to arrive in the west of Scotland in about the fifth century, and the language spread across Scotland, taking hold in the east following the ninth-century union of the two kingdoms of Pictland and Dalriada. It became the language of the entire country with the exception of the far north and parts of the south-east, which were Norse and Anglian respectively, and its decline did not begin until the aftermath of the Norman Conquest of England altered the political framework of the British Isles. This decline did not occur instantaneously, but gradually over many centuries, with Gaelic place-names being coined up to the present day. Gaelic is still spoken in parts of the north-west, and in these areas the place-names and street-names usually appear on road signs in both Scottish Standard English and Gaelic, not simply for the sake of clarity, but as a testament to cultural identity and heritage. The intimate connection between place-names and culture is not surprising when place-names are viewed as a component of language, and it is interesting to note that Gaelic ballad tradition is closely related to *dindshenchas* 'the lore of famous places', a form of folk-etymologising recorded in medieval verse and prose (Meek 1998: 148).

Considering the historical importance of Gaelic in Scotland, it is unsurprising that it has had a great influence on the toponymic record. For the historical linguist, this is particularly significant in the south of Scotland, since little is otherwise known of the form of Gaelic spoken there (Nicolaisen 2001: 158–9). Ó Maolalaigh (1998) discusses a variety of issues relating to this subject, including place-name evidence from Galloway from which it can be inferred that the system of eclipsis of *b-* to *m-* found in Ireland may also have existed in the Gaelic of Galloway. Examples of this phenomenon can be seen in Knockman, from *Cnoc na mBan*, and Drummuddioch, from *Druim (na) mBodach* (Ó Maolalaigh 1998: 30).

The Gaelic habitative element *baile* 'farm' is found in Balbeg AYR, Balnagowan ARG, Balmuir WLO, Balvannich INV and Balmacnaughton PER. Another common element is Gaelic *achadh* 'field', often anglicised to *Auchen-* or *Auchin-*, compounded with *breac* 'speckled' in Auchenbrack DMF and with *ruadh* 'red' in Auchenroy AYR (Nicolaisen 2001: 161).[13] Simplex forms are also found, a frequent example of which is *clachan* in Clachan ARG meaning 'village, settlement (with a church)' (Fraser 1999: 24). Other simplex names include Laggan BTE from *lagan* 'little hollow' and Dunan BTE from *dunan* 'little fort'.

ANGLIAN

'Anglian' is the dialect of Old English spoken by Anglo-Saxon settlers in the northern parts of England, many of whom began to move into southern Scotland in the seventh century. According to the currently accepted chronology, the earliest Old English names contain the element *hām* 'village, homestead', found in Twynholm KCB, Smallholm DMF, Ednam ROX, Midlem ROX, Oxnam ROX, Smailholm ROX, Yetholm ROX, Birgham BWK, Edrom BWK, Kimmerghame BWK and Leitholm BWK. Slightly later are names in *-ingahām* 'homestead of the followers of . . .' or 'homestead of the settlers at . . .', but only three Scottish examples have been securely established as containing this element: Coldingham BWK, Tynninghame ELO and Whittingehame ELO (Hough 2001a: 102). Names formed with the Old English derivational suffix *-ing* 'of, associated with', in the nominative plural form *-ingas* are thought to be later still, but there appear to be no instances of the use of this element in Scotland (Hough 2001a; Nicolaisen 2001: 89–92).

Other habitative generics include *wīc* '(dependent) farm', in compounds such as Hedderwick ELO 'heather farm'. Topographical vocabulary includes *sīde* 'side, slope of a hill or bank', in *le Wyteside* (c.1235), now Whitecraig MLO and in Birkenside BWK, recorded as *Birchinside* (1153–65). Other natural features represented in Old English names include plant and tree names. *Birken-* in Birkenside is from Old English *bircen* 'growing with birch-trees', and the first element in Saughton MLO (*Salectuna* c.1128), is Anglian *salh* 'willow'. Simplex names are also often topographical, as for example Dean MLO, recorded from the twelfth century, from Old English *denu* 'valley'.[14]

SCANDINAVIAN

Speakers of Scandinavian languages are thought to have begun having an impact on the British Isles from the eighth century onwards. The notorious attack on the monastery of Lindisfarne, recorded in the Anglo-Saxon Chronicle entry for 793, is generally taken as heralding the age of Viking invasions. Unfortunately, there are no native Scottish records documenting the events of this era, and so it is necessary to rely on the evidence provided by neighbouring lands. The Annals of Ulster tell of great destruction caused by Norse incursions in parts of the Hebrides in 794, and in the following year, raids are said to have taken place on the islands of Rathlin and Skye, and on the monastery of Iona.[15]

Over the next few centuries, many Scandinavian speakers arrived in the British Isles. In the far north of Scotland, the islands of Orkney and Shetland, and parts of the Hebrides, many Norse names were coined as a result of primary settlement. Old Norse place-name elements in the north include *vík* 'bay', found in the simplex Wick CAI and the compound Lerwick SHE 'mud-bay' from Old Norse *leir* 'mud'.[16] Scandinavian culture is reflected in Dingwall ROS, from Old Norse *þing-vǫllr* 'assembly-field', a name which signifies an important administrative site (Crawford 1987: 96).

Place-names in the south of Scotland may indicate that Hiberno-Scandinavians and Anglo-Scandinavians moved there from other parts of the British Isles which were affected by primary Norse influence or control. In the south-east of Scotland it is possible to find many examples of a type of compound place-name which has become known as a 'Grimston-hybrid'. This term arose from the study of habitative place-names in England which were formed by the addition of the Old English element *tūn* to a Scandinavian personal name, the commonest of which was *Grím*.[17] Scottish examples include Dolphinston ROX from *Dólgfinnr*, Ingliston MLO from *Ingjaldr* and Ravelston MLO from *Hrafnkell*.

Fellows-Jensen has commented on the geographical correspondences between Norse place-names in *bý* 'settlement, village, town' in the Central Lowlands of Scotland, and the distribution of eleventh-century Anglo-Scandinavian 'hog-back' tombstones. She argues that there may be a connection between the Scottish *bý* names and those found in the north of England, and suggests that these names may be late ninth or tenth century in origin, representing movement of population from the Danelaw.[18] Names of this type include the lost *Godfraby* DMF and Warmanbie DMF, which may contain the names *Guðfrøðr* and *Vermundr* respectively (Williamson 1941: 286).

SCOTS

The Scots language, being the subject of this volume, requires no introduction at this point. However, the label 'Scots' has often proven problematic for the toponymist, because of two conflicting points of view. On the one hand, a very large number of the elements which were used to coin place-names in areas where Scots was spoken can legitimately be termed 'Scots', considering that the language can be said to 'begin' in the twelfth century.[19] On the other hand, there is something of a tradition of labelling Scottish place-name elements according to their ultimate etymology, irrespective of the currency of those words in Scots.[20] Commentators tend to drift toward either of these extremes, and while it is easy to sympathise with the second approach on the grounds that it avoids the taxonomic nightmare of the first, the simplicity of this second approach fails to do justice to the Scots linguistic stratum.

Some distinctively Scots terms refer to measurements of land. A Scots *farthingland* was one such measurement, although its precise dimensions varied depending on the part of Scotland in which it was used.[21] It was equivalent to a 'quarter-pennyland' or 'quarter-merkland', and was also known as a *quarter-virgate*.[22] In Dumfriesshire, there are two notable examples of the *farthing*-element of this term being used in place-name formations: Fardingjames, recorded as *Fordiniames* (1523) and Fardingallan, recorded as *Firdenalane* (c.1450) and *Ferdenalane* (1451). Williamson suggests that these names denote farthinglands whose owners were 'James' and 'Allan', and notes that the order of the place-name elements follows the Celtic pattern (Williamson 1941: 206–7).

Terminology relating to land-use also includes *haining* 'enclosure', in The Haining SLK, recorded as *le Hayning* (1298–9) incorporating the French masculine definite article *le*, found in many historical forms of Scottish names in Latin contexts. The word is also recorded in the lost name *Haining* WLO.[23]

Scots *elbuck*, *elbok* 'elbow' appears to be the first element in Elbeckhill DMF, recorded as *Elbackhill* (1762), describing the shape of the land. *Gowk* 'cuckoo' is the first element in Gowkshaw Burn AYR, as is *puddock*, *paddock* 'toad' in Pottishaw WLO. In both of these examples the generic is *shaw* 'small wood, thicket' which is found in many other place-names including Birkenshaw WLO, Blackshaw DMF, Broadshaw MLO and Friarshaw ROX. *Craig* 'hill' is also attested in many names, including Craigend WLO and Craigshields DMF, compounded in the latter name with *shiel* '(shepherd's) temporary hut or shed, small house, pasture with a shepherd's hut' (Robinson 1985: s.v. SHIEL[1]).

Whitebaulks WLO is recorded as *Quhitbawkis* (1531), *Quhitbaukis* (1541), *Quhitbalkis* (1552), *Quhytbakkis* (1569), *Quhytbaikis* (1591) and *Quhitebaukis* (1583), and is a compound of the Scots elements *quhite* 'white' and *bauk* or *balk* 'unploughed ridge'. Later spellings, *Whytbalkis* (1656), *Whytbalks* (1656), *Whytebalks* (1696), and *Whitebalks* (1696) show the relatively sudden impact of anglicisation and standardisation.[24] Scots *Quh-* is replaced by *Wh-* and the representation of the vowel of the second element becomes increasingly consistent.

SCOTTISH PLACE-NAMES AND HISTORICAL LINGUISTICS

Place-name studies can tell us a great deal about language, in terms of early lexis, language contact, morphology and phonological development. At the same time, historical linguistics has informed toponymic studies, and each owes a debt to the other. There is much to be gained from a consideration of both disciplines and their areas of overlap, provided that a number of important caveats are borne in mind. Sources of early place-name spellings can be unreliable, and can fail to provide comprehensive coverage of diachronic changes. In the case of Scottish names, it is also unfortunate that very little extant documentary evidence pre-dates the twelfth century. However, considering that literary Scots is dated as beginning in 1375, place-name evidence often pre-dates other written sources, and is therefore particularly valuable to the historical linguist. Toponyms can preserve lexical items or senses which are otherwise unattested, as for example in Bemersyde BWK, which has been shown to contain Anglian OE *bēmere*, not with the meaning 'trumpeter', as attested in the literary sources, but with the meaning 'bittern' (Hough 1999). Phonological changes can also be traced. For example, the normal development of Old Northumbrian /tʃ/ is demonstrated by names in -*chester* (as opposed to -*caster*) in northern England and southern Scotland (Johnston 1997: 54).

Place-names form a special category of linguistic data because they do not 'behave' like lexical items, and are not subject to the same influences for change. They are used to identify specific locations, and this gives them a conceptual significance which is frequently very different from that of their component elements. Any semantic transparency that the naming elements may have had when the name was young may be lost or obscured over the course of time. It has been argued that 'place names which are lexically opaque are more likely to reflect changes in pronunciation earlier than words the lexical meaning of which is well known'.[25] While this can be supported by the historical spellings of particular names, the peculiar nature of place-names dictates that their morphological features often remain stable for longer periods of time than those of their component elements.

A good example of this phenomenon is provided by some recorded spellings containing reflexes of Old English adjectival forms which preserve the ending -*e*, long after this morphological distinction had fallen out of use in other linguistic contexts. Blackburn WLO is written as *Blakeburn* (c.1335) and *Blakeburne* (c.1424), and the lost name *Blakebec* near Howthat DMF appears in this form in the early thirteenth century (c.1218). Blackburn is also recorded in the forms *Blakburne* (c.1336) and *Blakburn* (1455), indicating that spellings without medial -*e*- were also acceptable during the same period, and *Blakburn* formations become increasingly more common from the fifteenth century onwards. The *Dictionary of the Older Scottish Tongue* provides further examples, including *Blakepol* (c.1190), *Blackedene* (c.1200), *Blackewel* (1220, a.1227) and *Blakeside* (c.1270) (Craigie 1937: s.v. BLAK a., BLAKE a.).

The conservative nature of place-names means that they can be very useful as resources for the dating of sound-changes. A datable place-name or group of names can often supply a *terminus ante quem* or *terminus post quem* for a specific sound-change, or provide some insight into historical language contact. For example, British place-name evidence has been used to calculate the likely dates of sound changes in West Norse by Eduard Kolb, who writes that 'the forms of a language transplanted to another linguistic environment can help us to determine the chronology of historical sound change, because on colonial soil they may have preserved an earlier stage of development' (Kolb 1969).

Place-names have been demonstrated to provide a useful supplementary source of historical data for linguistic studies, but there are fewer works which tackle the implications of the Scottish toponymic record than, for example, its Scandinavian and English equivalents. Scottish place-nomenclature remains, at present, a significantly under-used resource with the potential to yield much information which is directly relevant to the study of language change. In order to establish the areas of continuity between other sources of linguistic data and toponymic evidence, it may be useful to consider some typical examples.

In the Middle Scots period, the expected suffix of the present participle was -and, while -ing was used only for verbal nouns. The present participle hingand 'hanging', which may derive either from Old Norse hengja or Old English hangian, both meaning 'to hang', is used in place-names to indicate a sloping or steep hill-side. Hangingside WLO is written as Hingandsyde (1551), Hingandside (1551), Hingandsyd (1564) and Hingandsyid (1607).[26] Forms in -ing- only appear from the seventeenth century onwards, reflecting the more general processes of anglicisation which followed the Union of the Crowns; for example Hangingside (1667) and Hangingsyde (1691). The morphological changes in this place-name do not contradict the changes in Middle Scots lexis, and therefore support the argument that toponymic sources can be used to augment our knowledge of diachronic language change.

Similarly, developments in Scots phonology can also be traced in the historical corpus of place-name evidence. Prestonfield MLO appears as Prestisfelde (c.1375), showing the development of Old English prēost to prest. Later examples include Preistisfeild (1542, 1544, 1590), Preistisfield (1590), Preistfeild (c.1509, 1657, 1672), and Preistfield (1630, 1637, 1650), all of which show the development of the vowel of prest to /i/. Other later Middle Scots forms derived from Old English prēost also show pronunciations in /i/, as in Priesthaugh ROX (Preesthouch 1654). Priestinch WLO is Preistinche (c.1574) and Preistisinsche (1577) but later spellings like Prestinche and Prestinshe (1642) show that pronunciations in /ɛ/ were also available.[27]

Nicolaisen has used place-name evidence to examine the shift from /n/ to /ŋ/ in unstressed syllables and the loss of post-vocalic in -l after /ɔ/. Forms of the name Stirling STL in -lin, -line, -lyn and -lyne can be found alongside spellings in -ling and -lyng until the fifteenth century, when the -ng forms begin to become much more common, entirely replacing the -n and -ne spellings from around the late sixteenth century. Falkirk STL is derived from Old English fāg 'speckled, variegated' (which became Middle English fawe, faȝe) and Scots kirk 'church'.

Forms with medial -*l*- do not appear in the earliest spellings such as *Faukirk* (1298) and *Fawkirk* (1391), and are only recorded from the middle of the fifteenth century. Forms in -*l*- may therefore represent 'a hypercorrect spelling which only became possible or suggested itself after the -*l*- had been dropped in Scots, i.e. before 1458, the date of the first known *Falkirk* spelling' (Nicolaisen 1993: 312).

Nicolaisen notes that a similar pattern can be traced in a number of *Bal*- names, derived from Gaelic *baile* 'homestead'. Further evidence for the introduction of this medial -*l*- can also been seen in historical spellings of other place-names in *fãg*, including Falside ROX, recorded as *Faussyde* (1296), but later as *Falsett* (1568).[28] However, Fallsidehill BWK, which appears as *Fassethill* (1535) and *Fasyde Hill* (1654) has acquired its modern form through the introduction of -*l*- at a later stage, perhaps indicating a reshaping through folk-etymology.

CURRENT PROJECTS

In February 1996, in St Andrews, a conference on 'The Uses of Place-Names' saw many scholars from different disciplines explore some of the avenues open to toponymic studies. One of the outcomes of this conference was the founding of The Scottish Place-Name Society, which fosters co-operation between academics, local historians, researchers and those with a general interest in names.[29] Further information can be found at the society's web site (www.st-andrews.ac.uk/institutes/sassi/spns/).

One of the pioneers of the Scottish Place-Name Society is also the driving force behind the Scottish Place-Name Database, for which a Carnegie-funded pilot project has recently been completed. Dr Simon Taylor, of the University of St Andrews, has over the past few years, with expert technical support, been heavily involved in designing a database which is able to cope with the many different types of information associated with place-names. At present, the database contains details of about 8,000 place-names, and has the potential to become an invaluable resource for Scottish place-name research.[30]

DICTIONARIES, REFERENCE BOOKS AND FURTHER READING

At present, there is no comprehensive dictionary of Scottish place-names. Some attempts have been made to produce large-scale reference works, notably Johnston (1892) and Maxwell (1894), but these were written at a point when the study of Scottish place-names was very much in its infancy. The knowledge which can now be applied to the subject is much greater than it was over a hundred years ago, and many of the more exotic explanations can quickly be dismissed. However, had it not been for these early pioneers, Scottish place-name studies would be in a much poorer condition today.

The best introduction to the subject remains Nicolaisen's seminal work *Scottish Place-Names: Their Study and Significance*, first published in 1976 and now available in a new edition (2001). Nicolaisen has also written a substantial number of articles and chapters in books which are essential reading for any place-name student. For Celtic place-names, Watson (1926) is still regarded as a useful introductory text, even though many of the issues and etymologies he discusses have been subject to change and re-examination in more recent years. A number of general dictionaries of Scottish place-names are also available, although these are not comprehensive. Dorward (1995b) provides some introductory discussion for a large number of common elements, although he does not include historical spellings. Similarly lacking in chronological material is Darton (1994). It is axiomatic that all etymologies which are not supported by historical analysis should be treated with extreme caution.

Much raw data can be found in the archives of the Scottish Place-Name Survey, located within the Scottish Ethnology Section of the Department of Celtic and Scottish Studies at Edinburgh University. Three theses written in the first half of the twentieth century also provide data in the form of geographical place-name surveys, although these are not comprehensive, and many of the etymologies would benefit from twenty-first-century scrutiny. These works are Williamson's *The Non-Celtic Place-Names of the Scottish Border Counties* (1941), Dixon's *Place-Names of Midlothian* (1947), and Macdonald's *Place-Names of West Lothian* (1937). The study of Scottish place-names is not as advanced as the study of English place-names, largely because there are very few surveys of the individual counties of Scotland.[31] Research students therefore have the opportunity to redress this balance, and in tackling the vast body of available material the Scottish toponymicon will be created.[32]

NOTES

1. As in the following chapter, the Scottish counties listed in this chapter are those used before the reorganisation of local government in 1974. A summary of the changes in the governmental organisation of Scotland is provided by the Department of Geography at Edinburgh University (www.geo.ed.ac.uk/home/scotland/localgovt.html).
2. The dating of the change in element order of Celtic place-names to the ninth century was established by Jackson (1953: 225–7).
3. This situation is further complicated by the fact that Gaelic *cnoc* was borrowed into Scots as *knock*, and so a modern spelling in *knock* may reflect either an original Scots or original Gaelic place-name.
4. See further Nicolaisen (2001: 140–1).
5. Coates (1987) looks at a number of processes relating to this form of language change.
6. In accordance with standard practice, unidentified or lost place-names are given in italics.
7. Nicolaisen (2001) discusses this issue in some detail in chapter 9.

8. A recent example of a controversial publication on the subject is Cox (1999).
9. Confusingly, British P-Celtic place-name elements which occur in Scotland may appear in some texts with the labels 'British', 'Brittonic', 'Brythonic' (all three signifying P-Celtic spoken in the British Isles) and even 'Welsh'. For example, MacQueen (1990: 54): 'place-names provide fairly convincing proof that Welsh (Cumbric), and therefore ultimately British, was the language of SW Scotland before the arrival of Anglian settlers in the seventh century'.
10. However, this element is also found in the north of Scotland: see Taylor (1994: 8–9) and Taylor (forthcoming) 'Place-Names of Abernethy [Perthshire]' in *Pictish Reflections*, to be published by the Pictish Arts Society.
11. Examples from Nicolaisen (2001: 213–14).
12. For a recent discussion of the geographical distribution and morphological construction of place-names in *tref* and their significance, see Hough (2001b).
13. More accurately, the form *Auchen-* or *Auchin-* is from Gaelic *achadh-* plus the definite article which precedes the second element; see further Nicolaisen (2001: 161).
14. Early forms from Dixon (1947: 209, 153) and Williamson (1941: 144).
15. See further Crawford (1987) chapter 4.
16. Place-names in *-wick* may be derived from either Old Norse *vík* or Old English *wīc*, but few examples in Scotland remain ambiguous when early name-forms and known historical settlement patterns are taken into consideration.
17. While the term 'Grimston-hybrid' is still often used, many of the English places called 'Grimston' are no longer believed to derive from the personal name.
18. Fellows-Jensen (1990). She also offers the alternative view that these names may have been analogous formations, coined by Anglo-Scandinavians who travelled to Scotland in the twelfth century.
19. See the 'principal chronological periods in the history of Scots' (Robinson 1985: xiii).
20. Numerous examples can be found in early studies including Macdonald (1941), but it is also significant that while Nicolaisen (2001) has chapters on Scandinavian, Gaelic and English, the status of Scots is implied rather than stated. Part of the reason for this is the established model. For example, in Parsons, Styles & Hough (1997: xi): 'As is traditional in place-name scholarship, Old English forms are used as pegs on which to hang evidence from all dates'.
21. See further Robinson (1985), s.v. FARDEN, FARDING-LAND and PENNY-LAND.
22. As described in Adams (1976), s.v.; see further for other medieval measurements of land.
23. Early forms from Williamson (1941: 186) and Macdonald (1941: 79).
24. Early forms from Macdonald (1941: 65).
25. This theory is explored in Nicolaisen (1993).
26. Early forms from Macdonald (1941: 49).
27. Early forms from Dixon (1947: 187), Williamson (1941: 93) and Macdonald (1941: 23).
28. Early forms from Williamson (1941: 142, 146).
29. See further Taylor (1998).
30. See further in the edition of the newsletter of the Scottish Place-Name Society, *Scottish Place-Name News*, No. 11, Autumn 2001, p. 2.
31. County surveys have been produced by the English Place-Name Society since 1922. For a summary of the beginnings and developments in name-studies in the British Isles, see the introduction to Spittal and Field (1990).
32. I am very grateful to Philip Durkin, Anthony Esposito, Carole Hough, Joshua Pendragon, Tania Styles and Simon Taylor for their comments on an earlier draft of this chapter.

CHAPTER 3

Scottish Surnames

Carole Hough

INTRODUCTION

Surnames in Scotland date from many centuries later than the majority of place-names in present-day use. As in most Western European cultures, each person was originally identified by a single name, the need for a second emerging only as society became more complex, or the pool of available personal names too small to avoid confusion. The first stage in the process was the evolution of unstable 'bynames', which changed with each generation and were associated with individuals rather than with family groups. Some of these eventually developed into hereditary surnames, but many others fell out of use and have now been lost.

The main surnaming period took place between the twelfth and fifteenth centuries in Lowland Scotland and was not completed until still later in the Highlands, where the clan system both complicated and delayed the development of surnames passed down within the nuclear family. Even in the Lowlands, some families were without surnames up to the sixteenth century, while in Gaelic-speaking areas some clan names go back to the twelfth century but did not become hereditary surnames until the eighteenth, after the break-up of the clans following the defeat of the last Jacobite rising at the Battle of Culloden in 1746.[1] This means that the range of source languages is far more limited than for place-names. There is no question of surnames from Old English, Cumbric, Pictish or the pre-Celtic languages, except at one or more stages removed in the case of surnames derived from personal names or place-names. The languages most strongly represented in the surnames of Scotland are Gaelic in the Highlands and Scots or Scottish English in the Lowlands, with an admixture of Norse in areas of Scandinavian settlement such as the Northern and Western Isles. It is the first two in particular that distinguish Scottish surnames from those in other parts of mainland Britain, although the anglicisation of many Gaelic names for political reasons during the seventeenth and eighteenth centuries has often obscured their original derivation.

Other linguistic strata have been introduced through successive waves of immigration, from the French family names of the Anglo-Norman incomers encouraged to settle in Scotland by David I and other kings during the twelfth century, to the Irish surnames of the job-seeking immigrants from Ireland who arrived in large numbers on Clydeside and in other areas during the nineteenth. It is sometimes difficult to differentiate between surnames from Scottish and Irish Gaelic because of the close similarity between the two languages and the occurrence of similar formations in each. A few surnames of indubitably Irish origin are now common in certain parts of Scotland, as discussed below, but otherwise the term 'Gaelic' in this chapter should be taken to designate names which may occasionally be Irish but are in the main likely to be from Scottish Gaelic.

Surnames are conventionally classified into four main groups, according to whether the original denotation referred to the bearer's place of origin, parentage, occupation or nickname. The first type is historically characteristic of Lowland Scotland, the second of the Highlands, but all four contribute to the rich variety of surname types now found in varying proportions in most parts of the country. This chapter will discuss each of the main groups in turn, drawing for statistical information on the lists of common surnames compiled by the General Register Office for Scotland (1991 and web site) from the registrations of births, deaths and marriages. Table 3.1 at the end of the chapter shows distribution patterns for the four surname types in each region of Scotland and in the country as a whole, also based on the GRO figures.

LOCATIONAL SURNAMES

The earliest recorded surnames in Scotland are those of the Anglo-Norman families granted land by David I (1124–53) and his successors Malcolm IV (1153–65) and William the Lion (1165–1214) in a series of charters which are of the first importance in the study of surname history (Lawrie 1905; Barrow 1960; Barrow 1971). Some of these families already had hereditary surnames from the names of their estates in France, where surnames had begun to come into use by the beginning of the eleventh century. French place-names such as Bailleul, Brix, Coleville, La Hague, Quinci, Saint-Clair-l'Évêque and Somerville thus became established at an early stage as Scottish surnames, giving the modern forms Bal(l)iol, Bruce, Colville, Haig, Quincy, Sinclair and Somerville. Other incomers took surnames from their estates in England. These include Barclay (from Berkeley in Gloucestershire), Graham (from Grantham in Lincolnshire), Kerr (probably from Carr in Lancashire), Lindsay (from Lindsey in Lincolnshire) and Ramsay (from Ramsey in Huntingdonshire).[2] During the later twelfth and thirteenth centuries it became increasingly common for landed families to acquire surnames in this way, with many Scottish place-names similarly being transformed into family names such as Crawford (from Crawford in Lanarkshire), Cunningham (from Cunningham in Ayrshire), Douglas (from Douglas in Lanarkshire), Gordon (from Gordon in Berwickshire), Murray (from Moray) and Sutherland. Further down the social scale, many other Lowland families took local place-names as surnames from the fourteenth century onwards, and hence a wide variety of Scottish toponyms made the transition into a new onomastic context.

Surnames derived from place-names are known as 'locative' surnames, and they are often easy to recognise from the place-name generics discussed in the previous chapter. Although there are of course exceptions, surnames beginning in *Auchen-*, *Auchin-*, *Bal-*, *Inver-*, *Kil-* or *Strath-* are usually from Gaelic toponyms, those beginning in *Aber-* or *Pit-* from Pictish toponyms, those ending in *-burn*, *-chester*, *-don*, *-ford*, *-ham(e)*, *-house*, *-land*, *-ley*, *-lie*, *-ton(e)* or *-wick* from Old English toponyms, and those ending in *-beck*, *-bie*, *-by* or *-dale* from Scandinavian toponyms. Another characteristic is that locative surnames tend to cluster around the area from which they derive. Cockburn, Lauder and Renton, all from place-names in Berwickshire, are represented among the top fifty surnames in the Borders region only, and so too is Borthwick, from Borthwick in Roxburghshire. Kirkpatrick, from a place-name in Dumfriesshire, is in joint twenty-fourth place in Dumfries and Galloway but does not appear in the league tables for other regions. Surname occurrences outwith the area of origin sometimes make it possible to trace patterns of immigration and population movement, although the incidence of identical place-names in different parts of Britain means that many locative surnames have more than one potential source. The surname Leslie may derive from either of two places of that name in Aberdeenshire and Fife, Buick is from one of several Bewicks in northern England, and Pittendreich may derive from any of at least ten identically named places in various parts of former Pictland (Nicolaisen 1991–2: 15–16). Many occurrences of Johnston(e), now among the hundred most common surnames in Scotland,[3] are from Johnstone in Dumfriesshire, but some are from Johnstonburn in East Lothian and others from *St John's Toun*, a name used for Perth during the medieval period.[4] Certain recurrent place-names, such as Middleton, Morton and Newton, are so widespread across both Scotland and England that it is usually impossible to identify the origin of any individual surname.

As with Barclay/Berkeley, Buick/Bewick, Graham/Grantham, Kerr/Carr, Lindsay/Lindsey, Murray/Moray and Ramsay/Ramsey, locative surnames have sometimes developed a different modern form from the parent place-name, so that the source is not immediately evident. Furthermore, some surnames derive from place-names no longer in use. Leask, one of the four most common surnames in Shetland, is from a lost *Leask* in Aberdeenshire. Pringle, in joint fiftieth place in the Borders region, is from a lost *Hopringle* in Midlothian, and Snodgrass, a name with five entries in the 2001 telephone directory for Glasgow North, is from a lost *Snodgrasse* in Ayrshire. Like place-names, surnames are themselves liable to change, and hence surnames from a single origin may take a range of different forms. The surnames Arcus, Arkush, Harcus, Harkess, Herkes and Orcas all derive from the place-name Harcarse in Berwickshire, while Smeaton in Midlothian is the source of Smeaton, Smeton, Smieton and Smitton. Crombie in Aberdeenshire is an exception to the general rule that place-names ending in -bie are of Scandinavian origin, as it derives from a Gaelic river-name meaning 'bent stream'. The < b > is silent, and surname derivatives represented in the Glasgow North telephone directory include not only Crombie but also Cromey, Crommie, Crumey and Crummy.

Further complications are presented by the often complex inter-relationship between place-names and surnames. The surname Hamilton was brought to Scotland during the thirteenth century by a prominent Anglo-Norman family which took the name from one of its estates in England, probably Hamilton in Leicestershire. In the early fourteenth century, the Hamiltons were granted the barony of *Cadzow* in Lanarkshire, which was subsequently re-named after them and survives as the town of Hamilton near Glasgow. This in turn is the source of other occurrences of the surname. Similarly, the earliest bearers of the surname Melville were an Anglo-Norman family from Emalleville in France, but most modern bearers take it from the place-name Melville in Midlothian, itself derived from the family name.

Less common in Scotland than in England is another type of locational surname referring either to a feature of the landscape, as with Field, Ford and Forrest, or to a building, as with Hall, Kirk and Mill. These are known as 'topographical' surnames. Like locative surnames, they identify the place where the name-bearer lived; but unlike locative surnames, they derive from a word rather than a place-name. Among the hundred most common surnames in Scotland are Hill, Milne, Muir and Wood, respectively designating someone who lived at or near a hill, mill, moor or wood. Others are less transparent. Cross, among the top hundred surnames in Shetland, refers to someone who lived near a cross or at a crossroads, and Pirie, among the top hundred in the Grampian region and Orkney Islands, is usually taken to designate someone who lived by a pear-tree.[5] The problem here is that a similar range of topographical elements was used to coin the topographical place-names discussed in the previous chapter, so that it is sometimes difficult to differentiate between a topographical surname and a locative surname based on a topographical place-name. The surname Hay was introduced to Scotland during the twelfth century by Anglo-Norman incomers from La Haye in France, a topographical place-name meaning 'enclosure, hedge'. Most instances of the surname in England, however, are from a cognate term denoting residence by an enclosure or hedge, and this may also underlie some of the Scottish occurrences. Craig, the fifty-fifth most common surname in Scotland, may be topographical from a word for a crag, or locative from one of several place-names with the same derivation. Burns, in sixtieth place, may be topographical denoting residence near a stream, or locative from a place-name such as Burnhouse in Taynuilt, the origin of the family name of the poet Robert Burns. Wells, among the top fifty surnames in Dumfries and Galloway, may be topographical for residence near a spring or well, or locative from one of several place-names in England. Since topographical surnames are comparatively rare even in Lowland Scotland and largely absent from Gaelic-speaking areas, a locative source is usually the more likely alternative, but there is a danger of this type of argument becoming circular until the small corpus of minority formations is reduced almost to vanishing point.

A distinctive type of topographical surname in southern Britain comprises a topographical term with the suffix -er or -man. Bridger and Bridgeman denote residence by a bridge, Brooker and Brookman, residence near a stream, Hiller and Hillman, residence on a hill, and so on. These formations are common in central and southern England but rare in northern England and Scotland, and it is unlikely that any actually originated north of the present border. This means that where such names occur – Bridgeman, Brooker and Hillman, for instance, are all represented in the Glasgow North telephone directory – they can be taken to reflect immigration from other parts of Britain rather than being regarded as indigenous to Scotland.

It cannot of course be assumed that all holders of a surname are descended from a single original bearer. As with place-names, the same surname could be coined independently on a number of different occasions, or the same modern form develop from widely disparate origins. Recent work on English surnames has identified a single-family origin for a larger number than was previously recognised,[6] but in Scotland the names of important Lowland families have proliferated through the feudal custom of tenants adopting the surname of the land-holder, while in the Highlands an entire clan might assume the surname of its chief.[7] Clan names deriving from place-names include Bruce, Cunningham, Douglas, Forbes, Fraser, Gordon, Graham, Hamilton, Hay, Kerr, Murray, Ross, Sinclair and Sutherland, all now among the hundred most common surnames in Scotland. Many others derive from patronymics, another major surname type to be discussed in the next section.

SURNAMES OF RELATIONSHIP

Surnames of relationship most commonly derive from parents' forenames. Those from the father's name are known as 'patronymics'; those from the mother's name as 'metronymics'. The prototypical Highland surname is a patronymic with the prefix mac-, the Gaelic word for 'son'. This group accounts in total for about twenty per cent of Scotland's surnames (Dorward 1998: 116), including thirteen of the top hundred. Most have Gaelic personal names as second elements, although these have often been anglicised, as with MacDonald from *mac Dhomhnuill*, MacGregor from *mac Griogair*, MacKay from *mac Aoidh*, MacKenzie from *mac Coinnich* and MacLeod from *mac Leòid*, a Gaelic loan from Scandinavian *Liótr* 'ugly'. Others contain an occupational term, as with MacIntosh (*mac an toisich* 'son of the chieftain'), MacIntyre (*mac an t-saoir* 'son of the carpenter') and MacMillan (*mac mhaolain* 'son of the priest'). Further examples of both types occur within the top hundred names in individual regions, as with MacFarlane (*mac Pharlain*) in Central, Strathclyde, Tayside and the Western Isles, MacLaren (*mac Labhruinn*) in Borders and Tayside, and MacLa(u)ghlin (*mac Lachlainn*) in Strathclyde and the Western Isles, all from Gaelic personal names, and MacGowan (*mac ghobhainn* 'son of the smith') in Strathclyde and MacPherson (*mac a'phearsain* 'son of the parson') in Grampian, Highland and the Western Isles. Less common are English personal names and occupational terms, but in joint thirty-sixth place in the Western Isles is MacVicar, trailing the synonymous MacPherson in joint thirty-first place,[8] and the Glasgow North telephone directory also includes occurrences of MacAdam, MacIsaac, MacMichael, MacRobert, MacWilliam and others. In combination with a saint's name, as with MacAndrew, the meaning is sometimes 'devotee of Saint Andrew' rather than 'son of Andrew', and this is almost always the case with MacBride 'devotee of Saint Bridget', a name native to Arran but an Irish import to other parts of Scotland.

Paradoxically, many *mac*-names do not reflect a direct line of descent from an eponymous ancestor but an association with a particular clan. Some occurrences of MacDonald, the ninth most common surname in Scotland, may refer literally to the son of a man called *Dòmhnull* or *Donald*, but others designate members of the clan MacDonald. Other clan names now among the top hundred include MacGregor, MacIntosh, MacIntyre, MacKay, MacKenzie, MacLean, MacLeod and MacMillan. The capitalisation or non-capitalisation of the second element is a matter of personal choice, as is the variant Mc-, which originated as a printers' contraction. For the sake of consistency, forms have been standardised to MacX throughout this chapter.

Lowland patronymics, and those in areas of Scandinavian settlement such as Shetland and Orkney, are more commonly formed from a personal name with the suffix -*son*.[9] Among the ten most common surnames in Scotland are Anderson, Robertson, Thomson and Wilson, and the top hundred also include Davidson, Dickson, Donaldson, Ferguson, Gibson, Henderson, Jamieson, Morrison, Paterson, Simpson, Stevenson, Watson and Williamson. Characteristic of this group are surnames formed from shortened ('hypocoristic') forms of personal names popular during the main surnaming period, as with Dickson, Gibson, Simpson, Watson and Wilson, from hypocoristic forms of Richard, Gilbert, Simon, Walter and William. Many -*son* names are common to southern Scotland and northern England, but Donaldson, Ferguson, Henderson (from Henry) and

Paterson (from Patrick) appear to have originated exclusively in Scotland.[10] The first two may sometimes be translations of Gaelic *mac*-names (anglicised as MacDonald and MacFergus), and the same explanation has been suggested for other formations with Gaelic personal names such as Finlayson, among the top hundred surnames in the Highland region and Western Isles, and Malcolmson, in joint eighty-first place in Shetland.[11] Also among the top hundred in individual regions are Adamson (Fife and Shetland), Aitchison (Borders) from a hypocoristic form of Adam, Dawson (Shetland) from a hypocoristic form of David, Eunson (Orkney, Shetland) from Ewan, Georgeson (Shetland), Gilbertson (Shetland), Hughson (Shetland), Hutchison (Central, Fife, Tayside, Orkney, Shetland) from a hypocoristic form of Hugh, Jackson (Borders, Central, Dumfries and Galloway), Jacobson (Shetland), Johnson (Dumfries and Galloway, Shetland, Western Isles), Laurenson (Shetland), Lawson (Fife, Tayside) from a hypocoristic form of Lawrence, Manson (Orkney, Shetland) from a hypocoristic form of the Scandinavian name Magnus, Matheson (Highland, Western Isles) from a hypocoristic form of Matthew, Neilson (Central), Nicolson (Highland, Orkney, Shetland) from a hypocoristic form of Nicholas, Pearson (Shetland) from Piers, Peterson (Shetland), Richardson (Borders, Central, Dumfries and Galloway, Lothian), Robinson (Dumfries and Galloway) and Robson (Borders) from hypocoristic forms of Robert, Rogerson (Dumfries and Galloway), Sandison (Shetland) from a hypocoristic form of Alexander, Swanson (Highland) from the Scandinavian name Sveinn, Thomason (Shetland) and Walterson (Shetland).

A smaller number of patronymics comprises a personal name with no prefix or suffix. Among the top hundred names in Scotland are Aitken (from a hypocoristic form of Adam), Alexander, Allan, Christie (from Christian),[12] Duncan and Findlay (both from Gaelic personal names), Mitchell (from Michael), Ritchie (from Richard) and Watt (from Walter). Names of this type are recorded from as early as the thirteenth century and appear to pre-date surnames in -*son*, the predominant formation from the mid-fourteenth century onwards (McKinley 1990: 108). Again, hypocoristic forms are common, as also in Bartlett (Western Isles) and Beattie (Borders, Dumfries and Galloway, Grampian, Highland) from Bartholomew, Dickie (Western Isles) from Richard, Finnie (Shetland) from Finn, Greig (Grampian) from Gregory, Jack (Highland) from John, Nicol(l) (Fife, Grampian, Lothian, Tayside, Shetland) from Nicholas, Paton (Fife, Tayside) from Patrick, Petrie (Tayside) from Patrick or Peter, Rennie (Grampian) from Reynold, Robb (Tayside) from Robert, Sim (Grampian) from Simon and Watt (Central) from Walter. Beattie, Dickie, Finnie, Petrie and Rennie appear to have originated exclusively in Scotland, as does Ritchie,[13] and this is unsurprising since the construction of hypocoristic forms in -*ie* is characteristic of Scottish English, especially in the north east.

In some instances of apparently unsuffixed names, an original prefix has simply disappeared from the modern form. Kennedy, in fifty-eighth place overall, first appears as *mac Kenedi* in a charter of William the Lion, and although most occurrences of Martin, in thirty-third place, belong with the group discussed in the previous paragraph, a few may represent a shortened form of MacMartin (Black 1946: 393, 584). Sometimes the first two letters only of the *mac-* prefix have been lost, resulting in a name beginning with *C-* or *K-*, as with Cowen (Borders, Dumfries and Galloway), a shortened form of MacOwen from *mac ghille Chomghain*, or Keddie (Shetland), a shortened form of MacKeddie from *mac Adaigh*. The element *gille* 'servant' in many Gaelic personal names, often prefixed to the name of the saint on whose day the child was born, also gives rise to a number of characteristically Scottish surnames beginning with *Gil-*, as with Gillespie (Central, Fife) from *gille easbuig* 'servant of the bishop', Gillie (Borders) and Gillies (Highland, Western Isles) from *gille Iosa* 'servant of Jesus' and Gilmour (Strathclyde, Western Isles) from *gille Moire* 'servant of (the Virgin) Mary'. MacLean, in ninety-second place overall, is a contraction of *mac ghille Eoin* 'son of the servant of (saint) John'.

Surnames with the suffix *-s*, the southern English equivalent of *-son*, are not native to Scotland. Although both Hughes ('Hugh's son') and Jones ('John's son') are now among the top hundred, neither name is found in historical records, indicating that they have been introduced through immigration from England and Wales (Dorward 1995a: 149 and 163).[14] The same most probably applies to several other names among the top hundred in individual regions, including Adams (Dumfries and Galloway, Fife, Grampian, Western Isles), Collins (Fife, Orkney) from a hypocoristic form of Nicholas, Davi(e)s (Dumfries and Galloway, Western Isles), Edwards (Dumfries and Galloway, Tayside), Evans (Borders, Dumfries & Galloway), Harris (Orkney) from a hypocoristic form of Henry, Jenkins (Orkney) from a hypocoristic form of John, Roberts (Dumfries and Galloway, Tayside) and Williams (Dumfries and Galloway, Fife, Grampian). In some instances, however, the final *-s* may be a late addition to an originally non-suffixed name, or a reduction of *-son*. Another import is Kelly, the thirty-eighth most common surname in Scotland. This has two potential origins, as a locative surname from the place-name Kelly in Angus or Kellie in Fife, or as a surname of relationship from Irish Gaelic *Ó Ceallaigh* 'descendant of Ceallaigh'. It is significant that whereas Kelly ranks in thirteenth place in the Strathclyde region which represents a major centre of Irish immigration, and where the Irish surnames Docherty, Donnelly, Duffy, Gallacher/Gallagher, McGuire, Murphy, O'Donnell, O'Neill and Quinn also appear in the top hundred,[15] it is only sixty-second in the Tayside region (incorporating the old county of Angus) and only ninety-fifth in Fife. The implication is that Kelly is in the main a late Irish import into Scotland. At the same time, however, the absence of other Irish surnames from the top hundred in either Tayside or Fife (with the exception of Reilly, in joint ninety-sixth place in Tayside) suggests that in these regions the derivation may be locative.

Although the great majority of relationship surnames are patronymics, a sprinkling of other types does occur. The prefix *O* found in many Irish and some Scottish surnames refers to a descendant, sometimes specifically a grandchild, of the eponymous ancestor; and the Glasgow North telephone directory also yields instances of Brothers and Cousins, and of metronymics such as Annis (from Agnes), Cassie (from Cassandra), Catlin (from Catherine), Mabbs (from Mabel), Margison (from Margery), Marriott (from Mary), Megson (from Margaret), Mollison (from Molly), Sibson (from Sibyl) and Till (from Matilda).

It is important to realise that some surnames which are identical in their modern form may have developed from different origins in various parts of Britain. Highland occurrences of Shaw, one of the top hundred surnames in Scotland, represent a contraction of Gaelic *mac ghille Sheathanaich*. Lowland occurrences of the same surname, on the other hand, are locative from one of several place-names. Neave in England is a surname of relationship meaning 'nephew', but in Scotland is usually locative from the place-name Nevay in Angus. The patronymic Dawson in Scotland derives from a hypocoristic form of David, but in England from a hypocoristic form of Ralph.[16] Holland in England and most areas of Scotland is locative from one of several place-names, but in Glasgow is more likely to represent a shortened form of Mulholland, an Irish Gaelic surname of relationship from *Ó Maolchalann* 'descendant of the devotee of St Calann'. Similarly, Trainer in Glasgow usually represents an anglicised form of the Irish patronymic *mac Thréinfhir*, but elsewhere it means 'trapper', a surname of the occupational type to be discussed in the next section.

OCCUPATIONAL SURNAMES

Some of the earliest recorded occupational surnames in Scotland are found in the *Ragman Roll*, a document recording the deeds of homage made to Edward I by the people of Scotland in 1296 which lists the names of the nobility, barons, landowners, burgesses and clergy (Black 1946: xxi–xxii). Many are locational or relationship surnames, but alongside them are early forms of Marshall 'farrier, groom', Taylor 'tailor' and Wright 'carpenter', all now among the hundred most common surnames in Scotland, and of others such as Barbour 'barber', Barker 'tanner', Brewster 'brewer', Ferrar 'smith', Glover 'maker or seller of gloves', Goldsmith 'worker in gold', Lardner 'person in charge of the larder', Lister 'dyer', Mercer 'draper', Napier 'person in charge of table-linen', Porter 'door-keeper', Sergeant 'officer of the crown' and Spicer 'dealer in spices', which do not make it into the league tables but are still represented in the Glasgow North telephone directory. Occupational surnames are less common in Scotland than the locative or patronymic types, but are of particular interest for the information they preserve on early trades and occupations, and on the terms used for them. As many of these terms have now gone out of use, the meaning is not always transparent, but as a general rule most surnames ending in -er or -man – with the exception of the small group of topographical imports mentioned above – are likely to belong to this group. Hence entries in the Glasgow North telephone directory for names such as Bannerman, Bowman, Canter, Crowther, Dayman, Dempster, Fletcher, Gosman, Honeyman, Lorimer, Palfreman, Shearman, Speakman, Stalker, Trotter and Usher can be identified as occupational without knowing that the respective meanings are 'standard bearer', 'archer', 'cantor, singer', 'fiddler', 'dairy-man', 'judge', 'arrow maker', 'geese-keeper', 'maker or seller of honey', 'harness maker', 'groom', 'cutter (of woollen cloth)', 'advocate', 'stalker of game', 'messenger' and 'door keeper'. Some surnames contain -man in the sense 'servant', as with Addyman 'servant of Addy' (a hypocoristic form of Adam) and Hickman 'servant of Hick' (a hypocoristic form of Richard), so these too are occupational in origin. Less easy to recognise are unsuffixed nouns, designating an associated occupation by metonymy. Examples include Cant, with the same meaning as Canter, Day, with the same meaning as Dayman, and Besant, one of the top hundred surnames in the Orkney Islands, which appears to derive from the Middle English word *besant* 'gold coin' and to denote a moneyer.

The most common of all surnames in both Scotland and England is Smith, usually designating a blacksmith or farrier. Second in the order of frequency of occupational surnames in Scotland is Stewart 'steward', referring to one of the most important positions under the Crown in early medieval Scotland. Also among the top hundred are Clark 'cleric', Hunter, Millar/Miller and Walker 'cloth-treader'. Like many occupational surnames, the first three are common to both Scotland and England, although the spelling Millar is distinctively Scottish. Others have a regional distribution, as the same trade was known by different terms in different parts of Britain.[17] Walker refers to the occupation of 'waulking' cloth known as 'fulling' in south-east England and as 'tucking' in the south-west, where it gave rise to the surnames Fuller and Tucker.[18] Similarly, the Scots surnames Barker, Lister and Wright correspond to Tanner, Dyer and Carpenter in southern England.

Other occupational surnames represented in the top hundred in individual regions of Scotland include Armour 'maker of armour' (Western Isles), Bailey 'bailiff' (Western Isles), Baxter 'baker' (Western Isles), Chalmers 'chamberlain' (Fife, Tayside, Orkney, Shetland), Cook (Dumfries and Galloway, Fife, Tayside), Cooper/ Couper 'barrel maker' (Grampian, Orkney, Shetland),[19] Falconer (Highland), Gardiner 'gardener' (Tayside), Goudie 'treasurer' (Shetland),[20] Grieve 'bailiff' (Borders, Fife, Orkney), Harper 'harpist' (Grampian), Herd 'herdsman' (Fife), Hogarth 'shepherd' (Borders), Kemp 'warrior, wrestler' (Orkney), Lockyer 'lock-smith' (Orkney), Mas(s)on '(stone)-mason' (Grampian, Fife), Parker 'park-keeper' (Dumfries and Galloway), Pottinger 'maker of pottage (broth)' or 'apothecary' (Orkney, Shetland), Priest (Shetland), Purves 'purveyor of provisions' (Borders), Shearer 'cutter (of woollen cloth)' (Orkney, Shetland), Shepherd (Tayside), Slater

(Shetland), Spence 'worker in a larder or buttery' (Orkney, Shetland), Turner 'worker with a lathe' (Dumfries and Galloway, Fife, Lothian), Ward 'watchman' (Strathclyde, Shetland) and Webster 'weaver' (Grampian, Tayside). Also in this group are surnames referring to rank or status, as with Burgess 'freeman, citizen of a burgh' (Shetland) and Laird 'lord' (Central, Orkney). All are from Scots or Scottish English, and most also occur in England. However, the suffix -ster found in Baxter, Brewster, Dempster, Lister and Webster is particularly characteristic of northern formations.[21] So too are the phonetic development seen in Laird and the orthographic development seen in less common names such as Leiper 'basket maker' and Leitch 'physician', corresponding to Lord, Leaper and Leach in England.[22] Grieve is equivalent to the English surname Reeve, and Drever 'driver (of animals)', the second most common surname in the Orkney Islands from an Old Norse etymon, usually appears in southern Britain as Drover.

Occupational surnames from Gaelic are much rarer, represented in the league tables only by Dewar 'pilgrim, custodian of relics', in joint eighty-fourth place in Fife. Even here, some instances may be locative from the place-name Dewar in Midlothian. A few other Gaelic names occur with some frequency. The Glasgow North telephone directory has sixty-one entries for Gow, the Gaelic equivalent of Smith, with eight for Crerar 'sievewright', five for Caird 'craftsman, smith', four for Mavor 'steward', two for Grassick 'shoe-maker' and one for Clacher 'mason'.

Attention has often been drawn to the degree of specialisation evidenced in medieval surnames of occupation. Nicolaisen (1980: 122–4), for instance, presents an extensive list of names relating to the manufacture or sale of individual commodities, and points to a corresponding level of detail in those relating to animal husbandry. It would be misleading to assume, however, that an occupational surname necessarily designated the sole, or even the primary, employment of its bearer. Just as a locative surname might derive from any of several estates owned by the same land-holder and a surname of relationship from the forename of either parent, so too an occupational surname might designate only one aspect of the bearer's trade – possibly, as Fransson (1935: 31) suggests, 'an incidental occupation by the side of his ordinary trade' which served to distinguish him from other craftsmen. It is thus important to bear in mind while considering this group of names that some of the more esoteric terms may reflect particular skills or even sidelines rather than full-time occupations.

An additional complication is that it is sometimes difficult to distinguish occupational surnames from other types. Some occurrences of Milne may refer not to someone who lived by a mill but to someone who worked there, and Jardine, among the top hundred surnames in Dumfries and Galloway from an Old French word for 'garden', may similarly refer either to residence near a garden or to employment in one. An intriguing name is Barkman, in joint eighty-fourth place in the Western Isles. This does not appear in surname dictionaries and is not on record as an occupational term except as a nonce occurrence 'bargeman, lighterman' attested in 1599 and deriving from *bark* in the sense 'small ship'.[23] A similar meaning may be possible here; but bearing in mind that the suffixes -*er* and -*man* often form synonymous compounds from the same stem, as with Shearer and Shearman mentioned above,[24] comparison with the surname Barker suggests an alternative interpretation 'tanner'.

NICKNAME SURNAMES

Surnames derived from nicknames are a rich and varied group, covering a wide spectrum of attributes from physical features to personality traits, and ranging from straightforward description to metonymy and animal imagery. Colour terms are common, often referring to hair or complexion, as with Black, Brown, Reid, Russell 'red' and White.[25] Some occurrences of Gray 'grey' also belong in this category, but others are locative from a place-name in Normandy. Grant 'great' derives from the nickname of one of the early Anglo-Norman aristocratic families who settled in Scotland during the thirteenth century,[26] while by contrast King is more likely to be of lower-class origin, used either ironically or of someone who played the part of a king in a pageant. Also common are allusions to ethnic origin, as with Fleming, referring to a native of Flanders, Scott, referring to a Gaelic speaker, and Wallace 'welsh', referring to a Brittonic speaker from the old kingdom of Strathclyde. All are among the top hundred names in Scotland. So, too, is Young, although the corresponding Auld 'old' is represented among the top hundred in the Western Isles only. Gaelic in origin are Campbell 'crooked mouth', in sixth place overall, and Cameron, in thirty-fifth place, usually attributed to a Gaelic phrase meaning 'crooked nose'.[27] Both are clan names.

Whereas locative surnames tend initially to be associated with the land-holding classes and occupational surnames with skilled craftsmen, nickname surnames are more characteristic of the lower ranks of society. Like occupational surnames, some are common to Scotland and England whereas others reflect distinctively Scottish vocabulary or phonetic development. Based on Scots terms are Cruickshank 'bow-legged', in thirty-sixth place in Grampian region, and Todd 'fox', one of the top sixty surnames in Fife, presumably referring either to red hair or to some supposed characteristic of the animal such as slyness. Reid and Auld correspond to the English surnames Read(e) and Old, while Laing 'tall' (Fife, Grampian) and Rae 'roe-deer' (Borders, Central, Dumfries and Galloway, Fife) appear south of the border as Long and Roe.

Other nickname surnames of Scots or Scottish English origin represented in the top hundred in individual regions include Armstrong 'strong in the arm' (Borders, Dumfries and Galloway, Shetland), Beveridge 'drink' (Fife), Bird 'bird', less commonly an occupational surname 'bird-catcher' by metonymy (Western Isles), Bremner 'native of Brabant' (Highland), Cripps 'curly haired'

(Shetland), Darling 'loved one' (Borders), Drury 'sweetheart' (Orkney), Fairbairn 'fair child' (Borders), Goodlad 'good boy, i.e. servant' (Shetland), Halliday 'person born on a holy day' (Dumfries and Galloway), Hogg 'sheep', less commonly an occupational surname 'shepherd' by metonymy (Borders, Central, Lothian), Jolly 'merry' (Orkney), Little 'small' (Dumfries and Galloway), Noble 'noble' (Borders, Grampian), Sharp 'quick-witted' (Central, Fife) and Wiseman 'wise man' (Shetland). With the exception of Bremner, a surname reflecting the early settlement of traders and craftsmen from Brabant on the east coast of Scotland, all are also on historical record in England (Reaney 1997); but again it cannot be assumed that surnames of identical appearance will have the same meaning on both sides of the border. The term *hogg* refers in Scotland to a sheep but in England to a pig, and this affects the meaning not only of the nickname surname Hogg but of the occupational one Hogarth, meaning 'shepherd' in northern Britain but 'pig-keeper' in the south.

Nickname surnames from Gaelic are comparatively few and noticeably less imaginative, rarely extending beyond the most obvious physical characteristics such as size or hair colour. Represented in the regional league tables are only Bain 'white' (Highland, Lothian, Orkney, Shetland, Western Isles), Duff 'black' (Highland, Tayside) and Moir 'big' (Grampian). Others appearing in the North Glasgow telephone directory include Begg 'small', Dunn 'brown' (although some instances may be locative from a place-name in Angus), Gair 'short', Ogg 'young', Reoch/ Riach 'brindled, grey', Roy 'red' and Stronach 'prominent nose'.

A few nickname surnames derive from other languages. Blance, in joint thirty-sixth place on Shetland, probably derives from an Old French word for 'white'. Groat, among the top hundred in Orkney and Shetland, may be from Dutch *groot* 'tall'. Hardie 'brave', in joint seventy-eighth place in the Borders, is again from Old French; and Tait 'cheerful', joint thirty-first in the Borders, is from Old Norse.

DISTRIBUTION OF SURNAMES

Statistical information on the most common surnames in Scotland, as also on the most common forenames, has been published by the General Register Office in a series of surveys relating to the years 1855–8, 1935, 1958, 1976 and 1990. The GRO's website (www.gro-scotland.gov.uk) also provides listings of the most popular forenames in 1998, 1999 and 2000, and of the most common surnames in 1995. The 1995 data has been used as the basis of the statistics for Scotland as a whole referred to throughout this chapter and analysed in the first column of Table 3.1. As the website does not provide updated information on the top hundred surnames in individual regions of Scotland, the 1990 data published in the Registrar General for Scotland (1991) has been used for the regional statistics mentioned within the text and analysed in the remaining columns of Table 3.1.[28]

In practice, a discrepancy of five years is unlikely to be significant. Comparison of the top hundred surnames for 1995 with those for 1990 shows only six changes, with two locational surnames and four surnames of relationship being replaced by three other locational surnames and three other surnames of relationship.

Table 3.1 Derivations of the 100 most common surnames in Scotland (1995) and in the regions (1990)

Surname derivation	Scotland	Borders	Central	Dumfries & Galloway	Fife	Grampian
Place-name (Scotland)	10	18	16	12	11	13
Place-name (England)	2	3	2	2	6	2
Place-name (France)	5	1	2	0	4	4
Place-name (other)	1	0	0	0	0	1
Place-name (unclassified)	1	2	3	1	1	0
Topographical (Gaelic)	1	0	0	1	0	0
Topographical (ScoE)	4	2	2	6	5	4
Locational (unclassified)	2	1	2	1	1	1
Total locational	**26**	**27**	**27**	**23**	**28**	**25**
Relationship (Gaelic)	16	9	16	11	10	16
Relationship (ScoE)	26	28	23	31	30	27
Relationship (Norse)	0	1	0	0	0	1
Relationship (Irish)	4	0	2	2	0	0
Relationship (unclassified)	2	2	2	1	2	2
Total relationship	48	40	43	45	42	46
Occupational (Gaelic)	0	0	0	0	1	0
Occupational (ScoE)	10	14	11	14	16	13
Occupational (Norse)	0	0	0	0	0	0
Total occupational	10	14	11	14	17	13
Nickname (Gaelic)	2	1	2	1	2	3
Nickname (ScoE)	9	12	12	12	15	9
Nickname (Norse)	0	1	0	1	0	1
Nickname (French)	2	3	2	1	2	1
Nickname (other)	0	0	0	0	0	0
Total nickname	13	17	16	15	19	14
Unclassified	3	5	5	4	2	2
Total	100	103	102	101	108	100

Table 3.1—*cont'd*

Surname derivation	Highland	Lothian	Strathclyde	Tayside	Orkney	Shetland	West'n Isles
Place-name (Scotland)	15	12	11	11	41	27	11
Place-name (England)	1	4	3	5	1	1	5
Place-name (France)	4	3	2	4	3	7	6
Place-name (other)	1	1	0	0	0	0	1
Place-name (unclassified)	0	0	2	1	1	1	4
Topographical (Gaelic)	0	0	1	0	0	0	0
Topographical (ScoE)	3	5	2	3	5	3	1
Locational (unclassified)	0	3	2	1	0	0	1
Total locational	**24**	**28**	**23**	**25**	**51**	**39**	**29**
Relationship (Gaelic)	30	11	19	14	9	7	43
Relationship (ScoE)	22	26	18	29	22	37	17
Relationship (Norse)	3	0	0	0	3	1	1
Relationship (Irish)	1	2	12	1	0	0	0
Relationship (unclassified)	2	2	2	2	0	0	3
Total relationship	**58**	**41**	**51**	**46**	**34**	**45**	**64**
Occupational (Gaelic)	0	0	0	0	0	0	0
Occupational (ScoE)	10	11	11	14	15	15	10
Occupational (Norse)	0	0	0	0	1	0	0
Total occupational	**10**	**11**	**11**	**14**	**16**	**15**	**10**
Nickname (Gaelic)	4	3	2	3	2	0	2
Nickname (ScoE)	7	10	8	9	6	12	6
Nickname (Norse)	1	1	0	0	1	1	0
Nickname (French)	1	2	2	2	0	2	0
Nickname (other)	0	0	0	0	1	1	0
Total nickname	**13**	**16**	**12**	**14**	**10**	**16**	**8**
Unclassified	4	4	3	3	9	5	9
Total	**109**	**100**	**100**	**102**	**120**	**120**	**120**

Table 3.1 shows the relative proportions of surnames of different types and of different linguistic origins, both in Scotland as a whole and in individual regions. Anglicised spellings of Gaelic names, as with MacDonald from *Mac Dhomhnuill*, are treated as Gaelic, but English translations of Gaelic names, as with Donaldson (sometimes) from MacDonald, are treated as Scottish English (ScoE). Surnames of relationship are treated as Scottish English if they derive from personal names used in non-Gaelic areas, irrespective of the ultimate origin (such as Biblical,

classical, Germanic) of the personal name. Unclassified surnames are those of multiple or uncertain origin. An example of the former is Bell, the thirty-ninth most common surname in Scotland, which is variously topographical from a place of residence near a bell-tower, occupational by metonymy for a bell-ringer, or a nickname from French *bel* 'handsome'. An example of the latter is Gifford, in joint thirty-sixth place in Shetland, which is generally explained as a nickname from French *giffard* 'chubby-cheeked, bloated', but for which an alternative derivation from a French place-name has recently been suggested (Dorward 1995a: 112). Some surnames for which no single origin can be identified may nonetheless be assigned to a general category. As discussed above, the surname Hamilton, currently the twenty-ninth most common in Scotland, originally derived from an English place-name, but itself gave rise to a Scottish place-name from which later surnames derive. It has therefore been treated as an unclassified locative surname. Similarly, Craig is treated as an unclassified locational surname since it may represent either a place-name or a topographical description. Where there is a strong likelihood that a majority of occurrences derive from a single origin, that has been taken as the source. Hence the surname Hay is attributed to a French place-name despite the possibility that a few instances may be topographical, and Cameron is treated as a Gaelic nickname notwithstanding the alternative locative interpretation.

Although Table 3.1 presents a rough guide only, some interesting patterns emerge.[29] Locational surnames account for about a quarter of the total in all regions except Shetland and Orkney, where the figures are substantially higher.[30] Orkney in particular has a high proportion of surnames from local place-names, as for instance Breck, Clouston, Dearness (from Deerness), Firth, Flaws, Flett, Foubister, Garson, Hourston, Kirkness, Linklater, Mainland, Marwick, Meil (from Meal), Moar, Norquay/Norquoy, Rosie (probably from the Island of Rousay), Sabiston, Seatter, Stanger, Walls and Work.[31] Everywhere except Orkney, surnames of relationship are the largest category, representing nearly half in many areas, and more than half in the Highlands and Western Isles, the only regions where Gaelic surnames of relationship substantially outnumber those from Scottish English. Both occupational and nickname surnames are consistently few in number, and almost entirely from Scottish English. This is particularly interesting since the paucity of occupational surnames from Gaelic is often attributed to the fact that Scottish English was the language of the burghs where specialised trades were practised. While this may well be a factor, it fails to account for the corresponding paucity of nickname surnames from Gaelic, and it therefore seems that the imbalance may rather be attributable to the overwhelming preference for patronymics in Gaelic-speaking areas. Even in Lowland Scotland, however, where the evolution of surnames has more in common with England and where many individual names have counterparts or doublets south of the border, the proportion of both occupational and nickname types is relatively small.

Locational and relationship surnames together account for around seventy per cent or more in all regions as well as in the country as a whole, demonstrating that despite the many parallels with other parts of mainland Britain, Scotland has its own distinctive patterns of onomastic development.[32]

Dictionaries, Reference Books and Further Reading

The standard dictionary of Scottish surnames for more than half a century has been Black (1946). While still extremely useful, some of the etymologies are now in need of updating, and an emphasis on historical records may obscure the development of more recent forms. A much smaller and more selective dictionary is Dorward (1995a), which does not include historical spellings but offers generally reliable and up-to-date etymologies together with information on the geographical profile of individual surnames and on famous bearers. A good general surname dictionary is Reaney (1997). Despite the title, this includes Scottish as well as English surnames (previous editions were entitled *A Dictionary of British Surnames*), but it concentrates on names of Germanic rather than of Celtic origin. Also useful, particularly for tracing immigrant surnames, is Hanks and Hodges (1988), while Cottle (1978) contains some 12,000 names from various parts of the British Isles, classifying each according to the four main surname categories. All have been extensively used during the preparation of this chapter, especially the first three.

Some of the etymologies given in the dictionaries mentioned above have recently been revised, as for instance by Insley (1993) and McClure (1998). Moreover, the traditional method of linking early name forms with modern surnames has been challenged, most strongly by Redmonds (1997) and Hey (2000), both of whom advocate a multi-disciplinary approach based on localised evidence for the surname histories of individual families. Work along these lines has so far focused on English surnames, but it is clear that the new methodology may be equally applicable to Scotland.

The best general book on surnames is McKinley (1990), which discusses each of the main categories, with information on surname development and regional differences within discrete parts of England and Scotland. A good short account of the Scottish material is given by Dorward (1995–6). Despite the title, this is mainly about surnames, substantially repeating the introduction to Dorward (1995a). Distribution patterns for one hundred surnames in England, Scotland and Wales are mapped in Rogers (1995), and Hey (2000: 122–6) discusses surname evidence for immigration from Scotland to England. Selected articles of interest are included in the bibliography; others can be traced through the annual bibliography published in the journal *Nomina*. Also useful for identifying potential sources of locative surnames are the place-name dictionaries mentioned in the previous chapter.

NOTES

1. For the political background, see Lynch (1991: 318–39) 'Union settlement and Jacobite risings'.
2. Throughout this chapter as in most scholarly literature, place-names are identified by the counties preceding the local government reorganisation of the 1970s. Statistical information relating to the distribution of surnames, however, is based on the General Register Office tables, which follow the boundaries of the new regions of Scotland.
3 The GRO figures show Johnston in twenty-eighth place, with the variant spelling Johnstone in sixty-fourth place.
4. Still others represent a variant form of Johnson, one of the surnames of relationship to be discussed in the next section, with intrusive -t-. In some instances, the surname may have been adopted arbitrarily by members of a proscribed clan. Reaney (1997: liv) notes that 'In 1603 an Act was passed ordering the McGregors to renounce their name under pain of death. Some took the names of Johnestoun, Doyle, Menzies or Ramsay'.
5. An alternative derivation for the Orkney surname suggested to me by Professor W. F. H. Nicolaisen is a nickname from Orcadian *purie* 'small'.
6. See especially Redmonds (1997) and Hey (2000).
7. This did not always happen, of course. The latest discussion of the clan system, challenging many preconceptions relating to its influence on naming patterns, comments that 'the use of patronymics – that is stressing one's father, grandfather, etc. – was as likely as the notion of calling oneself by a collective clan name' (MacGregor and Mackillop 2001: 95).
8. This at any rate is the usual interpretation of MacVicar. On the other hand, Margaret Scott points out to me that *vicar* is attested in Middle Scots in the sense 'one acting, or appointed to act, in place of another, especially in administrative functions; a viceregent', and it may well be that this meaning is represented in the surname.
9. The possibility that the northern phenomenon of surnames in -*son* may result from Scandinavian influence has been much debated, although mostly with reference to English rather than Scottish evidence. For the latest discussion, see Postles (2001).
10. The entries in Reaney (1997) are based exclusively on material from Black (1946), suggesting that the names are not on early record in England.
11. This explanation is given for Donaldson, Ferguson and Finlayson by Black (1946: 215, 260, 265). It is put forward for Malcolmson by McKinley (1990: 45), but seems less likely here since the form *Malcomesson* is recorded as early as 1296 (Black 1946: 577).
12. Christian can be a feminine personal name in present-day Scotland (it is masculine in other English-speaking countries), and it could be either masculine or feminine in medieval times. The surname seems most likely to derive from the masculine form, but could conceivably be a metronymic.
13. The entries for Beattie, Dickie, Petrie and Ritchie in Reaney (1997) are based exclusively on material from Black (1946), while there is no entry for Finnie. Despite English attestations of Rennie and its variants, Reaney describes the name unequivocally as 'Scottish'.
14. Alternatively, as Hugh was regarded as the equivalent of the Celtic name Aodh, Dorward suggests that some occurrences of Hughes may represent disguised forms of Gaelic patronymics.
15. All are surnames of relationship.
16. This is demonstrated by McClure (1998: 123–8).

17. For an excellent discussion, see McKinley (1990: 143–7).
18. The present-day distribution of these surnames is mapped in Rogers (1995: 23, 40–1).
19. Alternatively, some instances may be locative from Cupar in Fife.
20. An alternative derivation as a metronymic from an unrecorded Old English feminine personal name *Goldgiefu* is also possible.
21. This is illustrated by, for instance, the distribution maps for the synonymous surnames Webb, Webber and Webster in Rogers (1995: 54–6). Occupational terms in -*ster* are often mistakenly stated to be the feminine equivalents of masculine formations in -*er*, but historical evidence as well as present-day distribution shows that the distinction relates not to gender but to geography.
22. Similarly, the patronymic Aitken mentioned above corresponds to Adkin or Atkin in England.
23. Simpson and Weiner (1989), s.v. *bark, barque* sb 2, sense 4. The citation is in the form *Barke-Men*.
24. Other examples are cited by Reaney (1997: xlii).
25. Although the surname Black is recorded in England from the early Middle Ages (Reaney 1997: 46), Rogers (1995: 134) points out that its distribution strongly suggests a Scottish origin.
26. Some instances of the surname may alternatively derive from Gaelic *grandd* 'ugly'. I owe this information to Derrick McClure.
27. The derivation is not universally accepted. Dorward (1995a: 36–7), for instance, prefers a locative origin from Cameron parish in Fife. This is no doubt correct in some instances: indeed, Black (1946: 128) identified the Fife place-name as the main source of the surname in the Lowlands, with the Gaelic nickname giving rise to the Highland clan name. Since, however, the surname seems to owe its present popularity to the proliferation of the clan name, and is still most common in the north-western half of Scotland (as is clear from the map in the Registrar General for Scotland 1991: 35), the Gaelic derivation is probably to be preferred for a majority of occurrences.
28. Some of the regional lists contain more than a hundred surnames, where there is a tie for hundredth place.
29. Different results would of course be produced by using a sample either larger or smaller than one hundred surnames for each region, or by factoring in the actual numbers of name bearers.
30. Again, different selection criteria would produce different results. Analysing the surnames listed in Black (1946) irrespective of the number of name bearers, Nicolaisen (1991–2: 9) estimates that about half are locative.
31. I owe some of these identifications to Doreen Waugh.
32. I am grateful to Ian Fraser, W. F. H. Nicolaisen, Margaret Scott and Doreen Waugh for their helpful comments on an earlier version of this chapter.

CHAPTER 4

Studying Scots Vocabulary

Caroline Macafee

INTRODUCTION

The vocabulary of Scots has a large overlap with that of English, including not only a core vocabulary that both inherit from Old English, but also shared loanwords from the language contacts of the Middle Ages. However, Scots has a larger proportion of loans from Old Norse than does Standard English, and in many cases has different loans from Middle Dutch, Anglo-Norman, Old French and Latin. The influence of Gaelic, though not large, is characteristic of Scots, with very little Gaelic influence having penetrated English. Scots also has a large and distinctive body of vocabulary of obscure origin, some of which may in fact be of unrecognised Gaelic origin, but most of which probably represents the linguistic creativity of speakers of Scots. Words of this kind tend to be regarded as colloquial or even as slang, at least when first coined, so they are more common in Scots and in the regional dialects of England than in Standard English. On sources of the vocabulary, see further Macafee and Anderson (1997), Macafee (1997a, revised in Macafee and Aitken 2002), and Tulloch (1997a).

The language contacts of the modern period – firstly in the Americas with Spanish and with native American languages, and later with the languages of the British Empire – have augmented the vocabulary of Standard English; and this lexicon, having no native counterpart, is also used in Scots. Similarly, the modern vocabulary of science, technology, industry and commerce generally has no specifically Scots equivalents. Indeed, much of this vocabulary, coined on Latin and Greek roots, is common to numerous European languages: Fishman (1980) calls it an 'econo-technical lingua franca'. We tend to think of such vocabulary as belonging primarily to Standard English, but it should be remembered that Scots were also active in the British Empire and in scientific and technological innovation. It was to make just this point that Murison added an appendix to *The Scottish National Dictionary* (SND) containing 'A list of scientific terms with

Scottish connections'. In general, however, the modern Scottish dictionaries from Jamieson (1808) onwards and including SND and *The Concise Scots Dictionary* (CSD) cover only material not shared with Standard English (though it may be shared with regional dialects of English), all of which reinforces the unfortunate impression that the shared vocabulary belongs to Standard English whereas Scots consists only of what is uniquely Scots.

The different degrees of overlap between Scots and Standard English are usefully captured in Aitken's (1979, 1984b) five-column model (see Figure 4.1). Column 1 consists of words that are found in Scots but not in Standard English, while Column 5 consists of the corresponding words in Standard English, often unidiomatic in Scots. Columns 2 and 4 correspond as different forms of cognate words in the two languages. The difference between these forms is one of phonology, but there are, of course, other types of difference between shared lexical items, particularly semantic differences and different ranges of parts of speech. Column 3 consists of the common core of shared vocabulary. The coverage of the Modern Scots dictionaries is restricted to Columns 1 and 2, but could in principle be extended to Column 3. The reason why this is not done is simply to save time and expense. There has been an increasing demand for a more inclusive Scots dictionary in recent years, though it must be said this comes largely from language activists with an ideological rather than a practical agenda. Such a dictionary might well have a beneficial effect on the quality of writing in Modern Scots, if it encouraged writers to make use of the Column 3 material rather than seeking out or inventing distinctively Scots words, often wrenching the sense in the process. A monolingual dictionary with the vocabulary of Scots defined in the Scots language is included in the future plans of Scottish Language Dictionaries (SLD), the successor body to the Scottish National Dictionary Association and the Joint Council for the Dictionary of the Older Scottish Tongue.

LEXICAL EROSION

Over much of the Lowlands, Scots is now at an advanced stage of language death. Part of this process is the erosion of distinctively Scots vocabulary. In terms of Figure 4.1, Column 1 vocabulary and Column 2 word-forms are increasingly lost, and as the Column 1 versus Column 5 and Column 2 versus Column 4 polarities cease to apply, what was Column 5 or 4 vocabulary (not Scots) becomes Column 3 (shared between Scots and Standard English).

Vocabulary is quite fluid over time and across language boundaries, because it is atomistic and not closely bound into larger structures. Nevertheless, some generalisations can be made about which types of vocabulary have survived better than others. As a consequence of anglicisation in the late sixteenth and early seventeenth centuries, few genres of writing continued in Scots. Learned and

Figure 4.1 A model of Modern Scottish speech (based on Aitken, 1984b: 520)

—Scots—			—English—	
1	2	3	4	5
bairn	hame	name	home	child
brae	hale	hole	whole	slope
kirk	mare	before	more	church
ken	puir	soup	poor	know
darg	muin	room	moon	job of work
cuit	yuis (n.)	miss	use (n.)	ankle
kenspeckle	yaize (v.)	raise	use (v.)	conspicuous
birl	cauld		cold	spin
girn	auld	young	old	whine
mind	coo	row	cow	remember
sort	hoose	London	house	mend
	loose	winter	louse	
	louse	feckless	loose	
ay	pey	bite	pay	always
gey	wey	tide	way	very
kye		tie		cows
een		feed		eyes
shuin	deed	see	dead	shoes
deave	dee	leave	die	deafen, vex
gaed	scart	agree	scratch	went
ben the hoose	twaw, twae	he	two	in or into the inner part
	no		not	of the house
		his		
	-na, -nae	they	-n't	
		some		

technical terms peculiar to Scots largely disappeared from use, apart from the distinctive vocabulary of Scots law (since the legal system was reserved by the Treaty of Union of 1707 as a distinctive Scottish institution). Much of this learned vocabulary was fairly recently borrowed from French and/or Latin, and a proportion (as in Standard English) would probably have proved ephemeral in any case. Perhaps more serious for the future status of the language was the fact that Scots now ceased to generate its own learned vocabulary, and this precisely at the point in time when many new discoveries and inventions were made and much of the modern vocabulary of Standard English was coined (cf. Finkenstaedt, Wolff et al. 1973).

Continuing losses of Scots vocabulary have naturally reflected changes in material culture since the Industrial Revolution and the opening up of markets by the railways, with agriculture and traditional crafts being transformed by industrial methods of production and mass marketing of consumer goods. A number of studies, of varying size and sophistication, have suggested that the recent rate of lexical erosion may be very rapid. The results are summarised in Figure 4.2.[1] It is not possible to construct a quantitative comparison between age-groups in Riach's studies of Galloway, but it is clear that there has been a considerable loss of vocabulary. The highest number of words known in any one school was thirty-six out of a possible 101 (Riach 1984) – these were items well known in Galloway amongst adults aged sixty years or more in his earlier dialect survey (Riach 1979–82). Hendry (1997) also used lexis collected from adults, aged 40–65, in his study of ten-year-olds' knowledge of Scots in Grampian Region. The average known to local children was sixty-one per cent.

Some studies asked about use as well as knowledge. For McGarrity's data on frequent use, a statistical regression on age showed an average loss of about one per cent for every six years of age. The decline in knowledge was even steeper (Macafee and McGarrity 1999).

When interpreting age differences, however, it is important to be aware of the phenomenon of age-grading, that is differences that are due not to change over time within the community, but to the different competences of different age groups. For instance, Lawrie (1991) notes that many of the terms used by her 10–12 age group are superordinates: for example *beastie* was given in response to 'beetle', 'caterpillar', 'earwig' and 'centipede', possibly indicating that the children's vocabulary was still limited, and allowing the possibility that further Scots vocabulary would be acquired as they grew older.

Despite obvious weaknesses in some of these studies, and allowing for the possibility of a certain amount of age-grading, the general trend is so uniform and so large that we must conclude that significant lexical erosion is taking place, certainly far more than can be compensated for by the limited amount of non-slang neologism. Scots is already a long way along a trajectory that is taking it towards integration with English as the continuum between the two shrinks,

Figure 4.2 Mean percentages of lexical items known and used in several studies

Study	Place	Source of Words	No. of Words	Elderly			Middle Aged			Adults			Young Adults			Teenagers			Children		
				n	% known	% used	n	% known	% used	n	% known	% used	n	% known	% used	n	% known	% used	n	% known	% used
Graham (1979)	Shetland	Jakobsen 1890s	360							1	29.1					1	18.1				
Wickens (1980)	Caithness	earlier dialect glossary	461							40	44.8	27.2				34	26.1	13.5			
Macaulay (1977)	Glasgow	'old Scots words'	10							16	78					16	33				
Pollner (1985c)	Livingston	"	23							47	45					9	26				
Nässén (1989)	Shetland	Jakobsen 1890s	323							35	c.20										
Hettinga (1981)	Fife	'old Fife words'	21	3	81	57.1										3	23.8		3	7.1	
Agutter and Cowan (1981)	Stirlingshire	LAS	33	10	77.3	52.1	3	52.1											10	52.1	33.6
Lawrie (1991)	Fife	"	20	16	23.3	12.2													16	9.8	6.9
McGarrity (1998)	Aberdeen	'old Doric words'	96	7	41	23	33	38	17				23	30	13						

Note: In most cases the percentages have been calculated from the published figures. Some figures have been calculated from lists. In the case of Lawrie (1991), only Scots responses have been counted. In the case of Wickens (1980), two items where 'knowledge' is higher than 'use' have been dropped (these were presumably misprinted). N = number of individuals.

apparently inexorably, towards the English pole. Nevertheless, the corpus of the language is so large that a great deal could be lost and some would still remain, as we see in residual Scotticisms present even in the speech of the anglicised urban middle classes (Aitken 1979, 1984a). Chambers (1992) suggests that the lexicon is both very vulnerable to erosion, and very resistant if not replaced early in the process of an individual's shift to a new dialect.

A number of specific processes of erosion can be identified:

(a) *active use gives way to passive knowledge*
As we would expect, use declines in advance of knowledge (see below). The generation for whom an item is becoming passive provides fewer opportunities to the next generation to learn it spontaneously in everyday use.

(b) *dialect becomes idiolect*
Comments from interviewees in Glasgow illustrate that words often become idiolectal, that is the property of particular speakers (or families), sometimes associated with reminiscences of specific individuals who used them strikingly or habitually (Macafee 1994).

(c) *limitation by register*
Words become fossilised in particular registers. Songs and rhymes are important categories in this respect, and can preserve passive vocabulary indefinitely.[2] We also find words preserved in anecdotes. For instance, it is jokingly said that when the *waggitywa clock* 'unencased pendulum clock' that gave the Waggitywa Pub in the East End of Glasgow its name was removed in the course of renovation, it had been there so long that the pendulum had left the mark of its swing on the wall.

(d) *derived forms survive best*
As Jakobsen (1897) observed in relation to Shetland Norn and Glauser (1974) in relation to the Borders, derived forms, metaphorical senses, idioms and compounds often survive while the stem in its basic sense is replaced by the Standard English word for that idea (or the idea itself becomes obsolete). This was also confirmed by several examples in Glasgow, such as the survival of *sugarallie* 'licorice' only in *sugarallie-waater* (Macafee 1994). However, Tulloch (1997a: 418) also gives a number of counter-examples, where only the more basic item has survived, such as *brave* 'splendid' but not *bravity* 'splendour'. Further research in this area would be valuable.

(e) *polysemy is eroded*
Aitken (1984a: 109) tells us that 'many words for common and permanent notions . . . in most of the areas of survival, no longer display their former,

full range.' Downie (1983) and Macafee (1994) confirm that for the less common items and those that are becoming old-fashioned, there is less consensus about meaning and there are more idiosyncratic associations to the word.

(f) *regional distributions become patchy*
See further below.

(g) *Scots and English forms become specialised to different senses*
Semantic differentiation sometimes develops between the original and incoming forms, such as Dieth's North-Eastern example of home-made *raips* but shop-bought *hempen ropes* (1932). In Glasgow I recorded *hame* in the basic sense, but only *home* with reference to institutions such as children's homes, and also in *home-help* (Macafee 1994). Such specialisation of competing forms is presumably brought about by use in different registers or social contexts.

LEXICAL INNOVATION

Scots continues to adopt new vocabulary from sources such as the mass media and brand names of products, while showing only limited renewal from its own internal resources. As noted above, neologisms often enter the language as slang in the first instance. Some areas of vocabulary are particularly productive of slang words, which remain in that register because of the taboo nature of the semantic field (for example words to do with sex, excretion, violence and drugs), or because of the deliberate forcefulness of the words (for example superlatives and insults). Children's language and the 'antilanguage' of delinquents and criminals (Halliday 1978) figure largely in any list of neologisms. Adults' slang and children's language have a great deal in common, particularly the practice of altering and mangling words. The same kinds of forms are created and used out of the contradictory motives of modesty (for example minced oaths), abuse, humour and sheer ebullience.

A number of recurrent creative principles can be seen at work in neologism, for example variations on a metaphor, on a phonological pattern or on a syntactical pattern. Some of these are listed in Macafee (1994: 161), and see further Tulloch (1997a):

(a) *-ie* is added with diminutive effect to the full or clipped form of a word, for example *haunnie* 'handstand'. There are also items of obscure origin with this ending, for example *hudgie* 'a hurl, a ride'.
(b) *-o* is added with emphatic effect to the full or clipped form of a word, for example *galdo*, a form of *gallus*.

(c) Forms resembling (often rhyming with) existing participial adjectives are coined, but the verb stem itself is not always found, for example *gingin* on the model of *mingin*, both meaning 'smelly'; *brammed up* on the model of *dolled up*.

(d) Metathesis, for example *occifer* 'officer'.

(e) Reduplication, often pairing front and back vowels, for example *mingmong* 'a smelly person'.

(f) Sound symbolism, for example the nasal consonants of *mingin*.

(g) Acronyms, for example *k.d.r.f.*, that is *kick-door-run-fast* (a prank).

(h) Spoonerisms, for example *chuckin fuckit*.

(i) Ad hoc elaborations, for example *swedgie-boo-boos*, a variation on *swedgers* 'sweeties'.

(j) *Eggie-language* forms, for example *jeginger* for *ginger* 'soft drink'.

(k) Rhyming slang, for example *Brussels sprouts* = *dowts* 'cigarette stubs', *chuckie stanes* (shortened to *chuckies*) = *weans* 'children'.

Interesting as such slang neologisms are in their own right, they do not replace the lexical losses in the mainstream of the language. Lexical erosion is of concern because it increases the gap between Scots as it exists in spoken forms and the literary culture and traditional folk-culture in the language. Lexical distinctiveness is also important to the question of whether Scots is a language, since it is the main barrier to intelligibility. Scots speakers are at least passively bilingual,[3] and Standard English monolinguals tend to expect from them, as a sort of courtesy, that they will make themselves intelligible by speaking Standard English. My research on working-class Glaswegian speech suggests that the direction of change (in effect, erosion) is towards greater intelligibility through the loss of distinctive lexis, while Scots grammar and word-form are relatively well preserved in comparison (Macafee 1994).

USING THE DICTIONARIES AND *THE LINGUISTIC ATLAS OF SCOTLAND* VOLS I AND II

The main resources for the study of Scots vocabulary are the two multi-volume historical dictionaries: SND (from 1700 onwards) and *A Dictionary of the Older Scottish Tongue* (DOST) (up to 1700); and the first two volumes of *The Linguistic Atlas of Scotland* (LAS). CSD is a one-volume digest of SND and DOST. It omits the distinctive material (mainly Norn loans) from Orkney, Shetland and Caithness. CSD also omits less well-documented items, namely those with fewer than three independent witnesses. It is nevertheless very useful. Its pronunciation entries (by the late A. J. Aitken) are more systematically phonemic than those of SND.[4] It is also a valuable bridge between the two historical dictionaries, as it is possible to find the main DOST headwords by looking up the Modern Scots forms in CSD, for example DOST *awin* 'own' adj. via CSD *ain*, DOST *builʒe* 'boil' v. via CSD *bile*[1], DOST *irne* 'iron' via CSD *iron* or the cross-reference entry for the more familiar Modern Scots form *airn*.

At the time of writing, work is in progress on the electronic conversion and tagging of SND and DOST, and an online dictionary combining material from the two historical dictionaries is expected to result. This should make it much easier to explore particular aspects of the lexicon in depth, although excellent work of this kind has already been done by hand, for instance Thun's (1963) study of reduplicative words, and Kries' (1999) study of the Scandinavian element in Older Scots. Some areas that warrant detailed quantitative, chronological and comparative studies in future include the various categories of word formation (on which see Tulloch 1997a), the etymologically obscure element, and the rate of turnover of the vocabulary (see Robinson 1987).

Other dictionaries that should be borne in mind as a source of information about Scots vocabulary are the *Middle English Dictionary* (MED) and *The English Dialect Dictionary* (EDD). An etymological dictionary of English – such as *The Oxford English Dictionary* (OED), *The Oxford Dictionary of English Etymology* or the more up-to-date concise edition of this, or Partridge (1966) – is needed to supplement the etymologies in the Scots dictionaries, if the prior history of Old English words or more detailed history of loanwords is required. MED can be useful for comparison, particularly in the poorly documented Pre-literary Scots period. EDD covers the whole of the British Isles, on the basis mainly of dialect literature and the input of voluntary correspondents. Its selection of quotations is independent of SND, so both this and OED can usefully be consulted if a wide range of quotations is required. The findings of the Linguistic Survey of Scotland (LSS), published in the three volumes of LAS (of which the first two are concerned with vocabulary) were not incorporated into the dictionaries, so the atlases – and especially the raw wordlists within them – should also be borne in mind as a source of lexical material not found elsewhere.

There are also many wordlists of varying degrees of sophistication covering local dialects.[5] Where these are earlier than SND, it will generally be found that they have been incorporated into the dictionary. Works subsequent to SND often have a few interesting items to add to the lexical corpus, but since the language is quite well documented across the range of dialects, the main value of these works is to sift out the material that is still current or within living memory. Lamb's (1988) Orkney dictionary is particularly well focused in this respect, and has a valuable new convention whereby an asterisk is used to mark those items that are still current (in contrast to the traditional use of a dagger to mark items that are obsolescent). The geographical area least well covered in SND is Ulster, and here there are two recent dictionaries that add considerably to the record. Fenton's (1995, 2000) dictionary of Co. Antrim Scots is discussed further below. The other is *A Concise Ulster Dictionary*. This covers the whole of Ulster, but unfortunately does not distinguish between Hiberno-English and Ulster Scots,[6] though it is often clear from its etymologies that certain items are of Scots origin.

SND omits the slang component of the language almost entirely, apart from a few items labelled 'Glasgow slang'.[7] The main reference works for slang are *A Dictionary of Slang and Unconventional English*, and the revised concise edition of this, and also the more arcane *Dictionary of the Underworld*.

The dictionary user should be aware of certain weaknesses of the multi-volume historical dictionaries. Both DOST and SND were produced over very long timescales. The first volume of SND appeared in 1931 and the final volume in 1975. The first volume of DOST appeared in 1937, and the last two volumes are in press at the time of writing. There have been changes over time in editorial practice, and also in coverage, with both dictionaries greatly increasing their range of source materials subsequent to the publication of the early letters of the alphabet. It is expected with dictionaries on this scale that material for the early letters will turn up after they have been published and will be collected in a final supplement. These supplements should always be consulted. (In DOST, as yet, supplementation consists only of additions at the end of some individual volumes.) However, supplementation cannot always rectify the lighter treatment of the earlier letters.

Computer-assisted methods were used to complete DOST, but the main darg, or 'work', of both dictionaries largely pre-dated computer methods. The material for the dictionaries was excerpted (largely by volunteer readers) from written sources, and each quotation was written out by hand on a piece of paper about the size of a postcard, called a dictionary slip. When writing a dictionary article, the editor has in front of him or her a pile of dictionary slips, which he or she sorts into one or more dictionary articles, with subdivisions by part of speech and sense. If the quotations are abundant, a selection is made of the ones to be used. Quite often, dictionary slips are sent forwards or backwards to other letters of the alphabet. The long timescale of sending forward can mean that cross-references are inaccurate. An editor may decide not to treat an item (for example a compound) at a particular point, and instead will indicate by a cross-reference where it can be found, but can only make a best guess at which spelling will be used for the headword when the item is edited, possibly decades later. It is of course impossible to send material back to previously published volumes – it can only be held over for a supplement.

A particular problem, of which SLD is very much aware, is the unreliability of the information on current regional distribution given in SND (and therefore in CSD and other derived dictionaries). The geographical labels are based on the occurrence of items, forms and senses in the written literature, supplemented by information received from a network of correspondents. As each letter of the alphabet was prepared, wordlists were sent out to these volunteers. The information on which the geographical labels are based is therefore patchy and unsystematic. The absence of attestation for a particular area is, of course, negative evidence, and should never be taken as conclusive. The information is summarised in CSD, but is seriously out of date, especially for the earlier letters of the alphabet, since citation of living witnesses in SND only implies that the word was known around the time that the relevant volume of the dictionary was published. CSD itself is now almost twenty years old, and there has certainly been a continuing erosion since it was published (although it is in the nature of obsolescent vocabulary that it can linger on at an idiolectal level for a long time (see above), and can therefore continue to be collected, while in practice it is moribund).

One of the geographical labels used in CSD is 'local'. These items have what is known in linguistic geography as a 'relic' distribution. Such a lexical item occurs over a large geographical extent, but only patchily, as if a length of fabric had disintegrated and gone into holes. This is what happens to a 'General Scots' word when it stops being general, so the 'local' category is likely to grow. Unfortunately, information about such distributions is particularly unreliable. Nässén (1989) made a study of Shetland weather words from Jakobsen's (1921) dictionary of Shetland Norn, the material for which was collected in the 1890s, mainly to see how modern geographical distributions compared with Jakobsen's for those words that had survived. What Nässén found is that where Jakobsen limited a word to a single area within Shetland, there was fairly good agreement with the modern distribution, if the word survived at all. If Jakobsen's distribution was patchy, the modern distribution was more likely to be patchy as well – but they were not the same patches. More than fifty per cent of these items occurred more in other areas than in the ones Jakobsen specified (Macafee 1991/92).

It cannot be denied that the Scots dictionaries – like other period and dialect dictionaries – are difficult to consult. The user may have to guess what the spelling is, or may have in front of him or her a spelling that is not one of those given in the dictionary. The Introduction to CSD gives suggestions of alternative spellings to try (pp. xix–xx), but many idiosyncratic problems remain. For instance, speakers of North-Eastern Scots have trouble locating the words *chaave* (s.v. *tyauve*) and *yockie* (s.v. *yeuk*). The CSD really is concise, and great care must be taken to understand its conventions before citing it as a source of information. Take, for instance, the word *feart* (see Figure 4.3). As a past tense and past participle this appears under *fear*, six lines down in the article, as the fourth item in a list of forms that begins *-ed*, meaning 'any of the forms listed at the beginning of the article + -ed'. The next article in the dictionary (apart from two cross-reference articles) is *feart*, which exists only as the root of a participial adjective *feartit*. The adjective *feartit* is found in Renfrewshire, Glasgow and Ayrshire. On the basis of this article – which, remember, is headed *feart* – the understandable mistake has arisen before now of claiming that *feart* is found only in West Central Scots. Even experienced scholars make mistakes through failure to follow up cross-references, failure to consult the supplement as well as the main dictionary and even (which is reprehensible) failure to consult the dictionaries at all. The dictionaries should be studied as if they were knitting patterns or circuit diagrams – every dot and comma is significant.

Figure 4.3 fear – feart (from CSD)

---

fear *18-*, **fere** &c *15–17* [fir; *Sh Ork nEC* fer] *n* 1
= fear *15-*. 2 a fright, a scare *19-*, *now Sh NE Fif Dmf*.
v 1 *vt* = fear *16-*. 2 frighten, scare *18-*. 3 *also vi*
~ o be afraid or fear for *19-*, *now Ags Fif*.
~ed *la16-*, **ferd** *la15-17*, ~it &c *la14-17*, **feart**
la18-: ~ed &c at, o, for frightened or afraid of
la14-. **feardie** &c, **feardie gowk** *chf child's*
word a coward *20-*. **dinna be** ~t o *humorous*
don't be so sparing with *20-*, *NE Fif Arg*. **ye're**
nae ~t *ironic* you are pretty brazen-faced *20-*.
~some &c frightening, terrifying *la18-*.
but ~ without fear *la15-16*. **nae** ~s! = no
fear! *la19-*.
fear *see* FEE, FIAR
fearsie *see* FIARCIE
feart [firt] *v* ~it *adj* afraid *la20-*, *Renfr Gsw Ayr*.
[f *feart* (*adj*) (FEAR)]

SURVEYING LEXIS

The pragmatic methodology of SND has already been mentioned. The problem for the dictionaries attempting to survey usage is the enormous extent of the wordlist, with perhaps 30,000 headwords in SND but more like 50,000 separate items when derivatives, compounds and phrases are included, many of these with numerous forms and further subdivisions of part of speech and sense. The lexicographer must, perforce, rely on finding a small number of dedicated and well-informed individuals to supply information about the speech of their communities. Linguistic geography and sociolinguistics, however, are looking for patterns and trends, and can therefore afford to concentrate on selected items of vocabulary. Even so, linguistic geography, with its need for wide spatial coverage, still relies on finding small numbers, or perhaps single individuals, to represent their speech communities. The LSS chose to increase the number of localities surveyed by using postal questionnaires for the lexical section, which is considerably cheaper than sending out field-workers. The questionnaires were sent to prominent individuals, such as schoolteachers, who were asked to find traditional dialect speakers to fill in the questionnaires. In some cases, the returned questionnaires were discarded because it was evident that they had been filled in by consulting a Scots dictionary. The returns that were used may well have been compromised, on occasion, in less obvious ways, but in the aggregate they generally produced coherent geographical distributions when mapped. The LSS was less tied than the Survey of English Dialects (the corresponding survey in England) to elderly informants, or to male informants – the bias that Chambers and Trudgill (1980) memorably captured in the nickname NORMs, that is 'non-mobile older rural males'. The data of the LSS can therefore be regarded as a fair picture of conservative speech recalled at a particular point in time, the 1950s. The questionnaire sought to elicit Scots translations of Standard English items, and the words collected may well have been passive rather than active in the respondents' vocabulary: the questionnaire asked the respondents to give first the most common local word, and in many cases what was given was the Standard English word. The introduction to LAS vol. I therefore instructs us to regard the language collected as 'potential'.

The items surveyed in the two postal lexical questionnaires were chosen, in consultation with the editors of the Scots dictionaries, as concepts that were likely to produce a wide range of regional words. The full data are given as wordlists in the atlases and a selection of items is mapped. Hatchings of different kinds are used to show the distribution of different responses. In the second volume of the atlas (based on the second postal questionnaire) isolated occurrences outside of the main distribution are also indicated, using point symbols. The edges of the hatched areas, although they are not drawn in as such, correspond to the linguistic-geographical concept of the isogloss,[8] a line drawn on a map to separate different linguistic responses.

Dialect areas are defined not by the distribution of responses to single questions, but by the accumulation of differentiae, seen on composite maps as isogloss bundles. There have been a number of such studies based on the data of the LSS, for instance Speitel's (1969, 1978) studies of the bundling of isoglosses in the vicinity of the Scottish-English Border. Glauser's (1974) study, based on his own fieldwork, also looks at the Border area. Macaulay (1997) has used the LAS data to address the question of whether Ayrshire has any integrity as a linguistic area (he concludes that it has). Macaulay (1985) is very critical of the presentation of data in the two lexical volumes of LAS, comparing the maps to abstract art. He would like to have seen more interpretation of the findings. One can see some obvious patterns, for instance the already known dominance of Norn-derived lexis in the dialects of Orkney, Shetland and Caithness; or the occurrence of some items with very limited distribution in the isolated river valleys of Galloway (helpfully brought out in the maps by taking the isoglosses round populated areas rather than through virtually unpopulated ones); but a great deal more work on the data is needed to bring out any other patterns, for which it will be necessary to add historical and etymological interpretations to the linguistic-geographical data.

LEXIS AND SOCIOLINGUISTIC RESEARCH

The methods of linguistic geography are based on the assumption of community norms, the reliance on a single individual (or at most two or three) to represent the speech of a whole community. But, as Labov (1966) demonstrated, when we wish to explain variability within the speech of individuals, it is necessary, paradoxically, to examine whole communities.

In many ways, lexis is unsuitable for sociolinguistic research in the Labovian paradigm. The ideal sociolinguistic variable, as Labov specifies, should be high in frequency, have a certain immunity from conscious suppression, be an integral unit of larger structures and be easily quantified on a linear scale (Labov 1966: 49). Hence the concentration on phonological variables. However, lexis has one property that makes it very useful in the sociolinguistic interview, namely its inherent interest as a topic of conversation. It was for this reason that I built my Glasgow interviews around the discussion of a lexical questionnaire (Macafee 1994). This allowed me to approach my interview subjects in good faith, as someone interested in their language, and willing to listen to their views about a level of language that they could discuss in everyday terms. Lexis is also, inescapably, an important aspect of linguistic variation, especially in the context of Scots (and the traditional dialects of England), where the vernacular has a much greater time depth and semantic content than it does for instance in urban New York or Norwich. It cannot be assumed that lexis varies in the same way as other linguistic levels: I found no correlation in my Glasgow data between a speaker's degree of Scotsness in the recorded interview and the same speaker's self-reported knowledge and use of old Scots words.[9]

The sociolinguistic researcher may be able to record enough Scots word-forms (the Column 2 items of Figure 4.1) for objective analysis,[10] but lexical items (Column 1) have to be elicited, either directly ('Do you know/use the word x?') or indirectly ('What is your word for y?'). The indirect method produces more reliable results, since it avoids suggesting the answer; but if there is a range of possible answers, there is a risk of false negatives (wrongly concluding that a particular item is not known). Some items are also difficult to translate into

English in order to frame an indirect question, and moribund items are difficult to elicit – prompting may be necessary, in which case it may be useful to keep a record of whether prompting was resorted to in particular cases.

The biggest problem is to select a well-motivated sample of the vocabulary. Widely different, and sometimes counter-intuitive, results can be obtained by selecting different types of vocabulary. Macaulay (1977: 55)[11] found that his middle-class interviewees knew more of his ten 'old Scots words' than his working-class interviewees. Pollner (1985a, 1985b) also found that his middle-class interviewees scored better on the more arcane terms, for instance those gleaned from LAS. Aitken (1979: 108) explained Macaulay's results in terms of the middle classes being better read in Scottish literature.[12]

The sociolinguistic approach demands that a representative group of individuals be administered the same sociolinguistic interview. They certainly cannot be preselected on the basis of their willingness and ability to provide information about local dialect vocabulary. It must be assumed that their time and patience is limited, and the questionnaire must be correspondingly short. One hundred words may be too many.

A number of approaches have been made to the problem of drawing valid generalisations from a necessarily small sample of lexis. In Macafee (1994) the lexical items were selected partly to present interviewees of both sexes and all ages with at least some words that each group would be likely to recognise, and which would therefore form a basis for discussion (and the collection of spontaneous speech). A distinction was made between active and passive knowledge. In most cases the interviewees were asked whether they knew a word – usually they were asked for a Glaswegian equivalent of a Standard English item, then prompted for specific items if they were not given spontaneously, but in the case of untranslatable items (for instance names for character types, such as *bauchle*) they were given a Glaswegian word and asked to define it. They were also asked whether they would use the word. Unfortunately, the opportunity was missed to distinguish between current and past usage, a point that the older speakers brought out in the discussion, many of them being aware of having dropped specific Scots items from their usage in the course of their lives.

The process of generalising from the data was similar to looking for isogloss bundles in linguistic geography; that is, the data were quantified in terms of age and sex,[13] and it was then possible to see that certain types of vocabulary tended to run along the same sociolinguistic gradients. Some of the patterns that emerged were:

(a) there was a decline of traditional vocabulary across the generations, with active use giving way to passive knowledge and thereafter to a rapid decline in knowledge and use;

(b) innovating items in children's speech were usually known to some adults, but used mainly by children and sometimes teenagers;

(c) some slang items were identifiable as male slang in their usage, though they were generally known to at least some of the females in the same age groups.

From this deliberately varied selection of lexical material, it was not possible to quantify the rate of decline of Scots vocabulary. In order to attempt this, we require a baseline against which to measure the data from the new study. Any reliable earlier studies can be used as a baseline (cf. Figure 4.2). One baseline that has been used (Agutter and Cowan 1981; Lawrie 1991) is the questionnaire of the LSS, or part of it, re-administered in or near to a locality surveyed in the original research. As expected, the results of these studies show a very steep decline, though it should be remembered that they are usually comparing ordinary speakers in the new study with 'good' speakers in the original study.

Another possible baseline, but one that gives less time depth, is the age stratification available within the social sample itself. Preliminary enquiries in the community can be used as a source of information about the traditional vocabulary of the area within living memory. Obviously, it is possible with this approach to exaggerate the rate of decline by inadvertently homing in on items that are salient to the community precisely because they are perceived as becoming moribund. Hendry carefully avoided this by the wording of his inquiries, asking for twenty to forty words 'which were in common everyday use when you were a primary school pupil' (1997: Appendix B).

Finally, there is SND. The dictionary has the advantage that it gives the whole picture, insofar as this is known, but, by the same token, the amount of material is unmanageably large. One approach would be to draw more systematically on the expertise of local dialect speakers by presenting the chosen arbiters with the material relevant to a particular locality. In principle, it should be feasible to extract this, when the planned electronic version becomes available.[14] If the local experts could stratify the non–obsolete material in terms of how moribund or current it was, the researcher could then take a sample from each stratum. Once refined by field-testing, such an instrument would in effect be a proficiency test in the local vernacular, the results of which would provide a whole dimension of sociolinguistic variability, which could be correlated with social factors and with linguistic data obtained by the analysis of tape-recorded speech.

Whatever the baseline, so many biases can be introduced by the selection of the lexical items that it is clearly desirable to select and yet, as far as possible, not select. The solution to this used by McGarrity (1998) was to take a complete semantic field. The field chosen was a subsection of the vocabulary of weather, namely terms for precipitation (rain, snow and so on). This semantic field was chosen because it was thought that it would be immune from change caused by external factors, and would therefore stand as good a chance of being preserved as any area of the vocabulary. In practice, it was soon realised that modern life insulates individuals to a great extent from the vagaries of the weather, and there is correspondingly less sensitivity to its nuances. Another suitable semantic field might have been parts of the body, but this is too delicate a subject for sociolinguistic interviews with strangers. McGarrity's research is discussed further below.

VOCABULARY AS CULTURAL HISTORY

Vocabulary can be of considerable value as a record of some aspects of cultural history. Such research is interdisciplinary in nature, and has more often been undertaken by ethnographers than by linguists, so it will only be mentioned briefly here.

In rare cases, the existence of a term may be the sole evidence for the existence of a cultural practice, for instance the words for 'animal manure used as fuel' cited by Fenton (1972). The existence of a wide range of synonyms is an indication of the importance of the referent in a culture: for instance, wild plants that are in some way useful (medicinally or as a food resource in times of scarcity) are more likely to have vernacular names, and more likely to have a wide range of different vernacular names in different dialects.

More subtly, language preserves many perceptions and insights, often humorous. These are embodied in the linkages made between one idea and another through metaphor, derivation and compounding. As Hugh MacDiarmid remarked, Scots contains 'a vast unutilised mass of lapsed observation made by minds whose attitude to experience and whose speculative and imaginative tendencies were quite different from any possible to Englishmen and anglicised Scots today' (1923: 210). But by the end of the nineteenth century, the dialect speaker with a fund of concrete imagery and proverbial wisdom – the product of a mental life circumscribed by local custom, tradition and dialect – became *rara avis*.

A source for the study of vocabulary in this perspective, of which little use has yet been made, is *The Scots Thesaurus*. Unfortunately, the *Thesaurus* covers only about half of the vocabulary contained in the CSD, on which it is based.[15] The *Thesaurus* can be used as an index to the multi-volume dictionaries, with their wealth of quotations selected from a very large corpus of literary and non-literary writings.

ADDITIONS AND CORRECTIONS TO THE DICTIONARY RECORD

As we have seen, studies of Scots vocabulary can make contributions to linguistic geography, sociolinguistics and ethnography or cultural history. Conversely, all of these, as well as descriptive studies specifically intended as contributions to lexicography, can provide additions and corrections to the dictionary record.

Even small studies or passing observations are valuable, and should be sent to Scottish Language Dictionaries, 27 George Square, Edinburgh EH8 9LD, or mail@sldl.org.uk. The absence of an item from SND ought to mean that it has been rejected as Standard English (on the authority of the OED) or as slang (for references, see above); this should be checked if possible before offering corrections and additions.

Although the dictionary record is fairly complete, and it is unlikely that many new items of traditional dialect vocabulary will turn up (as opposed to innovations, mainly slang), this is always a possibility. For instance, a student studying Scots at the University of Aberdeen recently collected the North-Eastern word *treelies* 'marbles (the game)', which is an otherwise unrecorded, but phonologically regular, form of *trule* (CSD), *trulis* (DOST) (and cf. SND s.v. *trow* v.[1]).

Additional information is more likely to be in a more subtle form: confirmation of the present-day regional distribution and currency of already-recorded material. The SLD encourages schools and individuals to compile wordlists with this in mind (and also, of course, as a consciousness-raising exercise and educational project: see the *Electronic Scots School Dictionary* and the 'Scuil Wab' at www.sldl.org.uk). A useful analogy can be drawn with the public interest in bird-watching. Isolated sightings that may be of little significance in themselves become meaningful when they are reported to a body that can combine the information into a composite picture. To extend the analogy, the British Trust for Ornithology has, over many years, built up the expertise of interested members of the public to the point where it can now call upon a large cadre of people to conduct quite sophisticated and statistically sound studies. The annual Garden Survey of birds also tries to stimulate interest and expertise amongst the next generation by encouraging schoolchildren to take part.

The SLD is always on the lookout, also, for linguistically knowledgeable and sophisticated individuals who have a good command of their local dialect, and who are willing to work systematically through the corpus of the CSD, commenting on currency.

Apart from monitoring the state – sadly, almost inevitably the decline – of traditional dialect vocabulary, it is possible to design studies at various levels of sophistication to monitor the ever-changing corpus of slang. As has already been mentioned, there are age and sex differences in the usage of slang and there are also interesting questions of pragmatics surrounding its appropriate and deliberately inappropriate use.

Another area where new material can be collected is what is sometimes known as 'folk-say', that is proverbs, catchphrases, weather rhymes and so on. This type of material is under-recorded in the dictionaries, forming as it does a transition zone between lexical items and texts. However, it is very difficult to elicit, as its use is often occasional, and it is not readily called to mind out of context. It is best collected over a long period of time by an insider who can record casual observations and draw on introspection. It is therefore unsuitable for small, time-limited projects.

CASE STUDIES

The two studies to be examined in more detail in this section represent the opposite extremes of methodology. Fenton's (1995, 2000) research is a particularly impressive example of a traditional exercise in dialect lexicography. McGarrity's (1998) research uses a sophisticated quantitative approach to estimate the rate of decline of traditional dialect vocabulary and attempts to explain this in terms of speakers' beliefs about and attitudes towards the local dialect.

Fenton's study of Co. Antrim Ulster Scots

A large part of the Ulster Scots area (as mapped by Gregg 1972, 1985) lies within Co. Antrim. Fenton (1995, 2000) used his own insider knowledge of the dialect and his extensive contacts with conservative dialect speakers to survey the currency of a very large and comprehensive corpus of material, published as an annotated dialect dictionary. The author and others of his generation, who are old enough to remember the years before the Second World War, still preserve in living memory the recollection of a rural way of life that has been swept away. Had Fenton not made this record of his traditional local dialect when he did, the opportunity would have been lost forever.

Fenton's data was obtained from a relatively small number of speakers, with whom he worked intensively over a long period of time. In order to establish a geographical core area of broad Antrim Scots, he used a checklist of Scots versus Standard English word-forms (following Gregg 1985). Lexical items collected from the transitional or 'mixed' area around the core are also listed in his dictionary, with their sources identified.

Fenton assembled his wordlist from his own personal knowledge, added to cumulatively by his interviewees, and also by thoroughly scouring the relevant dictionaries, including SND and Patterson (1880). A great deal of his long and patient research is thus concealed from the reader, as only those items authenticated by his survey as current within living memory are actually included – and geographically sourced – in his dictionary.

A useful innovation in the layout of his dictionary is the division of the material into what we have called Column 1 and Column 2 items (see Figure 4.1 above), with the former treated in detail and the latter treated briefly as a supplementary list without regional annotations. Other innovative supplements are a list of Standard English words not idiomatic in dialect speech (Column 5 items), for instance *afraid* (for which the normal terms are *feared* or *scarred*) and *child* (for which the normal term is *wain*); and lists of proper names and place names respelled to indicate pronunciation.

McGarrity's research on Aberdeen Scots (the Doric)

The research carried out in Aberdeen by McGarrity (1998; Macafee and McGarrity 1999) was an attempt to build on the Glasgow research of Macafee (1994), in which qualitative methods were used to explore language attitudes in relation to vocabulary maintenance. McGarrity attempts to put this relationship on a quantitative footing.

The voters' roll was used to take a random sample of the adult population in three socially differentiated areas of Aberdeen. An attitude questionnaire and a questionnaire asking for basic personal data were sent out by post. The people contacted were also asked if they would agree to an interview. Non-locals were eliminated when the postal questionnaires were returned, leaving sixty-two local individuals who agreed to be interviewed.

The interview included the administration of a lexical questionnaire. McGarrity's wordlist of terms for precipitation (see above) was compiled from *The Scots Thesaurus*, used as an index to CSD, and from recently published local wordlists, to provide a baseline of vocabulary traditional to the area. The questionnaire was in two parts, first (as a check on reliability) supplying the English words and asking for local equivalents, and then presenting the ninety-six North-Eastern words and word-forms, and asking if the person knew and used them.

'Use' was graded on a three-point scale from 'rarely' through 'occasionally' to 'frequently'. McGarrity found a relationship between both knowledge and use (in various degrees), on the one hand, and age, education and occupation, on the other. There was no relationship with gender.

The attitude questionnaire included questions of belief (for example, 'Women know and use more Doric words and phrases than men') as well as value judgements (e.g. 'The Doric is old-fashioned') and readiness for action (for example, 'Schools in the North-East should encourage their pupils to become better acquainted with the Doric and Scots language in general'). There were also factual questions about language (for example, 'I can understand the Doric in its written form'). The respondents were presented with a five-point scale from 'strongly agree' to 'agree' to 'neutral' to 'disagree' to 'strongly disagree'. The attitudes expressed were generally very positive (but see below), despite the sample being skewed (by uneven returns) towards the middle class. The professional and managerial group, and those with tertiary education, mostly disagreed, however, with the statement 'I speak the Doric'. Non-manual respondents, and those with tertiary education, were more likely to agree that they used Doric words in jest. Again, there were no significant differences by gender.

McGarrity attempted to reduce the thirty questions to a small number of measures of attitude, using a Principal Components Analysis. This is a statistical method of comparing the results from various questions in order to group together those that are, in some sense, measuring the same thing. The method is rather abstract, and it is not always clear what that thing is. Three factors emerged. From the questions that comprised them, they appeared to be measuring: how concerned people were about the preservation of the dialect (this was termed Defensiveness), how positive their value judgements were (Positiveness), and the extent to which they claimed to speak the dialect and take part in activities involving it (Participation). Individuals could then be given a score on each of these three measures, and correlations made with age, gender, occupation, and so on. However, there was only one significant relationship between these scores and social variables, namely Participation with occupation. This suggests that there are unidentified extra-linguistic factors at work. The three components together explain about half of the variance in the data, but they appear to be determined by some unknown aspects of life experience or personal preference that do not coincide neatly with age, gender, education or occupation.

One of the main goals of the research was to relate attitudes to language maintenance. This was done by giving each individual a score on each of the three attitudinal factors and correlating these scores with scores for lexical knowledge and use. There were only three significant correlations, all of them positive. The factor Positiveness correlated with one of the measures of lexical use. The factor Participation correlated with two of the measures of use. In general, however, just as the usual social variables did not go a long way towards explaining language attitudes in this community, language attitudes did not go very far in explaining lexical decline. The attitudes were largely positive, and this was shared by the middle as well as the working class, and yet the traditional vocabulary seemed to be rapidly disappearing from use.

There were, in fact, internal conflicts in speaker attitudes. Two of the few questions on which speakers did not, on average, have positive scores were 'Standard English speakers have more success in the modern world than dialect speakers' (there tended to be agreement with this); and 'Standard English should be spoken to children' (the response was neutral on average). The face-to-face interviews also brought out this familiar story of a tension between loyalty to the traditional dialect and the belief that it is a material handicap.

CONCLUSION

The similarity to bird-watching would seem to relegate lexicography to the very lowest ranks of the sciences, a taxonomic or 'butterfly catching' pursuit. Furthermore, it has to be admitted that those who study lexis do so more for its descriptive interest, as part of culture or history, than for its power to throw light on issues of linguistic theory. Nevertheless, just as taxonomy remains the backbone of the natural sciences, lexicography remains the backbone of dialectology. Lexis is the greater part of what makes Scots distinctive, and monitoring the lexis is an essential part of monitoring the state of the Scots language.[17]

NOTES

1. In most of these studies, the subjects were presented with the words under investigation; in others (Agutter and Cowan 1981; Lawrie 1991), they were given a definition and asked to supply local words. Some variation studies have also investigated lexis. As part of his Glasgow study, Macaulay (1977) asked his subjects if they knew ten 'old Scots words'. The average number known by the adults was 7.8 and by the fifteen-year-olds 3.3. Pollner's (1985a, 1985b) Livingston New Town study also included a lexical questionnaire. Forty-seven adults and nine thirteen-year-olds were presented with a list of twenty-three Scots words and were asked whether they knew any of them. Since the New Town population did not represent a single dialect area, the questionnaire was designed to include items from all over the Lowlands. The adults knew forty-five per cent of the items, the children twenty-six per cent.
2. An interesting parallel to the survival of passive Scots lexis is the retention of archaisms in written Standard English. *Thou* and *thy*, for instance, are quite common in newsprint (mainly in quotation and idiom, and in playful extensions of these), but the transmission of such archaisms is dependent on shared cultural references, in this case passed on through education and the pulpit (Minugh 1999). See Lenz (2000) on obsolete Scots vocabulary in Modern Scottish plays and Douglas (2000) on newspapers.
3. Except perhaps in cases of senile reversion.
4. The pronunciation entries also cover Older Scots.
5. For some references, see my online bibliography of the Scots language (details at the beginning of the Bibliography).
6. Because of the geographical vagueness of some of the main sources of its material.
7. Mainly from McArthur and Long's novel, *No Mean City* (1935).
8. Really, strictly speaking, a heterogloss, since it separates points that are different, rather than joining those that are the same.
9. Identified as those showing the pattern of age-related decline.
10. Great care must be taken in the construction of the sociolinguistic variables, because of the intricacies of lexical incidence – for instance, not every /u/ in Scots corresponds to an /au/ in Standard English (see Macafee 1997b). There is also a great deal of lexical conditioning, with some items much more likely to occur in their Scots form than others (cf. the remarks above on the erosion of column 2, and see Macafee 1994: chapter 5).
11. See note 1 above.
12. In Lawrie's study also, a slight difference between males and females seemed to be attributable to females having read more in Scots than males (1991: 22).
13. Class was not a variable as all of the interviewees were working-class Glaswegians.
14. The abortive North-East Language Project attempted to extract the North-Eastern material (including General Scots and local material found in the North-East) from the electronic files of the CSD.
15. The process of creating the *Thesaurus* was an experimental one, and as much as possible was done within the constraints of time and funding.
16. Items with no regional annotation are to be understood as general within the study area.
17. I am grateful to Iseabail Macleod for her comments on this chapter.

CHAPTER 5

Syntax and Discourse in Modern Scots

Jim Miller

INTRODUCTION

Since the eighteenth century speakers in Scotland have had at their disposal a range of structures varying from Broad Scots at one end to Standard English at the other. Different speakers make different choices in different situations but this chapter focuses on structures towards the Broad Scots end of the range. The chapter deals with syntactic structures, the combination of words into phrases and phrases into clauses. Words too consist of smaller units; some aspects of word structure are relevant to clause structure and will be described below. Speakers typically combine clauses into larger chunks which are called discourse or text. (The latter term is nowadays applied to both spoken and written language.) We will look at discourse insofar as Scots has phrases and clauses which are central to its organisation.

The data is taken from a number of sources: a 220,000-word digitised body of conversations collected in Edinburgh and East Lothian and described in Brown and Miller (1982) (the Edinburgh Corpus of Spoken Scottish English, or ECOSSE); a 12,000 word subset of a body of dialogues produced by West of Scotland speakers carrying out a task – the Map Task corpus, or MTC; the data from Macaulay (1991), which analyses a set of narratives collected in Ayr; the excerpts from narratives in Bennett (1992) but excluding the narratives from speakers from the Highlands and Islands; data in Häcker (1999); data in Beal (1997) and data obtained by elicitation tests (see Miller and Cann 1994). For the sake of comparison with older structures, still used by the oldest speakers, we consulted Murray (1873) and Wilson (1915, 1923, 1926).

The data in ECOSSE was collected mainly by two field-workers from school pupils aged seventeen or eighteen. Three schools took part, a state school in Edinburgh, a state school in East Lothian and a fee-paying school in Edinburgh. The same field-worker visited a given school and recorded conversations with the same four or five pupils. The occasional one-to-one conversation took place but mostly the field-worker was talking to two or three pupils.

Much of the data was not collected in the most relaxed and informal of circumstances but the hope was that field-worker and pupils would get to know each other and produce relaxed conversations. It was also the only way to collect a large quantity of data, analyse it and write up the results in the two-year time limit associated with the research grant. The method worked, most spectacularly in the state school in East Lothian. The initial conversations are awkward, with much of the data contributed by the field-worker (who was from north Edinburgh and a speaker of Scottish English) but the majority are produced by participants at ease with each other and talking openly, and sometimes scurrilously, about their teachers and other pupils. One field-worker recorded conversations at home with members of his family, a sister of fifteen, a brother of nineteen and his wife (in her early twenties). The author collected data from five eighteen–year-old undergraduates from East Lothian; informality was created by making the recording as the participants sat round his kitchen table having a meal.

The Map Task Corpus was collected in 1989–90 in the Human Communication Research Centre at the University of Edinburgh. The task required two participants. One had a map with a route from a starting point to a finishing point. The other had a map with just a starting point. Both maps had landmarks, such as mountains, rivers, meadows, smiddies and caravan parks. One map had landmarks that the other map did not and one map had two occurrences of a given landmark while the other map only had one. The participant with the complete route had to explain to the other participant how to draw the route. Neither participant could see the other participant's map. Although the task was carried out in a formal setting, at a special table in the Psychology Department at the University of Glasgow, the cognitive demands of the task distracted the participants' attention from their language. The participants were all first-year students from Glasgow.

Digitised bodies of spontaneous speech are an essential for the investigation of non-standard language but have a serious disadvantage: even a corpus of several million words may contain only one example, or no examples, of a particular construction. This gap can be filled by the use of elicitation tests, designed by the investigator to elicit examples of a specific usage. Consider the account of HAVE TO and MUST in English in which HAVE TO is used for conditions imposed on someone from outside, by a higher authority or *force majeure*, while MUST is used for conditions which people impose on themselves. One elicitation test consists of examples such as *I ___ read this article because I like the author's ideas* (condition imposed by the speaker on himself or herself) vs *I ___ read this article because otherwise I will fail the degree exam* (condition imposed by circumstances/ *force majeure*). Participants in an elicitation test are asked to use HAVE TO in one example and MUST in the other. Alternatively they are given a free choice and the two examples are separated from each other in the questionnaire to prevent direct comparison. A third test provides *I must read this article because* ____ and *I have to read this article because* ____ and participants are asked to complete the examples.

Two caveats are required. The first is that Modern Scots is essentially a spoken variety. Recent research on various languages demonstrates that spontaneous spoken language has its own structures and that certain properties are found across different (spoken) languages. The properties, outlined in the following section, are found in all non-standard varieties of English, a fact which should not cause surprise given that non-standard varieties of any language are typically spoken but not written. (Properties associated with spontaneous spoken language are also found in spontaneous spoken Standard English in England.)

The second caveat is that, apart from the general properties of spontaneous spoken language, a number of (morpho-)syntactic structures used by Scottish speakers are not unique to Scots but occur in other varieties, especially Northern English and the English of the southern USA. Structures found in the above-mentioned bodies of data are referred to as Scots; many of them are not unique to Scots and possibly none of them is.

Why bother with a grammar of Scots? We need to record non-standard varieties of English (and other languages) to make sure that theories of syntax, typology, language change and language acquisition are based on adequate data. We also need to record essential socio-cultural facts. The structures described here are the everyday language of many speakers in Scotland but differ greatly from the structures of standard written English. They form a different system – see Häcker (1999: 11–12, 241) on this matter. Their survival is worth recording, their role in the construction of Scottish identity and the identity of individuals is central even if sadly neglected by researchers, and they bear directly on education, employment and social exclusion. (This point is ignored by politicians and many educators, despite recent comments by the Secretary of Education for England and Wales on the link between social class and academic achievement.)

MORPHOLOGY

We look first at words, in particular at the past tense and past participial forms of verbs. The same lexical verb may have irregular (strong) forms in both Scots and Standard English but the irregular forms may differ – *seen* (Scots) versus *saw* (Standard English). The same lexical verb may be strong in Standard English but weak in Scots – compare *sold* (Standard English) and *sellt* (Scots). Similarly, the same lexical noun may have an irregular plural in one variety but a regular plural in the other – compare *wolves* (Standard English) and *wolfs* (Scots).

The lists of words are illustrative, not exhaustive.

Past tense forms of verbs

seen (= saw)	*taen* (= took)	*come* (= came)	*writ* (= wrote)
done (= did)	*killt* (= killed)	*sellt* (= sold)	*driv* (= drove)
tellt (= told)	*brung* (= brought)	*sunk* (= sank)	*run* (= ran)

Past participles

broke (= broken)	*gave* (= given)	*took* (= taken)
went (= gone)	*forgot* (= forgotten)	*fell* (= fallen)
saw (= seen)	*knew* (= known)	*feart* (= frightened)
rose (= risen)	*froze* (= frozen)	*beat* (= beaten)
came (= come)	*gotten* (= got)	*stole* (= stolen)
blew (= blown)		

Seen, done and *taen* result from a tendency to generalise the past participle form to the past tense. These forms of English irregular verbs settled only in the eighteenth century, and in different patterns in different varieties. *Sellt* and *tellt* indicate that irregular verbs can be made regular. *Sellt* is simply *sell* + *ed* (*ed* → *t* after *l* and *n*).

Broke and *forgot* are past participles in Earlier Modern English. *Went* occurs as a participle in Dunbar's poem 'Celebrations' (late fifteenth century). *Gave* and *knew* are 'incomers'; the original verbs are *gie*, with past tense *gied* and past participle *gien*, and *ken*, with *kent* as past tense and past participle.

Plural nouns

Scots used to have plural forms such as *een* (= eyes), *shin* (= shoes) and *treen* (= trees). (The author last heard *shin* in West Lothian in 1963, *een* is still in regular use, and *treen* is long gone.) In modern Scots the forms worthy of note are *wifes, knifes, lifes, leafs, thiefs, dwarfs, loafs, wolfs*. The relationship between singular and plural is regular, unlike the Standard English *wife* and *wives* – but not *rooves* and is it *hoofs* or *hooves, dwarfs* or *dwarves*?

Pronouns

Scots has a second person plural *yous* or *yous yins*, avoided by educated speakers. *Us* is regularly used instead of *me*, particularly with verbs such as *give, show* and *lend*, for example *Can you lend us a quid?* This usage is informal but widespread.

The possessive pronoun *mine* corresponds to *mines*, which is analogous to *yours, his, hers, ours* and *theirs*.

Himself and *themselves* correspond to *hisself* and *theirselves*. The latter generalise the pattern of *yourself*, *herself*, and so on consisting of a possessive pronoun, such as *your* + *self* or *selves*.

Note *Me and Jimmy are on on Monday our two selves* (= by ourselves). *Two* occurs between *our* and *selves*, which raises the question whether *myself* etc. should be considered as one word or two.

Demonstrative adjectives

Corresponding to Standard English *those*, Scots has *thae*, as in *Thae cakes was awfy dear* (= These cakes were very dear). *Thae* is still alive but the most frequent form is now *them*: *Them cakes was awfy dear*. (*Thae* and *they* derive from different words in Early English.) Wilson (1915) gives *thir* as the plural of *this*. Macaulay (1991) gives no instances of *thir* but there is one occurrence in ECOSSE, from a young East Lothian speaker.

Adverbs

Like all Germanic languages (except Standard English), Scots does not add *-ly* to adjectives to create adverbs: *They got on real good*, *Drive slow* (on a sign at a roadworks), *Drive quick*.

SYNTACTIC LINKAGE

Words combine into phrases and phrases combine into clauses. Syntactic linkage is the term for the different ways in which the connections between words and phrases are signalled. The simplest link is mere word order but in many languages nouns come in different shapes in order to signal their relationship to the verb in a clause; they take singular or plural suffixes depending on whether the verb is singular or plural and they may take different (case) suffixes to signal whether they are the subject or the direct object of the verb. The differences between Scots and Standard English concern the signalling of number; singular forms of the copula BE combine with plural subject nouns and numerals are not always followed by plural nouns either.

Number agreement

Plural subject nouns usually combine with *is* and *was*.

1. the windies wiz aw broken (= the windows were all broken)
2. the lambs is oot the field (= the lambs are out of the field)
3. And I mean there are employers that's harmful to the workers just the same (Macaulay)

Wilson (1915) gives *Ma glassiz iz broakun* (my glasses are broken) and *is they yours?* (are these yours?).

We was is frequent. *We is* does not occur.

Educated speakers avoid the above but use *is* and *was* with plural nouns in the existential construction in (4) and (5).

4. there's no bottles
5. is there any biscuits left?

Macafee (1983: 50), describing the Scots of Glasgow, cites *was* combining with *you*: *an they'll look at you as if you was a Dalek or something* and *goes* (and other verbs in -*s*) as a narrative form: '*Naw*', *I goes, near screaming, you know?* Macaulay (1991) gives examples of *there* (= *there's*) and *there were* (= *there was*). Wilson (1915: 77) cites the example in (9); the construction is not new and not confined to Ayrshire.

6. There naebody going to force them
7. and there a gate just after you go ower the brig takes you intae this field
8. in fact there were a fellow doon there Andy Smith you caw'd him – he belonged to Girvan
9. There no sic a thing hereaway

Measure phrases

Numerals from two upwards regularly combine with singular nouns: *five mile long, two foot high, weighs eight stone, two year old.*

Macaulay (1991: 110) says that forty-one out of ninety measure nouns in his data are plural. *Minute, day, week, shilling, inch* and *yard* are always plural after numerals greater than one. The percentage of inflected plurals for other nouns is *pound* – eighty-nine per cent, *month* – eighty-six per cent, *year* – sixty-eight per cent, *ton* – fifty per cent, *mile* – seventeen per cent. Wilson (1915: 62) cites *three gless o' whiskay, a guid wheen month* and *five acre*, not to mention *broth, porridge* and *kail*, which were plural.

There is regularly no preposition between the measure nouns *bit* and *drop* and a following noun: *a bit paper, a bit steel, a drop water*. These constructions are typically Germanic: compare Standard German *zwei Meter lang* (= two metres long), *ein Stück Papier* (= a piece (of) paper).

Less and not *few* is normal with plural count nouns, as in *less cars*. Note too *much more cars* (= many more cars).

CLAUSE STRUCTURE AND FUNCTION

Number agreement as discussed above has to do with the structure of clauses; it signals the link between not only the subject noun but the phrase containing the subject noun, and not just the verb but the phrase containing the verb. Many phenomena which distinguish Scots from Standard English relate to the structure of clauses; examples are the kinds of modal verbs or modal expressions that combine with main verbs, the means by which clauses are made negative, different types of subordinate clause constructions, and the devices which mark the organisation of clauses into larger chunks of text (all of which are described below).

Syntactic analysis sets out to show how words combine into phrases and how phrases combine into clauses; how clauses combine into larger units; what kinds of unit can function as the subject of a clause. Clauses describe situations or events; syntax is concerned with how clauses are made negative (the speaker is asserting or denying an event), with how tense and aspect are signalled (the speaker places an event in past, present or future time and presents the event as ongoing or as completed), with how modality is signalled (the speaker presents an event as factual, merely possible or necessary) and with the constructions by means of which speakers ask questions or give commands.

The first paragraph of this section ends with the phrase 'the organisation of clauses into larger chunks of text'. Two problems arise. One concerns the larger chunks of text. In the analysis of written language clauses are said to combine into sentences. If someone writes *When Morag arrived at the house, she found it locked and empty*, we are dealing with one sentence consisting of two clauses. If someone writes *Morag arrived at the house. She found it locked and empty*, we are clearly dealing with two sentences, each consisting of a single clause.

The Scots data described in this chapter is informal and spoken and the first problem is that the unit of analysis called the sentence is not applicable to spontaneous spoken language and has been abandoned by most analysts in the field. In spontaneous speech there are no reliable clues of rhythm, pausing or intonation as to where one sentence ends and another one begins. Even provided with an unpunctuated transcription of an impromptu narrative to which they are listening, listeners offer different divisions of the transcript into sentences. (See the discussion and references in chapter 2 of Miller and Weinert (1998).)

We can tell from a particular verb which other words and phrases go with it to form a clause, but it is often not clear whether we can analyse a sequence of clauses as a single sentence or not. A number of analysts employ the notion of a clause complex, a series of clauses in various relationships to each other. Clauses specify, for example, reasons for a situation (*because*), conditions (*if*), and times (*when, as, while*).

Clause complexes bring us to the second problem, or at least the second syntactic property that has to be captured in any account of spontaneous spoken language (whether standard or non-standard). Clauses are organised into clause complexes but the latter typically do not evince the tight syntactic links to be found in written text. Using the currently fashionable term, the syntax of clause complexes is 'unintegrated'. This property is exemplified and discussed in relation to (10) – (17). Consider (10).

10. I only wear shoes which don't throw me forward on my toes

The relative clause *which don't throw me forward on my toes* is linked to *shoes* by the relative pronoun *which* and is thereby integrated into the main clause. The utterance actually produced is in (2).

11. I only wear shoes that I'm not thrown forward on my toes

In the apparent relative clause *that I'm not thrown forward on my toes, that* is an invariable conjunction. That is, it does not change shape or alternate with another conjunction, in *th-*. Relative clauses can also be introduced (but this is typical of writing) by *wh-* words; *which* is used in relative clauses modifying inanimate nouns (*the books which*, not **the books who*) and in formal written English *who* is used if it is the subject of the relative clause but *whom* if it is the object (*the thief who escaped* versus *the thief whom we caught*). In (11) the relative clause has no pronoun linking back to *shoes* – compare the possible constructions *I only wear shoes that/which do not throw me forward on my toes* or *I only wear shoes in which/ with which I'm not thrown forward on my toes.*

In (12a) *who* is the direct object of *recognise* but functions as a clause-initial complementiser and picks up the human head noun *person*. (12b) has the invariable conjunction *that*, and *recognise* has no overt object. In (12c), the actual utterance, *recognise* has the direct object *them*. That is, the main clause and the relative clause are each complete, with subject, verb and object and set down one beside the other. (12c) is easy to interpret, precisely because the relative clause is not integrated into the main clause.

12. a tracking down a person who you would think someone would recognise
    b tracking down a person that you would think someone would recognise
    c tracking down a person that you would think someone would recognise
      them

(13), from a radio discussion, exemplifies another construction.

13. Everyone knows Helen Liddell how hard she works

The direct object of *knows* is *Helen Liddell*. As direct object, the noun phrase is central in the clause complex and highlighted. Appended to (13), with no formal linking apart from order, is the clause *how hard she works*. Central to the communication is a property of Helen Liddell. The human entity is mentioned first and then the property. That is, whereas a written text would have, for example, *Everyone knows how hard Helen Liddell works*, the spoken text separates the two major pieces of information and highlights both.

WH complements can also be appended at the end of equative clauses, as in (14), from a radio news interview. The written version – *What they're doing to the union is unfair* – has a complex subject and complex subjects are avoided in spontaneous speech. (14) conveys the main information – 'it' is unfair – unimpeded by a complex initial phrase; what exactly is unfair is highlighted at the end of the sequence.

14. it's unfair what they're doing to the union

(15) is another example of unintegrated syntax, from a television documentary.

15. A what are you doing to these?
    B what we're doing we're hanging them up to drouth

B produces a WH cleft. The classic written WH cleft is exemplified in (16).

16. What he does is interrupt all the time

In (16) the initial WH clause, *What he does*, is followed by *is*, followed in turn by a phrase containing the bare verb *interrupt* – *interrupt* (*all the time*). (16) can be thought of as created by the combination of two complete clauses; one is *what he does* and the other is *he interrupts all the time*. As part of the combining process the subject *he* in the second clause is deleted; repeated words and phrases are typically deleted in writing when two or more clauses are combined into a sentence or a clause complex. (15) exemplifies the spoken WH cleft, in which the WH clause is followed directly by a whole clause containing a subject and tense/aspect – *we're hanging them up to drouth*. The two clauses *what we're doing* and *we're hanging them up to drouth* are side by side, linked only by the repetition of *we're*. The repeated subject *he* is not deleted, whereas in writing we would expect *What we're doing is hanging them up to drouth*.

As a final example of unintegrated syntax consider (17), from Bennett (1992: 69).

17. It was an old Scottish custom, well it was still carried on in Glasgow – when a baby was taken out to be christened the custom was ye made up what was called a 'christening piece'

Like spoken WH clefts, (17) contains an introductory noun phrase, *the custom*, followed by *was*, followed by a complete clause with subject and tensed verb, *ye made up what was called a 'christening piece'.* In writing we would expect *the custom was to make up what was called a 'christening piece'.* Here the phrase *the custom was* is followed by an infinitive phrase *to make up. . .* The infinitive phrase has no subject and can be thought of as resulting from a full clause from which the subject, *you* or *they*, has been removed. The full clause contains a verb that is marked for tense – *made up.* The reduction of a full clause to an infinitive phrase requires the removal of tense. The removal of the subject and of tense yield a reduced structure, *to make up what was called a 'christening piece'*, and this structure is integrated into the sentence precisely by the disappearance of the subject and the tense.

In spite of non-integration we can recognise main and subordinate clauses, since subordinate clauses are subject to restrictions on word order which do not apply to main clauses. For example, the main clause *The dog came into the kitchen* can be remodelled as *Into the kitchen came the dog.* In *When the dog came into the kitchen, the cat leapt onto the window sill*, the subordinate *when* clause cannot be remodelled to **When into the kitchen came the dog . . .* (See Miller 2002, chapter 6.).

The clause *when the dog came into the kitchen* specifies the time of another event, the cat leaping onto the window sill, and is called an adverbial clause of time. *When* signals the joining of the adverbial clause to the main clause; it is called a conjunction because it serves to conjoin the two clauses and it is called a subordinating conjunction because the adverbial clause of time is subordinate to the main clause. This example provides an excellent illustration of why the syntax of spoken language should not be analysed as if it were identical with the syntax of written language. The example describes two consecutive events, the dog coming into the kitchen and the cat leaping onto the window sill. The speaker or writer presents the leaping as the main event and describes it with the main clause; the entry into the kitchen is presented as secondary and is expressed by the subordinate clause of time. Note too that the adverbial clause precedes the main clause; the temporal setting is established before the main event is placed in it. This complex set of relationships is shown in Figure 5.1.

Figure 5.1 Event sequence and sentence structure in speech (i)

EVENT 1:   EVENT 2:
[dog come into kitchen]   *[cat leap onto window sill]*

SECONDARY EVENT: MAIN EVENT:
[dog come into kitchen]   *[cat leap onto window sill]*

When the dog came into the kitchen,   the cat leapt onto the window sill.

The speaker or writer could have produced the clauses in the reverse order: *The cat leapt onto the window sill* + *when the dog came into the kitchen*. In writing, the clauses could be separated by a comma or merely juxtaposed. When they are merely juxtaposed – *The cat leapt onto the window sill when the dog came into the kitchen* – the interpretation is the same as for the example above; the *when* clause establishes the temporal setting for the dog's entry into the kitchen. In spite of the reverse order of clauses, the cat leaping onto the sill is presented as the main event by means of the main clause. In other words, the dog's entry into the kitchen is still presented as the secondary event by means of the subordinate *when* clause; that the *when* clause is subordinate is shown by the fact that in spite of the change in order it is still impossible to remodel the clause to **when into the kitchen came the dog*. This set of relationships is shown in Figure 5.2.

Figure 5.2 Event sequence and sentence structure in speech (ii)

EVENT 1:   EVENT 2:
[dog come into kitchen]   *[cat leap onto window sill]*

SECONDARY EVENT: MAIN EVENT:
[dog come into kitchen]   *[cat leap onto window sill]*

The cat leapt onto the window sill   when the dog came into the kitchen.

However, when the clauses are separated by a comma, a different interpretation and a different syntactic analysis emerge. Note first that *The cat leapt onto the window sill, when the dog came into the kitchen* has the interpretation that the cat jumped onto the sill and then the dog came in. That is, the dog's entry is not presented as a secondary event which is merely the temporal setting for the main event; the events are presented as equal in status and the cat's leap onto the window sill is followed by the dog's entry into the kitchen. Note too that the *when* clause can be remodelled: *The cat leapt onto the window sill when into the kitchen came the dog*. In other words, the *when* clause is not a subordinate clause but a main clause. These relationships are shown in Figure 5.3.

Figure 5.3 Event sequence and sentence structure in speech (iii)

EVENT 1:   EVENT 2:
[dog come into kitchen]   *[cat leap onto window sill]*

MAIN EVENT 1:   MAIN EVENT 2:
[dog come into kitchen]   *[cat leap onto window sill]*

The cat leapt onto the window sill,   when the dog came into the kitchen.

The above construction is regularly either misinterpreted or excluded from written English. A thirteen year-old wrote in an essay *She shone the light along the dark passage when suddenly she saw a big rat*. Figure 5.4 shows the order and relative status of the events.

Figure 5.4 Event sequence and sentence structure in speech (iv)

EVENT 1:	EVENT 2:
[She shine light along dark passage]	*[she see big rat]*

MAIN EVENT 1:	MAIN EVENT 2:
[She shine light along dark passage]	*[she see big rat]*

| She shone the light along the dark passage, | when suddenly she saw a big rat. |

Her teacher wanted to change the sentence to *When she shone the light along the dark passage, she suddenly saw a big rat*. The order and status of events for the revised example are in Figure 5.5. The original version has the interpretation 'She shone the light and then she saw a big rat' (giving equal importance to both events) whereas the teacher's version has the interpretation 'When she shone the light/once she shone the light, she saw a big rat' (giving more importance to seeing the rat).

Figure 5.5 Event sequence and sentence structure in speech (v)

EVENT 1:	EVENT 2:
[She shine light along dark passage]	*[she see big rat]*

SECONDARY EVENT:	MAIN EVENT:
[She shine light along dark passage]	*[she see big rat]*

| When she shone the light along the dark passage, | suddenly she saw a big rat. |

This example demonstrates clearly how a common construction in spoken Scots can be excluded because an arbiter of written English takes an over-narrow view of what is acceptable in writing.

   Complement clauses and *that* relative clauses occur regularly, but subordinate adverbial clauses occur less regularly. In connection with adverbial clauses the following points are worthy of mention.

(i) *Because* or *cause* clauses typically follow the main clause – *We lent them our car because the garage couldn't fix theirs right away*; in writing they both precede and follow the main clause – *Because the garage couldn't fix theirs right away we lent them our car*. Chafe (1984) suggests that preceding *because* clauses act as signposts, whereas following the main clause they merely provide a reason. The position of the *because* clauses may reflect the lack of signposting in spoken Scots because of the nature of the interaction. Clauses in narrative can be more complex because narrators have more planning time; they can pause to organise what comes next without running the risk of losing their turn. In conversation, participants who pause risk losing the floor to someone else.

(ii) Clauses of condition and time (as in the cat and dog example above) also tend to follow the main clause. An additional problem is that in conversation and in the map-task dialogues many of the clauses introduced by *if* are not straightforward subordinate adverbial clauses of condition. Many convey an instruction – *if you just draw the line two centimetres below the cave* – and constitute a complete discourse. Conversely, imperative clauses can be used to express conditions, as in *tell a lie an they'll believe you* (Häcker 1999: 119).

(iii) Concession clauses, introduced by *although*, are missing altogether. The participants in the conversations conceded a point with clauses introduced by *but*, with clauses containing *though*, usually in clause-final position – *they're not going to shut the factory – they're making a loss though*. The speaker uses the first clause to reject the idea that the factory is to be shut but uses the second clause to concede a point, that they are making a loss. Another construction for the conceding of points is exemplified in (18).

18. But eh customs is a' changed noo. You still see them in Glasgow right enough
     (Bennett 1992: 110–11)

(iv) Consider *If Shona is coming to the party, I'm going to stay at home*. The *if* clause is the starting point or theme of the speaker's message. The speaker states a condition first, making it prominent. In Scots this can be done with the construction *See if Shona is coming to the party – I'm going to stay at home*. A similar construction is used with *when* clauses: *see when we get into the gardens, can we go up the tower?* This *see* construction strongly highlights the time or conditional clause and breaks up the integration of subordinate and main clause which we find in the initial example above.

(v) Adverbial clauses of time can be introduced by *frae* or *fae* (= *from*) instead of *since*. The examples in (19) are from Macaulay (1991) and the author has heard similar examples in West Lothian.

19. a my it's a while fae I heard that (= since I heard that)
     b the first time I ever was idle fae I left the school (= since I left the school)

(vi)   Time clauses can be introduced by *tae* (= *to*), as in (20), from Macaulay (1992). There is an example in the Map Task dialogues.

20. wait here tae I come oot (= till I come out)

Häcker (1999: 172–3) highlights the use of adverbial time clauses introduced by *till* with a purposive meaning, as in (21).

21. a Turn on the wireless till we hear the news
     b an that wis wait till I think where that [was]
        [= wait so that I can think where that was]

(vii) Häcker (1999: 161, 192) comments on the use of gerunds introduced by *with* to express reason, manner or accompanying circumstances. (22) is from ECOSSE.

22. but he didnae like to take it [a job] with him being a friend

SYNTAX

Relative clauses

(i) Restrictive relative clauses help the hearer or reader to pick out which entity is referred to. In *Have you read the book that Gordon recommended?* the relative clause *that Gordon recommended* restricts the referent of the phrase *the book*. Such clauses are introduced by *that*, but also by *where: just about that other place where I started*. Relative clauses modifying time nouns such as *day*, *month* and so on do not usually contain *that*: *the day she arrived* or *the day that she arrived* . Only the first version occurs in ECOSSE. (Macafee (1983: 52) notes that restrictive relative clauses in the Broad Scots of Glasgow are occasionally introduced by *what*: *like the other birds what takes Dexedrine.*)
(ii) Relative clauses can be used to convey information about a whole event, as in *my Dad came to an Elton John concert with us which at the time we thought was great*. What was thought great was the event of the speaker's father coming to the concert. Event relative clauses are introduced by *which*, never by *that*.
(iii) Instead of *whose*, *that* + possessive pronoun is used: *the girl that her eighteenth birthday was on that day was stoned, couldnae stand up* (as opposed to *the girl whose eighteenth birthday was on that day . . .*).
(iv) The shadow pronoun is a typical feature of complex relative clauses: two examples recorded informally are *the spikes that you stick in the ground and throw rings over them* and *an address which I hadn't stayed there for several years*. The

formal spoken version is *the spikes that you stick in the ground and throw rings over* and *an address where I hadn't stayed for several years* or, in writing, *an address at which I hadn't stayed for several years.* The possessive example in (iii) above is also an example of a shadow pronoun. This construction is not an accident of fast speech but is frequent and of long standing, examples being cited in Murray (1873) such as *the man that his wife's deid.*

(v) Prepositions always occur at the end of the relative clause (*the shop I bought it in*, not *the shop in which I bought it*) but are frequently omitted: *of course there's a rope that you can pull the seat back up* (*with* omitted) and, noted in a radio discussion, *I haven't been to a party yet that I haven't got home the same night* (with *from* omitted).

(vi) Existential constructions have no relative pronoun or conjunction; in writing, *that* or *who* would be in the square brackets in (23).

23. a my friend's got a brother [ ] used to be in the school
    b there's only one of us [ ] been on a chopper before

(vii) Relative clauses may be used not to restrict the reference but merely to add information. They are known as non-restrictive relative clauses. In writing, they are separated by a comma from the noun they modify – *the book, which Gordon recommended, is excellent*; the interpretation is 'the book [which we both know about] is excellent, and by the way Gordon recommended it'. In speech, a short pause separates non-restrictive clauses from the nouns they modify and the clauses have their own intonation pattern. In Scots (and possibly in spoken English generally) non-restrictive relative clauses are notably scarce. MTC and ECOSSE have no non-restrictive relative clauses with *who*. University under-graduates and seventeen–year-olds at an Edinburgh private school produced nineteen non-restrictive relatives with *which*. Adults and sixteen- and seventeen-year-olds at state schools produced three such clauses. Macaulay (1991: 64) comments that in his middle-class interviews twenty per cent of the relative clauses are non-restrictive; in the working class interviews five per cent.

Instead of non-restrictive relative clauses, speakers of Scots use coordinate clauses: *the boy I was talking to last night – and he actually works in the yard – was saying it's going to be closed down* (not *the boy . . ., who actually works in the yard, . . .*).

The relative complementiser *that* is not a pronoun but a conjunction, which developed historically from a pronoun. *Which* is following the same path. Consider the second *which* in (24).

24. you can leave at Christmas if your birthday's in December to February which
    I think is wrong like my birthday's March and I have to stay on to May *which*
    when I'm 16 in March I could be looking for a job

The second *which* – *which when I'm 16 in March* – does not link a relative clause to a noun but signals that the preceding chunk of text is connected to the following one. This construction too is old, occurring in Dickens and in *Punch* throughout the nineteenth century.

Finally in this section, we should note that shadow pronouns occur in another construction that can be heard on radio and television. Consider (25):

25. a in New York on Manhattan Island there is a theatre there that . . .
    b out of the twenty four traditional medicine shops they visited rhino horn
       was for sale in nineteen of them

Speakers use the initial phrases – *in New York on Manhattan Island, out of the twenty four traditional medicine* shops – to announce what is important and the theme or starting point of the message. The phrases are independent 'flags' which do not belong to the following clause, although the clauses contain the shadow pronouns *there* and *them* referring back to them.

NEGATION

In Scots verbs are negated by the independent words *no* and *not* , as in (26), or by the suffixes *nae* and *n't*, as in (27).

26. a She's no leaving
    b She's not leaving
27. a She isnae leaving
    b She isn't leaving

Is attaches to the preceding pronoun and is reduced. In ECOSSE *no* is most frequent with 'BE' – *She's no 'phoned yet*, with *'ll* (= *will*) – *she'll no be coming to the party* , and with *'ve* (= *have*) – *I've no seen him the day*. *Nae* is added to all the modal verbs and to 'DO' – *He doesnae help in the house, She cannae knit*. Educated speakers prefer *not* or *no* and use *not* in negative interrogatives such as (28).

28. Are you not coming with us?

The typical Scots tag question has *not* or *no*, as in (29).

29. that's miles away is it no?

Educated speakers occasionally use *amn't*, as in (30).

30. I'm coming with you amn't I?

Nae is suffixed to modal verbs if it applies to the modal verb: *He cannae come to the party* = *He is unable to come to the party*. *No* and *not* do occur with modal verbs, but apply to the phrase following the modal: *You can no come to the party if you dinnae want tae* = *You are able not to come to the party* . . .

Macafee (1983: 47) cites *will you not put too many on there in case they fall in the street please*. Here *not* applies to *put too many on there*. *Won't you put too many* . . . has precisely the opposite force: the speaker asks for too many to be put on.

Where there is no auxiliary verb, as in *I got the job*, the sentence is made negative with 'DO': *I didn't/didnae get the job*. In Scots the normal negative with past tense verbs is *never*, as in (31).

31. a . . . I could've got the job . . . but I telt them I couldnae leave till the end of May so I never got it
   b I sat down to that tongue slips essay at 7 o'clock I never got it started till nine

Never is regularly not emphatic, unlike Standard English *You will never catch the train tonight* (= It is utterly impossible that . . .). As *never* acquires the meaning and function of *not* many speakers express the meaning 'at no time' in general with *never ever*. *Never* is used as a pro-verb, where Standard English has *didn't*: *I added water and it fizzed I done it again and it never* (pupil to teacher).

There is an emphatic negative construction with *nane* (= *none*), as in (32)

32. Rab can sing nane

The interpretation is not just that Rab does not sing but that he is completely useless at singing.

Finally, we turn to the relationship between *not*, *n't*, and so on, and the quantifiers *all*, *each* and *every*. Consider (33):

33. all the hotels take British guests

The whole sentence can be negated and interpreted as 'It is true of all the hotels that they do not take British guests'. This meaning can be expressed by *None of the hotels take British guests*. In contrast, just the phrase *all the hotels* can be negated, giving *Not all the hotels take British guests* (= some do and some do not). In Scots, this meaning is expressed by (34), which was observed in conversation and in the context could only have the latter meaning. *n't* modifies *all* but is attached to *do*.

34. All the hotels don't take British guests

Note also (35):

35. a It is not democratic, because every member is not consulted on the decision
    b We all don't have to be there

In context, (35a) clearly means that some members are consulted but not others, and (35b) is used as justification for not attending a meeting – colleagues of the speaker would be there.

MODAL VERBS

The system of modal verbs in Scots is massively different from that of Standard English.

(i) Scots lacks 'SHALL', 'MAY' and 'OUGHT'. There is not a single occurrence in ECOSSE, though these modal verbs do occur in writing and in formal announcements, as in the notice in an Edinburgh butcher's window *This shop shall be open on Monday* and in train announcements such as *This train shall stop at Paisley Gilmour Street, Johnstone* etc. The source of this usage may be legal and the examples are imbued with some sort of institutional force. The butcher was binding himself to be open on the Monday and the train operators are binding themselves to stop the train at the stations mentioned.

    In spoken Scots, however, SHALL is missing both as a marker of future tense – *We shall arrive in the morning* – and as an expression of promises – *You shall have the money tomorrow* (= *I promise you*). Permission is expressed by CAN, GET TO and GET + gerund as in (36).

36. a You can have this afternoon off
    b the pupils get to come inside in rainy weather
    c they got going to the match

SHOULD replaces OUGHT, but WANT is often used, as in (37), uttered by a judo instructor.

37. you want to come out and attack right away

(ii) MUST is restricted to epistemic modality. In Standard English MUST expresses conclusions, as in (38a), and obligation, as in (38b), to be glossed as 'It is necessary for you to be at the airport by nine'.

38. a You must be exhausted (= I conclude from your appearance that . . .)
    b You must be at the airport by nine or you will lose your seat (= It is necessary for you to be at the airport by nine.)

In ECOSSE, MUST expresses only the conclusion meaning; obligation is expressed by HAVE TO and NEED TO.

MUST is said to express internal compulsion, whereas HAVE TO is said to express external compulsion; one is compelled by someone or by circumstances. Elicitation tests show that Scottish undergraduates (and some English ones too!) have no clear intuition about MUST versus HAVE TO, but use HAVE GOT TO for external compulsion and WILL HAVE TO for milder compulsion, which can even be self-compulsion, as in (39).

39. I'll have to write to Carol because she wrote to us six months ago

HAVE TO is less strong than HAVE GOT TO. It also expresses conclusions, as in (40):

40. that has to be their worst display ever

(iii) NEED behaves like a main verb; Scots has *Do you need to leave immediately* and *You don't need to leave immediately* (but not *Need you leave immediately?*, *You needn't leave immediately*). NEED occurs in the progressive, as in *They're needing to paint the windows*. NEED expresses only obligation, and is equivalent to HAVE TO. (41a) and (41b) are typical of answers produced by university undergraduates who were given, e.g. *I must be back at midnight because* ____ and asked to complete the sentence.

41. a I must be back by midnight because I need to switch off my electric blanket
    b I have to go to the library because I need to do my French essay today

NEED can express external compulsion as in (42), from ECOSSE:

42. you'd need to go down there and collect her and drop her

In Scots *mustn't* expresses 'I conclude that not', as in (43). Some descriptions of Standard English suggest that only *can't* has this interpretation.

43. a this mustn't be the place
    b I mustn't have read the question properly
       [all observed in conversation]

Obligation is also expressed by SUPPOSED TO or MEANT TO, as in (44).

44. a you're supposed to leave your coat in the cloakroom
    b you're meant to fill in the form first

MEANT TO also occurs with the meaning 'It is said that': *The new player is meant to be real fast.*

(iv) *Can't, cannot* and *cannae* all express 'not have permission to'. To express 'have permission not to', speakers of Scots indeed use *don't need to, don't have to* and *are not allowed to.*

(v) Scots has double modals, as in (45):

45. a he'll can help us the morn/tomorrow
    b They might could be working in the shop
    c She might can get away early

Note the acceptable interrogative *Will he can help us the morn/tomorrow?* and the unacceptable **Might they could be working in the shop?* There are grounds for supposing that *might* in (45b) (45c) is developing into an adverb, syntactically equivalent to *maybe*: note sentences such as *They maybe could be working in the shop*, with *maybe* in the same position as *might.*

Might occasionally combines with *should* and *would*, as in (46):

46. a you might would like to come with us
    b you might should claim your expenses

Here again *might* is equivalent in meaning and position to *maybe*. Note too the parallel between (47a) and (47b):

47. a he might no could do it
    b he maybe no could do it

The double-modal sequence *will can* is relatively old, being mentioned by Wilson (1915). The double-modal construction in general may be in decline. Some of the examples cited above were provided by speakers from East Lothian who recognised the construction as occurring in their communities but did not themselves use it. McIver (1997) found that in Orkney the over-60s used the construction, speakers in the age-group 25–60 recognised only some of the sequences but did use *will can*, and the under-25s neither used the construction nor recognised all the combinations.

(vi) Modal verbs occur after the infinitive marker *to*, as shown in (48). This too is not a new feature but is mentioned by Grant and Main-Dixon (1921).

48. a you have to can drive a car to get that job
    b I'd like to could do that

According to an informant born and brought up in Galloway, examples such as (49) are common.

49. ah would uh could uh done it (= I would have been able to do it)

Apart from the two instances of *uh* – presumably equivalent to *'ve* or *have* – the unusual feature is *could* preceded by *have*.

TENSE AND ASPECT

Progressive

In Standard English a set of stative verbs is recognised, such as KNOW, LIKE, SEE and HEAR. These verbs denote states; the main (animate) participant is not an Agent. Stative verbs either do not occur in the progressive at all or only rarely, as shown in (50), and they do not occur in the WH cleft construction, as shown in (51). (50a) and (50b) with ordinary verbs in the progressive are correct while (50c) and (50d) with KNOW and LIKE in the progressive are incorrect.

50. a Kirsty is writing the answer
    b Archie is reading this book
    c *Kirsty is knowing the answer
    d *Archie is liking this book

(51a) and (51b) are correct, being examples of the WH cleft construction with ordinary verbs; (51c) and (51d), with KNOW and LIKE, are incorrect.

51. a What Kirsty did was write the answer
    b What Archie did was read this book
    c *What Kirsty did was know the answer
    d *What Archie did was like this book

KNOW behaves in the same way in Scots but other stative verbs occur regularly in the progressive, as in (52):

52. a I wasnae liking it and the lassie I was going wi wasnae liking it [ECOSSE]
    b we werenae really wanting to go last year but they sent us a lot of letters to come [ECOSSE]
    c he's not understanding a single thing you say [TV]
    d they're not intending opening the bottle tonight surely
       [informally recorded in conversation]

Intending opening in (52d) is known as the 'double *-ing*' construction because of the two verbs ending in *–ing*. Some grammarians believe that the double *–ing* construction is unacceptable but it is frequently used in Scots.

Standard English (at least, the written variety) has a contrast between the progressive aspect and the simple aspect. In *Soapy is washing the dishes* WASH is in the progressive, *is washing*, and is used to present the action as in progress. *Soapy washes the dishes* contains the simple aspect *washes*, which is used to present an action as habitual or repeated – *Soapy usually washes the dishes*, *Soapy washes the dishes after the evening meal*. (The usage is actually far more complex but the above simple analysis is sufficient for our purposes.) A change is under way in Scots whereby use of the simple aspect is decreasing. Younger speakers and writers use the progressive where older speakers, including the author, have to use the simple aspect. The examples in (53) are from essays and examination answers by undergraduates at Edinburgh University. The author would have to use *don't learn* in (53a), *recognise* in (53b) and *forget* in (53c).

53. a Today, educational establishments are still trying to teach a standard. Many school children are not learning the standard outwith school.
   b Each time we mention something we are recognising that there is a relationship between a word and a class of objects.
   c The code is often changed and students are forgetting the new number [minutes of Liaison Committee written by a student]

Many languages, for instance Russian, have only one set of verb forms (called 'imperfective') for presenting an action as in progress or as habitual; *Ivan chitaet Tolstogo* corresponds either to 'Ivan is reading Tolstoy' or 'Ivan reads Tolstoy'. If the usage exemplified in (53) spreads and establishes itself, the aspect system of Scots will become not unlike the aspect system in Russian. Such a change is not unusual; in many languages progressive constructions have developed into imperfectives.

Past and Perfect

In written English the Perfect typically excludes time adverbs denoting a definite past time: **We have seen the exhibition this morning* and **We have been to New York last year*. In speech the Perfect occasionally occurs with definite time adverbs, as in (54). Since they have no pauses or breaks in intonation between the perfect and the adverb, the adverb cannot be seen as an afterthought.

54. a I've seen him last year
   b I've been to the exhibition last year

Combined with the progressive, the perfect refers to recent past time. *Kirsty has been working with the Royal Bank* is appropriate either if Kirsty is still working with the bank or was working with the Bank until quite recently. Speakers of Scots can refer to a recent, completed event by the past progressive + *there*, as in (55).

55. a I was speaking to John there
    b I was speaking to John on Friday there
    c Somebody was just kicking your car there

Deictics such as *there* point to entities or locations visible to speaker and hearer. Its use in (55) can be interpreted as the speaker presenting the event of speaking to John as metaphorically visible to the listener and therefore close in time. The Friday referred to in (55b) is the Friday in the past closest to the time of utterance.

The Standard English *The electrician has just phoned* puts an event in the immediate past. In Scots the same effect is conveyed by *The electrician just phoned*, with the simple past and *just*. (56) exemplifies the same usage. The person addresses Bob immediately after the latter has bought a round of drinks (Macaulay 1991: 197–8).

56. and one of the men happened to comment he says 'Bob' he says 'you forgot the boy' 'No' he says 'I didnae forget the boy'.

In Standard English the perfect can refer to an event which someone has experienced at some indefinite time in the past, as in *Have you ever been interested in football?* or *I have visited Prague.* In Scots the Simple Past also conveys this experiential meaning, as in (57).

57. you said you enjoyed fishin   were you ever interested in football?

A third major use of the perfect in Standard English is to convey the result of a past action. If Fiona has written her essay, the result is that the essay is written (and ready to be handed in). The perfect contains participial forms such as *written* which were originally participles of result. In Scots, results of past actions are often expressed by constructions which are not the perfect, may not contain HAVE, but do contain a resultative participle. (58) and (59) exemplify the resultative structure from which the perfect is supposed to have developed.

58. You have access to a vein gained and a cardiac analysis done within one minute [Radio discussion]
59. I was wanting to borrow her hoover but she'll have it put away [conversation]
    A common structure is *there's* plus resultative participle.
60. there's something fallen down the sink

Speakers often report the completion of an action by referring to its result. They use a construction known as a 'reverse cleft' which consists of *that's* or *that was* plus a noun phrase plus a resultative participle. In (61), from Kennedy (1994), the noun phrase following *is* is the 'direct object' of the action.

61. That's the letters written and posted

The examples in (62), from Macaulay (1991), show reverse clefts in which the noun phrase following *is* is the 'subject' of the action.

62. a but that's me seen it (= I've seen it now)
    b and he says 'That you left the school noo Andrew?' (= Have you left school now?)

The equivalent of a pluperfect is in (63).

63. he just lay doon on the settee and turned over and that was him gone (= he had gone)

Resultative participles also occur in the construction in (64).

64. a I need the car repaired by midday
    b She needs collected at four o'clock
    c I'd get out of the way, Mr Lawrence. You don't want burned, do you? (Kennedy 1994)

Pluperfect

The pluperfect is rare in main clauses in Scots, and absent from certain subordinate clauses. The examples in (65) were written by secondary school pupils and 'corrected' to the pluperfect by their teacher.

65. a He said his mum had brought him the fireworks but she really didn't [hadn't]
    b . . . he . . . was angry I didn't stay in the cafe [= hadn't stayed]

Tense and aspect in conditional clauses

(66a) and (64b) are typical of modern Scots.

66. a If she would come to see things for herself
    b If she would have come to see things for herself

The corresponding Standard English construction replaces *would come* with *came* – *If she came to see things for herself she would understand our difficulties*. *Would have come* corresponds to *had come* – *If she had come to see things for herself, she would have understood our difficulties*. Interestingly, examples like (66) are making their way into written English, as shown by (67), from *The Times*.

67. Suppose further that all Conservative and Labour voters in England would have given the Alliance as their second choice . . .

The standard canon requires *had given*.

Another conditional construction, exemplified in (68a), replaces the pluperfect with *had* + *'ve* (= *have*). The same construction, as in (68b), is also found in clauses introduced by *wish* presenting an event as no longer possible.

68. a I reckon I wouldnae have been able to dae it if I hadnae 've been able to read music [= hadn't been able]
    b I wish he'd 've complimented me, Roger [= had complimented]

Häcker (1998) discusses how anteriority (one event preceding another) is expressed by means of *once* + simple past, e.g. *once her children left home, she got a job* [example devised by the author].

INTERROGATIVES

(i)   Scots regularly uses *how* where Standard English uses *why*.

69. a A: Susan, how's your ankle?
       B: I can walk on it I think how? [= why?]
    b how did you not apply? [in the context = why?]

(ii)   *Whereabouts* is used instead of *where* and is regularly split into *where* and *about*. *How* + *about* relates to quantity.

70. a Whereabouts did you see him?
    b Where does she stay about?
    c How old was he about?

(iii) *What time . . . at?* frequently replaces *when?*, as in *What time does it finish at?* (iv) In Standard English, *which book?*, for example, asks about one of a set of known books; *what book?* asks about one out of the set of all books. In Scots *what* fulfils both functions, as in (71).

71. a What book have you been buying? [Addressee is carrying a book.]
    b What book is being published next year?

(v) In writing, indirect questions have the structure WH word + subject pronoun + auxiliary verb, as in (72).

72. The teacher asked what book they had read
    [Cf. What book have you read?]

In Scots indirect questions have the word order of direct questions, as in (73), which involved no hesitations or changes in intonation but were uttered as one chunk.

73. a If they got an eight they had to decide where was the best place to put it
    [ECOSSE]
    b you sort of wonder is it better to be blind or deaf [conversation]

(vi) Scots has various tag-questions. Speakers use the same tags with repeated auxiliary as Standard English does as in (74).

74. a John has left, has he no?
    b John's no left, has he?

They also use *e*, added to both positive and negative declarative clauses, as in (75a) and (75b), and the tag *e no*, added to positive clauses, as in (75c).

75. a . . . we know him quite well by now e? [= don't we]
    b it's no too dear e? [= It's not too dear, is it?]
    c you're taking her to the pictures e no? [= aren't you]

e occurs in imperatives, converting them to requests, even coaxing requests. In questions the tag asks the addressee to agree with the speaker's statement; in imperatives the tag asks the addressee to agree with (and act upon) the speaker's request. Compare (76a) and (76b).

76. a let me tie my lace e
    b put it down there e

When added to (76a) and (76b) *won't you* can increase the sharpness of a request — *let me tie my lace won't you, put it down there, won't you,* but *e* always reduces the sharpness. That is, *e* in imperative clauses mitigates the command or request and makes it more polite. The tag *e* mitigates requests and increases politeness even where the request is conveyed not by a clause but by a phrase. A customer (male, over 50) came into a fish and chip shop in Leven in Fife. The woman behind the counter asked him what he would like and the reply was *a mini fish supper e?* The *e* carried interrogative intonation and the only Standard English equivalent would be *could I have a mini fish supper, please?*, which also involves the use of an interrogative construction. (The exchange was observed by the author in February 2002.)

A positive clause can be followed by a positive tag, as in (77). The force of these tags in context seems to be that speakers expect a positive answer to their question.

77. a A: aye that's cos I didnae use to go
      B: did you start skiving did you?
    b are you still working at Woolie's are you?

Other tags available in Scots are illustrated in (78). (78f) is from Bennett (1992: 115), (78a), (78b) and (78e) are from ECOSSE, and the others are from conversation.

78. a you don't go for that sort, no?
    b you've mentioned this to him, yes?
    c they're not intending opening the bottle tonight surely?
    d he's not trying to make all of it, not really?
    e he's coming on Monday, right?
    f have you not heard of rubber trees, no?

(78a) expresses the speaker's strong confidence that the addressee does indeed not favour that sort of man. (78b) expresses the speaker's strong confidence that the addressee has mentioned 'it' to the other person. Particularly strong confidence is displayed by speakers who put *sure* or *e* at the beginning of a declarative clause (which has the intonation of a question). Compare (79), and note that (79a) is not equivalent to 'Are you sure that Harry supports Celtic?' but 'I'm certain you can confirm my confident belief that Harry supports Celtic'.

79. a Sure Harry supports Celtic?
    b E Harry supports Celtic?

THE DEFINITE ARTICLE AND POSSESSIVE PRONOUNS

A well-known characteristic of Scots is the use of *the* with nouns denoting institutions, certain illnesses, certain periods of time, quantifiers such as *both*, *all*, *most* and *one*; games; family relatives and modes of travel. (Data from the author's files, Macaulay (1991: 70–1) and Wilson (1915).)

80. a the day [= today], the morn [= tomorrow], the now [= now]
    b She has the hiccoughs/the shivers/the 'flu/the measles/the chickenpox
    c They are at the kirk [= at church]/at the school/in the jail/in the hospital/ at the college (not necessarily a specific school, etc.)
    d in the house [= at home], through the post [= by post], up the stair [= upstairs], down the stair, over the phone [= by phone]
    e Cathy helps Trisha . . . and the both of them get on really good
    g The hale three of them's back on it [= the whole three]; the maist of the farmers; When the one supporter run on the field
    h going to the bingo, a game at the bools, the beds [= hopscotch], the peeries [spinning tops]
    i the wife, the lassie [= my daughter], the boy [= my son]
    j wi the train, with the bus, with the car

Examples of possessive pronouns are given in (81).

81. a Look Cathy, I'm off for my dinner [= to have dinner]
    b After our tea we all went to our bed [= to bed – not a communal bed!]
    c I went to France on my holidays [= on holiday]
    d to get ready to go up to your work [= to work]

COMPARATIVES

What intervenes between *more than* and *as much as* and a following clause, as in (82).

82. a more than what you'd think actually
    b you've as much on your coat as what you have in your mouth

Macaulay (1991: 102) cites similar examples along with *and of coorse the traffic wasnae as strong as what it is noo*. Wilson (1915) gives examples with *nor* instead of *than* but the only examples in any of the sources came from Macaulay's (1991: 103) two oldest speakers – *well it was better then nor what I think it is noo* and *you couldnae get any mair nor two pound*.

Comparative forms are used only before *than*: *Sue is bigger than Jane*. Elsewhere the superlative is used, as in *Who is biggest, Sue or Jane?*

GERUNDS AND INFINITIVES

In English generally some verbs take infinitives, as in (83a), while others take gerunds, as in (83b).

83. a We hope to leave next week [not *we hope leaving . . .]
     b Bob resents spending money on books [not *Bob resents to spend . . .]

Other verbs take either an infinitive or gerund, as in (84).

84. The children started to quarrel/quarrelling

Verbs and adjectives that take either infinitives or gerunds in Scots are shown in (85).

85. a It's difficult to know/knowing how to start this letter
     b They always continue to work/working until the bell goes
     c He started to talk/talking to his friend
     d It was daft to leave/leaving the puppy in the house
     e Try to eat less/eating less if you are putting on weight

Elicitation tests (see the introduction to this chapter) were administered to Scottish and English secondary pupils and to Scottish and English teachers. They showed that the gerund is more frequent in Scots where there is a choice. For (85a) to (85e) Scottish pupils had (statistically) significant numbers of gerunds while the English pupils did not. Some Scottish pupils used only gerunds. Teachers preferred infinitives, with English teachers showing a stronger preference than Scottish teachers.

In Scots the infinitive is regularly marked by *for to*. Macaulay (1991: 106) gives the examples in (86).

86. a we had the clear road for to play on [infinitive relative]
     b you don't need to faw ten thousand feet for to get killt [purpose/result]
     c and aw these hutches was sent out to the bing for to be couped you see [purpose]
     d you werenae allowed at this time for to go and take another job on [verb complement]
     e but my own brothers was all too old for to go [comparison]

His two youngest working-class speakers have no *for to* infinitives, whereas the two oldest use them most frequently. The construction may be in decline, certainly in all except the most informal circumstances.

Some verbs are followed by *and* plus a verb phrase, as in (87).

87. a try and do your homework by tomorrow [= try to do]
    b remember and bring her back by 12 o'clock
    c she tells us to mind and dae what we're tellt [to remember]

This construction has become a catchphrase in a television comedy show, *Chewing the fat*. The catchphrase is *gonna no dae that*, which is probably a distortion of *go and no dae that*, the negative of *go and dae that (right the noo)*. Infinitives can follow AWAY: *I'm away to the shops, I'm away to ask her to dance.*

REFLEXIVES

The reflexive pronoun *myself* is frequently used in speech and writing where Standard English requires just *me* or *I*.

88. a He was just two years younger than myself
    b There wasn't one policeman on duty at the time and if it hadn't been for myself, no evidence either
    c Myself and Andy changed and ran onto the pitch

PREPOSITIONS AND ADVERBS

The prepositional system of Scots has yet to be studied in detail, but the following points can be made.
(i) The typical prepositions in passive clauses are *from, frae/fae* [= from], *off (of)* and *with*.

89. a heh, ah'm gonna get killt fae ma maw [by my Mum]
    b we were all petrified frae him
    c ah'd rather hae no job than bein beat frae pillar tae post aff a that man [by that man]
    d . . . except when it's their weans that get battert wi some other weans [= by some other kids]
    e there was always a lot of shouting going on between carters getting jammed up wi coal lorries
    f she [a dog] was attacked with a Labrador, a big rusty-coloured dog

(ii) *Off*, not *from*, generally expresses the source of something – *I got the book off Alec. From* expresses cause, as in *Many old people die from hypothermia*, but so does *off*, as in *I'm crapping myself off you* [because of you], uttered sarcastically. *Off* has yet to be studied in detail.

(iii) In its location sense *by* is infrequent; *at*, *beside* and *next to* are used. *By* is also infrequent in its directional sense, *past* being used instead – *They drove past the house on their way to the airport.* Attempts to elicit *by* from undergraduates in examples such as *We went to Inverness _____ Stirling* elicited *via* (perhaps because buses have *via* on their destination boards).

(iv)   *In* and *out* are not followed by *to* or *of* after verbs of movement – *She ran in the living room, . . . because she's just walked out the shop with it.* Macaulay (1991: 111) gives similar examples.

(v) Likewise, *down* and *up* do not require TO – *We're going down the town, go down the shops.* After verbs of location they do not require *at* – *One day I was down the beach, They were up the town yesterday.*

(vi) *Outside* is regularly followed by *of* – *outside of the school*

(vii) Miscellaneous examples: *shout on someone* [to someone], *over the phone* [by phone], *through the post* [by post], *wait on someone* [for someone], *fair on someone* [to someone], *married on someone* [to someone], *think on something* [think of/ about].

Macaulay (1991) gives examples with *to* – *he worked to Wilson of Troon, I'm labouring to a bricklayer.*

ORGANISATION OF DISCOURSE

Speakers combine clauses to form large texts, tailoring them to suit the contributions of other speakers. Scots has a range of devices for highlighting items. Because they belong to speech the devices differ from those of the written language but are no less subtle or consistent.

(i)   Speakers often announce a new topic, possibly contrasting with another topic, by means of left-dislocation, a noun phrase followed by a complete clause. Left-dislocation is not primarily associated with problems in planning and producing syntactic constructions; it occurs frequently with simple noun phrases and with no pause between the noun phrase and the clause. The noun phrase may be introduced by *there's*, as in (90d).

90. a it's not bad – *ma Dad* he doesn't say a lot
    b *the driver* he's really friendly – you get a good laugh with him
    c And *the minister*, ye just gave him five shillings. But on the way out we met a wee girl and we gave her the christening piece. [Bennett 1992: 69–70]
    d and *there's one girl* she's a real extrovert

The initial noun phrase can be quite complex – *well* another maths teacher that I dinnae get *he must've corrected my papers* – or may be separated from the main clause by a subordinate clause, as in (91).

91. But a lot of people, *although they didnae have a gift*, it was a coin that they would give them [Bennett 1992: 48]

(ii) English possesses the IT cleft, WH cleft and reverse WH cleft constructions exemplified in (92).

92. a It was Aongais that left (IT cleft)
    b What I want is a large cup of coffee (WH cleft)
    c That's what you should read (Reverse WH cleft)
    d What he does is interrupt all the time (WH cleft)

The IT cleft picks out an entity from a set of possible candidates – Aongais as opposed to Ruaridh. The second clause, *that left*, is a relative clause. The complementiser is usually *that* and the highlighted word can be a lexical noun, as in (92a), or a pronoun, as in (93), from Macaulay (1991: 79).

93. a It was *him* that led the band
    b it's *me* that's het [hot]

There may be no complementiser, as in (94), from Macaulay (1991:121).

94. a It was *Jimmy Brown* was the fireman
    b and it was *my mother* was daein it

Compare *It was Jimmy Brown* that *was the fireman* and *and it was my mother* that *was daein it*.

Seventy-seven per cent of Macaulay's IT clefts are in the working-class interviews. Miller and Weinert (1995) found that IT clefts in general were very rare in both ECOSSE and MTC, although interrogative IT clefts occur regularly in ECOSSE, as in (95).

95. a where is it he works again?
    b who is it that's been murdered?

As a native speaker the author has the intuition that the IT clefts both make the question less abrupt and highlight the WH word, but the construction awaits detailed investigation.

In Scots the WH cleft in (92b) is rare. The WH cleft in (92d) does occur; the key properties are the initial WH clause, *What he does*, followed by BE, followed by an infinitive phrase or a bare verb, *interrupt* in (92d). (96) shows the most common WH cleft, as discussed above (in the section on 'Clause Structure and Function') with respect to (15) and (16).

96. a so what you had to do was you got a partner and you got a match . . .
    b but what you did in the evening you carried a sandwich or two

Reverse WH clefts are frequent in MTC and occur in ECOSSE. They highlight some point that has been agreed and draw a line under a section of discussion. Many discussions of the route in MTC are closed with remarks such as *that's where you should go*. The construction is introduced by *that* or, much less often, *this* followed by a WH clause. Macaulay's narratives (1991: 78–79) contain reverse clefts introduced by *that* or *this* followed by a pronoun and a modifying phrase, as in (97).

97. a so that was me on the rope-splicing
    b that was him idle
    c and this was him landed with a broken leg

The reverse clefts in (97) highlight pronouns. First mentions of entities (animate or inanimate) employ full nouns but subsequent mentions employ pronouns. Reverse clefts are used to complete pieces of narrative, that is, not for first mentions but for subsequent mentions. This explains why all Macaulay's examples contain pronouns following *was*.

Examples of left-dislocation were given in (90) – (91) above. Macaulay (1991: 91) also discusses right-dislocation but its discourse function is unclear and there seem to be two constructions. One is exemplified in (98).

98. a In fact he offered me a job Mr Cunningham
    b She was a very quiet woman my mother
    c I was asking John if he ever heard of it Cabbies Kirk

In (98a) to (98c) the final noun phrases, lying outside the clause, are right-dislocated – *Mr Cunningham my mother*, and *Cabbies Kirk*. They appear to confirm the referents of pronouns inside the clause rather than highlight them. The other construction does seem to have a highlighting function; the final extra-clausal noun phrase is a pronoun repeating a pronoun inside the clause. The referent is not only confirmed but reinforced. Examples are in (99).

99. a He was some man him
    b But she was a harer her
    c Oh it was a loss it

Right-dislocation is less frequent than left-dislocation and almost absent from the middle-class interviews. Macaulay suggests that middle-class speakers are more likely to use emphatic stress than the repeated pronouns, that is with stress on *he* in *he was some man*, on *she* is *she was a harer* and on *it* in *oh it was a loss*. (iii) Various focusing devices highlight items (or propositions) that the speaker wishes to introduce into the discourse. *See* in (100a) is close in meaning to the perception verb *see*, more distant in meaning in (100b).

100. a see those old houses . . . this area was all houses like that right round
     b A: there's a car park
        B: aye – see I hate going in there

See highlights the noun phrase *those old houses* in (100a) and the clause *I hate going in there* in (100b). In the MTC, examples such as *see the bridge below the forest* are always understood as questions: the reply is *uhuh* or *aye* or *right*. *See* does not normally occur in the imperative except in special phrases such as *see here! I've had enough of this nonsense!*

In the MTC speakers use *see* when they treat a landmark as given; that is, they assume the hearer can find the landmark or knows about it, either because it is prominent on the map or has already been mentioned. *See* always takes a definite noun phrase: *see the fast-flowing river* but not **see a fast-flowing river*. To introduce items suspected of not being given or findable, speakers use, for example, *can you see a fast-flowing river?* or *do you see a fast-flowing river?*

See can highlight entire clauses. Examples from the MTC are in (101).

101. A: right see if you come down straight down right see if you come round
        the left of the hills right
     B: uh huh
     A: see if you go straight down but not go straight to the aeroplane right see
        where the see where the pilot would go that wee bit

Macafee (1983: 48) cites *see you* as a type of vocative: *see you, you're just a pain in the neck*.

In the MTC, items are introduced by KNOW: *know the bridge across the fast-flowing river*. As with SEE, these utterances are understood as questions, and contain only definite noun phrases. Thus, **know a bridge across the fast-flowing river* is not possible.

Know is equivalent to the Scots *ken* [= *know*]; you can *ken* someone and *ken* how to do something. *Ken* can highlight new items, including new topics of conversation. Examples are given in (102).

102. a ken John Ewan – he breeds spaniels
     b the estate up at Macmerry – ken there's a big estate there – it's got a
       gamekeeper

Ken in (103) introduces a proposition by way of explanation.

103. she's on the machine until they can get another kidney for her – ken to have a transplant

Macaulay (1991: 160) says that *ken* often accompanies background or orientation clauses (as in (103)) and marks interactional solidarity. That is, checking that your partner in conversation knows what you are talking about is a good way of bringing them into the conversation. Some of Macaulay's examples are in (104).

104. a And they turned it on hard and ken brushed aw these things
      b Oh they washed aw the dirt oot for ken Hogmanay
      c And an auld wuman come oot wi wan of them hearing horns mind ken

Interestingly, Macaulay (1991: 145) notes that *you know* occurs at the rate of 2.1 per thousand words in the speech of his middle-class speakers and 2.3 per thousand words in the speech of his working-class speakers. 'Interestingly', because this contradicts Bernstein's claim that it is working-class speakers who use large numbers of meaningless interjections.

Propositions and properties are highlighted by *the thing is, thing is*. They highlight a point which the speaker feels might be overlooked.

105. a but the thing is – at our age what is there what sort of facilities can you provide
      b thing is he's watching the man he's not watching the ball
      c the thing about school is that you can get them to relax

(iv) There are two constructions with *like*. The older one dates from at least the early nineteenth century, since the first occurrence in print, according to the *Oxford English Dictionary*, is in 1819 in a novel by Walter Scott. This construction has *like* in clause-final position and is used by speakers use to provide explanations and forestall objections as in (106).

106. he's back in hospital he's in for observation like [as opposed to an operation]

(106) was uttered by a research assistant (Mike Cullen, now a successful writer of plays for theatre and television). His father had been suffering from a heart problem. One afternoon he announced *he's back in hospital*, referring to his father, and continued with *he's in for observation like*. When it was pointed out that he had provided another example of *like*, Mike answered that he had used that construction in order to counter the inference, which he could see from the listeners' expressions, that his father was seriously ill again.

The above analysis fits the other declarative clauses with *like* in ECOSSE. (It also fits *like*-final clauses in dialogue in Trollope's novels and in Dorothy Sayer's novels. In both cases the examples are uttered by characters speaking non-Standard English.) Another Scots example is in (107).

107. you had a wooden spile – you bored on the top of the barrel . . . and then you had ready a spile, which was a wooden cone about that length . . . and a soft wood naturally was porous and it would help to get this froth to let it work down – you had to be very careful you didn't take it right down *like*/it went flat

The inference being countered by the *like* in (107) is 'Surely the beer would go flat if you bored a hole in the top of the barrel?' The speaker points out that this inference is incorrect, because the operation was carried out very carefully precisely to prevent the beer going flat.

Like occurs not just in clauses but in noun phrases, as in (108). (The double plus sign in (108) signals a medium pause, as opposed to a short pause – see also (110a) and (110d).)

108. we've decided to produce a news sheet at the end of the year + + just something to leave a memory of us like

The phrase *just something to leave a memory of us like* counteracts any potential inference that the proposed unofficial news sheet is to be big and remarkable. It will be a modest production, not a trend-setter but simply a memento from the pupils who are about to leave school.

Like occurs in interrogative clauses, as in (109).

109. A1 got a bairn have you?
    B1 aye – Nicole's eh three
    A2 three?
    B2 aye – I was married young
    A3 aye – you must have been – how old are you *like*

(109) with emphatic stress on *are*, relates to B's exact age, that is, to the detail that A needs in order to understand the surprising information that B's daughter is three. A can be interpreted as suddenly suspecting that he has wrongly inferred B's age.

The second construction with *like* is more recent. In it *like* occurs in any position except at the end of clauses. It precedes and highlights clauses (110a) and phrases (a prepositional phrase in (110b), a noun phrase in (110c) and a gerund phrase in (110d)) – all from MTC.

110. a I mean and *like* + you've not got any obstacles here have you?
     b you go *like* round it
     c to the lefthand side of East Lake? *like* the very far end of East Lake?
     d you want to be sort of *like* + going + + up + and then curving right
        round the fast flowing creek

Many analysts treat the second *like* construction as a pause filler but Miller and Weinert (1995) show that it does not occur at pauses or where the speaker has problems planning the syntax. Moreover it occurs where WH or IT clefts could – note *what I want to ask is you've not got any obstacles here?* as a paraphrase of (110a), and *is it the very far end of East Lake I go to?* as a paraphrase of (110c). (The pause-filler view does not of course apply to clause-final *like*.)

Like regularly highlights items constituting an explanation or leading to an explanation, as in (111a). In interrogatives, as in (111b) it focuses on requests for information on particular points, here whether the addressee's parents insist that she returns home by a particular time in the evening.

111. a like I knew I couldnae apply for Edinburgh because I didnae have an O
        level language so I just didnae do it
     b like are there strict rules about coming in and all this?

CONCLUSION

This chapter has set out the major syntactic and discourse structures of modern Scots, avoiding large-scale comparisons and contrasts with Standard English. It is worthwhile reminding ourselves of two things. The first is that while Scots shares some, possibly many, of the structures with other non-standard and spoken varieties of English, it has its own mix of morphology, syntax, discourse organisation and vocabulary. Secondly, but more importantly, the differences between Scots and standard (written) English are systematic and far-reaching, and crucial to problems of education, employment and social identity.

That said, there has been little progress in the study of Scots grammar since the initial flurry of activity in the late seventies. New bodies of data on computer, such as the SCOTS archive at the University of Glasgow (www.scottishcorpus.ac.uk), have to be exploited. The systematic collection of data by cassette recorder and elicitation techniques has yet to be undertaken. Map Task dialogues help to build up our knowledge of structures currently in use but represent a different genre from spontaneous conversation. Some accounts of Scots are based on dialogues in novels; it is essential to determine which structures are peculiar to such dialogues and which are still in active use.

But in active use where? The morphology and syntax of Buchan Scots, we may suspect, is different from that of Edinburgh and the Lothians, which is what this account is based on. How different in grammar are the varieties of Scots spoken in Glasgow, in Ayrshire, in the Borders, in Dumfries and Galloway? How different in grammar are the varieties spoken in large urban centres, in smaller towns and in small villages? In ex-mining communities, fishing communities and farming communities? How is grammar and discourse organisation affected by variation in formality, for example in relaxed domestic conversation as opposed to narratives or political discussions. What structures and vocabulary are used by members of different socio-economic classes and by different age-groups? The participants in the ECOSSE conversations are now approaching forty and the participants in the MTC are now approaching thirty. What is the spoken language of the 15–25 age group in different situations? Is there an effect of gender on the use of Scots grammar and vocabulary? What do people from different age groups and socio-economic classes write, in diaries, in personal letters, in work reports and so on? There is a small army of questions; where is the small army of researchers?

CHAPTER 6

The Phonology of Modern Urban Scots

Jane Stuart-Smith

INTRODUCTION

A. J Aitken's 'model of modern Scottish speech' (for example 1984b: 519f.) famously models language use in Scotland along a 'bipolar stylistic continuum' ranging from 'Scots' to 'English' (see Macafee, Chapter 4, Figure 4.1). In his model, 'Phonology (system and rules of realisation)' exists in column 3, as a '"common core" of invariants' which Scots speakers share with Scottish Standard English speakers as the basis of their phonology, supplemented by recourse to the outer columns containing possible 'variants or options of selectional phonology' (p. 519). The degree to which speakers select from columns 1 and 2, which contain either distinctive Scots words or Scots cognates or equivalents, will determine the depth of the vernacular that they use. He observes that the common practice of many working-class speakers, and hence most speakers of Modern Urban Scots, is frequent selection from column 2 (for example *hoose* rather than *house*), less frequent from column 1 (for example *wean* rather than *baby*) and 'inconsistency for many other items' (p. 521). They may also style-drift up and down the continuum according to context or interlocutor.

Again, in his discussion of Scottish English vowels earlier in the same book (1984a: 94f.), the vowel system is described as 'largely shared' across the two extreme varieties of vernacular Scots and Scottish Standard English. He goes on to note (p. 94) that alongside those who tend to select for Scots 'there exists also a very large body of Scottish speakers who variously compromise – in system, realisations, selections – between the fully vernacular variety of Scots . . . and . . . SSE [Scottish Standard English]'. Describing and accounting for this 'compromise', which I would suggest is now the norm for the majority of Urban Scots speakers, in my view presents one of the greatest challenges for those working on Scots phonology today.

This chapter is concerned with precisely this – the adequate description and explanation of the observable phonological behaviour of Modern Urban Scots. Aitken's observations provide a number of cues for investigation. What do speakers actually show in terms of system, phonetic realisation and lexical incidence? Is it possible to find Urban Scots speakers who just use 'the vernacular'? What is this compromise linguistically? How should it be described – as the 'mixing' of two systems, or one integrated system, or something else? To what extent can we talk of 'common' or 'shared' phonological categories such as vowels and consonants between Urban Scots and Scottish Standard English? How much are Scots lexical options used by speakers? What words are involved? How consistent is the speech of working-class speakers? And so on.

The work presented here does not – and cannot – answer these questions. However, I hope to make a start, and to encourage others to continue, by considering them with explicit reference to existing evidence. Given my own limited experience with Modern Urban Scots I discuss here in detail only aspects of Glaswegian speech, thus here 'Urban Scots' generally refers to the speech of the working classes of Glasgow. The results will be comparable to other varieties of Modern Urban Scots found across the Central Belt, as far as dialectal and sociolinguistic differences will allow (cf. for example Macafee 1994: 23f. for the main differences between East and West Central Scots; see also Johnston 1997b: 440f.).

I begin by considering a number of methodological issues, and then provide a brief outline of the phonology of Urban Scots, considering suprasegmentals, vowels and consonants. My aim is not to present a phonetic and phonological description of Glaswegian, since these exist in some detail elsewhere (for example Macafee 1983: 31; Macafee 1994: 26f., 224f.; Johnston 1997b: passim; Stuart-Smith 1999a; Stuart-Smith and Tweedie 2000), but rather to sketch a descriptive outline and consider in more detail certain features, in particular the vowel alternation /ʉ ~ ʌʉ/ as in e.g. *hoose/house* and the realisation of postvocalic /r/ as in, for example, *car*, which present some thought-provoking results.

METHODS

If we are to describe Urban Scots phonology in practice, we need to work with examples of actual speech, which entails gathering speech data, and in turn certain methodological assumptions (and problems).

We begin with the linguistic context. We assume here that the Urban Scots of Glasgow continues a form of West Central Scots, which has changed and is continuing to change mainly through processes of dialect contact and levelling with Scottish Standard English. Glasgow has had its own distinctive history of urbanisation and in-migration, and with it has come linguistic change (see, for example, Macafee 1994: 26f.). In terms of language use, Urban Scots in Glasgow enters into a similar relationship with Scottish Standard English as in Aitken's model.

The speakers who are of most interest for us are working-class, living in now relatively tight-knit communities, which have witnessed substantial geographical and social upheaval from the city's housing policies during the mid-twentieth century, and sharp economic deprivation from the decline of heavy industry. The data we consider avoids 'problems' of dialect contact with forms of English other than Scottish Standard English (cf., for example, the interesting results of Hewlett et al. 1999 whose Edinburgh sample contained children of English parents).

We assume here that the main methodological approach which is useful for tackling questions of Urban Scots phonology is variationist, that is the investigation of speech by means of quantification of linguistic elements and correlation of these with extralinguistic factors (for a similar position for the work in Belfast, cf. L. Milroy 1982: 142). The 'Labovian' approach has been met with varying degrees of enthusiasm in Scotland (less so by, for example, Macafee 1994: 34f.; more so by, for example, Johnston 1983; most so by, for example, Romaine 1975: 225). The results presented here support a variationist (as opposed to strictly Labovian) approach with appropriate modifications required by this particular linguistic context. Differing lexical incidence, or the selection of a sound for a particular word, is a key characteristic of Urban Scots. Constructing variables to describe Urban Scots therefore requires reference to lexical incidence as appropriate (see L. Milroy 1987: 131f.). Quantifying variables can also be awkward, though in the data discussed here using separate percentages for separate variables seems most useful, and avoids forcing possibly discrete elements into a continuum (cf. L. Milroy 1987: 121f.).

The speech data that forms the basis for the discussion occurs in three datasets collected by Ronald Macaulay, Caroline Macafee and myself, in 1973, 1984–5 and 1997 respectively (available in Macaulay and Trevelyan 1973; Macaulay 1977; Macafee 1988, 1994; Stuart-Smith 1999a; Stuart-Smith and Tweedie 2000).[1] Each speech corpus is rather different as a result of the differing goals and approaches of each investigator.

Macaulay's work used the classic Labovian approach with the aim of describing phonological variation and change in Glaswegian. He worked with forty-eight speakers in three age groups (adult, fifteen years, ten years), male and female, grouped into social classes I, IIa, IIb, III (from higher to lower status) according to occupation (see p. 18f.). Interviews with Macaulay at home and at school resulted in 'careful, rather formal speech' (p. 21); some read speech was collected. Five phonological variables were analysed: (i) (u) (a) (gs) (au) [his labels].

Macafee's corpus includes sixty-two working-class speakers, male and female in five age groups (10–15; 16–25; 26–45; 46–65; 66 +). Recordings of generally broad Urban Scots were made during interviews with the investigator and informants outside the home and were usually made in groups. The study concentrated on Scots lexis in Glasgow, combining qualitative and quantitative methods (the field-work is described in some detail in 1994: 42–55). Sixteen variables of lexical incidence are analysed: /wa/ /ʌ~ʌu/ /e~o/ /ɛr/ /aŋ/ /ɪ~u/ /u~ʌu/ /ɔ~a/ /ɛ~a/ /i~ɛ/ /a~ɔ/ /e~u/ /l/ /v/ /nd/.

My own corpus was recorded in the spring and summer of 1997, with the help of a Scottish field-worker, Claire Timmins, who is from Edinburgh but who had lived and worked in Glasgow for four years. Thirty-two speakers were involved, male and female, younger (thirteen to fourteen years) and older (forty to sixty years), working class and middle class. Self-selected pairs of the same sex talked alone for up to forty-five minutes, and then read a wordlist (see Stuart-Smith 1999a: 204). The spontaneous speech for most speakers was casual and seems to have benefited from not having an 'outsider' present during the recording. The goal of the data collection was to consider phonological variation and change in Glasgow, with an added emphasis on detailed phonetic analysis (including instrumental). In a subsequent research project based on this data eleven consonantal variables were analysed: (t) (th) (dh) (s) (x) (hw) (l) (r-realisation) (r-postvocalic) (k) (w).[2]

We may make a few observations about these corpora:

- Both Macaulay and I collected middle-class speech. Given that we intend to describe Urban Scots (working-class speech) one might assume that only working-class speech is needed. However, it becomes clear from the examples below that if we wish to describe Urban Scots as it is used now, data from middle-class speech can act as a useful foil to demonstrate the patterns that are characteristic and, sometimes the exclusive domain, of Scots. This contrast is particularly important in a city such as Glasgow where both the middle and the working classes work hard to remain separate.

- We assume that the activities of reading and speaking are different (cf. e.g. Macaulay 1977: 53). We therefore tend to focus on conversational or spontaneous speech, which is necessary when considering phonological alternations of lexical incidence (such as *hoose/house*), since these are usually inhibited when reading, as a result of Scottish Standard English as the dominant variety in school and thus for the acquisition of literacy.

- While there are differences in context, field-worker, topic and so on across the three corpora, within these we can probably assume that the factors commonly regarded as contributing to different 'styles' were rather similar. There is therefore little discussion of stylistic differences here (the most extensive discussion of style in Urban Scots is Johnston's 1983 analysis from Edinburgh).

– The unnaturalness of being recorded, whether the field-worker is present or not, is bound to place some contraints on the speech captured. For the purposes of this work we have to assume that these speech corpora are in some ways representative of usual speech patterns, though with reservations. (A related point is that the speech of 132 individuals collected across twenty-five years from a city with a current population of around 600,000 is hardly going to be representative of the city as a whole.)

– Problems are obviously going to be encountered when attempting to compare data from these three very different corpora. Thus all comparisons made here are to be regarded with caution (even when this is not explicitly stated).

The fine analysis of phonological variables is time-consuming. The prospects for narrow phonetic transcription are far better today with high-quality digital recording, and the possibility of digitising speech into computers, but it remains very difficult. Cross transcription, at least of a sample, is usually necessary, as is the categorisation of the inevitably vast array of variants identified. Acoustic analysis of variation using spectrography and other forms of spectral analysis is appropriate for many variables (see, for example, Docherty and Foulkes 1999 on consonant analysis). To date I have found it most effective when considering (s) – where hints of a gender difference from the auditory analysis immediately emerged in the acoustic analysis – and (x) and (hw) – where phonetically intermediate variants exist (see, for example, Lawson and Stuart-Smith 1999).

Statistical analysis was not performed on the phonological data in Macaulay and Macafee (the variables discussed here). It formed a substantial element of the project on my own data, and we were fortunate to have the statistician Fiona Tweedie as a member of the research team, whose task it was to find the appropriate statistical tools for testing hypothesised differences and for exploring how the data themselves formed clusters of speakers (for more details, see Stuart-Smith and Tweedie 2000).

SUPRASEGMENTALS

We know little about suprasegmental aspects of Urban Scots. The research that exists on intonation in the speech of Edinburgh and Glasgow shows a difference between the two cities, with terminating mid- to low-falls in Edinburgh (e.g.

Brown et al. 1980), and a tendency towards high rising patterns in Glasgow (e.g. Macafee 1983: 36; Stuart-Smith 1999a: 211). The extent to which these continue patterns from earlier forms of Scots is not known, though Northern Irish influence may be invoked to some extent to explain distinctive Glaswegian patterns (Macafee 1983: 37). Even less has been said about rhythm in Scottish English (but see Abercrombie 1979: 67f.).

My study of voice quality in Glaswegian (Stuart-Smith 1999a: 211f.) investigated the extent to which reported features of jaw protrusion and harshness were present in the 1997 corpus. Using a perceptual analysis of voice quality based on the work of John Laver (for example, most recently 1994: 391f.), I established a voice quality profile for each of the thirty-two speakers and then analysed this data. The results showed little evidence for the stereotypical Glasgow voice, but at the same time a specific constellation of settings typical of working-class speakers (more open jaw, raised and backed tongue body with possible retracted tongue root, whispery voice), which tended to be absent in middle-class speakers. We can only speculate about the extent to which this working-class Glasgow voice quality continues voice qualities of earlier forms of (West-) Central Scots, though it seems likely that developments in segmental realisation were related to particular voice qualities. Certainly this seems to be the case now; cf., for example, the vocalisation of postvocalic /r/ to a vowel with velarised secondary articulation described below.

VOWELS

Describing Urban Scots vowels is helped by reference to two idealised vowel systems, those of Scots and Scottish Standard English. In terms of phonemic categories, as Aitken points out, both systems share an inventory: /i ɪ e ɛ a o ɔ ʉ ʌ əi ae oe ʌʉ/. An outline of the expected Scots lexical incidence is given in Table 6.1 (after Johnston 1997b: 453, with some modifications for subsets), together with Aitken's vowel numbers to enable reference to the historical discussion in Macafee (Chapter 7), corresponding RP vowels, assumed Scots vowels, and assumed corresponding Scottish Standard English vowels (lexical incidence for these may be found in Figure 7.2, Macafee, Chapter 7). Between the two, the vowels and vowel alternations that are found in Urban Scots.[3] Two more alternations should be added which are relevant in Glasgow: /ɛ~a/ in, for example, efter/after, and within the Urban Scots of Glasgow, /e~ɛ/ before /r/ in, for example stair (see Macafee 1994: 225f.). In general both Scots and Scottish Standard English show specific and different treatments of vowels before /r/; for details see Johnston 1997b; Abercrombie 1979: 78f.

Table 6.1 An outline of Scottish English vowels (after Aitken, 1984, Table 1, Macafee Chapter 7, Figure 7.2, Johnston, 1997, 453). ↔ indicates vowel alternation.

keyword	no.	Scots (Glasgow)		SSE	RP
MEET	2	i	i	i	i
BEAT	3	i	i	i	i
(DEAD)		i	i ↔ ɛ	ɛ	ɛ
MATE	4	e	e	e	eɪ
(BOTH)		e	e ↔ o	o	əʊ
BAIT	8	e	e	e	eɪ
PAY	8a	əi	əi ↔ e	e	eɪ
BOOT	7	ɪ	ɪ ↔ ʉ	ʉ	u
DO		e	e ↔ ʉ	ʉ	u
BIT	15	ɪ	ɪ	ɪ	ɪ
BET	16	ɛ	ɛ	ɛ	ɛ
OUT	6	ʉ	ʉ ↔ ʌʉ	ʌʉ	aʊ
COAT	5	o	o	o	əʊ
COT	18	o	o ↔ ɔ	ɔ	ɒ
OFF		a	a ↔ ɔ	ɔ	ɒ
CAT	17	a	a	a	a
(LONG)		a	a ↔ ɔ	ɔ	ɒ
(WASH)		a	a ↔ ɔ	ɔ	ɒ
HAND		ɔ	ɔ ↔ a	a	a
START		ɛ	ɛ ↔ a	a	a
CAUGHT	12	ɔ	ɔ	ɔ	ɔ
(SNOW)		ɔ	ɔ ↔ o	o	əʊ
CUT	19	ʌ	ʌ	ʌ	ʌ
(PULL)	6a	ʌ	ʌ ↔ ʉ	ʉ	ʊ
NEW/DEW	14	jʉ	jʉ	jʉ	ju
BITE	1s	əi	əi	əi	aɪ
TRY	1l	ae	ae	ae	aɪ
EYE	11	i	i ↔ ae	ae	aɪ
LOIN	10	əi	əi ↔ oe	oe	ɔɪ
VOICE	9	oe	oe	oe	ɔɪ
LOUP 'jump'	13	ʌʉ	ʌʉ	(ʌʉ)	–

An important aspect of Scottish vowels not represented is vowel length. The Scottish Vowel Length Rule (SVLR, also called 'Aitken's Law') refers to the phenomenon whereby vowels are phonetically long in certain environments: before voiced fricatives, before /r/ and before a boundary, including a morpheme boundary. Thus the vowels in *breathe, beer, bee, agreed* are longer than in *brief, bead, greed*. The SVLR arose during the history of Scots (see Macafee Chapter 7) and still operates in most varieties of Scots. Recent accounts of the SVLR based on durational data (some of it from the 1997 Glasgow corpus) conclude that the monophthongs /iʉ/ and the diphthong /ai/ are subject to the SVLR (for details and reviews of earlier empirical analysis, see Scobbie et al. 1999a; Scobbie et al. 1999b). Scobbie's analysis of the Glasgow data revealed no durational differences between middle-class and working-class speakers, but some differences of vowel quality.

The representation of the vowel systems for Scots and Scottish Standard English is not controversial, though observations from the data discussed below might make us question whether we could ever encounter a speaker who actually shows the Scots system as given (even if our data were maximally 'broad'). Thus we might assume that the Scots pole is now an idealisation. The same is probably not true of Scottish Standard English. The real question is just what to make of the middle column of Table 6.1, since this represents the actual practice of many Urban Scots speakers in Central Scotland. While I left the heading blank, perhaps it should be 'Urban Scots', since this is what is found in Urban Scots speakers. But this then has the problem of giving this set of possible vowels a name, even of implying that it might be an independent system. It is usual to regard the practice of combining common vowels and alternating vowels in Urban Scots as the result of dialect systems in contact (cf. the discussion in Romaine 1975: 15f.). Certainly from a historical point of view, it is 'dialect mixture'. We will return to what it might be synchronically in due course.

However we wish to describe how the vowels appear to act in concert, we can identify in Urban Scots two main types of vowel, those which are common or shared, whose phonetic realisation is felt to be continuous, and those which are alternating or optional, and whose realisation is felt to be discrete (this distinction also applies to consonants, and the alternation is a direct consequence of independent developments in the history of Scots).[4] The table gives the impression that both types are equally likely, but as we shall see, they are not, and lexical frequency plays a key role. From the point of view of the continuation of historical Modern Scots reflexes, the alternating vowels are of some interest, and we discuss these with specific reference to /ʉ ~ ʌʉ/.

/ʉ ~ ʌʉ/ as in e.g. *hoose/house*

In Macafee's study of alternating vowels, /ʉ ~ ʌʉ/ was used most frequently. This alternation may be considered stereotypical of Scots, and Urban Scots in particular (for the historical derivation, see Vowel 6 in Figures 7.1 and 7.5, Macafee Chapter 7). The alternation, and the realisation of /ʌʉ/, has also been a variable for studies from the three Glasgow speech corpora: (au) in Macaulay (1977: 40f.); /u ~ ʌu/ in Macafee (1994: 229), and OUT in Eremeeva (2002).

Table 6.2 Frequency of /ʉ ~ ʌʉ/ words and usage of /ʉ/ across the three Glasgow studies. (Figures taken from Macaulay 1977, 168-70; Macafee 1988, Fig. 2.3, Eremeeva 2002. Macaulay and Eremeeva limited the number of tokens transcribed, and so these figures are given in brackets.)

	Macaulay fieldwork 1973 pub. 1977		Macafee fieldwork 1984/5 pub. 1994	Eremeeva fieldwork 1997 (un)pub. 2002	
	all	working class	working class	all	working class
no. of speakers	48	32	62	16	8
possible /ʉ ~ ʌʉ/ sites (no. words)	(1266)	(822)	1059	(429)	(207)
average /ʉ ~ ʌʉ/ sites (no. words/speaker)	(26)	(26)	17	(27)	(26)
overall use of /ʉ/ (no. words)	433	400	749	156	130
overall use of /ʉ/ % of possible sites	34	49	71	36	63
total corpus (no. words)			c.57,000		
possible /ʉ ~ ʌʉ/ sites % of corpus			c.1.9		

For a comparison of the three studies, see Table 6.2. Macaulay transcribed (au) in all his speakers, with a limit of three instances of each word to avoid bias used more often with monophthongs (Macaulay personal communcation). Macafee too considered the alternation in all of her sixty-two speakers. Eremeeva transcribed the first thirty tokens, removing all instances where unstressed position in an utterance led to reduction (and hence potential monophthongisation of intended diphthongs). Her small sample per speaker was determined by the other goal of her study, an acoustic analysis of all the tokens. At the time of writing Eremeeva was just completing her transcription, thus the figures presented here may vary slightly from those in her dissertation. In all cases descriptive statistics (percentages) are presented.

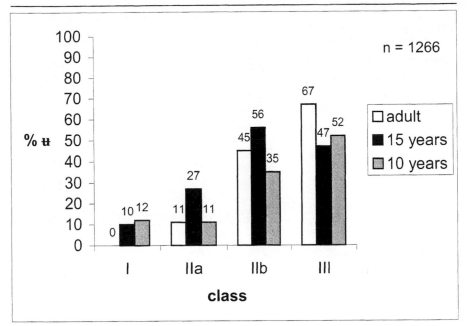

Figure 6.1 Percentage of monophthongal pronunciations of OUT in forty-eight Glaswegian speakers in 1973 – from Macaulay 1977, tables 7–9

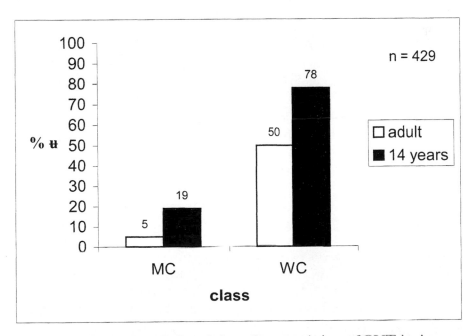

Figure 6.2 Percentage of monophthongal pronunciations of OUT in sixteen Glaswegian speakers in 1997 – preliminary figures are taken from Eremeeva 2002

Figures 6.1 and 6.2, and Table 6.2 (fifth row – overall use of /ʉ/) show the extent to which /ʉ/ is used. This gives us our first main finding for this data: Urban Scots can and does use the Scots option frequently. The highest figure is for the working-class adolescents in Eremeeva, though Macafee's overall average of seventy-one per cent will hide higher amounts for some individuals. The selection/grouping of the informants contributes to a dramatic contrast between working-class and middle-class speakers for Eremeeva, while for Macaulay usage increases as class lowers. Attempting any type of real-time comparison between 1973 and 1997 is difficult. Assuming Eremeeva's working class correspond to Macaulay's IIb/III (Macaulay personal communication), the numbers are rather similar for adults, and higher for adolescents in 1997. Whether this could possibly represent change is difficult to say, especially because Macaulay's data collection was more formal and his analysis different. It is difficult to know the extent to which observed increases in non-standard variants in adolescents will persist into adulthood. What does seem to emerge is that across the last twenty-five years the use of /ʉ/ is rather stable.

There is a related finding from considering the alternation, which, while obvious, should be noted: for all speakers there is always an alternation.[5] Thus alternating these vowels is an obligatory part of speaking Urban Scots, even in data which is broad (as Macafee) or casual without an outsider present (as Eremeeva). These alternations are difficult to describe in terms of stylistic shift, though it is likely that topic may account for some instances. This gives rise to the 'inconsistent behaviour' noted by Aitken (1984b: 522) found in Romaine's 1975 study. Do we have to live with a degree of 'inherent variability' (as Romaine 1975: 224f.)? Further close analysis of exactly what might provoke alternation is needed.

Macaulay's decision to present (au) in terms of a (socio)phonetic continuum rather than alternating variants was met with the criticism (see, for example, Romaine 1975: 121f.) that this was a variable where the alternation based on historically different developments was tantamount, and hence it is necessary to present variation in terms of diphthongal versus monophthongal data. However, Macaulay's data presented as it is without pooling the diphthongal variants are revealing (see figure 6.3). As he points out (p. 29), they show a clear sociolinguistic continuum.[6] The three diphthongal variants show different patterns: (au-1) [qʊ] and (au-2) [ʌu] are used mainly by Class I, while (au-3) [əu] is the preferred diphthongal variant for Classes IIb and III. Macafee (1997b: 521) too is convinced of the existence of a phonetic continuum from wider through narrower diphthong to monophthong, and she argues for the 'very narrow' option either as an 'intermediate' form, or perhaps better the preservation of an earlier development.

Whatever the derivation of (au-3), what is striking about this variant is that it is used most often by those who alternate with /ʉ/, that is, Class IIb/III and Class IIa speakers (who alternate infrequently). This shows that while these speakers alternate to a diphthong, and so 'away' from the Scots reflex, what they alternate

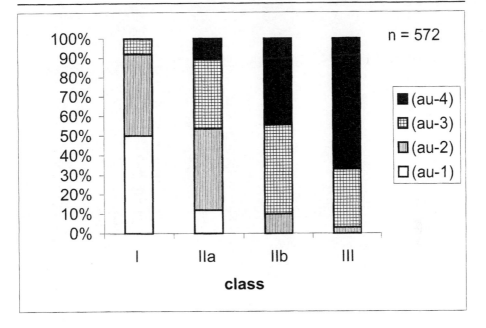

Figure 6.3 Percentage of each variant of (au) according to social class in adults in Macaulay's 1973 Glasgow data (figures from Macaulay 1977, table 7)

to is not typical of Scottish Standard English speakers. Thus we see that whilst producing a diphthong, these Urban Scots speakers are systematically using a variant which is not frequent in Scottish Standard English. Hence, though they have moved to a phonologically shared category, they continue to maintain a different pronunciation, which is then characteristic of Urban Scots.[7] If we accept Macafee's explanation, these speakers would be exploiting a peripheral variant resulting from the historical development of Vowel 6.[8] This interpretation also allows us to speculate about the IIa speakers. They appear to be aiming at the Class I pattern, in the shared use of (au-2), but they persist in using (au-3), possibly indicating a recent working-class background. (Johnston too found stratification in the realisation of /ʌʉ/, which he investigated using two variables, separately considering the social stratification of the first and second elements; Speitel and Johnston 1983: 19–21.) The important finding from the diphthongal variation is that the common vowel of the alternation is likely to have a different realisation from that of the 'same' category in Scottish Standard English.

We are able to consider the lexical distribution of this alternation thanks to Macafee's painstaking analysis (Macafee 1988, Figures 5.1, 5.2, 5.3 and Macafee 1994, Figure 5.1).[9] Figure 6.4 shows that only seven different words are involved to any degree, and of these only six show /ʉ/ more than fifty-nine per cent (and *oor/our* has only twenty-five tokens overall). An additional eight words were found infrequently (*mooth/mouth*; *croon/crown*; *hoor/hour*; *Toonheid/Townhead*;

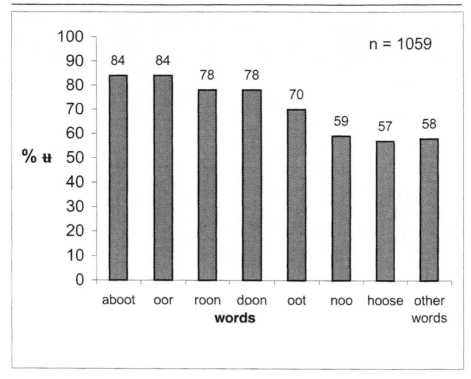

Figure 6.4 Lexical distribution of percentage of monophthongal pronunciations for the variable /u ∼ ʌu/ in sixty-two Glaswegian speakers in 1984–5
(figures from Macafee 1988: Figure 5.3)

Sooside/Southside; *coont/count*; *pooder/powder*; *goon/gown*). Thus her data split into
six common items (around 100 tokens or more), one less common, and eight
which are rare. My impression from Eremeeva's data confirms Macafee's main set
as frequent, and a few more word alterations (such as *poond/pound; foon(d)/
found; groon(d)/ground*) may be added.

Some cautionary comments are necessary in assessing these figures. It is
common practice to discount alternating items which could alternate but which
do not occur within the corpus (cf. Macafee 1994: 215), which means that to a
certain extent the corpus defines and delimits (and probably also reduces) the
possible lexical distribution of an alternating variable. This is probably also
affected by the context of the data collection, topic of discussion and so on. Thus
our finding from these results is cautious: very few words are involved in the
alternation, and some are very much more frequent than others.

The final observation that I would like to make here concerns overall lexical
frequency and the /ʉ ∼ ʌʉ/ alteration. Again, Macafee's work helps here (see the
last two rows of Table 6.2). Of the several low-frequency alternating vowel
variables, /ʉ ∼ ʌʉ/ is used the most frequently. However, even for this alternation

the number of possible sites (words) for alternation is only about two per cent of the entire corpus. Again, we have to be cautious about this figure, but even being generous, we may note another finding, namely that: this alternation affects a tiny percentage of overall lexical frequency. Given that the other alternations are even less frequent, we can predict that overall the number of alternations represents a very low percentage of the possible items encountered.

If we reconsider the middle column of Table 6.1, this means that while the alternations might appear 'equal' to shared vowels, in terms of frequency they are very much less common. If this is so, how do the alternations achieve such salience (both to Urban Scots speakers and outsiders)? Part of the answer may lie in general effects of frequency. In general what seems to be important from a frequency point of view are either features that are very infrequent, or alternatively those which are very frequent (see, for example, Bybee 2000). It is possible that the alternations are salient precisely because they are now so infrequent.[10]

Other (related) factors affecting alternating vowels (and also consonants) are lexical transfer and erosion, in other words the replacing of a Scots word with its Standard English cognate, for example *ground* for *groon(d)*, or the loss of a non-comparable Scots word, for example *bouk* 'bulk'. The consequences of lexical drain (Johnston) on the phonology of Urban Scots are difficult to predict though we would assume that it can only increase the rarity of alternation and gradually pull lexical incidence towards that of Scottish Standard English (see Harris 1985: 128f. on lexical transfer in Belfast). In particular, lexical transfer of a once frequent item such as *oor* will have the effect of drastically reducing the overall potential frequency of the alternation. That so few words now belong to lexical sets potentially showing Scots vowels, and therefore inversely that so many show Scottish Standard English incidence, explains why it would be so difficult to find an Urban Scots speaker with the Scots distribution in Table 6.1.

Apparently less interesting for the continuation of Urban Scots in terms of historical reflexes is the realisation of the common or non-alternating vowels. However, as we have seen from the common variants of /ʉ ~ ʌʉ/, the realisation and patterning of the common vowel in Urban Scots is socially and phonetically particular to Urban Scots, and different from that of the 'same' vowel in Scottish Standard English. This observation can also be made for the common vowels in general (cf. Johnston 1997b: 453–99). Examples from observable data are found in Macaulay's analyses, for example that of the variable (i) (BIT), which appears in Class IIb and III speakers as a split in pronunciations between (i-2) [ɛ/ɪ] and (i-3) [ɛ̞/ɪ̞] (see Macaulay 1977: Figure 3, p. 37).[11] A similar impression of lowered and backed variants occurs in the 1997 data (Stuart-Smith 1999a: 207), and this fits with the historical development of this vowel in Scots (see Macafee's Figure 7.5, Chapter 7).

This cursory discussion about a tiny proportion of the vowels of Urban Scots provokes the following observations which may supplement the information in the middle column of Table 6.1:

– alternating vowels always alternate
– the common category of an alternation does not share a common pattern of realisation
– alternations occur in very few words, which are themselves rare overall
– alternations may appear more salient because they are infrequent
– common vowels do not share common patterns of realisation
– these findings rely on methods drawn from the variationist approach, namely quantification and correlation with external factors.

Thus our impression of Urban Scots vowels is that while categorically they may be 'shared', in all other respects they are not. This conclusion is pretty much what one might expect from previous discussions. However, my intention here is to draw attention to differences in realisation and patterning, which certainly have consequences for the impression of Urban Scots accents, and which may also have implications for their phonology. After all, when the realisations of a category pattern differently from another category which is supposed to be the 'same', one might start to wonder to what extent it is 'the same', especially when this extends across the entire inventory.

CONSONANTS

Again, in terms of inventory, Urban Scots and Scottish Standard English show a large number of common consonants: /p b t d k g f θ v ð s z ʃ ʒ x ʍ h tʃ dʒ r l m n ŋ w/. Of these, /x ʍ/ are not generally found in southern accents of English English and RP. Having said that, the extent to which these categories are intact for some speakers of Urban Scots is doubtful. Macafee's (1983: 32) observation of [k] and [w] as possible realisations in localised Glasgow speech was confirmed for the speech of the working-class speakers in 1997, especially the adolescents, for whom [k] and [w] are the majority forms (Lawson and Stuart-Smith 1999; Stuart-Smith and Tweedie 2000). [x] and [ʍ], which we might expect to be characteristic of Urban Scots, were more common in middle-class Scottish Standard English speakers.

There is a much smaller group of alternating categories based on Scots lexical incidence and arising from particular developments in the history of Scots: /l ~ V/, e.g. *fitbaw/football*, /v ~ Ø/, e.g. *gie/give*, /θ ~ Ø/, e.g. *wi'/with*, /nd ~ n/, e.g. *staun/stand*; /t ~ d/, e.g. *bastart/bastard*. As for the vowel alternations, Macafee's investigation (1994: figure 5.1) revealed that each consonant alternation is represented by a handful of items used to any degree. Just as for the vowel alternations, consonant alternations alternate, the overall number of alternations is very low and occurs in only a few words.

A large amount of data now exists on the realisation of consonants in Glaswegian as a result of our recent project (Stuart-Smith and Tweedie 2000; publications are still being prepared). When considered as a whole, exploratory statistical analysis of all the variants for all eleven variables grouped speakers into two polarised groups – middle-class adults and working-class adolescents, with working-class adults and middle-class adolescents ranged between them. The two extremes showed a good deal of consistency in speech behaviour (cf. the linguistic focussing in Belfast discussed by, for example, L. Milroy 1982). Working-class speech in this data showed a tight-knit group of adolescents using non-standard features (both local 'Scots' and non-local 'English' ones including the infamous [f] for [θ] in, for example, *think*) while adults were more loosely grouped, and showed a higher spread of variation in consonant realisation, which again is reminiscent of the greater range found in lower status speakers in Belfast (cf., for example, Milroy 1982). It is clear from these overall results that consonants common to Urban Scots and Scottish Standard English do not show common realisations or patterns of realisation. Also, Urban Scots speakers may exhibit varying degrees of linguistic consistency.

For the rest of this section we restrict the discussion to two aspects of realisation from the 1997 corpus, briefly T-glottalling which gives insight into an apparently common variant in Scots and Scottish Standard English, and then in some detail and for the first time, postvocalic /r/, which gives a good illustration of the nature and range of possible realisations of a common consonant in Urban Scots.

T-glottalling, the realisation of /t/ with a glottal stop, is a stereotype of Glasgow speech and Urban Scots more generally (cf., for example, Macafee 1994: 27; Macafee 1997b; Stuart-Smith 1999b; Johnston 1997b: 500f.). T-glottalling is clearly evidenced in Macaulay's data with the lower classes using glottals extensively (ninety per cent for Class III). An analysis of the 1997 Glasgow data revealed similar patterns, and a cautious real-time comparison across the two suggested some increase in working-class speakers, especially girls (though with the already high numbers in 1973 there was little room for manoeuvre).

More interesting here perhaps are the qualitative patterns of T-glottalling which were found from a close analysis of the 1997 corpus (Stuart-Smith 1999b). When we talk of T-glottalling, whether in Scottish Standard English or Urban Scots, we might think that Urban Scots will simply show more glottals – and that impression is certainly gained from the 1973 and 1997 results. However, when the patterning of glottalling in working-class speakers and middle-class speakers was examined according to phonetic environment, looking at the usage in prepausal position (e.g. *but#*) compared with prevocalic (for example, *a lot of#*) and intervocalic (for example, *water*), a striking difference emerged. When all instances where [t] was used (exceptions to T-glottalling) were considered, it became clear that T-glottalling is the norm for working-class speakers: we could even say obligatory for working-class adolescents. All exceptions are clearly motivated. Middle-class speakers, however, show a different pattern. For them [t] is the norm, and T-glottalling optional. What was also revealing was that style-shifting up or down resulted in unsuccessful attempts to match the pattern of the other group. Thus working-class speakers reflect a particular pattern of T-glottalling, which given the attestation of glottalling in Glasgow for more than a century (for example, Macafee 1994: 27, n. 20) is likely to continue patterns inherited from earlier forms of Urban Scots (Macafee personal communication). The observation to be drawn from this data is this: common consonants may be realised with the 'same' phonetic variant, but even this may pattern differently from that in Scottish Standard English.

postvocalic /r/, e.g. *car*

The consonant /r/ is common to both Scots and Scottish Standard English. The traditional Scots articulation is given as a tap or a trill, while Scottish Standard English speakers are said to prefer the central approximant [ɹ], which is now trickling into Scots (for example, Johnston 1997b: 510). Rhoticity, or the pronunciation of postvocalic /r/ in words such as *car*, *card*, *better*, is also a shared characteristic of the two systems. The loss, or perhaps better, vocalisation of postvocalic /r/ (R-vocalisation) was not generally thought to be a feature of Scottish English, but Johnston (1997) extends it as a rule for the entire Central Scots region. Two variationist studies in Edinburgh have confirmed R-vocalisation in working-class speakers. Romaine (for example, 1978) found r-lessness (with taps) as a feature of working-class boys, while girls preferred an approximant articulation. Johnston (Speitel and Johnston 1983: 28f.) again found taps and pharyngealised vowels mainly used by working-class speakers (males). He also observed that intervocalic and word-initial /r/ maintained the expected Scots taps in working-class speech, with the latter position reflecting a 'self-identification with vernacular culture or with Scottish ethnic identity' (p. 26).

Our pilot investigations of the 1997 Glasgow speech corpus indicated realisational differences and r-vocalisation. At the outset of the project on the data, considering the realisation of /r/ as a variable in its own right was not included in the original research schedule. However, the complexity of the variation that emerged from looking at the loss of postvocalic /r/ was so great (eleven variant categories) that we decided to construct two /r/ variables:

R-realisation: a summary overall picture of the sociolinguistic patterning of the articulatory possibilities for /r/ (across all phonetic environments, reducing all vocalic variation to a single category [V])[12]

R-vocalisation: an investigation of the variation and change of postvocalic /r/ (separating phonetic environments, reducing all articulatory variation to a single category [r])

The matching of these two variables is slightly awkward in that the articulated [r] variant category of *R-vocalisation* does not correspond exactly to the data analysed for *R-realisation* (hence differing raw and percentage figures). However, visual inspection of the transcribed data for both variables did not reveal obvious sociolinguistic or phonetic differences in articulation according to position in the word, and thus articulated [r] in *R-vocalisation* may be expanded by referring to the findings of *R-realisation*. Given the focus of this chapter, we concentrate on reporting those findings particularly relevant for Urban Scots (although as this chapter is the first published statement, in each instance all data is given).

We begin with *R-realisation*. All words containing /r/ in the wordlist were transcribed for all speakers. At first all instances of /r/ in the conversations were transcribed, but the high frequency of the sound forced us to reduce this to all instances for the first ten per cent of the duration of all conversations for all speakers, giving a total number of 1,474 variants. The range and subsequent categorisation of articulatory variants for /r/ is shown in Figure 6.5.[13] No instances of labialised /r/ articulations occurred outside labial contexts, and so no independent 'labial [r]' category was constructed (for the spread of labialised /r/ in England, see Foulkes and Docherty 2000).

[r] – central approximant:
[ɹ] [ɹ̟] [ɹ̠.] [ɹ̠] [ɹ̥]

[R] – retroflex approximant:
[ɻ] [ɻ̠.] [ɻ̠] [ɻ̃] [ɻʷ] [ɻ...]
[ɻ̥] [ɻ̥.] [ɻ̟] [ɻʰ] [ɻʰ.]
[ɻʰ..]

[rt] – alveolar tap:
[ɾ] [ɾ̥] [ɾ̠.] [ɾ̠..] [ɾ̠.ʰ] [ɾ̟] [ɾ̟ʰ] [ɾʰ] [ɾ̩] [ɾ̟..]
[ɾ̥..] [ɾ̪] [ɾʷ] [ɾʷ] [ɾ̟] [ɾ̟.]

[Rt] – retroflex tap:
[ɽ] [ɽ̥] [ɽ̠] [ɽ̟]

[Ru] – uvular fricative:
[ʁ]

[rtt] – alveolar trill:
[r]

[V] – vowels:
Under this category fall all variants of rhoticised and velarised vowels, and vowels without obvious secondary articulation which were detailed under variable *R-vocalisation*.

[m] – miscellaneous:
[ʇ] [0] [d]

Figure 6.5 Articulatory variants in the realisation of /r/ (*R-realisation*) and their categorisation for this study (from an original table prepared by C. Timmins)

The auditory data were statistically analysed to test for the main factors of CLASS, AGE, GENDER using log-ratio linear modelling, a technique that takes account of the potential difficulty caused by multivariate data of this type.[14] Subsequent testing with Bonferroni-corrected p-values was carried out to test differences across groups (for example working-class girls from middle-class men), and within variants. Note that the range of variation is such that apparently large differences in means are not necessarily statistically significant. We worked with the assumption that reading and speaking are different activities, rather than points on a continuous stylistic continuum. As a result, we made no attempt at quantitative comparison between the two forms of data.

Table 6.3 Variation in the pronunciation of /r/ in read speech from the 1997 Glasgow speech dataset (n = 1834)

	[r]	[R]	[rt]	[Rt]	[Ru]	[V]	[m]
MCYF	6.64	64.6	23.45	0	0	5.31	0
MCYM	5.17	41.38	30.6	0	0	22.84	0
MCOF	13.42	58.87	21.64	0.87	0	5.19	0
MCOM	11.25	44.15	29	7.36	0	8.22	0
WCYF	12.66	0	29.69	0	0.44	56.33	0.87
WCYM	7.92	2.2	37.44	0	0.44	51.54	0.44
WCOF	13.85	20.78	44.59	4.76	0	16.02	0
WCOM	12.61	0.43	60.87	0	0	26.09	0

Note that the numbers in this and following tables result from the transformation of the data by log-ratio linear modelling, and can be considered similar to percentages. Effects of CLASS, AGE and their interaction were significant, as were the interactions of AGE/GENDER and AGE/CLASS/GENDER. Across variants working-class girls differentiate significantly from all four groups of middle-class speakers. Not surprisingly, working class girls are significantly different from all middle-class speakers, and working-class women in their use of [R].

The results are presented in Tables 6.3 and 6.4. In general, the realisation of /r/ shows complex sociolinguistic patterning, with a range of phonetic variation within and across speakers. Statistical analysis identifies working-class girls as a group distinct from the middle classes in read speech. Otherwise, only tendencies can be noted. Groups tend to be divided from others by clusters of variation, as opposed to the presence or absence of a specific variant. For example, /r/ in conversations is generally articulated as central or retroflex approximants and taps by both working-class and middle-class adults, but the distributional patterns of these shared realisations tend to be different for different groups of speakers. Taps are common for all speakers, and are the most common form of articulated

Table 6.4 Variation in the pronunciation of /r/ in spontaneous speech from the 1997 Glasgow speech dataset (n = 1474)

	[r]	[R]	[rt]	[Rt]	[Ru]	[rtt]	[V]	[m]
MCYF	13.71	60.48	22.58	0	0	0	3.23	0
MCYM	14.71	52.21	28.68	0	0	0	4.41	0
MCOF	23.10	52.71	21.66	0	0	0	2.53	0
MCOM	12.37	64.21	10.37	0	0	0	13.04	0
WCYF	14.84	4.52	20.00	0	0	0	60.00	0.65
WCYM	2.17	19.57	28.26	0	2.17	0	45.65	2.17
WCOF	11.00	39.23	26.79	2.39	0	0	20.57	0
WCOM	18.39	44.44	23.75	0	0	1.15	11.88	0.38

Note that the effect of CLASS emerged as significant, as did the interaction between all three effects, AGE/CLASS/GENDER. There were no significant differences within or across variants.

/r/ for working-class adolescents (and working-class men in read speech). Retroflex approximants are predominantly middle class, but also occur in working-class speakers. Central approximant articulations were occasional across speakers. The other variants were sporadic, and mainly occurred in working-class speakers, increasing their range. The main difference between read and spontaneous speech appears in the retroflex approximant, whose frequency reduces dramatically in working-class speakers, with a corresponding increase in taps (or vowels for adolescents). Any direct comparison with Johnston's findings for Edinburgh is difficult given the difference in analysis procedures. However, we can confirm that from our analysis the realisation of /r/ as a tap is still maintained in the Urban Scots of Glasgow (especially in read speech), but with the observation that it is found as one of a number of possible variants.

We move now to *R-vocalisation*. All instances of postvocalic /r/ were transcribed in the wordlists, and for all speakers for the duration of all conversations, resulting in 8,179 tokens. The data was analysed separately according to phonetic environment:

preconsonantal, e.g. *card*
prepausal, e.g. *car*, *better*, which was further subdivided according to the stress condition of the syllable which /r/ closes:
   stressed, e.g. *car*
     with subdivisions in conversational data into phonetic environment within the utterance – prepausal/turn-final, e.g. *car#*, prevocalic, e.g. *car and*, preconsonantal, e.g. *car could*.[15]

unstressed, e.g. *better*
    with subdivisions in conversational data into phonetic environment
    within the utterance – prepausal/turn-final, e.g. *better#*, prevocalic,
    e.g. *better and*, preconsonantal, e.g. *better could*.

We predicted a ranking in R-vocalisation across the main phonetic environments, perhaps with phonetic and phonological constraints playing a role, namely that R-vocalisation would be most likely in preconsonantal position, for example *card* (loss of articulation more likely in a consonant cluster), less so in prepausal unstressed position, for example *better* (loss of articulation – or perception of an articulation – when closing an unstressed syllable), and least likely in prepausal stressed position, for example *car*. For phonetic environment in the utterance, we predicted a ranking similar to that found by Romaine, namely most R-vocalisation in prepausal position, for example *car#*, then preconsonantal position, for example *car could*, and least in prevocalic position, for example *car and* (for the last, compare the feature of 'linking r', as in, for example, RP *far away* [fɑɹ ə'weɪ], persisting even in non-rhotic accents).

The extensive phonetic variation was assigned to the following variant categories:

-   [r]: types of articulated /r/ (cf. *R-realisation*)
-   [V]: vowel variants, [V]: a range of monophthongs and diphthongs without obvious auditory secondary articulation
-   [r/V]: an 'inbetween' category: variants which were difficult to assign to either [r] or [V]
-   [V^]: 'velarised' vowel variants: vowels produced with (or at least heard as produced with) some accompanying secondary articulation, which we felt to be largely caused by secondary raising and backing of the tongue body, though some slight auditory pharyngealisation was also audible
-   [Vr]: rhotacised vowel variants, which are common in rhotic accents (see, for example, Ladefoged and Maddieson 1996: 313).

Statistical analysis as detailed above was carried out for all phonetic environments, and across all environments. A brief summary of the findings is presented here.

The results for all instances of postvocalic /r/ in read and spontaneous speech are presented in Tables 6.5 and 6.6. While the patterning is more complex in spontaneous speech than read speech the overall impression remains the same. The main findings can be appreciated more clearly when presented in a chart (see Figure 6.6). Middle-class speakers use articulated /r/ with a scattering of vocalised variants. Working-class speakers use a much wider spread of variation, with working-class adolescents, in particular girls, preferring vocalisation.

Table 6.5 Variation in the pronunciation of postvocalic /r/ in read speech in the 1997 Glasgow speech dataset (n = 1103)

	[r]	[V]	[r/v]	[V^]	[Vr]
MCY	81.41	6.32	0.00	5.58	6.69
MCO	88.21	1.43	0.36	1.43	8.57
WCY	17.56	50.54	2.15	25.81	3.94
WCO	62.91	17.45	2.55	9.82	7.27

Note that there is a significant effect of CLASS. Working–class adolescents are significantly different from all middle–class speakers. These differences persist within [V] and [V^].

Table 6.6 Variation in the pronunciation of postvocalic /r/ in spontaneous speech in the 1997 Glasgow speech dataset (n = 8179)

	[r]	[V]	[r/v]	[V^]	[Vr]
MCYF	93.03	2.92	0.16	0.00	3.89
MCYM	89.39	4.22	0.22	4.65	1.52
MCOF	94.33	4.12	0.14	0.07	1.35
MCOM	92.02	3.71	0.00	2.23	2.04
WCYF	5.82	76.33	1.50	15.15	1.20
WCYM	22.13	50.50	2.21	17.51	7.65
WCOF	69.07	22.45	0.86	2.42	5.20
WCOM	75.38	12.94	0.51	6.85	4.32

Note that all main effects and their interactions are significant. The group and variant differences are complex. Across groups working–class girls are different from all others except working–class boys and women; working–class boys are polarised from middle–class men and girls.

The complex sociolinguistic and phonetic patterns of variation persist for working–class speakers in the different environments analysed. This is illustrated by showing the results for the three main conditions (see Tables 6.7, 6.8 and 6.9). In preconsonantal position (for example *card*), working–class girls favour plain vowels, while boys also use velarised vowels. In stressed prepausal position (for example *car*), the adolescents tend to pattern together, but then move apart again for unstressed prepausal position (for example *better*), where working–class girls use plain vowels almost exclusively. (This becomes virtually categorical when the environment is truly prepausal after the other utterance environments – pre-consonantal/prevocalic – have been taken away.)

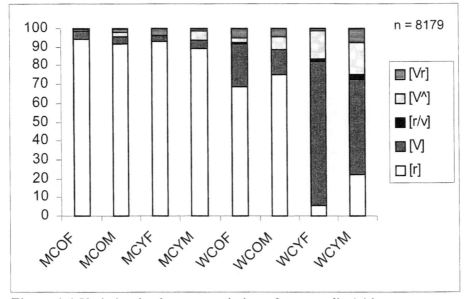

Figure 6.6 Variation in the pronunciation of postvocalic /r/ in spontaneous speech in the 1997 Glasgow speech dataset

Table 6.7 Variation in the pronunciation of postvocalic /r/ in spontaneous speech in preconsonantal position (e.g. *card*) in the 1997 Glasgow speech dataset (n = 3271)

	[r]	[V]	[r/v]	[V^]	[Vr]
MCYF	85.14	4.05	0.00	0.00	10.81
MCYM	85.97	3.12	0.00	7.53	3.38
MCOF	93.49	3.41	0.00	0.16	2.95
MCOM	91.00	3.74	0.00	2.21	3.06
WCYF	7.32	73.17	0.00	18.12	1.39
WCYM	21.56	38.92	2.40	19.76	17.37
WCOF	66.74	16.32	1.24	2.48	13.22
WCOM	74.19	8.33	0.41	8.13	8.94

Note that all main effects are significant, as are the interactions AGE/CLASS and CLASS/GENDER. Working-class boys and girls are again distinct from most middle-class speakers (except boys), mainly through the use of [V], [V^] and from each other through the use of [V], [r] and [V^]. Working-class women are also distinct from all middle-class speakers through the use of [r], [V] and [Vr].

Table 6.8 Variation in the pronunciation of postvocalic /r/ in spontaneous speech in stressed prepausal position (e.g. *car*) in the 1997 Glasgow speech dataset (n = 2886).

	[r]	[V]	[r/v]	[V^]	[Vr]
MCY	93.91	4.06	0.17	1.86	0.00
MCO	93.46	5.50	0.23	0.57	0.23
WCY	13.48	64.15	2.52	17.63	2.22
WCO	76.49	18.24	0.52	4.32	0.43

Note that the main effects of CLASS and AGE and their interaction are significant. Working-class adolescents are polarized from the other three groups in the use of [r].

Table 6.9 Variation in the pronunciation of postvocalic /r/ in spontaneous speech in unstressed prepausal position (e.g. *better*) in the 1997 Glasgow speech dataset (n = 2022).

	[r]	[V]	[r/v]	[V^]	[Vr]
MCYF	97.69	1.54	0.77	0.00	0.00
MCYM	93.36	4.27	0.47	1.42	0.47
MCOF	97.34	2.37	0.00	0.00	0.30
MCOM	97.14	0.32	0.00	1.90	0.63
WCYF	1.93	93.72	1.93	1.93	0.48
WCYM	10.06	71.01	0.59	17.75	0.59
WCOF	65.54	30.77	0.92	0.92	1.85
WCOM	83.79	11.31	0.31	3.06	1.53

Note that all main effects are significant. Working-class girls are distinct from middle-class females, and working-class men are distinct from all middle-class speakers except boys.

Our prediction of variation according to phonetic environment in the utterance was confirmed. Articulated /r/ was least likely prepausally (for example *car#*), then before a word beginning with a consonant (for example *car could*), and most likely before a word beginning with a vowel (for example *car and*); see Figure 6.7.

Our prediction according to main phonetic environment was complicated by finding a range of vowel variants such that R-vocalisation (for those who participate) is not simply a matter of using plain vowels, but rather an interaction between plain

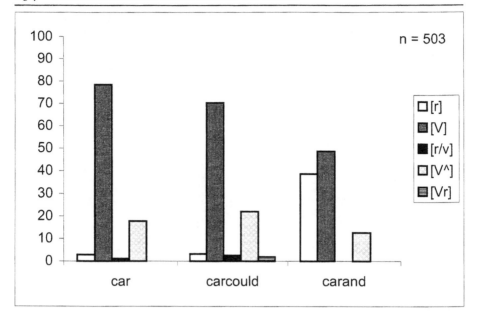

Figure 6.7 The distribution of variants of postvocalic /r/ in spontaneous
speech in working-class girls in prepausal stressed position according to
following phonetic environment: before a pause/turn final (e.g. *car#*), before a
word beginning with a vowel (e.g. *car and*), and before a word beginning with
a consonant (e.g. *car could*). (There are no significant differences.)

and velarised vowels (used differently by different speakers). The type of ranking
we found was similar for read and spontaneous speech, and is illustrated by that
for spontaneous speech in working-class boys in Figure 6.8. It is clear that plain
vowels increase from preconsonantal (for example *card*) to unstressed prepausal
(for example *better*) position, while velarised vowels show the reverse pattern.

The findings for R-vocalisation may be summarised:

– extensive R-vocalisation is attested in working-class speakers, especially
  adolescents
– R-vocalisation involves a complex interaction of vocalised variants, showing
  differing patterns according to social group
– R-vocalisation proceeds differently according to phonetic environment
– velarised vowel variants are common, especially for working-class boys, and
  in preconsonantal positions
– more frequent still are plain vowels, used most by working-class girls.

We can therefore confirm Johnston's observations that R-vocalisation is increasingly common in Glasgow, but with the reservation that vowels with and without
secondary articulation occur, and that those who vocalise most tend to show plain

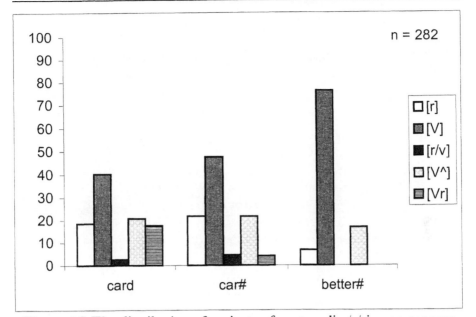

Figure 6.8 The distribution of variants of postvocalic /r/ in spontaneous speech in working-class boys according to phonetic environment: preconsonantal (e.g. *card*), stressed prepausal before a pause/turn final (e.g. *car#*), unstressed prepausal before a pause/turn final (e.g. *better#*). (There are significant differences in the use of [V] and [V^] across environments.)

vowel variants. Our interpretation of the secondary articulation as velarised rather than pharyngealised is different from Johnston's, perhaps reflecting a genuine difference in place, though some auditory pharyngealisation was present for some speakers. Whether /r/ should be analysed as fully deleted is debatable. It may be for certain individuals but not others (Macafee's rhyming evidence (1994: 29), for example 'Wee Linda, a boattle i ginger' cited by Johnston is suggestive). The Glasgow corpus is rather different from that of Romaine, and unlike the subjects of her findings, the working-class girls in our sample lead in R-vocalisation.

This detailed analysis of a single consonant, and even of one aspect of that sound, allows us to add the final observations to those being collected throughout the chapter:

- the realisation of a common consonant can show the same variant types in Urban Scots and Scottish Standard English, but relative distribution may differ
- the realisation of a common consonant can be very different in Urban Scots from in Scottish Standard English
- the realisation of a common consonant can change within Urban Scots
- these observations from such numerous and complex data are made possible through quantitative methods.

CONCLUSION

We can now draw together the findings that have emerged from this brief discussion of a few aspects of Urban Scots phonology in spoken data (assuming a descriptive distinction between alternating and common sounds, where the two assumed descriptive systems are Scots and Scottish Standard English):

- all speakers show both alternating and common sounds
- alternating sounds always alternate
- the common variant of an alternation does not necessarily share a common realisation or pattern of realisation
- alternations occur in very few words, which in turn occur rarely
- the infrequency of alternations may contribute to their salience
- there are no indications of loss of alternating words
- common sounds do not necessarily share common realisations or patterns of realisation
- common realisations of common sounds may not show similar proportional distribution of variation across speakers, or the same patterning across phonetic environments
- within Urban Scots, common sounds may be changing
- Urban Scots speakers can show differing degrees of linguistic consistency.

These comments depend much on, among other things, the data discussed (the corpora from which they are drawn) and in particular on my interpretation of them. However, if we return to the questions raised in the opening paragraphs we can begin to attempt some answers (which in turn lead to more questions). Urban Scots phonology in practice supports the assumption of alternating and common sounds being used together. The detailed analysis shows clearly that while sounds may be common in categorical terms (and perhaps also in terms of contrast), very little else is shared. If the very substance of a category is fundamentally different from that of another which is presumed to be the 'same', can we still regard it as shared? Ultimately this depends on one's theory of phonology, though we suspect that data as complex as this is rarely considered by theoretical phonologists (but see Harris 1985; see also Docherty and Foulkes 2000).

I finish by returning to the issue of the phonology of Modern Urban Scots as a 'system'. We noted before that it is usual to talk in terms of the mixing of two dialect systems, which is certainly appropriate when thinking of historical derivation. Synchronically, this seems more difficult. Using a variationist approach allows us to describe and make sense of the patterns that are observed, but I am not sure that it really helps us resolve the question of system in the way that that term is generally understood by phonologists. If we find, for example, a pattern of variation that includes the Scots variant of an alternating vowel, in some senses this remains a Scots variant. What we have done is to describe it more adequately in its synchronic context. However, if we allow the patterns themselves to become recognised as parts of a system/set of systems, then we may talk of Urban Scots phonology as a system in its own right. But this in itself might mean departing from variationist theory which usually observes variation alongside the premise of acceptable or at least usual linguistic structures. Having said this, if this data does not form part of a system, it certainly has many features which are systematic. This question, and the others raised here, need much more empirical research if we are to get any closer to a resolution.

NOTES

I am grateful to Viktoria Eremeeva for allowing me to present her data in this chapter, and to her, Paul Johnston, Caroline Macafee, Ronald Macaulay and Jim Scobbie for comments on a draft of this chapter. All errors and views remain my own. I am also grateful to the Leverhulme Trust and the Arts and Humanities Research Board whose financial assistance supported the research presented here and its writing up respectively.

1. I concentrate here on those aspects of the corpora which were used for phonological analysis by Macaulay and Macafee.
2. This was funded by the Leverhulme Trust, grant no. F/179/AX.
3. In all cases more details may be found about Scots vowels in, for example, Johnston 1997: 453f., about alternating vowels in, for example, Macafee 1983: 37f.; 1994: 224f., about Scottish Standard English vowels in Abercrombie 1979.
4. The categorisation of 'common' and 'alternating' vowels used here is a descriptive generalization based on predominant patterns of Scots lexical incidence. At the same time, we acknowledge that sound changes during the history of Scots mean that absolute mappings of lexical incidence across Scots and Scottish Standard English are not always possible (see Macafee forthcoming b).
5. Some speakers may use only one vowel for a particular word, but across the lexical set alternation will always occur.
6. It is perhaps worth noting that articulatorily and acoustically these discrete variants exist on a number of intersecting continua. Eremeeva's acoustic study will provide interesting data towards this point.
7. Similar tendencies have been found in Northumberland dialects (Johnston personal communication).
8. Macaulay (1977: 29) makes the point from the other end, that is by pointing out that those who use mainly diphthongs can show differences in quality.
9. Eremeeva had not yet completed her lexical analysis by the time of writing.
10. I am grateful to John Coleman for this reference. Macafee (1994: 215) argues that the alternations are salient because they are dialectal.
11. Although Macaulay used index scores he also presents all data as raw and percentage figures.
12. An informal analysis of lexical distribution of transcribed occurrences indicates that about two-thirds of the data was postvocalic.
13. An independent acoustic analysis was also carried out for both variables; this data awaits interpretation.
14. All the tables for /r/ presented here were prepared by Fiona Tweedie.
15. This data is equivalent to that reported in Romaine 1978.

CHAPTER 7

The Phonology of Older Scots

Caroline Macafee, incorporating material by the late
A. J. Aitken

This chapter is based on the writings of A. J. Aitken on the pronunciation of
Older Scots (Aitken 1977, [1996a], [1996b], 2002), with additional background
material from Macafee and Aitken (2002).[1] It is intended as a general account of
Older Scots phonology, and should enable the reader to pronounce Older Scots
with reasonable accuracy, depending on the level of detail aimed at. It concludes
with some sample transcriptions as examples. The emphasis is mainly on the
vowels, as these have changed more between OE and OSc and between OSc and
Modern Scots than have the consonants.

THE VOWEL NUMBERING SYSTEM

The vowels are referred to below by the numbers that Aitken gives them. This
numbering system, he claims, is a convenient and unambiguous way of referring
to any item at any chronological stage, in any dialect, without having to specify a
particular realisation. It therefore avoids the ambiguity of traditional labels such
as ī, which is the OE value of *time* (Vowel 1), but by OSc is the value of *meet*
(Vowel 2); or the clumsiness of unambiguous labels such as 'the sixteenth-century
Scots reflex of OE ī'. This system is more easily grasped than anything before: it is
less complex, and the user is not presented with a confused plethora of data
relating to a plethora of categories, but with a limited set of categories for
reference. It is directly focused on Scots, and is not a by-product of the history of
Standard English. This enables us to see the development of Scots as a separate
whole, not as occasional footnotes to RP. Likewise, it is of direct relevance to
events in the later phonological history of Scots. Use of the Aitken system does
not, of course, exclude the use of other reference points, for example the OE or
ME system, when necessary to make a particular point. The system has been used
by several scholars, including Kuipers (1964), van Buuren (1982, 1997) and

Jonathan Glenn (1987) (some of whom combine it with the traditional system), as well as the present writer, and is, of course, employed in Aitken's definitive treatment of the subject (Aitken 2002). The only reasonable alternative is a system of keywords. Wells' (1982) system is widely used for Standard English and its varieties, but it is unsuitable for Scots (and for many dialects of England) because of the time-depth and complexity of the differences from the Standard English model. Johnston (1997a, 1997b) has adapted Wells' approach for Scots.[2] Keywords have the advantage over numbers of being more transparent. There is, however, a danger that the reader will give them Standard English rather than Scots values, for example taking OUR to refer to a diphthong (as in Standard English) rather than a monophthong (as in Scots). When keywords are used also for sub-categories, for example HAND as a sub-category (before /nd/) of CAT, the reference of the superordinate term (CAT) becomes ambiguous: it can be unclear whether it is to be taken as including the subordinate category (HAND) or not, in particular contexts. In what follows, we shall accordingly use the established numbering system, as set out in Figure 7.1, which gives a rough historical outline of the vowel systems, with the main OSc spellings. The reader will no doubt find it necessary to make frequent reference to this. Figure 7.2 lists the modern Scottish Standard English correspondences of the OSc vowels.

It is possible to reconstruct with some confidence the segmental phonology of OSc: the systems of speech sounds (phonemes) and the distribution of each sound in the lexicon (also referred to as selection or lexical incidence), and the patterns of stressed and unstressed syllables in words. Aitken uses the standard approaches to reconstruction: the contemporary evidence of spelling, rhyme, and metre together with comparison of the reflexes (outcomes) in modern dialects and extrapolation backwards to a common ancestor, within the framework of the accepted reconstructions of OE and early ME, and of languages contributing loanwords, particularly ON and OF. The borrowing of words into other languages, notably Gaelic, can also be informative. Contemporary comment, unfortunately, is much less copious than for English, but there are, for instance, representations by Elizabethan dramatists (see Aitken 2002: §§20.2, 20.7).

We can also arrive at reasonable estimates of the phonetic realisation of the phonemes, but this is necessarily more speculative.[3] Other aspects of pronunciation are little known, even for the modern dialects. Their systematic investigation often requires not only tape-recordings but laboratory equipment. These are the suprasegmental features: habits of voice quality and articulatory setting (harshness, nasality and so on), loudness, intonation patterns, rhythm and tempo; and the pitch-changes that are characteristic of accentuation, as well as variations from the norm in all of these to signal special attitudes and moods.

Figure 7.1 Vowel systems of Scots: a rough historical outline

Vowel number	Early Scots (to 1450)	Middle Scots (to 1700)	Modern Scots	Principal Older Scots graphemes
1	iː ————	ei ————	ae / əi	iCe, yCe, y; yi, ay: y#
2	eː ————	iː ————	i	e, eCe, eC-; ei, ey, ea: e(e)#, ey#, ie#
3	ɛː ⟨ or			
4	aː ————	eː ————	e	a, aCe, aC-; ai, ay, e, ea: a#, ay#, ae#
5	oː ————	oː ————	o	oCe, oC-, o; oi, oy: o#, oo#
6	uː ————	u ————	u	ou, ow; (ul): ow#
6a	ul			ul(l), (w)ol: ull#
7	yː ————	øː ————	ø	oCe, oC-, oi, oy, o(me), o(ne), (w)o, uCe, uC-, wCe, wC-; ui, uy, wi, wy, ou, ow, oo: o#, oe#, oo#, ou#, ow#, u(e)#, w#
		or ————	i	
		or ————	e	
		or	e / I	
8	ai ————	ɛi ————	eːə	ai, ay, aCe, aC-, ae, ei, ey; e, ea
		or	e	
8a	ai# ————	ɛi# ————	əi#	ay#, ey#
9	oi ————	oi ————	oe	oi, oy
10	ui ————	ui ————	əi	oi, oy; ui, uy, wi, wy, i, y, iy

Figure 7.1—*cont'd*

Vowel number	Early Scots (to 1450)	Middle Scots (to 1700)	Modern Scots	Principal Older Scots graphemes
11	ei# — eː# — iː#	————	i#	ey#, e#, ee#; ie#
12	au — ɑː		ɑ	au, aw; (al): aw#, a#
			or ɔ	
12a	al			al, all, aul; au, aw, a: aw#, a#
13	ou — ou		ʌu	ou, ow; (ol): ow#
13a	ol			ol, oul: oll#
14a, 14b(i)	iu ——— iu		iu	eu, ew, uCe: ew#, ue#
			or (j)u	
14b(ii)	ɛou ———— iʌu ———— (j)ʌu			eu, ew; ou, ow: ew#, ow#
15	ɪ ——— ɪ ——— ɪ			i, y
16	ɛ ——— ɛ ——— ɛ			e
17	a ——— a ——— a			a
18	o ——— o		o	o
			or ɔ	
19	u ——— u ——— ʌ			u, o(m), o(n), w(o); ou

Note: The word 'or' is used to indicate divergences between and amongst dialects. In the lists of graphemes, the semi-colons divide spellings dominant in ESc from those which become common only in MScots; the colon precedes word-final spellings. Vowel 14b(ii) is an alternative dialectal development, probably more widespread than in ModSc. Aitken (2002) uses more phonetically specific symbols (as in Figure 7.5) when referring to the values of phonemes 5, 18 and 19, and diphthongs/triphthongs including them. Here we simplify and use broader symbols.

Figure 7.2 Modern English correspondences to the Scots vowels (adapted from Aitken [1996a]: table 3)

Vowel number	ModSc	Corresponding English items, as pronounced in Scottish Standard English
1 long	ae	/ae/ as in *rise, byre, buy, cry, ay* 'yes'
1 short	əi	/əi/ as in *bite, price, mind*
2	i	/i/, especially as spelled <ee> as in *meet, deed, queen, here, tree, see*
3	i	/i/ as in *seat, steal, ear*; /ɛ/ as in *breath, deaf, dead*
4	e	/o/ as in *boat, oath, both, load, whole, more, go, so*; /e/ as in *gate, late, scathe, fade, ale, care*
5	o	/o/ as in *coat, coal, close, before*
6	u	/ʌu/, spelled <ou, ow> as in *about, mouth, loud, foul, down, hour, cow*
6a	u	/ol/ or /ul/, spelled <(o)ulC> or <ull> as in *coulter, shoulder, multure, bulk, bull, full, pull*
7	ø etc.	/(j)u/ as in *boot, good, fool, moon, moor, move, do, fruit, suit,* and *duke, sure, pure, sure, use, refuse, fortune, measure*
8	e	/e/, chiefly as spelled <ai> or <ay#> as in *bait, braid, pail, rain, pair, day, say, pray, away*
8a	əi	/e/ as in *May, pay, aye* 'ever, always'
9	oe	/ɔe/ (chiefly from Old French /oi/) as in *Boyd, avoid, noise, boy, joy*
10	i	/ɔe/ (chiefly from Anglo-Northern /ui/) as in *oil, spoil, join, point, poison, quoit*
11	i	/ae/ as in *eye, die, flie, high, lie* 'a falsehood, to tell falsehoods'
12	ɔ	/ɔ/ spelled <au, aw> as in *laud*; /o/ spelled <ow>, as in *low, show, snow*; /ol/ as in *old, bold, cold*
12a	ɔ	/ɔ(l)/ as in *chalk, salt, all, ball*
13	ʌu	no clearly corresponding English item: Scots examples include *nout* 'cattle', *gowk* 'cuckoo', *loup* 'jump', *lown* 'calm', *louse* 'loose', (all from Old Norse /au/), and *bow* 'the weapon', *chow* 'chew', *grow, four, owre* 'over' (from various sources)
13a	ʌu	/o(l)/ as in *folk, colt, gold, solder, knoll, roll*
14	(j)u	/(j)u/ as in *dew, few, new, Jew, steward, blue, due, true, virtue, duty, rule, adieu, beauty*
15	ɪ	/ɪ/ as in *bit, sit, lid, chin, mill*. Note that *bind, blind, find, wind* had this vowel in Older Scots, but *kind, mind, sind* 'to rinse' and *strind* 'generation, race' had vowel 1[a]
16	ɛ	/ɛ/ as in *get, bed, men*
17	a	/a/ as in *cat, lad, man, pass, dance*
18	o	/ɔ/ as in *cot, God, on*
19	ʌ	/ʌ/ as in *cut*; /u/ as in *put, push, bush, pudding, bullet*

[a] As a result of Homorganic Cluster Lengthening (see below).

THE SOUNDS OF OLDER SCOTS

Sound change

Sound changes are classified as being either conditional, where the change depends on the phonetic environment (usually the immediately preceding or following sound), and unconditional, where the change takes place regardless of phonetic environment. In this outline treatment, we cannot deal with the many conditioned changes (some of which apply only in particular dialects, sometimes only to a very small group of words). For a full treatment, see Aitken (2002).

Consonants

Consonants change less over time than vowels, and consequently also show less regional variation. We shall therefore pay most attention below to the vowel systems. Besides initial consonant clusters, mentioned above, the main points to note are:

- /ŋg/ was simplified to /ŋ/ in all positions, thus /fɪŋər/ *finger* rhyming with *singer* (as in Modern Scots)
- ESc had the additional palatal consonants /ʎ, ɲ/, known as l-mouillé and n-mouillé, in words of French and Gaelic origin, for example *bulʒe* 'boil', *cunʒe* 'coin', and the proper names *Culzean, Menzies*. These consonants are still separate in Barbour's rhyming practice. At an unknown period, /ʎ/ became /lj/; and /ɲ/ became /nj, ŋj/, or in some cases, /ŋ/, for example *ring* 'reign'. There was a wide range of spellings: < nʒe, ngʒe, nʒhe, nyhe, ny(i)e and so on >, and similarly < lʒe, lʒhe, lyhe, ly(i)e and so on >.[4]

Some other points would be taken into consideration in a full-scale reconstruction:

- /ʍ/, written < quh >, was pronounced [ʍ];[5]
- /r/ was most probably a strong trill
- most dialects probably had dental rather than alveolar /n, r, l, t, d/.

Number of syllables

In ESc, the inflectional ending -*is* /ɪs/ (later /ɪz/) was still pronounced as a syllable in some contexts, but in others was beginning to be reduced to a mere consonant. Poetic licence allowed ESc and early MSc poets to follow speech in these contexts (and reduce the inflection) or tradition (and retain it as a syllable), a convenient way of adjusting the metre.

The inflection is always reduced after an unstressed syllable or one with only secondary stress, such as *dowcot*, *labour*, *profit*, *questioun*.[6] After vowels, the inflectional vowel had likewise been absorbed before ESc: cf. rhymes such as *rais* p.t. 'rose': *gais* 'goes' (Barbour's *Bruce* 7, 349–50), and the metrics of lines such as: *Yai bar all oyer-wayis on hand* (Barbour's *Bruce* 1, 62).[7]

After stressed syllables ending in fricatives there was never reduction: for example *facis*, *raisis*, *fechis*, *jugis* 'judges' (as in ModEng).

After other consonants, it seems that, by the time of Barbour, retention of the vowel in this ending was optional, though down to the sixteenth century unreduced syllabic forms seem to predominate.

Similarly, the inflection *-it* could be reduced to a consonant if the root ended in a vowel, for example *cryit*. This was probably already the spoken form in early MSc. The ending was also optionally reduced after nasals and liquids, for example *answerit*. After the fricative consonants, metrical licence already allowed the inflection *-it* to be reduced in the second half of the fifteenth century (cf. van Buuren 1982: 112), but it generally remains syllabic even into the modern period after the plosive consonants, for example *stoppit*, *biggit*.

The loss of /v/ in words like *deil* 'devil' and *our* 'over' reduces the number of syllables by one. This may be concealed by spelling. Although used with restraint (and apparently regarded as colloquial), such 'cuttit short' word-forms were available for occasional metrical licence in certain genres (see Aitken 1971, 1983; Macafee and Aitken 2002).

Unstressed vowels

OE had a number of different vowels in inflections, which were later replaced by a single vowel, written < e >, conventionally interpreted as /ə/. Final *-e* was lost in the ME period,[8] earliest north of the Humber. Chaucer uses *-e* optionally to fit the metre, but Barbour does not.[9] In Pre-literary Scots (and northern ME), < e > changed to < i >, conventionally interpreted as /ɪ/, starting in the thirteenth century.

The promotion of unstressed syllables to rhyme with stressed ones is a poetic licence available to OSc poets, though in MSc mainly with suffixes of Romance origin. Many suffxes, such as *-ure* (for example *scripture*) and *-ude* (for example *plenitude*) may still have taken full vowels in speech (in these examples, Vowel 7). Aitken observed that in Modern Scots there is less contrast between stressed and unstressed syllables than in most dialects of English, which suggests that the ongoing process of unstressed vowel reduction may have proceeded more slowly in Scots than in English.[10] In the transcriptions below, unstressed vowels are shown as /ɪ, ə/, /ø/ shortened in the absence of stress, and (in the sixth transcription, the 'Record of an oral deposition, Lanark') /i/. (In *The Concise Scots Dictionary* (CSD), the unstressed vowels are shown without distinction as /ə/.)

Stressed vowels

Vowel Length
For most vowels in Scots (and partly also in Scottish Standard English), vowel length is governed by the phonetic environment following the vowel, rather than being intrinsic to the vowel. For example, in Modern Scots the originally long vowel /u/ (Vowel 6) is still long in *doo* 'dove', but short in *dout* 'doubt'. The rule for vowel length, known as the Scottish Vowel-Length Rule (SVLR) or Aitken's Law, has been described in Stuart-Smith's chapter (this volume). Here it is only necessary to note that the vowel systems of OE and OSc had long and short vowels, in pairs that were originally close enough to each other in quality to capture words from each other in processes of lengthening and shortening, and to permit occasional near-rhymes of long with short vowels in ESc. A number of sound changes, culminating in the Great Vowel Shift (below), disrupted this parallelism by altering the qualities of the vowels. It then became possible for new 'shorts' to be created by the SVLR in the second half of the sixteenth century. Thus the SVLR shortening of *dout* results not in **dut* (Vowel 19, as with OE shortenings) but in *dout*, still with Vowel 6, though shortened in realisation. It is probably this disruption of the traditional quantity system that we see reflected in late MSc spelling habits (cf. Meurman-Solin 1999a), where long vowel spellings (final < e > and digraphs) are used for traditionally short vowels, for example < cate, cait > 'cat', and short vowel spellings (double consonants) are used for long vowels, for example < fatte, faitt > 'fate'. Double long spellings partly solve the problem, that is, both final < e > and a digraph, for example < faite > but these are not always reserved for long vowels either, so < caite, caitte > 'cat' is not impossible.

Lengthenings and shortenings in the OE period
There were a number of length adjustments in the OE period. (For examples, see Figure 7.6.) Short vowels were lengthened in a process known as Homorganic Cluster Lengthening (HOCL). Homorganic clusters of consonants are clusters pronounced at the same place of articulation, for example /nd/ (dental/alveolar) and /mb/ (labial). There were some lengthenings in Scots by this change, but also many failures to lengthen. Long vowels were shortened before double consonants (hence the use of double consonants as an orthographic marker of short vowels), non-organic consonant clusters, and when two unstressed syllables followed.

Open Syllable Lengthening
In the Pre-literary Scots period, Open Syllable Lengthening (OSL) lengthened short vowels (by this time including loans from OF) in stressed syllables followed by an unstressed syllable, where the stressed syllable was 'open', that is, when it ended in a vowel. These conditions were met in many words with inflectional

endings that were later lost, for example *name*. The retention in spelling of a lost final vowel gives us the characteristic orthographic convention of Scots and English whereby a silent final < e > modifies the vowel in the preceding syllable. By the time of OSL, the short vowels had apparently lowered (apart from the already low Vowel 17), so the lengthenings do not match up with the long vowels in the same way as the earlier HOCL (see Figure 7.3):

- Vowel 15 > 2, for example ON *gifa* > *geve* 'give', *stice* > *steiche* 'stitch'; also (unusually) before two unstressed syllables in MF loans, for example *ministre* > *menister* 'minister'
- Vowel 16 > 3, for example *brecan* > *breke* 'break', *stelan* > *stele* 'steal'
- Vowel 17 > 4 (as HOCL), for example *nama* > *name, gaderian* > *gaither* 'gather', *labour*;
- Vowel 18 > 5, for example *þrote* > *throte* 'throat', *col-* > *cole* 'coal'
- Vowel 19 > 7, for example *lufu* > *lufe* 'love', *duce* > *duik* 'duck' (for the later development of Vowel 7 before voiceless velars, see below).

OSL often left doublets without lengthening, for example *gif* 'give', *brek* 'break', *gadder* 'gather', *throt* 'throat', *mak* alongside *make*.[11] A following syllabic consonant could also provide an environment for OSL, for example *heofone* > *hevin* 'heaven', *sadol* > *saiddle* 'saddle'.

Figure 7.3 Open Syllable Lengthening

1 iː				uː 6
2 eː ←——— ɪ 15		19 u ———→ oː 7		
3 ɛː ←——— ɛ 16		18 o ———→ ǫː 5		
4 aː ←——— a 17				

The Great Vowel Shift

The most important sound shift in the history of Scots, as in that of English, is the Great Vowel Shift (GVS), which was completed in Scots by about the middle of the sixteenth century. Crudely, the effect of this was to raise long vowels. As one consequence, Scots and English spelling is out of line with continental sound values for historically long vowels: compare the vowels of the loanwords *estate*, *noble*, *complete* with their Modern French equivalents *état*, *noble*, *complet*. Since the GVS affected only long vowels, the shortening and lengthening sound changes that preceded it take on added significance: they determine whether groups of words are part of the input to the GVS or not. For example, in Scots (and Northern English) *blind* was not lengthened by HOCL, and consequently not affected by the GVS, thus Modern Scots /blɪn(d)/.

Two other important changes preceded the GVS, one north of the Humber, affecting Scots and Northern English dialects, the other south of the Humber. The northern change results, by the late thirteenth century, in front vowels in words such as *mune* 'moon' < OE *mōna* (Vowel 7);[12] the southern change results in a back vowel in words such as *home* < OE *hām* (= Scots *hame*, Vowel 4). Scots and English therefore differ in the input to the GVS. There are also differences in the details of the sound shift. In particular, Scots does not shift Vowel 6, for example *doon*, *hoose*, preserving it as a monophthong /uː/.

In some late loans from French, MF *ī* is equated with Vowel 2, by then raised to [iː], for example *baptese*, *oblege*. There are generally doublets borrowed earlier as Vowel 1 (when it had the [iː] value, prior to its diphthongisation), for example *baptise*, *oblige*.

Figure 7.4 shows the two main alternative forms of the GVS in Scots, with Vowel 3 merging either with Vowel 2 or Vowel 4 (the latter characteristic, for instance, of David Lindsay, from Fife).[13] The high front vowel, Vowel 1, which cannot raise any further, becomes a diphthong, as in English. In OSc, it has not yet split into two distinct phonemes as in Modern Scots.

Figure 7.4 The Great Vowel Shift in Scots

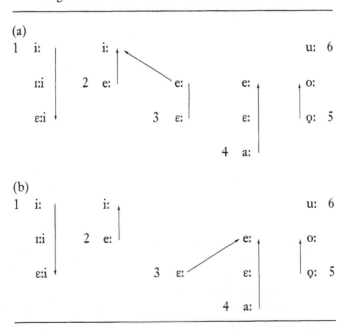

L-vocalisation

A group of conditioned changes known as l-vocalisation took place in the late fourteenth or early fifteenth century. When /l/ was preceded in a stressed syllable by one of the three short back vowels (including Vowel 17 as a back vowel) and fell within the same closed syllable as the vowel, it vocalised to [u]:

- /al/ > /au/, merging with Vowel 12, for example *all*, *salt*, *hals* 'throat', *calk* 'chalk', *halch* 'haugh, river-meadow', *wannot* 'walnut'
- /ol/ > /ʌu/, merging with Vowel 13, for example *knoll*, *folk*, *golf*, *colpindach* 'young cow'; also before /d/, in, for example, *gold*, *mold* 'earth'[14]
- /ul/ > /uː/, merging with Vowel 6, for example *full*, *pull*, *pulpit*, *schulder*, *fulth* 'plenty'.

Unvocalised doublets in /al/ are visible in many rhymes of words such as *all*, *fall*, *small* with the Latinate suffix *-all* (in such words as *celestiall*): there is no indication that this suffix ever underwent l-vocalisation. The verb *sall* 'shall', which also participates in this set of rhymes, never displays a vocalised form.[15]

The doublets /fʌl/ beside /fuː/ *full* and /pʌl/ beside /puː/ *pull* are widespread throughout Modern Scots.

Some further sound changes

Other conditioned sound changes include:

- OF *a* before nasal combinations has a variety of outcomes, but is most usually Vowel 12, for example *aunt*, *ensaumpill* 'example', *chaumer* 'chamber'. However, between /tʃ/ or /r/ and /ndʒ/, there are variants with Vowel 3, for example Modern Scots *cheenge* 'change', *reenge* 'range'. The Vowel 3 forms of *change* and so on produce further variants in Vowel 1, thus *chynge* and so on
- some time in the Pre-literary Scots period, Vowel 17 was lengthened to Vowel 4 before /r/ followed by any consonant. In most cases the outcome seems to have been doublet unlengthened and lengthened forms, and also sometimes Vowel 16 forms, presumably by the shortening of Vowel 4 at the GVS [ɛː] stage, for example *sharn*, *shairn*, *shern* 'dung'; *cart*, *cairt*, *kert*. OSc spelling does not usually reflect the Vowel 16 forms, however
- conversely, Vowel 16 was lowered to Vowel 17 in the fourteenth century before /r/, again producing doublets, for example *serk* and *sark* 'shirt', *stern* and *starn* 'star', *ger* and *gar* 'to cause'
- Vowel 7 diphthongises before the voiceless velars /k, x/ to merge in some dialects with Vowel 14a, in others with /j/ + Vowel 19, for example Modern Scots /ən(j)ux, ən(j)ʌx/ 'enough' and /hjuk, hjʌk/ 'hook'. In OSc there were apparently also undiphthongised Vowel 7 doublets

- there is an early shortening of Vowel 7, before its fronting, to Vowel 19 in certain words, with a subsequent development to Vowel 15 (see next), for example *fit* 'foot', *sit* 'soot', *wid* 'wood', *ither* 'other', *brither* 'brother' and *mither* 'mother'. A few Vowel 19 doublets remain in Modern Scots dialects, for example *fut* 'foot'[16]
- from the fifteenth century onwards, an allophone of Vowel 19 is captured by Vowel 15, for example *dissone* 'dozen', *hinnie* 'honey', *kimmer* 'godmother', *nit* 'nut', *simmer* 'summer'
- an allophone of Vowel 18 is captured by Vowel 19, so that *broche*, *loge*, *sojourn* and *motioun* /motju:n/ appear in the fifteenth century as *bruche* /bruʧ/, *luge* /luʤ/, *sudgeorn* /suʤərn/, *mudgin* /muʤən/
- an allophone of Vowel 18 in labial environments is captured by Vowel 17, so that *crop*, *croft*, *loft*, *off*, *bonnet* appear in the fifteenth century as *crap*, *craft*, and so on
- certain words with Vowel 8 finally, which would otherwise have continued as a diphthong (Vowel 8a), have a separate development (Vowel 8b, see Figure 7.5) and are captured by Vowel 4, for example *day*, *may*
- Vowel 4 after /w, ʍ/ rounds to merge with Vowel 12 in all dialects except West Central and southern East Central, for example *twa* 'two', *quhar* 'where', *awa* 'away'
- in late MSc, initial Vowel 4, as in *ane* 'one' and *ale*, develops to /jɪ/ in most of Scotland south of the Forth-Clyde line, thus *yin*, *yill* and so on.[17]

PRONOUNCING OLDER SCOTS

In his 1977 paper, Aitken listed and discussed a number of models for the pronunciation of Older Scots, some of which represented existing (sometimes bad) practice and some of which were his own recommendations. He accepted that different models were suited to different purposes, and did not try to gloss over the difficulty of achieving a full-scale reconstruction. It remains true that virtuosity is required to read such a reconstruction aloud both consistently and fluently. However, Aitken's work since 1977, and the completion of DOST, have brought what was then possible only for a tiny group of specialists within the grasp of any scholar in this field.

Models

Before setting out Aitken's general recommendations for reading OSc aloud, we shall look briefly at the models he outlined:

- **the Chaucerian or Middle English Model**: it was formerly the practice for university students of English to be taught a pronunciation of ME which enabled them to read the writings of Geoffrey Chaucer, for example, in a plausible reconstruction. Since ESc writers, notably John Barbour, were contemporaries of Chaucer, and ESc shared many features with Chaucer's English, this has been used for ESc, although there are, as we have seen, important differences between the South-East Midland dialect of ME and ESc

– **the Early Scots Model**: the spelling system of ESc was more regular than it later became, and the spellings of vowels had their continental values with realisations close to the values assigned to the cardinal vowels in the International Phonetic Alphabet. That is, ESc orthography is simpler and more 'phonetic' (actually phonemic) than that of MSc, and consequently a reconstruction suitable to this period is fairly easy to learn, especially for anyone with a knowledge of another European language. But it is not suitable for reading sixteenth century Scots (any more than the Chaucerian model is suitable for reading Shakespeare). Still, as Aitken said, if it is done with consistency, it is preferable to an unprepared rendition

– **the Modern Recitation Scots Model**: the Modern Recitation Scots Model is probably the most accessible for those who have grown up in the tradition of reading, reciting and singing in Modern Scots. The recitation register is somewhat different from spoken varieties of Modern Scots in daily use.[18] This well-established tradition of performance allows speakers to avoid the unintentional nuances that might be imported by using, for instance, a broad Glaswegian accent.

To make this model acceptable as a substitute for MSc pronunciation, especially in poetry, certain restorations of earlier forms need to be made. In order to preserve the scansion, words such as *patience*, *nation*, *special* and many noun plurals, for example *deidis* 'deeds', need to be given the additional syllable that they had in the early sixteenth century and before. The inflexional ending *-is* is variably syllabic in many phonetic contexts, according to the requirements of scansion (see *Number of syllables* above).[19] The main adjustment that needs to be made to ensure that poems rhyme as intended is to pronounce the ending *-ie* or *-y* in some words such as *rethorie* and *poetrie* with the same final vowel as words like *dry* and *cry* (Vowel 1). A careful reader in the Modern Recitation Scots Model will also pronounce the /k/ in the consonant cluster /kn/, for example *knicht*; the /g/ in the cluster /gn/, for example *gnaw* and the /w/ in the clusters /wr/, for example *wrang*, and the rare /wl/ for example *wlonk* 'lady'.

Apart from these differences, the pronunciation of Scots by the end of the sixteenth century was similar enough to that of the early twentieth century to make the Modern Recitation Scots Model acceptable as a representation of MSc. This was Aitken's recommendation for the reading of MSc, for most purposes, by native Scots speakers. It demands much less preparation and very much less phonetic virtuosity than the Full-scale Reconstruction Model, resulting in a more fluent as well as an easier performance. He was considerably less happy with it as a model for reading ESc, which is so much more distant from Modern Scots.

The performer in the Modern Recitation Scots Model will aim to reproduce the words of the OSc text not with the exact phonetic realisations they had in OSc, but with the present-day Scots reflexes of the OSc phonemes. In the case of words now obsolete, or replaced by their English cognates (for example *door* or *tool*, both Vowel 7), the word is given the pronunciation it would have had if it had survived:

- the **Rough Approximation Model**: an alternative which is perhaps more accessible than Modern Recitation Scots to the many non-Scots who have occasion to read OSc aloud, and wish to do so as realistically and consistently as possible, is the Rough Approximation Model, which can be achieved by reading off the values from Figure 7.1, using OSc spellings and the spellings of cognate words in Modern English (see Figure 7.2) as a rough guide to the selection of phonemes;[20]
- the **Full-scale Reconstruction Model**: this model differs from the Rough Approximation Model both in the level of phonetic detail (see Figure 7.5) and in the pains taken to ascertain the phoneme selection in individual words (see Figure 7.6 and refer to CSD, DOST and the index to Aitken (2002)). Of these, phoneme selection is the more important. The realisations in the ESc column are conventionally reconstructed as being closer to the values of the spellings; the values in the MSc column are interpolations between these values and the observed modern ones. The earlier values cannot be known precisely, and readers may therefore be excused for modifying their renderings towards the sounds of their own accents. There is, however, no point in attempting a narrow phonetic transcription if the phonemic selections are only approximate.

General considerations

Aitken's discussion of the performance models includes some of the following general points.

A prerequisite for a reasonably correct performance is preparation. Nobody can expect to pick up an edition of an OSc text and produce a spontaneously accurate reading in any model, though some philologists would do better than most. All of us need time to prepare our reading, to work out whether a set of rhymes, for instance, is of Vowel 3 with Vowel 2, or of Vowel 3 with Vowel 4; whether a particular word contained Vowel 4 or Vowel 8; to remind ourselves that < oi > more often than not represented Vowel 5 rather than Vowel 9 or Vowel 10. A large number of OSc words have several alternative pronunciations (and spellings): for example, the word 'great', spelled < grete, greit; gret(t); grite, gryte; girt; gert; gart > had all of the following pronunciations in MSc: /grɛːt; grɛt; greit; gɪrt; gɛrt; gart/.[21] This may or may not matter in a particular context, but a decision has to be made. Sometimes a scribal copyist or an early printer has preferred a spelling that reproduces his own favoured pronunciation rather than that of the author, resulting in an apparently false rhyme, which we may be able to correct by restoring an alternative form. MSc poets also used occasional anglicised forms, such as < go > for < ga(y) > 'go' or < more, moir, moyr > for < mare, mair, mayr > 'more'. In some cases, the rhyme will confirm that this is the author's own anglicisation; in other cases, it has been introduced by a later hand in contradiction to the rhyme. In these cases we may need to rehearse in advance our own decision as to which is the correct pronunciation.

Some common errors include:

- *fleche* 'to cajole' should be pronounced /fliʧ/, not /*flix/
- *our* 'over' should be pronounced /ʌur/, not /*uːr/
- conversely, the possessive pronoun *our* is correctly rendered /uːr/
- by mistaking Scots spelling practice, the indefinite article is often wrongly read as /*en/, rather than /ə(n)/, the /n/ being pronounced only before the vowels, as in modern speech[22]
- the feminine pronoun *scho* is often mistakenly read as the wholly spurious /*ʃoː/, rather than OSc /ʃøː/ or Modern Scots /ʃeː/ (Vowel 7).

Some thought must be given to phrasing and intonation, which will, of course, be influenced by the punctuation of the copy. Many OSc texts are devoid of punctuation in the originals, and the punctuation of modern editions is supplied by the editors.

The need to pay attention to the number of syllables has already been mentioned. Another aspect requiring consideration is stress placement. There was still some variation in the stressing of loanwords from OF. Most disyllables from this source must have been borrowed as iambs, but this conflicted with the native language, and gradually most of them have been made trochaic. For a long period, certainly in poetic usage, such loans remained variable, so, for instance, a MSc poet could stress *nature* or *river* on different syllables on different occasions.[23]

Aitken emphasised that there are no short cuts to the reading of OSc with authenticity, that is with the correct selections of sounds and the correct phrasing. Nevertheless, by taking sufficient pains, it is perfectly possible to achieve an acceptable performance – though he added with regret that very few modern performers of OSc, including (with further regret) many professional scholars of OSc, even attempt this.

Does it matter?

Aitken's 1977 paper was originally given at an international conference. Kinsley, in a review of the conference proceedings, recalled the effect that the paper had on the audience:

His original *tour de force* . . . had consequences immediate and devastating. Native scholars, accustomed to read the 'makars' aloud in some brand of Modern Scots, were disconcerted; non-Scots were in disarray. The bars and lounges were for a time thinly peopled, as those with papers still to read struggled in decent privacy to relearn their lines; and the results were sometimes more hilarious than comprehensible. However, we 'ken noo'. (1980: 356–7)

When he revised the paper in 1996, Aitken was entitled to take the view that 'the excuse advanced by some that we know nothing about how OSc was pronounced is simply not tenable', in view of his 1977 paper, and his contributions to CSD, including a lengthy section on pronunciation in the Introduction, and pronunciation entries throughout the dictionary (for obsolete as well as current Scots lexis).[24] Nevertheless, he saw no reason in 1996 to withdraw the strongly worded criticisms that he had made twenty years earlier: in those scholars who professed special interest in OSc language and literature, slipshodness in these respects seems, he said, to betray a dilettante, even a meretricious, attitude to the literature they are professedly interpreting to others. He did not believe that this criticism was disarmed by disclaiming from the outset any pretence to competence in this area of their study, by openly adhering to what he generously called the Modern English Model – though he also said that by performing in this manner one is not reading OSc at all, but simply delivering a rough and ready sight translation into ModEng. OSc, he reiterated, deserves a degree of professional commitment by those who claim to profess it.

SPECIMEN TRANSCRIPTIONS

The transcriptions below are in the Full-scale Reconstruction Model, following the values given in Figure 7.5. A full-scale reconstruction demands that the pronunciation of each word be ascertained, as far as possible, rather than hypothesised on the basis of familiar (Standard English and/or Modern Scots) forms and the notoriously *laissez-faire* spellings of OSc. The pronunciation entries in CSD and the index to Aitken (2002) have already been mentioned as sources for the pronunciation of individual words. Otherwise, the procedure is one of triangulation amongst the etymological forms, the modern forms, and those suggested by (or compatible with) the OSc spellings. It is necessary to know what the expected reflexes of the various OE, ON and OF (AN) vowels are (see Figure 7.6), and to be aware of the many conditioned developments that lead to deviations from these (see further Aitken 2002). Figure 7.5 shows the main developments from ESc to Modern Scots. Figure 7.6 summarises the sources up to the beginning of the PreSc period, at which point

Figure 7.5 Vowel-systems of Scots in more detail

vowel number	ESc c.1375	early MSc c.1500	late MSc c.1600	modSc	notes	examples
1	iː	ɪi	ei	ɛ(ː)i	aˑe (aːi)	SVLR-long	*rise, fire*
			ɛi	əi (ɛi, ʌi)	SVLR-short	*bite, mine*
2	eː — eˑ	iː	iˑ	i(ː)		*here, green*
	before /r/					
3	ɛ	ɛː	eː	ɛ	in a few N dialects	*year, lean* adj.
4	aː	æː	ɛː	e(ː)		*mare* 'more', *stane* 'stone'
	(i)				(i) after labials merges in some dialects with Vowel 12	
5	o̩ː	oː	oː	oː (o̩ː)		*store, loan* 'lane'
				o (o̩)	SVLR-short, merges with Vowel 18	
6	uː	uː	uː	u(ː)	LV	*hour, doun* 'down'
6a	ʉɫ# / ʉɫC	ʉɫ	öɫ	ʌɫ		*full, multure*

7

y: —— ø:

ø: —— ø(:) —— e: (ë:, ɛ:)

ø —— ı (ë)

(ii), (iii)

- SVLR-long, merges in some dialects with Vowels 4/3/8 — *use v., muir*
- SVLR-short, merges in some dialects with Vowel 15 — *use n., muin* 'moon'
- (ii) in N, merges with Vowel 2
- (iii) before /x, k/, merges in most dialects with Vowel 14

8a ai# —— æi# —— əi# (ɛi#, ʌi#) merges with SVLR-short Vowel 1 — *hay*

8 ai —— æi —— ɛi —— e: (ë:, ɛ:) (e:) merges in most dialects with Vowel 4 — *pain*

8b ʔä:, ʔɑ: —— a: —— ë: —— ë:ə (ë:) undergoes GVS — *day*

9 ǫi —— o̧i —— oi — *noise, void*

10 ui —— u̧i —— öi —— əi (ɛi, ʌi) merges with SVLR-short Vowel 1 — *point, join, doit* 'the coin'

Figure 7.5—cont'd

vowel number	ESc c.1375	early MSc c.1500	late MSc c.1600	modSc	notes	examples
11	ei — eː				merges with Vowel 2	hey 'high', drey 'endure'
12	au —— a:ʷ	ɑː (aː)	ɑː (aː) →	ɔː	LV	hawk, faut 'fault'
12a	al# / alC }	al	al	al	remains in some dialects	balk 'beam', salt, call
13	ɒu	ɒu		ɒu	LV	gowk 'cuckoo', lown 'calm'
13a	ol# / olC }		ol			folk, bolt, knoll
14a	iːu / eːu }	iu	iu / juː — (j)uː	iu (ɪu) / (j)uː		knew, stewart, duty
14b	ɛːu	iąu	ia (ja)	(j)ʌu	in some dialects	dem, beauty
	ʔɛau	ia (ja)			up to eighteenth century	OSc lauté 'loyalty'

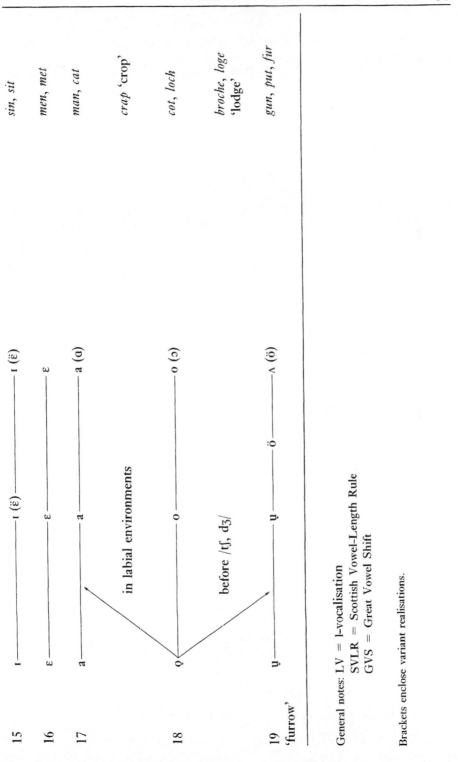

15   ɪ ———————— ɪ (ï) ———————— ɪ (ï)   *sin, sit*

16   ɛ ———————— ɛ ———————— ɛ   *men, met*

17   a ———————— a ———————— a (ɑ)   *man, cat*

in labial environments

    crop 'crop'

18   ǫ ———— o ———— (ɔ) o   *cot, loch*

before /tʃ, dʒ/

    broche, loge 'lodge'

19   ụ ———— ö ———— ʌ (ö)   *gun, put, fur*
'furrow'

General notes: LV = l-vocalisation
                SVLR = Scottish Vowel-Length Rule
                GVS = Great Vowel Shift

Brackets enclose variant realisations.

Figure 7.6 Stressed vowels in OE, ON and OF (AN), and their reflexes in ESc. Note that unconditioned developments follow conditioned ones.

Source	Developments, with examples	ESc vowel
OE *ī*, *ȳ*	OE shortenings, e.g. *fīfte* > *fift*, *cicen-* > *chikkin*	15
	before *w*, e.g. *spīwan* > *spew*	14a
	irregularly, e.g. *wīr* > *were* 'wire'	3
	otherwise, e.g. *bite*, *fire*, *drȳge* > *dry*	1
OE *ē*, including Anglian *ē* = WS *ēa* and WS *ǣ¹* (but see below)	OE shortenings, e.g. *grēttra* > *gretter* 'greater', *hēhþu* > *hecht*, 'height' *cēpte* > *kept* p.t. hence *kep* 'keep', *blētsian* > *bles*	16
	irregularly, e.g. *gēotan* > *ȝett* 'pour' var. of *ȝete*	16
	before final *g* /j/, e.g. *hēg* > *hay*, *cǣg* > *kay* 'key'	8
	before *g* /j/ + V, e.g. *drēogan* > *dre* 'endure', *ēage* > *e* 'eye', *cǣg-* > *key*; including *g* for *h* in inflected forms, e.g. *hēag-* > *he* 'high'	11
	otherwise, e.g. *hēr* > *here* 'here', *hēran* > *here* 'hear', *scēp* > *schepe*	2
OE *ēo*	var. rising diphthong *eō*, see *ō*	
	before *w*, e.g. *trēowþ* > *treuth* 'truth', *nēowe* > *new*	14a
	otherwise as *ē*, e.g. *dēop* > *depe*, *sēoc* > *seik* 'sick', *cēosan* > *chese* 'choose'	2
OE *ǣ¹*	normally as Anglian *ē* (see OE *ē*)	
	exceptionally, e.g. *brǣþ* > *brethe*	3
OE *ǣ²*	OE shortenings, e.g. *brǣmblas* > **brammill* 'bramble'	17
	word-final, e.g. *sǣ* > *se* 'sea'	2
	inconsistently before *d*, *n*, *l*, *r*, e.g. *clǣne* > *clene*	2
	before *w*, e.g. *slǣwþ* > *sleuth* 'sloth'	14b(i) 14b(ii)
	before *g* /j/ e.g. *clǣg* > *clay*	8
	otherwise, e.g. *hlǣne* > *lene*, *ǣr* > *ere* 'before'	3
OE *ēa*	var. rising diphthong *eā*, see *ā*	
	exceptionally, e.g. *lēaf* > *leve* 'permission'	2
	grēat > *grete* (alongside metathesised forms with shortened vowel)	3
	before *w*, e.g. *dēaw* > *dew*, *scēawian* > *schew* 'show'	14b(i) 14b(ii)
	otherwise, e.g. *dēad* > *dede* 'dead'	3

Figure 7.6—cont'd

Source	Developments, with examples	ESc vowel
OE *ā*	OE shortenings, e.g. *hālfmǣsse* > *lammes* 'Lammas'	17
	before *w*, e.g. *cnāwan* > *knaw* 'know', *sceāwian* > *schaw* 'show'; includes *g* /ɣ/ > w/, e.g. *āgen* > *awn* 'own' v.	12
	before *h* /x/, including *h* for final *g* /ɣ/, e.g. *daich* 'dough' dial. *deuch*	4 14b(i)
	otherwise, e.g. *stān* > *stane* 'stone'	4
OE *ū*	OE shortenings, e.g. *hūsbonda* > *husband*, *sūðerne* > *sutheron*	19
	irregularly, e.g. *clūd* > *clud* var. of *cloud*	19
	before *h* /x/, var. shortening, e.g. *ruch* var. of *rouch* 'rough'	19
	with vocalisation of *v*, e.g. *dūfa* > *dow* 'dove'	6
	otherwise, e.g. *mūþ* > *mouth*, *trūwian* > *trow* 'believe', *būgan* > *bow* 'bend' v.	6
OE *ō*	OE shortenings, e.g. *ōhsta* > *oxter* 'armpit', *þōht* > *thocht*	18
	before *w*, e.g. *grōwan* > *grow*, *treōwþ* > *trowth* 'truth'	13
	before *g* /ɣ/ + V, e.g. *bōgas* > *bewis* 'boughs' pl.; including *g* for *h* in inflected forms e.g. *clōg-* > *clewis* 'ravines' pl.	14a
	otherwise, e.g. *gōd* > *gude* 'good', *ceōsan* > *chuse* 'choose', *hōh* > *heuch* 'hough', *bōg* > *beuch* 'bough'	7
OE *i, y*	HOCL, e.g. *wilde* > *wild*, *cynde* > *kind*	1
	ic > *I*	1
	before *w*, e.g. *siwan* > *sew*	14a
	before *g* /j/, e.g. *stigel* > *stile*, *-ig* > *-y* as in *haly* 'holy'	1
	belated HOCL, e.g. *cild* > *chelde* 'child'	2
	inconsistently before *l, n, d, sc* /ʃ/, e.g. *glida* > *gled* 'kite, the bird'	16
	otherwise, e.g. *biddan* > *bid*, *hyll* > *hill*; including failure of HOCL, e.g. *blind*	15
OE *e, eo*	HOCL, e.g. *eldu* > *eild* 'old age'	2
	final in monosyllables, e.g. *he*	2
	wel > *wele* 'well' adv.	2
	var. before *h* /x/ + *t*, e.g. *feohtan* > *ficht* var. of *fecht* 'fight'	15
	before final *g* /j/, e.g. *weg* > *way*; before *g* /j/ + C, e.g. *regn* > *rain*	8
	before *g* /j/ + V, e.g. *swegan* > *swey* var. *swe* 'sway'	8 11
	otherwise, e.g. *bedd* > *bed*; including failure of HOCL, e.g. *mend*	16

Figure 7.6—cont'd

Source	Developments, with examples	ESc vowel
OE æ	var. before alveolars, e.g. *glæs* > *gles* var. of *glas*	16
	before *h* /x/, e.g. *hlæhhan* > *lauch* 'laugh'	12
	before *g* /j/, e.g. *dæg* > *day*, *hægl* > *hail*	8
	otherwise, e.g. *græf* > *graf* 'grave' n.	17
OE ea	*beard* > *berde*	3
	before *h* /x/, e.g. *eahta* > *aucht* 'eight'	12
	before alveolars, e.g. *ears* > *erse*	16
	otherwise, e.g. *eall* > *all*	17
OE a, including Anglian *ald* = WS *eald*	HOCL, e.g. *camb* > *kame* 'comb', *-ald* as in *cald* 'cold', etc.	4
	before *w*, e.g. *clawu* > *claw*; including /ɣ > w/, e.g. *lagu* > law 'law'	12
	otherwise, e.g. *catt* > *cat*; including failure of HOCL, e.g. *band*	17
OE o	HOCL, e.g. *bord* > *buird* 'board'	7
	dial. before *h* /x/, e.g. *dohtor* > *douchter* 'daughter'	13
	before *g* /ɣ > w/ + V or syllabic C, e.g. *boga* > *bow* 'the weapon', *logn* 'calm';	13
	after *w* in *geswogen* > *swoun* 'swoon'	6
	otherwise, e.g. *dohtor* > *dochter* 'daughter', *loc* > *lok*; including failure of HOCL, e.g. *gold*	18
OE u	HOCL, e.g. *bunden* > *bound* p.p.	6
	before *w*, including *g* /ɣ > w/, e.g. *fugol* > *foul* 'bird'	6
	after *w*, e.g. *wucu* > *(w)ouk* 'week'	6
	otherwise, e.g. *cuman* > *cum* 'come'; including var. failure of HOCL, e.g. *bunden* > *bund*	19
ON í, ý	as OE ī, ȳ, e.g *knífr* > *knife*	1
ON é	as OE ē, e.g. *sér* > *sere* 'separate'	2
ON œ́	e.g. *sœ́ma* > *seme* 'seem'	2
ON ǽ	as OE ǣ, e.g. *sǽti* > *sete* 'seat'	3
ON á	as OE ā, e.g. *báðir* > *bathe* 'both'	4

Figure 7.6—cont'd

Source	Developments, with examples	ESc vowel
ON *ú*	as OE *ū*, e.g. *drūpa* > *droup* 'droop'	6
ON *ó*	as OE *ō*, e.g. *lōfe* > *lufe* 'palm of the hand'; Norn *óðal* > *outhall* 'udal'	7 6
ON *i, y*	as OE, e.g. *kirkja* > *kirk*, *byggja* > *big* 'build'	15
ON *e*	as OE, e.g. *klegge* > *cleg* 'horsefly'	16
ON *a*	as OE, e.g. *kasta* > *cast*; *mav-* > *maw* 'gull', *maðkr* > *mauch* 'maggot'	17 12
ON *o*	as OE, e.g. *toft* 'homestead'	18
ON *u*	as OE, e.g. *buski* > *bus* 'bush'	19
ON *ei, ey*	e.g. *þeir* > *thai* 'they', *leyna* > *lain* 'conceal'	8
ON *au*	e.g. *gaukr* > *gowk* 'cuckoo'; *haukr* > *hawk*	13 12
OF *ī*	e.g. *pris* > *prise* 'price'	1
OF *-y*	e.g. *mercy*	1
AN *ō̄* = OF *ue*	*boef* > *befe*, root-stressed forms of *mover*, *prover* > *meve* 'move', *preve* 'prove'	2
AN *ē*, including = OF *ie*	e.g. *pece* 'piece', *frere* 'friar'	2
OF *-é*	e.g. *cite* 'city'	2
OF *-ée*	e.g. *cuntre*, var. *cuntray*	2 8
Latin *ē*	e.g. *redeme*	2
OF *ę̄* from Latin *ē*	e.g. *remede* 'remedy'	3

Figure 7.6—cont'd

Source	Developments, with examples	ESc vowel
AN *ē* = OF *ai* and countertonic *ei*	e.g. *pese* 'peace', *fede* 'feud'; exceptionally, e.g. *praise, laisere* 'leisure'	3 8
OF *ā*	e.g. *estate*	4
AN *ã*	e.g. *aunt, branche, change, danger*	17 12 ?4
OF *ǭ*	e.g. *estore* > *store, glore* 'glory'	5
OF *ū*	e.g. *flour* 'flower', *prisoun* 'prison'	6
OF *ō*	e.g. *povre* > *pure* 'poor', *mover* > *muve, prover* > *pruve*	7
OF *ǖ* including AN *ǖ* = OF *üi*	final, e.g. *valew* 'value'; var. (? sociolectal) *valow*	14a 6
	in hiatus, e.g. *cruel*	14a
	dur > *dour*	6
	var. in *juge, justice*	19
	otherwise, e.g. *use, fruit, duc* > *duke*	7
OF *i*	before /ʎ/ borrowed as /l/, /ɲ/ borrowed as /n/, e.g. *famyle* 'family', *desyne* 'design'	1
	otherwise, e.g. *riche, ligne* 'lineage'	15
OF *e*	before /ʎ/ borrowed as /l/, /ɲ/ borrowed as /n/, e.g. *feign*	8
	breme 'bream', *preche* 'preach'	3
	before *r* + C, e.g. *perce* 'pierce'	2
	otherwise, e.g. *serve, det* 'debt', *menȝee* 'company'	16
OF *a*	before /ʎ/ borrowed as /l/, /ɲ/ borrowed as /n/, e.g. *fail*	8
	otherwise, e.g. *fasch* 'vex', *falȝe* 'fail'	17
OF *-al*	e.g. *bestiale*	17 4

Figure 7.6—cont'd

Source	Developments, with examples	ESc vowel
OF *o*	before final C, e.g. *los* 'praise' n.	5
	before *st*, e.g. *host* 'army'	5
	otherwise, e.g. *joly*	18
OF *u*	before /ʎ/ borrowed as /l/, /ɲ/ borrowed as /n/, e.g. *boil, oyll*	10
	tonic in closed syllables, e.g. *trubill, numir,*	19
	var. *trouble, noumer*	6
	otherwise, e.g. *buket, cunʒe* 'coin', *ulʒe* 'oil'	19
AN *ai* including = OF *ei*	e.g. *faith, verray* 'true'	8
OF *ǫi*	e.g. *joy, noise, voice*	9
	var. e.g. *voice*	10
AN *ui* = OF *oi*	e.g. *point*	10
OF *au*	e.g. *faut* 'fault', *sauf* 'safe'	12
	Lowrence	13
OF *ou*	e.g. *couper* > *cowp* 'overturn', *poulenet* > *powny* 'pony'	13
OF *eu, iu,* AN *iw*	e.g. *bleu* > *blew* 'blue', *griu* > *grew* 'Greek', *pursiwer* > *persew*	14a
OF *eau*	e.g. *lewtee* 'loyalty';	14b(i)
		14b(ii)
	var. (?sociolectal) *laute*	14b(iii)

the changes described above have still to take effect. There are many minor changes that affect only small groups of words, or are confined to particular dialects, and there are also many unpredictable developments and by-forms, where a vowel has captured items from a contiguous vowel (including irregular long and short forms). Where the OSc spelling seems to suggest such a by-form, the modern pronunciations can be consulted to confirm its existence (see CSD).[26] See also Aitken (1971, revised in Macafee and Aitken 2002) for the relationship between orthographic and phonological variation. Specimen readings, including the texts below, in a variety of models, can be heard on a tape recorded by Aitken (1996b).

Barbour's Bruce, c.1375 (ESc)

Aitken (1977) took Barbour's *Bruce* as a specimen of NE dialect, but it is no longer thought that Barbour was himself a north-easterner. In any case, one of the few distinctive features in the 1977 transcription no longer applies, as Aitken's more recent reconstruction assumes an ESc value [yː] for Vowel 7 in all dialects, and not just the NE.

ˌxwɛn ðat ðɪ ˈgyːd ˈkɪŋ ˈbeːriːt ˌwas
ðɪ ˈɛrl o̞f ˈmy̞ref, ˈʃɪr ˈto̞ˌmas,
tyːk ˈal ðɪ ˈland ɪn ˈgy̞verˌnɪŋ,
ˈal o̞ˈbaɪt tɪl hɪs ˈbɪˌdɪŋ.
and ðɪ ˈgyːd ˈlo̞ːrd o̞f ˈduːglas ˈsiːn
gɛrt ˈmak a ˈkaːs o̞f ˈsɪlvɪr ˈfiːn,
ɛˈnamɪlɪt ˈθruː ˈsy̞tɪlˈteː
ˈθaːrɪn ðɪ ˈkɪŋɪs ˈhart dɪd ˈheː
and ˈai aˈbuːt hɪs ˈhals ɪt ˈbaːr
and ˈfast hɪm ˈbuːnɪt fo̞r ty ˈfaːr
hɪs ˈtɛstaˈment dɪˈviːzɪt ˈheː
and o̞rˈdainɪt ˈhuː hɪs ˈland sy̞ld ˈbeː
ˈgy̞vernɪt xwɪl hɪs ˈgain ˈky̞mɪŋ
o̞f ˈfreːndɪs, and ˈal ˈyːðɪr ˈθɪŋ
ðat ˌtɪl hɪm perˈteːnɪt ˈo̞niː ˈwiːs,
wɪθ ˈsɪk ˈfo̞ːrˌsɪxt and ˈsaː ˈwiːs,
o̞r hɪs ˈfy̞rθ ˈpasɪŋ o̞rˈdainɪt ˈheː
ðat ˈnaː θɪŋ ˈmɪxt aˈmendɪt ˈbeː.
and ˌxwɛn ðat ˌheː hɪs ˈleːv had ˈtaːn
ty ˈʃɪp ty ˈbɛrwɪk ˌɪs heː ˈgaːn
and wɪθ a ˈno̞ːbˌl ˈky̞mpaˈniː
o̞f ˈknɪxtɪs and o̞f ˈskwiːɛˈriː
heː ˈpy̞t hɪm ˈθaːr ty ðɪ ˈseː
a ˈlaŋ ˌwai ˈfy̞rθwart ˈsailɪt ˈheː
fo̞r bɪˈtwɪks ˈko̞rnˌwail and breˈtaːɲ
heː ˈsailɪt and ˈleft ðɪ ˈgryːɲ o̞f ˈspaːɲ
o̞n ˈno̞rθ ˌhalf ˌhɪm.

(John Barbour, *Bruce* XX, 299f., Edinb. MS.)

Holland's Howlat, c.1450 (early MSc)

For the Orcadian Holland, writing in Morayshire c.1450, Aitken assumed a stage early in the GVS. Taking the dialect as NE, we still have [y:] for Vowel 7 (shortly to unround to [iː]). The capture of Vowel 4 after labials by Vowel 12 is seen in *quhare*.

ðɪ 'hɛrt 'kǫstlɪːi hę: 'kuːθ 'klǫːz ɪn ə 'klęːr 'kæːs
and 'hɛld aːʷ 'hæːl ðɪ bɪ'hɛst hɪ 'hɛxt ty ðɪ 'kɪŋ,
'kụm ty ðɪ 'hæːlɪːi 'græːv θru 'gǫdɪz 'grɛt 'græːs,
wɪθ 'ǫfrandz ənd 'ǫrɪzuːnz ənd 'al 'ụðɪr 'θɪŋ,
uːr 'salvə͵tuːrz 'sɛpul͵tyːr and ðɪ 'sæːmɪn 'plæːs
xwaːʷr hę: 'ræːz əz wę: 'ręːd 'rɪxtwɪːis ty 'rɪŋ,
wɪθ aːʷ ðɪ 'rɛlɪks 'ræːθ ðat ɪn ðat 'ruːm ͵was
hę: gart 'halǫu ðɪ 'hart and 'sɪːin kuːθ ɪt 'hɪŋ
ə'buːt hɪz 'haːʷs fụl 'hęːnd ənd ǫn hɪz 'aʷːn 'hart.
ǫft wụːd hę: 'kɪs ɪt ənd 'krɪːi
ǫ: 'fluːr əv aːʷ 'ʧɛvəl͵rɪːi,
xwɪːi 'lęːv ɪːi a'las, 'xwɪːi,
ənd 'ðuː 'dɛːd art?
mɪːi 'dęːr, kwǫd ðɪ 'duː͵glas, art ðuː 'dɛːd 'dɪxt,
mɪːi 'sɪŋyːlɪr 'suvɪ͵ræin, əv 'saksǫnz ðɪ 'wand,
nuː bụt ɪːi 'sɛmbl͵ fər ðɪːi 'saːʷl wɪθ 'sarazɛnz 'mɪxt
sal ɪːi 'nɛvɪr 'sęːn 'bę: ɪnty 'skǫt͵land.

(Richard Holland, *The Buke of the Howlat*, 469 f., Asloan MS.)

Dunbar c.1500 (early MSc)

This is assumed to be an advanced form of southern East Central Scots, as spoken at court. The language of serious verse was conservative, however, in avoiding l-vocalised forms. For *of*, doublet /of/ and /o/ forms are shown, the latter evidenced from the fourteenth century on (see DOST s.v.). The pronunciation /ɪn/ for the verbal noun ending *-ing* is likewise attested from ESc on. In this dialect, Vowel 4 remains after labials (for example *quhairfoir*). The realisation of Vowel 18 is shown as closer than in the next example, from further north.

tø 'speːk of 'seːiɛns, 'kraft ər 'seːpɪ͵ɛns,
o 'vɛrtiu 'moral, 'kụnɪŋ ər dok'treːin,
of 'ʤøːr, o 'wɪsdøːm ər ɪn'tɛli͵ʤɛns,
of 'ɛvreːi 'studeːi, 'leːr ər 'dɪskɪp͵leːin –
'al ɪz bụt 'tɪnt ər 'rɛdeːi fər tø 'teːin,

'not 'øːzɪn ɪt əz ɪt suːd 'øːzɪt 'biː,
ðɪ 'kraft ɛk'sɛrsɪn, kon'sɪdɛrɪn not ðɪ 'feːin.
ə 'parɪlʉs 'siːknɛs ɪz 'vɛin proˈspɛrɪˌtiː.

ðɪ 'køːrɪʉs proˈbeːsɪuːn 'loʤɪˌkal,
ðɪ 'ɛloˌkwɛns of 'ornat 'rɛtoˌreːi,
ðɪ 'neːtøːraːl 'seːiɛns 'fɪloˈsofɪˌkal,
ðɪ 'dɪrk aˈpiːrɛns of aˈstronoˌmeːi,
ðɪ 'θiːoˌloːgz 'sɛrmuːn, ðɪ 'feːbɪlz of 'poːɛtˌreːi,
wɪˈθuːt 'gøːd 'leːif 'al ɪn ðɪ 'sɛlf døːz 'diː,
əz 'mɛi 'fluːrz døːz ɪn sɛpˈtɛmbɪr 'dreːi.
ə 'parɪlʉs 'siːknɛs ɪz 'vɛin proˈspɛrɪˌtiː.

'xwɛːrfor, jiː 'klarks ənd 'grɪtɪst of konˈstans,
'fʉlɪst o 'seːiɛns and o 'knɑːleʤˌɪn,
tø 'ʉz biː 'mɪruːrz ɪn juːr 'gʉverˌnans
and ɪn 'uːr 'darknɪs biː 'lampɪz in 'ʃeːinˌɪn,
or 'ðan ɪn 'frustrar ɪz juːr 'laŋ 'lɛrnˌɪn,
ˌgɪf tø juːr 'sɑːz juːr 'diːdɪz 'kontrar 'biː,
juːr 'meːst əˈkøːzər səl 'biː juːr 'aːn 'kʉnˌɪn.
ə 'parɪlʉs 'siːknɛs ɪz 'vɛin proˈspɛrɪˌtiː.

(From *The Poems of William Dunbar* ed. Priscilla Bawcutt, Glasgow: ASLS, 1998, no.82.)

The Complaynt of Scotland, c.1545 (transcribed as late MSc)

This text, from Dundee, represents northern East Central Scots. An opener realisation is assumed for Vowel 18 than in the previous transcription. *Thai* 'they' is shown as retaining the original Vowel 8a, rather than Vowel 4 (which it has acquired in all dialects since the fifteenth century). In the environment before /r/, Vowel 4 merges in this dialect with Vowel 8, rather than vice versa, thus *thare* 'there' merges with *thair* 'their'. The writer who produced the printer's copy was rather consistent in writing the inflection -(*i*)*s* as < is > after stressed syllables, in contrast to mostly < s > after unstressed syllables, suggesting that the unreduced vowel persisted in his idiolect in, for example, /rɪˈpøːtɪz, 'ɪŋlɪz, 'skɒtɪz/, though not in, for example, /'neːsjuːnz/.

'fɒr 'ɛvrɪ 'neːsjuːn rɪˈpøːtɪz 'ɪðɪrz 'neːsjuːnz tø beː barˈbeːrɪɛnz xwan ðɛiːr
'twɑː 'neːtøːrz ənd kɒmˈplɛksjuːnz ər 'kɒntrər tɪl 'ɪðɪrz. and ðɛiːr ɪz 'nɒxt
'twɑː 'neːsjuːnz ʉndɪr ðɪ 'fɪrməmɛnt ðat ər 'meːr 'kɒntrər ənd 'dɪfɪrɛnt
freː 'ɪðɪrz nɒr ɪz 'ɪŋlɪzˌmɛn ənd 'skɒtɪzˌmɛn huːˈbiːɪt ðat ðɛːi 'biː wɪθɪn
'eːn 'eːil ənd 'nɪxbuːrz ənd əf 'eːn 'laŋeːʤ.

Reported speech, Fife, c.1560 (late MSc)

For this somewhat later passage in a dialect not very different from that of the previous passage, a much more progressive speech form is assumed. The SVLR is taken to be fully established. (Vowel lengths are shown, though strictly this is now unnecessary, as they are predicted by the environmental rule.) Vowel 3, as in *meat*, merges in this dialect with Vowel 4, not Vowel 2. A Vowel 7 form of *brother*, obsolete in Modern Scots, is shown. *Smaik* has Vowel 8.

mɛːi 'brøðɪr ɪz ən 'sal 'biː 'vɪkər ə 'krel xwɛn 'ðuː sal 'θɪg ðɛːi 'met 'fɑːs 'smeik. ɛːi səl 'pöl ði ut ə ði 'pupət bɪ ðɪ 'lögz ənd 'ʧes ði 'ut ə ðɪs 'tun. (From *The Register of the Ministers, Elders and Deacons of St. Andrews*, Scottish History Society 4, 1889: 106–7.)

Record of an oral deposition, Lanark, c.1610–20 (late MSc)

As in the previous passage, vowel lengths are included, but the SVLR is assumed. A distinction is shown between the vowels of *-in(g)* and *-an(d)*.

'ʤon 'kampbɛl kom'plinz ənd rɪ'ports tø jör 'wözdömz ðət 'æːi 'biːɪn öpon 'mönənde: wəz on 'ɔxt 'deːz økø'pæːɪt wɪθ mæːi 'kraft ən 'kalin 'kömɪn 'hem tø 'get ət 'in sɪk 'porʃön əz 'god 'sɛndɪt 'ɪn 'köm ə 'man ðət æːi 'nɛvɪr 'knjuː o bɪ'foːr ənd ɪn'kontɪnent 'ðeːr'eftɪr 'ɪn 'kömz 'tomǝs 'moǝt ənd 'seːz, 'goː 'pei jör 'lɔːin ənd 'hi 'seːz ɪ wəd 'noː fər 'hɪm. ənd 'sweː or æːi 'wɪst ðeː wɪr ɪn 'ɪðɪrz 'lögz. and 'ɪn 'kömz 'ʤon 'moǝt ənd 'seː ðeː wɪr 'rɛd wɪ'θut 'skeθ.

(From a transcript of an undated document on a single sheet, bound in with the 1590–1615 vol. of the MS Lanark Town Council Records: see *Extracts from the Records and Charters of the Royal Burgh of Lanark*, Glasgow, 1893: 121–2.)

NOTES

1. Aitken (2002) is also summarised in Macafee and Aitken (2002). (The notes below are by Macafee unless otherwise indicated.)
2. Johnston's (1997b) analysis of the Modern Scots dialects is excellent (though the phonemic outline is sometimes obscured by the phonetic detail), but his historical reconstructions (1997a) are not based on the same extensive knowledge of OSc orthography and rhyme as Aitken's.
3. Johnston (1997a) often attempts more detailed reconstructions of phonetic realisation than Aitken has done.

4. The spellings in < ʒ > were subject to confusion with < z > in print.
5. Cf. the much quoted comments of Alexander Hume (c.1617) (Hume 1865: 18).
6. But when the preceding syllable consists of a fully unstressed vowel + a liquid or nasal, it seems that optionally the unstressed stem syllable rather than the inflection might undergo syncope: e.g. *eldris* 'elders', *noblis, watrys, lipnis* (pres. t. of *lippin* v. 'trust'); this is exemplified from the earliest ESc texts onwards – AJA.
7. References are to McDiarmid and Stevenson's (1980–5) edition.
8. Subsequent to Open Syllable Lengthening (see below).
9. A curious exception is the word *jugement*, which is generally counted as three syllables in ESc verse. However, this anomaly was corrected in MSc by changing the word to *jugisment*.
10. Two related phenomena of Modern Scots unstressed vowels may go back to the OSc period: terminal stress and vowel harmony. Terminal stress, most fully described by Wettstein, is:

> an increased rhythmic or emphatic stress on final unaccented syllables . . . [which] is most apparent at the end of breathgroups, where it may easily amount to a full stress or more and be coupled with a considerable reduction of a preceding accented syllable. (1942: 16–17)

e.g. [hedz 'bro'ken]. It is a noticeable marker of modern Central Scots working-class speech. Vowel harmony (Dieth 1932; Hill 1963) is a predictable variation in the realisation of unstressed /ɪ/ according to the stressed vowel in the syllable preceding, for example in Buchan:

> [spidi, dɪnɪr, doθɛr]

Although it is now characteristic only of some non-Central dialects, vowel harmony was perhaps once more general – AJA.
11. In some, but not all, cases, the unlengthened forms correspond to uninflected forms (see Aitken 2002: §4.1).
12. There is thus no ō /oː/ in Scots to raise to /uː/ by the GVS (as in ModEng *moon*).
13. In a few modern dialects, Vowel 3 remains distinct.
14. There is also a variant Vowel 7 form *muild*, in which the vowel was previously lengthened by Homorganic Cluster Lengthening.
15. Unvocalised forms of *all* and so on also continue in some peripheral modern dialects.
16. This interpretation follows Aitken (2002), in contrast to Aitken (1977), which in turn followed Luick (1903), who posited a direct change from Vowel 7 to Vowel 15 (paralleling the later change in most of Central Scots), subsequent to fronting.
17. However, /j/ in /je/ *ae* 'one' adj. appears to be a rare survival of an earlier change, which left the vowel unaffected. Possibly the link with *ane* helped to preserve this form.
18. For instance, Vowel 18 realised *anglice* as [ɔ] rather than [o].
19. By the end of the sixteenth century the modern syllabifications of all of these words were established – AJA.
20. Aitken (1996a) gives additional tables with the Modern Scots vowels arranged in quasi-alphabetical order, and the Modern English correspondences to the Scots vowels listed, by Modern English spelling.
21. That is, Vowels 3, 16, 1, 15, 16, 17.
22. Aitken (1996b) suggests that 'it is possible that the indefinite article < ane > was

sometimes read or recited during the MSc period by some readers as /eːn/ as a spelling-pronunciation . . .', which 'was at best a minority affectation in MSc times'. Unfortunately, he does not cite the evidence for this suggestion. There is no trace of the pronunciation in any of the modern dialects, which we might have expected to find if it had been current in any form of colloquial MSc. Aitken had earlier pointed out that reverse spellings like *ane-levin* (for 'eleven', see DOST s.v.), *ane mendis* (see DOST s.v. *mendis* n. 2) and *ane mis* 'amiss' (see DOST s.v. *mis* n. 6) suggest that this was a merely conventional practice (1971: n. 53).

23. When Barbour treats Anglo-Norman loans as end-stressed, it is not unlikely that these were living pronunciations, since he is still fairly close in time to the period of borrowing.

24. Both the *Pocket Scots Dictionary* and the much more comprehensive *Concise Scots Dictionary* give directly, or by implication from the spelling, when this is unambiguous, pronunciations for every word entered, which in the case of CSD, comprises almost all of the distinctive vocabulary of Scots. It is true that a very few words with distinctively Scots pronunciations did not qualify for inclusion in CSD: examples are *juice* /ʤɪs/, *habit* OSc /haˈbiːt/, *position* /pəˈziːʃən/, *puncture* /ˈpʌŋktɪr/. But it is surprising just how many words which one might have expected to have escaped entry in CSD because of not apparently being distinctively Scots are in fact, for one reason or another, included, so that their pronunciation is in fact given. A fully exhaustive dictionary of Scots pronunciation has yet to be compiled. Until it is, CSD is a very useful resource indeed – AJA. The index to Aitken (2002) also contains pronunciation information, including some for words not found in CSD.

25. The transcriptions have been revised to make them consistent with Aitken's latest thoughts on the subject (Aitken 2002). A few typographical corrections have also been made, and a more recent edition of Dunbar preferred.

26. For those prepared to grapple with it, Volume III of the *Linguistic Atlas of Scotland* also provides relevant information. In general, it is best to by-pass the maps and refer directly to the lists. For advice on how to interpret the data, see Johnston (2000).

27. The subsequent loss of distinction between *-ing* and *-and* (the ending of the present participle), though no doubt influenced by anglicisation, was also at least facilitated by this and by the reduction of *-and* to *-an*.

CHAPTER 8

Corpus-based Study of Older Scots Grammar and Lexis

Anneli Meurman-Solin

INTRODUCTION

This chapter focuses on how the methods of corpus linguistics allow us to reconstruct Older Scots grammar and lexis. Modern linguistic research more and more frequently extracts data from large electronic databases, and aims to provide evidence of the statistical significance of the findings. In addition to briefly introducing general issues related to the reconstruction of the language of the past and the identification and definition of language-external factors conditioning linguistic choices, this chapter discusses some recent research based on diachronic corpora of Scots, especially the Helsinki Corpus of Older Scots (HCOS), 1450–1700, with some data extracted from two text corpora being compiled at present, the Corpus of Scottish Correspondence (CSC), 1500–1800, and the tagged Edinburgh-Helsinki Corpus of Older Scots (E/HCOS), 1450–1650. The HCOS (c.850,000 words) comprises chiefly non-literary texts representing the following fifteen genres: Acts of Parliament, burgh records, trial proceedings, histories, biographies, travelogues, diaries, pamphlets, educational treatises, scientific treatises, handbooks, private letters, official letters, sermons and the Bible. This corpus has been structured by including information about variables such as genre, text category, level of formality, audience and the author's age, sex and social rank (cf. Kytö 1996).

The lexicographically defined description of Older Scots lexis has been achieved by the completion of the Dictionary of the Older Scottish Tongue (DOST). This information can be usefully complemented by quantitative analyses based on text corpora, and by identifying further linguistic and extra-linguistic factors that can be related to specific features of the lexis. Ideally, unlike the dictionary, this research will draw data from texts checked against manuscript. Considerably more work still needs to be done in the field of grammar. In fact, it is only gradually becoming possible to write a comprehensive account of Older Scots grammar as large geographically and socially representative electronic corpora based on diplomatic editions of texts are being made available (see the important discussion of editing principles in the introduction to LALME, the Linguistic Atlas of Late Middle English). The focus here is thus on how to proceed in this descriptive process: that is, what tools and alternative or complementary methodological approaches are available. Beside the list of references at the end of the chapter, the bibliography on the internet can be consulted for information about the literature (www.unibg.it/anglistica/slin/scot-bib.htm).

Older Scots is a 'text language'. While discussing theoretically, methodologically and ideologically problematic issues in historical linguistics, Fleischman (2000: 34) defines this useful concept in the following way:

> The term 'text language' is intended to reflect the fact that the linguistic activity of such languages is amenable to scrutiny only insofar as it has been constituted in the form of extant *texts*, which we might think of as its 'native speakers', even if we can't interrogate them in quite the same way as we can native speakers of living languages. Another crucial difference between text languages and living languages is that the data corpus of a text language is finite; new data only become available when previously unknown documents are discovered, whether in the form of manuscripts, printed texts, tablets, etc.

Despite limitations on the availability of data, '[both] the synchronic and the diachronic approaches to historical linguistics are essentially data-driven and data oriented', in contrast with the 'theoretical approach', which 'extrapolates from the data in order to identify general principles and mechanisms of language change' (ibid.). Given the recent advances in corpus linguistics, polarisation of this kind is no longer always justified since data extracted from large electronic text corpora provides statistically significant evidence for both a detailed description of linguistic variation, with a particular interest in how this variation can be related to language-external variables (geographical area, genre, gender, social rank, mobility and so on) and the identification of mechanisms of change reflected in the chronology, rate and direction of change. For example, research on grammaticalisation processes (see, for instance, Traugott and Heine 1991; Hopper and Traugott 1993; Rissanen et al. 1997; Palander-Collin 1999; Brinton 2000) and studies recording the shape of change over time (see, for instance, Devitt 1989; Nevalainen and Raumolin-Brunberg 1996; Nurmi 1999; Nevalainen 2000) illustrate that the two approaches can be integrated in various relevant ways. In other words, a thorough descriptive analysis of the data allows us to see patterns reflecting systemic developments that can ultimately be used to formulate theories about language variation and change.

What are the prerequisites of a genuinely data-driven and data-oriented approach? The concern here is to examine the data available for the reconstruction of the text language called Older Scots and, just as importantly, to provide at least some direct and indirect evidence of what the major gaps are. In other words, in addition to a good understanding of what is presently available in the text corpora of Older Scots, we will have to keep in mind what Mittendorf and Poppe 2000: 127) refer to as 'a notional corpus', a database that would in theory comprise the full range of once functional texts relevant for expressing the communicative purposes of the various speech and discourse communities in a given geographical area, but which will in practice remain beyond recovery (Meurman-Solin 2001a; as regards Scottish women's writings, see Marshall 1983: 57; see also Houston 1985). In historical linguistics, irrespective of language or variety, it can be 'difficult for the analyst to separate out the effects of diachrony from the effects of genre' (Herring et al. 2000: 3). This problem is aggravated when genres are unevenly represented over time, space and social milieu. In the case of Scots, the history of periphrastic *do* (Meurman-Solin 1993b) and the relative pronoun *who* (Meurman-Solin 2000c), for instance, illustrate a pattern of change in which the early uses have been attested in specific genres, so that the spread is from these to a wider range of genres. However, since there are gaps in historical data in the earlier periods in particular, the claim that genre is the primary conditioning factor in the introduction and spread of a specific linguistic feature is valid only in so far as the database from which the evidence is extracted can be considered fully representative. In addition, statistical tools (Meurman-Solin 1994, 1997d) are needed to identify reliably the language-external factors that condition the choice of linguistic features. Apart from the relative scarcity of early texts in Older Scots, the range of genres varies in the different areas of Scotland, and thus the goal of creating a perfectly balanced reconstruction of geographical, social and stylistic variation cannot be achieved (Meurman-Solin 2001a: 15–18).

Even though corpus compilers may refer to large multi-genre corpora as general-purpose databases, also suggesting that these are representative as a result of diversity – whether assessed by register variation, dialectal variation or subject matter (Biber et al. 1998: 248), the validity of a database is dependent on the questions we want to ask in our research. Beside carefully examining whether a database is applicable to the study of a specific topic, the assessment of validity is also necessary to ensure that there is no theoretical and/or methodological contradiction between the approaches of the corpus compiler and the corpus user. Thus it is only with caution that we can apply methods developed by, for instance, modern sociolinguistics, dialectology or discourse stylistics to data that has not been compiled within the theoretical framework of these fields. A good example of a corpus that has been structured to reflect recent theoretical and methodological developments in historical sociolinguistics with due rigour is the Corpus of Early English Correspondence (Nevalainen and Raumolin-Brunberg 1996).

Those who study Scots tend to favour an approach that compares it to English. In fact a comparative approach is often preferred for any language variety which is used in a geographically restricted area and is in direct contact with another variety of the same language, especially one that, at some stage, achieves the status of a widely used written standard. However, since the history of Scots consists of stages reflecting varying degrees of internal heterogeneity and developments over time and space, taking various directions of change, a detailed description of Older Scots should first be available before conclusions can be drawn about how it relates to other varieties of English. The perspective chosen in earlier studies (Devitt 1989; Meurman-Solin 1993a, 1997a, c) can perhaps be justified where the focus is on language differentiation and standardisation processes, but a wider range of perspectives is necessary to write about diachronic developments in the grammar and lexis of Older Scots. While language contact phenomena in the reconstruction of Scots provide us with a set of extremely interesting research topics, it is important to examine system-internal pressures on variation and change as well. As Herring et al. point out, '[different] dialects may have been differentially affected by contact with other varieties (Weinreich 1964), necessitating that texts produced in those dialects be analyzed separately from those in other varieties, even though they are nominally from the "same" language' (2000: 22).[1]

To conclude this introductory section. Aitken (1971) highlights features of Older Scots in a way that is, thirty years later, still very perceptive and relevant. My discussion of how corpus linguistics methods can shed more light on the grammar and lexis of Older Scots is indebted to Aitken's views on variation and variety. To identify continued variation and multidirectional processes of change in a text language is a complex process, but the task of reconstructing the past stages of Older Scots has been greatly facilitated by the new technology now available. In addition to corpus-based descriptive work that has allowed us to produce tools such as linguistic atlases, dictionaries and thesauri, recent developments in fields such as historical dialectology (Laing 1991, 1993, 2000; Williamson 1992–3, 2000), historical pragmatics (Jucker 1995), historical sociolinguistics (Nevalainen and Raumolin-Brunberg 1996; Tieken-Boon van Ostade 1987, 1994) and historical stylistics (Taavitsainen 1997a, b) have provided us with a number of new perspectives and methodological approaches. While the Older Scots variety must be described as an integral part of the history of the English language, close attention should at the same time be paid both to how contacts with other languages and varieties have shaped it over space, time and milieu, and to the role played by system-internal pressures. In my view, any language variety can be considered functional, that is, serving the communicative purposes of its users, and therefore fully fledged. Some varieties may be internally more uniform than others, and some may resort to the borrowing or recontextualisation of elements taken from another variety or varieties more readily or more extensively than others, but each variety should first be depicted in its own right rather than selectively in terms of how it converges with or diverges from some other variety.

ELECTRONIC TEXT CORPORA

Diachronic databases of Scots

At present the HCOS is the only multi-genre corpus of Older Scots available internationally, but there are numerous ongoing projects (ECOS, CSC, E/HCOS, CESWW; see below), which will significantly expand electronic databases of Scots. The Older Scots Textual Archive, an early collection of digitised Middle Scots texts, established by A. J. Aitken to serve as a resource for DOST, is now part of the Oxford Text Archive (www.ota.ahds.ac.uk). Beside DOST, the major dictionary projects, especially the Scottish National Dictionary (SND), have part of their data in electronic form, and ongoing work is producing electronic versions of the present printed volumes of these dictionaries (www.sldl.org.uk; see also Chapter 4, this volume). Hyperlinks will make dictionaries of this kind very useful as tools for finding data. Moreover, the Scottish Archive Network project is making 3.3 million electronic images of the last wills or testaments of Scots (1500–1875) linked to 475,000 index entries available, thus creating a database of a new kind. The primary sources listed in various studies (Devitt 1989; Caldwell 1974; Romaine 1982; Moessner 1997) can also suggest useful guidelines for data selection.

One of the problems in corpus studies at present is that manuals tend to restrict the information given to lists of texts included as well as technicalities such as conventions used in the mark-up of texts. The users of corpora will often need more information about textual histories, and a critical examination of how the language-external variables have been conceptualised and defined may also be necessary (Meurman-Solin 2001a).

Representativeness

Since the rationale of a corpus, such as its relevance and applicability to the study of specific research questions, is not always defined in sufficient detail by its compiler(s), the user will have to assess its relevance by applying particular criteria. An important question in this assessment is whether a corpus is diatopically representative, that is, whether it contains consistently and coherently selected texts that originate from specified localities that together ensure a virtually comprehensive coverage of a wider geographical area. It is noteworthy that, despite their shared geographical origin, a group of texts will probably be linguistically heterogeneous since linguistic choices in them are also affected by a number of other language-external as well as linguistic conditioning factors. For example, a localised text may not be diatopically representative if its language is strongly influenced by discourse-specific conventions widely shared by any texts belonging to the same genre, irrespective of which geographical area their writers come from. Some linguistic features may also have been borrowed from discourses created in communities foreign to a specific locality. In general, careful linguistic analysis of texts sharing the same place of origin suggests that they can be positioned on a continuum depending on the degree to which their linguistic features converge with or diverge from the common core: that is, the most frequently attested usage in that locality.

The diatopic relevance of findings will be questionable if the data is extracted from non-diplomatic editions of texts. Any degree of normalisation or emendation changes the original text into a second-order construct (Lass 1997: 101): 'emendation is not in fact creative, but destructive; it obliterates part of the record, and substitutes for it an invention of another time, place and culture' (ibid.: 100). Similarly, the expansion of contracted forms without clearly indicating the principles applied in doing so (cf., for instance, *The Prose Works of Sir Gilbert Hay*, vol. 3: xii–xiii, Scottish Text Society, fourth Ser. 21) makes patterns of linguistic variation unrecoverable. The editorial principles should be carefully considered when using corpora based on editions. If such principles are not described in detail in the editions, it is usually necessary to reconstruct them by comparing the original and the edition. A decision can then be made as to whether the edited text can be used for data in the analysis of a specific research topic. While some topics in the fields of lexis and, doubtfully, syntax can perhaps utilise corpora based on editions not checked against manuscript, research questions in the fields of orthography, phonology and morphology can only be examined by extracting data from diplomatic editions or transcriptions of manuscripts.

Variation, including the use of variants interchangeably by the same writer in the same text, is typical of numerous Older Scots texts – the aim of research based on large corpora is to highlight such variation, not to downplay it. The Edinburgh Corpus of Older Scots, 1380–1500 (Institute for Historical Dialectology, University of Edinburgh; Williamson 1992–3, 2000), the Corpus of Scottish Correspondence, 1500–1800 (Research Unit for Variation and Change in English, University of Helsinki; Meurman-Solin 2001c), and the Edinburgh-Helsinki Tagged Corpus of Older Scots (E/HCOS) will contain only texts checked against manuscript. The ECOS aims at both diatopic and diachronic representativeness since its rationale is to serve as a resource for the Linguistic Atlas of Older Scots. In contrast, the HCOS is not diatopically representative as it chiefly focuses on the Central Scots area, with only a few texts originating from the Northern Scots area (first and foremost Aberdeen records). However, the Corpus of Scottish

Correspondence is being compiled giving priority to both time and space as criteria by which representativeness is assessed. Meurman-Solin (2000b) examines the spread of *i*-digraphs in the diatopically relatively representative selection of autograph letters addressed to Mary of Lorraine (*Correspondence of Mary of Lorraine*). This study shows that differences between the various dialect areas can be significant.

A further point of relevance when considering geographical variation is how the 'space' variable relates to what we mean by a text. In the HCOS, for instance, texts such as the *Complaynt of Scotland* contain numerous passages more or less closely translated from French (Meurman-Solin 1993a: 72–4); some texts are compilations written by various writers or a number of scribes (for instance Acts of the Parliaments of Scotland and burgh records), and some (letters) have been dictated to an amanuensis. Features of this kind have to be carefully considered in examining the findings from a diatopic perspective.

A database is diachronically representative when at least in some respects language-externally uniform texts can be positioned on a continuum covering a relatively long time span. In other words, a diachronic database of this kind would allow the study of the evolution of texts sharing the same or similar social function and communicative purposes. Whether such comparability can be achieved is another matter as, for instance, the range of genres may vary considerably over time (Biber et al. 1998: 252; Meurman-Solin 2001a, b; on the evolution of genres, see Nevalainen and Raumolin-Brunberg 1989; Biber and Finegan 1988, 1992; Taavitsainen 1993, 1997; Meurman-Solin 1994, 1995c, 1997d, 1999b). Corpus compilers have usually divided the time span into sub-periods, seventy years in the Helsinki Corpus of Older Scots. However, in the forthcoming corpora of Older Scots no sub-periodisation will be used. Like any periodisation in language history, the one in the HCOS is arbitrary, and even important dates such as those of the Scottish Reformation (1560) and the Union of the Crowns (1603) are clearly not unambiguously reflected in the anglicisation process (Meurman-Solin 1997a, 2000a; Hagan 2002).

Interpreting variation and change over time means considering the extent to which conventionalised discourse features influence the degree of linguistic conservatism of a text. A time-lag in the spread of change may also be due to the social function of a text or genre being restricted to a tightly knit speech community, or rather text community (for instance, legal and administrative documents produced in administratively self-contained localities or regions; Meurman-Solin 1997b, 2000a). However, the maintenance of linguistic features can also be explained with reference to a writer's relatively low degree of geographical or social mobility as compared with those with numerous weak ties with members of other speech communities (Meurman-Solin 1999a, 2000b, 2001c). We would find the early adopters of incoming variants among social aspirers (for more information on social mobility as a conditioning factor in language variation and change, see Nevalainen and Raumolin-Brunberg 1996).

The size of multi-genre diachronic corpora available at present allows the identification of trends in variation and change, and they are useful in pinpointing areas of interest for further research. However, both larger corpora and focused corpora, that is, those tailored to provide quantitatively and qualitatively representative data for more specific purposes, are essential for elaborating arguments and for drawing conclusive evidence. In addition to assessing quantitative and qualitative representativeness, it is necessary to pay attention to the degree of internal heterogeneity in categories (genre, text category, level of formality and so on) defined by language-external criteria (Meurman-Solin 2001a, b). The presentation of data by a specific category, the listing of frequencies and distributions of a linguistic feature by genre, for instance, should be avoided 'where a hypothesis about the relevance of an association or correlation pattern between specific linguistic features and genre has not been formulated' (Meurman-Solin 2001a: 8). Among focused corpora representing Scots, the single-genre Corpus of Scottish Correspondence could be mentioned; other varieties of English can be examined using the Corpus of Early English Medical Writing (Taavitsainen and Pahta 1997) and the Corpus of Early English Correspondence (Nevalainen and Raumolin-Brunberg 1996), for instance (see the ICAME web page for further information on text corpora).

Another feature relevant to assessing the quality of a database is the type of search it allows. The degree of sophistication as regards search tools is chiefly dependent on whether the texts are tagged or not, that is to say whether each item is supplied with information about grammar and lexical morphology. There are no completed databases of Scots that have been lexico-grammatically tagged. However, Keith Williamson at the Institute for Historical Dialectology, University of Edinburgh, has created software for tagging texts in the ECOS, and these programs are now also used for tagging the HCOS, the CSC and the E/ HCOS. A tagged database allows the orthodox application of the variationist approach, as pre-selection or judgement sampling of data is no longer necessary for reasons of research economy or other pragmatic concerns. The time put into tagging is amply compensated by increased efficiency and reliability in analysing the data as well as the availability of more sophisticated tools for the presentation of findings. In variation analysis all variants are given equal status, irrespective of how they have been treated in earlier descriptions of a language variety; item lists created from tagged texts are complete inventories of the variants of a specific linguistic feature occurring in a database (Williamson 1992–3, 2000). Thus earlier descriptions or grammars of the variety do not dictate which are the so-called main variants and which are peripheral. It also becomes possible to reconsider which variants can be claimed to be paradigmatic. The importance of reconsideration can be illustrated by the practice adopted in numerous text-books of depicting a change as the replacement of one form by another. This seems to reflect the general assumption that the 'minor' variants can be put aside as sporadic, irregular or transitional, and therefore marginal, irrespective of the fact that there may be items among them that continued to be used as main variants in some geographical areas or in some other extra-linguistically definable context (Meurman-Solin 2001c, 2002a; for examples, see also the section below on the reconstruction of morpho-syntax).

Language-external variables conditioning language variation and change

Structured electronic corpora differ from compilations of digitised texts as research material in that they contain information about language-external variables related to the texts. Herring et al. (2000: 1) introduce the concept of 'textual parameters', listing as examples 'text type and genre, poeticality, orality, dialect, writer demographics, scribal influence, cultural status, and whether a text is a translation from another language'. From a corpus compiler's perspective, such variables are a useful device for ensuring a desired quality, which, as mentioned above, in the world of corpus linguistics is generally assessed by epithets such as 'representative' and 'balanced'.

However, Herring et al. pertinently point out that '[the] choice of the word 'parameters' is intended to suggest that such factors exercise a partially deter-mining or constraining influence on the choice of linguistic expression within a given text, and moreover that this influence is in principle systematic and predictable, given sufficient understanding of the parameters themselves' (ibid.). I would like to stress the word 'partially' as it is not always possible to conclude that the choice of a specific linguistic feature or the co-occurrence patterns of a number of features are conditioned by a particular language-external variable or set of variables. Thus while a value of the parameter 'dialect' (for example south-east, north-east and so on) may usefully summarise the attested convergence of linguistic preferences in texts originating from a specific geographical area, these texts may also contain features that are foreign to that dialect, occurring exclusively in a restricted set of contexts. Such features may have been introduced as part of conventionalised, perhaps stylistically prestigious expressions such as epistolary formulae. To illustrate this further, the earliest uses of the relative pronoun *who* in Older Scots (Meurman-Solin 2000c) occur in the final formulae in letters: 'as knawis god **quha** mot haue *z*our grace *in* keping e*t*ernalye' (CSC 1543 Elizabeth Keith, Countess of Huntly, NAS SP2/1: 17).[2] The spread of variants of the present participle in -*ing* instead of -*and* (Meurman-Solin 2002a) has been first attested in contexts of a specific kind such as the very frequent collocate *in times coming* in legalese, lexicalised items such as *notwithstanding* or verbs such as *praying* and *beseeking* in letters: 'Maist hum*m*elie **beseking** *z*our grace no^{t}w^{t}standing ony laub*ouris* of o*ur* contray p*artiis* t^t yair be na p*art* th*arof* disponit to yame bot at all the samy*n* \ Remane haill i*n* zo*ur* grace hand*is* q^{lk}*is* doand Is zo*ur* grace hono*ur* & p*r*offett' (CSC [1545?] Lord Methven, SP2/2: 102); 'praying god to conserve zoure grace' (HCOS 1546/7 Adam Otterburn, SP2/2:127). It has also been shown that spelling practices such as -*tht* instead of -*th* are introduced into public documents earlier than texts representing other genres, reflecting a direction of spread from above, that is, from formal texts with a public social function to those written in less formal and private settings (Meurman-Solin 1997b, 2000a). The importance of genre-specific conventions varies because a text may contain a number of different contextual styles, and the constraining influence may be related to properties of discourse rather than genre (on genre and discourse, see *European Journal of English Studies* 2001, Vol. 5, No. 2; Diller and Görlach 2001).

It is also important to bear in mind that since the variables used in structuring text corpora are usually rather loosely defined, the user of a structured corpus will always have to give a more precise definition of or perhaps redefine each variable that is hypothesised to affect or condition the occurrence of a linguistic feature or features selected as a research topic. In addition to specifying how the language-external variables have been conceptualised, it is necessary to assess how independent each of the variables is in the set chosen to structure a corpus. There are varying kinds of interrelatedness or even overlapping that have to be considered in interpreting linguistic findings (Meurman-Solin 2001a). In the HCOS, 'genre' is directly linked with 'level of formality' so that legal documents, including recordings of trial proceedings, and official letters have been classified as formal, and diaries and private letters as informal. There may also be a direct link between 'genre' and 'audience', for example in the case of some handbooks (Alexander Huntar, *A Treatise of Weights, Mets and Measures of Scotland*) and scientific treatises (George Sinclair, *Hydrostaticks*), but this correlation is not always as straightforward as Gilbert Skeyne's treatises, for instance, show. However, we tend to speculate that *Ane breve descriptioun of the pest* (1568) presumably addresses a more professional audience than *Ane breif descriptioun of the qualiteis and effectis of the well of the woman hill besyde abirdene.*

The parameter values supplied by the corpus compiler should be understood to be tentative, especially where no thorough previous research is available to establish specific criteria of classification. To further illustrate the complexity of the issues, the definition of the audience of, for instance, Skeyne's treatises would have to be based on a large-scale comparative study of medical writing in Scotland, England and Europe, including treatises written in other languages. It is also noteworthy that the variable 'sex' has been incorporated in the HCOS even though it is obvious that language use is conditioned by the social construct of gender rather than biological sex (Meurman-Solin 1999a, 2001a, c).

Nor can the variable distinguishing between speech-based texts, scripts and other written texts be directly appealed to as a conditioning factor. In the HCOS, the parameter value 'script' has been used in the genre of sermons, and the value 'speech-based' in the genre of trial proceedings, but a close analysis of a variety of different ways of reconstructing speech, ranging from direct speech, and mixed types, to indirect speech is relevant to discuss how the parameter 'speech-based', for instance, conditions the choice of linguistic features (Biber and Finegan 1992; Kytö, 2000; Meurman-Solin 1993b, 2002a). Herring et al. (2000: 18) point out that:

> Oral features may be present if the text was originally produced in the
> spoken modality and subsequently transcribed, or they may be
> introduced into a text produced in writing, either unconsciously (e.g. as
> a reflex of the writer's spoken language practices) or deliberately (e.g. in
> scripted dialogue).

In the HCOS, the former type would occur in the witness statements in the recordings of trial proceedings and the latter in the letters of less stylistically competent writers or texts written in dialogue form (such as William Lamb's *Ane Resonyng of ane Scottis and Inglis Merchand Betuix Rowand and Lionis*, 1550). As punctuation is often changed in editions, syntactic units reflecting spoken discourse are difficult to identify without examining the manuscripts (for an example, see Meurman-Solin 2001a: 20–2).

As regards the 'genre' variable it is useful to apply concepts similar to those developed for describing speech communities (Milroy 1992; Chambers 1995) to types of discourse communities (Meurman-Solin 2001a, b). Some discourse communities are tightly knit professional coalitions whose members share expectations related to an exclusive insider practice of writing, while some others are more loosely constructed, with members who perhaps borrow only certain features, or apply the practices less consistently. Aside from the density and multiplexity of their ties with a discourse community or communities, the linguistic and stylistic competence of writers significantly influences how faithfully they succeed in writing in a certain generic tradition (on heterogeneity as regards linguistic and stylistic performance in letters, see Meurman-Solin 2001c). A further important point is that genre models have spread unevenly across Scotland both geographically and socially. A more restricted range of genres may be relevant and functional in certain areas (consider the scarcity of genres in culturally homogeneous localities) or among certain writers (for example, sixteenth-century women, who chiefly benefited from their literacy in keeping household accounts and in their correspondence with relatives).

To sum up: firstly, genre categories in electronic corpora such as the HCOS are based on the co-application of different criteria, that is to say, texts are grouped by topic (for instance, travelogues and autobiographies), or by function (for instance, handbooks and sermons), or a combination of the two (for instance, educational treatises) (Meurman-Solin 2001b). Herring et al. call genre a multiple textual parameter (2000: 2). Other multiple variables in the HCOS are 'prototypical text category', [the author's] 'age' and 'social rank', 'description of audience', 'relationship to spoken language' and 'participant relationship'. Variables may also be binary (in the HCOS, 'verse' and 'prose', 'interactive' and 'non-interactive', the latter marked by x). In the present version of the corpus, the 'dialect' variable has also been used as a binary parameter to distinguish between Central Scots and Northern Scots texts, but, as pointed out earlier, a corpus in which data has not been checked against manuscript cannot be used as a tool in historical dialectology. In a number of variables the value x has been used in cases where information is not available to allow a more specific value (for instance, 'setting': formal, informal, x; 'description of audience': professional, non-professional, x). Herring et al. (2000: 2) give 'degree of scribal influence' and 'degree of contact with other languages' as examples of scalar variables. Even though the variables and reference points provided by the parameter values illustrated above reflect a tendency to compartmentalise, this should perhaps be seen as a technical failure to introduce a system in electronic corpora that would successfully convey the scalar nature of language-external variables. Many corpus compilers are fully aware of the problems, Nevalainen and Raumolin-Brunberg, for instance, stressing that the categorisation of texts into genres 'involves a scalar notion of genrehood with some nearly invariant generic structures at one end (letters, statutes) and some quite loosely structured ones at the other (book-length treatises on different topics)' (1989: 95; see also *European Journal of English Studies* (2001), Vol. 5, No. 2). The user of corpora will have to position carefully an individual text on the continuum only partially described by values ascribed to a variable. Moreover, while some texts can be given the value 'translation' (in the HCOS the *Mar Lodge Boece*, the *Porteous of Noblenes*), others contain only some passages that are more or less direct translations (for instance, the *Complaynt of Scotland*). Some information about the texts in the HCOS has been provided in Meurman-Solin (1993a: 86–124), but further study is usually necessary as well.

Secondly, the more precisely definable variables such as 'time' and 'space' can be given a more central role in compiling a database (for instance, the ECOS), or in assessing the validity of a specific database for the analysis of a specific research topic (Williamson 2002). Describing the advantages of their textual parameters approach, Herring et al. (2000: 4) point out that:

> when the conditioning parameters are themselves well understood, the analyst may abstract away from their influence in order to focus on structural (phonological, morphosyntactic, etc.) phenomena, and by comparing data subsets within a language, arrive at more nuanced generalisations about such structures than would otherwise be possible.

The strength of a conditioning factor can be weighed by using statistical tools (Butler 1985; Woods 1986; Biber 1988, 1995; Meurman-Solin 1994, 1997d, 1999b; Taavitsainen 1993; Kytö 2000).

RECONSTRUCTION OF MORPHO-SYNTAX

In addition to surveys of the grammar of Older Scots of various dates (Murray 1873; Smith 1902; King 1997; Moessner 1997), a number of valuable studies focusing on specific texts can be consulted (for example, text editions such as Kuipers 1964 and van Buuren-Venenbos 1982). Studies analysing specific linguistic features in a corpus of texts have examined the relative pronouns and the verb phrase (the subject-verb rule, *do*-periphrasis and the progressive, for instance) (Caldwell 1974; Romaine 1982; Devitt 1989; Meurman-Solin 1992, 1993b, 1997b, 2000c, 2002a; Montgomery 1994 and Dons and Moessner 1999). See also Aitken 1991.

Presentation of data

The sample size in the HCOS varies from short complete texts to relatively large samples such as those extracted from the Acts of Parliament. Thus *Vertewis of the Mess* has only c.800 words of running text and Skene of Hallyard's *Of husbandrie* c.1,600, whereas the sample from the Acts of Parliament dating from the period 1570–1640 is c.50,000 words. In the presentation of findings, normalised frequencies should be given, often together with absolute numbers (the raw frequencies) and percentages (Biber 1988: 14, 75–8). Information about the non-normalised frequencies is useful as these figures allow assessment of the general frequency of a feature and normalised frequencies enable comparison between texts of varying length, while percentages facilitate the conceptualisation of relative frequencies. However, normalisation per 1,000 words of running text, for instance, can be misleading if the sample is small. Lack of uniformity in categories such as genre justifies the presentation of data per text as well as category (Meurman-Solin 1994). The diffusion of specific variants takes place at a varying rate in different texts (Devitt 1989; Meurman-Solin 1997a, 2000a), and the presentation of findings per sub-period can only be justified if the general trend attested over a long time-span is also discussed, providing more detailed information about how individual texts deviate from one another. Even though long-term developments may seem unidirectional, as is often illustrated by anglicisation processes, a closer analysis of individual texts may reveal a more complex pattern of spread (for examples, see the following section; see also Meurman-Solin 2000c and 2002a). As regards the conventions used in the mark-up of the HCOS (e.g. +t for a thorn in the edition), a useful source of information is the manual to the Helsinki Corpus of English Texts (Kytö 1996 and www.hd.uib.no/corpora.html).

The variationist approach and the study of morpho-syntax

In general, the degree of orthographic variation in non-diplomatic editions tends to be lower than that in manuscripts (see the comparison of the HCOS and the E/HCOS below). For example, it has generally been considered acceptable to replace the graph *y* by *i* for the vowel /i(:)/ or to substitute modern equivalents for the often interchangeable graphs of *v* and *u*. Despite the streamlining effect of some questionable editorial principles applied in a number of texts in the HCOS, the identification of all the relevant variants of a specific feature can be a relatively laborious task. Further problems are caused by the editors' disparate practices as regards the expansion of contracted forms. In the HCOS, contracted forms have not been expanded where this is also the practice in the text editions; thus, in the Acts of Parliament, variants such as *p ~ nce*, *p ~ liame ~ t*, *c ~ c ~ ni ~ g* and *s ~ ve* have been used instead of *presence, parliament, concerning* and *serve*). To illustrate the degree of variation in the E/HCOS corpus, where texts have been checked against manuscript, variants of *afore* as adverb, conjunction and preposition can be listed: *affoir, affor, afoir, afor, afore, afoyr, effor* and *effor ~*. The result of the search for these variants provides information about the word *afore* occurring exclusively in Bellenden's translation of Livy (1533) and in letters dating from 1543–57 (cf. *before* attested in contemporary Acts of Parliament, 1526–43, and letters as well as in numerous later texts (see Table 8.2)).

The search for all the variants of a specific item varies from quite demanding tasks, such as numerous features related to the structure of the verb phrase, to the recording of variation where a prevailing form is replaced in later texts by another form, both having relatively easily identifiable variants. The latter task can be illustrated by the subordinator of time *after*, a substitute of the variant *efter* typical of earlier texts. The variants *efter(e)*, *eftir(e)*, *eftir ~*, *eftyr*, *eftyir*, *effter*, *efftir*, *eft ~*; *after, aftir, affter* have been attested in the HCOS. Developments over time can be illustrated by Table 8.1:

Table 8.1 Percentages of the variants of *efter* and *after* as subordinators of time in the HCOS

Period	efter	%	after	%	Total
1450–1500	15	100	—		15
1500–1570	47	96	2	4	49
1570–1640	60	71	25	29	85
1640–1700	6	5	114	95	120
Total	128	48	141	52	269

As Table 8.1 illustrates, variants of *efter* are almost exclusively used in the first two sub-periods. After a transition period reflecting a relatively slow rate of change (cf. Meurman-Solin 1997a: Figures 1.1–1.4), *after* is shown to have become the prevailing variant. This is confirmed by the E/HCOS corpus based on manuscripts, only two instances of the variant *after* having been attested in pre-1650 texts.

Earlier descriptions of the Scots language, dictionaries in particular, provide indispensable tools for searching the HCOS for relevant variants of a specific linguistic feature but the data cannot be restricted to such pre-selected items; rather, a careful analysis of the alphabetically ordered item list provided by the WordCruncher search engine is always necessary, either by examining the whole corpus (HSCOTS in the bookshelf), or each sub-period (HSC0, HSC1, HSC2, HSC3) separately.[3] The identification of all the variants of a specific item is facilitated by knowledge of orthographic and phonological variation in Older Scots (Aitken 1971, 1977, 2002; Macafee in this volume; Kniezsa 1997; Johnston 1997; see also Meurman-Solin 1999a, 2001c), and by information about editorial practices (usually commented on only very briefly if at all in many of the earlier editions).[4] In an untagged corpus, the process of selecting items relevant to the study of a specific item or a string of items usually also requires analysis of high-frequency items in contexts of varying lengths provided by WordCruncher. Consider, for instance, the task of distinguishing between uses of *and* and *or* as co-ordinating conjunctions and those where *and*, 'if', introduces an adverbial clause of condition, or *or*, 'before', an adverbial clause of time:

> Alssua and ('if') the office of knychthede / yat sa mekle is lufit and
> prisit and honourit / war' till derub / and destroy the pore folk / and all
> sik peaceable personis / and till dissaue wedowis / yat has na defence
> bot god and the office of knychthede / And till mysgouerne jn thair'
> gudis and heritagis and dissaue the faderles and moderles barnis / And
> ('if') all thing yat war' falsate barate wikkitnes and trechery war'
> poyntis of the said office / And ('if') the office war' alsmekle honourit
> for euill dedis / and wickit lyfing / as jt is now for gude dedis /- Thare
> suld ma press' to tak the said ordre / and office / na thare dois now /.
> (HCOS 1456 G. Hay: 21)

> Item mair iiij pundis till giue for iiij pair of schoune, quhilk I gait or
> ('before') ever Vattie Scot furnishit me at your avine command. (HCOS
> 1540 Patrick Waus: 2)

The nature of the selection process can also be illustrated by the occurrences of *its*, which, apart from being the possessive form of *it*, is sometimes the contracted variant of *it is* (for example, Sir John Lauder's *Journals*) (cf. *thers* or *theirs* for *there is* in the HCOS).

In the study of numerous features of Older Scots grammar and lexis it is necessary to pay attention to transitional variants such as *quich* and *quisch*, 'which' (see below), and hypercorrect variants such as the type *publict* (Meurman-Solin 1997b) or *resing*, 'raisin', and *metting*, 'mitten' (Meurman-Solin 2002a). A macro-level presentation of data per sub-period (Table 8.1) or genre (Table 8.4), for instance, can usefully provide information about diachronic developments, but findings in a quantitative analysis of this kind must be complemented by a discussion based on a detailed linguistic analysis of individual texts. Besides providing information about degree of deviation between texts representing a time period, a genre or some other variable used to group texts, such an analysis also allows us to examine the role of transitional variants. Rather than *quhilk* being replaced by *which*, both of these having a number of orthographic and/or phonological variants, an interesting and relatively long period of transition is reflected in the use of the following variants in some of the sixteenth- and seventeenth-century texts in the HCOS: *quhelk, qwehlk, qwhelkis, qwelk(es)* (1542–60 Corr. ML); *quich(e), quhich(e), q^{ch}* (1542–60 Corr. ML, 1562/a 1578 Wishart's trial, 1598 James VI, *Basilicon Doron*, 1625 Earl of Haddington, Lord Binning, 1629 James Law, 1631–2 Alexander Leslie, 1678 Stirling records, 1650 Spalding, 1681–5 Acts of Parliament); *quilk* and *quisch* (1613–29 Juliana Ker, Lady Binning); *whilk, whilks* (1571 Fergusson's sermon, 1600–10 James Melville of Kilrenny, 1638 Row's sermon, 1665–76 Lauder's *Journals*, a 1669 Skene of Hallyard's *Of husbandry*, 1670 Aberdeen records, 1682 Donald McDonald of Moydart) (see also Devitt 1989: 45). The letters in the CSC allow us to examine processes of change of the following kind: in his early letters to his Countess and in two later letters, Alexander, sixth Earl of Eglinton, exclusively uses the variant *quhilk* (contracted to *qlk*, 1642, 1644); however, in other letters dating from the 1640s he chooses *whilk*, and in even later letters (1648, 1653, 1658, 1658) *which* (for further examples, see Meurman-Solin 2001c). The MS-based E/HCOS has the following variants *quhilk, quhylk, quilk, qlk, q^{lk}, quhilk, quhlk, qwelk, qwhilk, qvilk; quhiche; vhilk; which, whitch, wich* and *wiche*.

A search of word-final items allows the study of present participles ending in *-and* (Dons and Moessner 1999). It is also possible to create files by combining items that occur at varying distances in a text so that, for instance, the occurrence of BE + *-and* or *-ing* or their variants can be searched for to find all the instances of the progressive in the corpus (Meurman-Solin 2002a). This feature is also useful in the study of collocates in the texts of the HCOS (Dossena 2001b).

An interesting case is variation reflected in the formation of present and past participles and the verbal noun and gerund (Meurman-Solin 2002a). Beside the frequent variants such as *failzeand or failzeing* (DOST), the variant *failyene* has been attested (other present participles in *-in(e), -yn(e), -en(e)* in the Helsinki corpora of Older Scots include *mendin, seine, wreten* and *walken*, 'mending', 'seeing', 'writing' and 'walking'). In this context, it is, however, important to notice that similar forms also occur as variants of the verbal noun and gerund (*doine*, *fencin* and *reyeddin*, 'doing', 'fencing' and 'riding'), and also as a past participle form *be vphalding*, 'be held up'.

In the E/HCOS ninety-two per cent of the forms of the verbal noun (533 occurrences) end in *-ing* or *-yng*. With the exception of sporadic instances in the Acts of Parliament (1525–6; three occurrences) and the *Complaynt of Scotland* (one occurrence), the variants in *-en*, *-in(e)* and *-yn(e)* (eight per cent; forty-five occurrences) have been exclusively attested in letters. In this corpus, the variants of the past participle representing the present-day English type *given*, *taken* and so on end in *-en*, *-in*, *-ine*, *-yn*, *-yne*, *-n* and *-ne* (for example, *reden*, 'ridden', *commen*, 'come', *schauin/schewin*, 'shown', *vrytine*, 'written', *knawyn*, 'known', *gyffyne*, 'given', *mistaekn*, 'mistaken' and *gotne*, 'gotten'), but, interestingly, there are also variants of the past participle in *-ing*, *-inge*, *-yng* and *-ynge* (*cumynge*, *speking*, *halding*, *geving*, *ryd(d)yng*, *gottyng*, *wrytinge* and so on; 'he is cumit and stollyng yis benefice', 1551 John Hamilton, archbishop of St. Andrews, SP2/3: 239; 'ye nixt parliament to be begunnyng and haldin at Edinburghe', 1525 Acts of Parliament, NAS PA2/8: f22v). The past participle forms of the verb *come* in the E/HCOS further illustrate the great degree of variation: *com*, *come*, *cum*, *cum*, *cume*, *cwme*, *cowm*, *coum*, *cowme* (forty-seven percent); *cumin*, *cumin*, *commen*, *cummin*, *cummyn* (thirty-one per cent); *cumynge* (two per cent); and *comit*, *cumit*, *cumit*, *cumit*, and *coumid* (twenty per cent). In this context, a further finding based on the E/HCOS can be commented on. The use of *be* instead of *have* as the auxiliary in compound tenses (for example, 'I fear it **is** not **come** to your hands yett', 1612 Anna Livingston, GD3/5/33) occurs with a wide range of verbs of motion (*come*, *go*, *pass*, *(de)part*, *ride*, *fall*, *ascend*, *descend*, *arrive*, *return*, *flee*, *cross*, *enter*) in eighty-nine per cent of the occurrences; among the rest of the examples the frequency of *be become*, 'have become', is particularly interesting ('my brethir **ar becum** onmerciful tirrans touart me', *Complaynt of Scotland*, f100v).

As I have concluded elsewhere, '[the] study of correlation patterns between form and function in varieties of English can shed light on whether variants previously marginalised as irregular or sporadic may be viewed as candidates for paradigmatic status in the grammar of a specific regional or local variety'. Thus in idiolectal grammars, instead of being used interchangeably, the variants of the present participle have been attested as having specialised distributions (Meurman-Solin 2001c).

Even in an at present relatively small manuscript-based corpus, it has been possible to identify some patterns in the distributions of the rich variety of forms that Older Scots pronouns have. For instance, while the *Complaynt of Scotland* exclusively has *sche*, 'she', contemporary texts use *scho*, *shew* and *schow*. The prevalence of *thae* (variants *tha*, *thai*, *þa*, *þai*, *þaj* and *þay*), instead of *those*, and of *thir* (variants *thyr*, *ther*, *ȝir*, *yer*), rather than *these*, in the E/HCOS confirms the finding based on the HCOS, in which the increase in *these* and *those* has been attested in post-1570 texts.

To summarise some areas of special interest that have been identified in the various preliminary studies on Older Scots grammar, the following observations can be made. Despite some evidence of dialect area as a conditioning factor (see Meurman-Solin 1997c, 1999a, 2000b, c, 2001c), a quantitatively and qualitatively valid diatopic description will become a feasible exercise only when the Edinburgh Corpus of Older Scots is available. On the basis of the restricted amount of data at present available in the CSC, the hypothesis of geographically conditioned variation has been shown to be less significant than language use that can be related to social, cultural and economic factors. This is particularly obvious when examining how women's socio-economic status influences their language (Meurman-Solin 2001c). Only on a very general level has it been possible to record that anglicising trends spread more rapidly in Acts of Parliament than in burgh records. A comprehensive account of regional and local variation in legal documents will be given in the forthcoming Linguistic Atlas of Older Scots.

It is discourse-specific factors that significantly influence the introduction and spread of *who*, so that the earliest uses have been attested in formulaic expressions in letters (see example on p. 178). The spread of *who* and variants in Older Scots illustrates how the macro-level semantic category of modality correlates with type of reference signal in various types of discourse. The earlier use of *who* with generic reference ('whoever', 'anybody who') prevailing in legalese, for instance, is in negative correlation with its use to refer to a specific antecedent – mostly animate and positioned either adjacently or otherwise. In the latter case *who* can function as subject, prepositional complement and so on in an independent proposition instead of introducing a modifier clause. This use has typically been attested in narrative discourse strategies in histories, diaries and witness statements in the HCOS (Meurman-Solin 2000c). The following examples illustrate the developments over time:

> ITEM ane ~ t ~ rede fische it is ordanyt Þᵗ **quha** sa beis c ~ uickit of slaucht ~ of rede fische in tyme forbodyn be Þe lawe Þe doar and he Þᵗ bidd ~ it be done sall pay x l ~ i for Þe vnlawe but remissione (HCOS 1457 Acts of Parliament: 51.C2)
>
> *Item.* He affirmit, That in Setoun, my Lord Bothwell callit on him, and sayd, 'Quhat thought you quhen thou saw him blowen in the ayre?' **Quho** answerit, 'Alas! my lord, quhy speak ye that? For quhen ever I heare sic a thing, the wordes wound me to death, as they ought to do you!' (HCOS 1567 Criminal Trials: 500)

Research into the spread of *who* shows that it is

necessary to distinguish between both the relative frequencies of specific linguistic features per genre and the occurrence of linguistic features motivated by type of discourse. In diachronic studies, the analysis of frequencies of occurrence with reference to discoursal properties also provides evidence of a pattern of spread that may be essentially different from that exclusively based on changing frequencies over time and space. (Meurman-Solin 2001a: 18)

Complex sentences

In the study of subordinators of time in Older Scots, various methodological approaches in the search for the data prove useful (Meurman-Solin 2002b). Since the untagged HCOS does not allow a distinction, for instance, between *when* used as an interrogative and as a subordinator of time, or between *while* as a noun and a subordinator, a WordCruncher View List containing all instances was examined to create files of relevant items (Selected List files) for further analysis, sometimes also introducing a further sub-classification. For example, the list of all items for Older Scots *quhil(l)* and *quhile* in the HCOS consists of the following variants: *qll, quheil, quheill, quhil, quhile, quhill, quhyl, quhyle, quhyll, qwil, qwl, qwyl, q^{ll}, wheyll, whil, while, whill, whille, whyle, whyll* (cf. the variants of the subordinator *quhill*, 'up to the time when', in the E/HCOS: *qll, q^{ll}, quhil, quhill, quhyll, whill*). When used as a subordinator, *quhill* is sometimes followed by *as* or *that*.

When all the subordinators have been selected, a wider linguistic context may be necessary to group them according to whether they introduce a subordinate clause where the time reference in the subordinate clause is 'up to a point of time when' or indicates the ultimate result or outcome of continued action expressed by the principal clause (posteriority; cf. *till* and *until*) or whether the subordinate and matrix clause situations overlap (cf. *while*, 'during the time that' and so on). In WordCruncher the length of the preceding and following context needed for such an analysis can be specified. The data can then be further classified by semantic criteria, and the occurrences of each subordinator compared with the semantically closely related ones in Older Scots (*till, until* and *unto*, for instance). In my view, choosing the variationist approach requires examination of all the realisations of a semantic role. Thus, in this specific case of subordinators of time, the identification of all the members of a variational paradigm can most reliably be achieved in terms of major semantic roles such as posteriority and anteriority, so that all the conjunctions indicating that the main clause situation occurs at a time before or after the subordinate clause situation will be discussed rather than a selected subset of such conjunctions (cf. Häcker 1999).

Table 8.2 illustrates the distributions given in absolute numbers and percentages of four semantically associated subordinating conjunctions of time: *afore, before, ere* and *or*, including all their variants in the HCOS. To highlight the significant differences between texts, the data is given per each text with occurrences of these subordinators. It is also noteworthy that some texts are shown not to use any of them; further study is then necessary to find out whether this can be explained by discoursal properties that influence the degree to which the semantic role of posteriority is present in texts or perhaps by the use of some other – non-conjunctival – realisations of this role in them (cf. Meurman-Solin 2002b).

Table 8.2 Relative frequencies and percentages of the subordinators *afore*, *before*, *ere* and *or* and their distributions in individual texts in the HCOS. N = number of texts.

(a) Period: 1450–1500

Text	*before*	%	*or*	%	Total
Acts of Parliament	–		2	100	2
Peebles records			1	100	1
Craft of Deyng			1	100	1
G. Hay	1	9	10	91	11
Dicta Salomonis	–		3	100	3
Total	1	6	17	94	18

Mean frequencies (N = 11) *before* 0.01, *or* 0.18

(b) Period: 1500–1570

Text	*before*	%	*afore*	%	*or*	%	Total
Acts of Parliament	1	100					1
Edinburgh records					1	100	1
Peebles records			1	20	4	80	5
Aberdeen records					2	100	2
Fife Sheriff Ct. Bk.					2	100	2
St. Andrews Kirk S.					1	100	1
Criminal Trials	3	60			2	40	5
Complaynt of Sc.					3	100	3
Lamb, *Resonyng*					1	100	1
Kennedy, Tracts	1	11	7	78	1	11	9
Boece, history					6	100	6
Private letters					2	100	2
Official letters					10	100	10
Bible	2	100					2
Total	7	14	8	16	35	70	50

Mean frequencies (N = 17) *before* 0.03, *afore* 0.04, *or* 0.17

(c) Period: 1570–1640

Text	before	%	or	%	ere	%	Total
Acts of Parliament	10	100					10
Aberdeen records			1	100			1
Huntar	3	100					3
Skeyne, *Pest*	1	100					1
Basilicon Doron	9	90	1	10			10
Bruce, sermon	2	100					2
Row, sermon					1	100	1
St. Andrews Kirk.S.	5	71	2	29			7
Criminal Trials	1	50	1	50			2
Roy trial	1	100					1
Fowler	1	100					1
James VI, *Tobacco*	1	100					1
Birnie					1	100	1
Lesley, history	2	67	1	33			3
Pitscottie, history			4	100			4
Lithgow, travelogue	2	50			2	50	4
Waus, diary	1	50	1	50			2
Melville, diary	1	33	2	67			3
Birrel, diary	3	75	1	25			4
Johnston, diary	4	100					4
Lesley, diary	2	67	1	33			3
Melville, biography			2	100			2
Private letters	5	83	1	17			6
Official letters	2	100					2
Total	56	72	18	23	4	5	78

Mean frequencies (N = 30) *before* 0.19, *or* 0.06, *ere* 0.01

(d) Period: 1640–1700

Text	before	%	or	%	ere	%	Total
Acts of Parliament	7	100					7
Stirling records	2	100					2
Aberdeen records	1	100					1
Skene, handbook	1	100					1
Reid, handbook	8	73			3	27	11
Sinclair, science	9	100					9

(d) Period: 1640–1700—*cont'd*

Text	*before*	%	or	%	ere	%	Total
Sinclair, narrative	6	75			2	25	8
Welsh, sermon	2	100					2
Standsfield trial	6	86			1	14	7
Presbyterian Eloq.	1	100					1
Apology for Clergy	2	100					2
Spalding, history	1	100					1
Prince of Tartaria	1	50			1	50	2
Lauder, *Journals*			3	75	1	25	4
Lamont, diary	1	100					1
A. Brodie					1	100	1
J. Brodie					1	100	1
A. Hay, diary	1	100					1
Somerville, biography	4	100					4
Turner, biography	4	100					4
Private letters	19	95	1	5			20
Official letters	3	75	1	25			4
Total	79	84	5	5	10	11	94

Mean frequencies (N = 23) *before* 0.32, *or* 0.02, *ere* 0.04

Bearing in mind that the general frequency of features of this kind is relatively low in individual texts, the findings in Table 8.2 can be summarised as follows. In the 1450–1500 period there are no occurrences of these subordinators in fifty-five per cent of the texts, and two of them, *afore* and *ere*, have not been recorded at all. The subordinator *or* is chosen in ninety-four per cent of the total. There is co-variation only in Hay (with *or* prevailing). The general frequency of these subordinators remains low in the 1500–1570 period, there being no occurrences in twenty-four per cent of the total of seventeen texts. While *or* continues to dominate (70 per cent), interesting co-variation patterns have been attested in Peebles records (*or* eighty per cent), Criminal Trials (*before* sixty per cent) and Kennedy's Eucharistic Tracts (*afore* seventy-eight per cent). There are no examples of *ere*. In the 1570–1640 period the general frequency of these subordinators does not change significantly (no occurrences in twenty per cent of the texts). However, a dramatic change has been recorded in the relative frequencies of *before* and *or*: an increase from fourteen to seventy-two per cent and a decrease from seventy to twenty-three per cent respectively. There are no examples of *afore*. In the last sub-period their general frequency has increased from 0.26 to 0.38 (the frequency of *before* has somewhat increased, and there is only one text where there are no occurrences of any of them). There are no instances of *afore*, while *or* occurs only in Lauder's *Journals* and two letters, and *ere* in two diaries, two travelogues, a handbook, a witchcraft narrative and a trial. Co-variation patterns have been attested in ten texts altogether. *Before* and *ere* co-vary in four texts, and *or* and *ere* in Lauder, letter writers in this period using *before* and *or*. There are no instances of *afore*. The subordinator *afore* is also rare in the E/HCOS corpus (one instance).

As discussed in Meurman-Solin (2002b), beside items categorised as conjunctions in present-day Scots, a wider range of items functioning as temporal links should be looked at. For example, it would be useful to investigate items that articulate the sense 'up to a point of time that', such as *to*, *unto*, *unto the time (that)*, *quhill þe tyme (at)*, *quhil on to the tyme that*, *until the/such tyme (that/as)* and *till such(e) tyme as*, *ay (and) quhil*, *quhil(l)/while*, *till* and *until*. Some clause combining devices in older Scots have been discussed in Meurman – Solin (forthcoming c) from a typological perspective.

ON THE STUDY OF LEXIS

As pointed out above, the completion of DOST is by far the most important achievement in the study of Older Scots in recent years. It may therefore be justifiable to restrict the focus and, within the very limited scope of this outline, only point out some features of the corpus-based study of lexis. Apart from valuable surveys on the history of lexis in English such as Nevalainen (1999), Macafee (1997a) provides good introductory reading on Scots. The corpora available at present are not necessarily sufficiently large for the study of individual lexical items, but there are high-frequency items and some other relatively frequent items that can be examined, especially if grouped together as members of a specific semantic category (for instance, modal adjectives or adverbs in Meurman-Solin 1995c, 1997d, 1999b; Dossena 2001b), or by some other criterion such as origin (Meurman-Solin 1989). A corpus, unlike a dictionary source, often allows the identification of uneven distributions of lexical items across genres (for example, nine of the eleven examples of *recommendation* in the HCOS occur in initial formulae in letters).

Lexis can be studied from several different perspectives. To mention only a few examples, in the thesaurus framework we are interested in features such as legal terminology, in the discourse-pragmatic approach terms of address, interjections, hedging devices or modality or epistolary formulae and so on (Dossena 2001b; see also Nevala 1998, forthcoming), and in the onomastic approach in personal names and place-names. In the discourse-stylistic approach we can examine lexical choices in texts representing various levels of formality, features of argumentative discourse or stylistically marked borrowings (Dossena 2001c, forthcoming b,

Meurman-Solin 1989). A further area of study is scotticisms (Dossena forth-coming a).

The study of lexical morphology will be facilitated by the ECOS and E/HCOS corpora, where prefixes, suffixes and compounds have been tagged. In the texts of the preliminary version of the latter, the great degree of variation typical of Older Scots has again been attested. The variants of the suffix -*ous* are as follows: -*es*, -*is*, -*iss*, -*os*, -*ous*, -*ouse*, -*ouss*, -*ous*, -*us* , -us, -*use*, -*uss*, and -*yse*. Table 8.3 gives information about adjectives with the suffix -*ous* and its variants in the HCOS. The two main groups of variants consist of the type *gracious, glorious* and so on and the type *ambitius, dolorus* and so on, the latter being particularly frequent in texts such as the *Complaynt of Scotland*.

Table 8.3 Mean frequencies and distributions of the adjectival suffix -*ous* in the HCOS

Period	-*ous*	/1,000	-*us*	/1,000	Other	/1,000	Total	/1,000
1450–1500	135	1.4	32	0.3	2	0.02	169	1.8
1500–1570	109	0.5	49	0.2	37	0.2	195	1.0
1570–1640	461	1.5	66	0.2	2	0.01	529	1.7
1640–1700	382	1.5	2	0.01	-		384	1.6
Total	1087	1.3	149	0.2	41	0.05	1277	1.5

Considering individual texts in the period 1450–1500, the mean frequency per 1,000 words varies from 3.5 in Hay's prose works and 4.5 in *Porteous of Noblenes* to 0.4 in the Acts of Parliament. Considerable standard deviation has also been attested in the following periods: 1500–70 from 3.3 (Boece's history) to 0.1 (Peebles records), 1570–1640 from 10.1 (Fowler's *Answer to Hamilton*) to 0.2 (St Andrews Kirk Sessions and Lesley's diary) and 1640–1700 from six (*Prince of Tartaria*) to 0.2 (Welsh's sermon). On the basis of information provided in Table 8.4, it is possible to argue that the use of adjectives of this type may be conditioned by genre.

Numerous adjectives in -*ous* are evaluative, and their high frequency in argumentative discourse such as pamphlets and in narratives recording experiences and observations from the perspective of subjective evaluation such as travelogues and biographies can be related to earlier research on correlation patterns between attitudinal expressions and genre and type of discourse (Meurman-Solin 1999b).

Table 8.4 Adjectives with the suffix -*ous* in the various genres in the HCOS. N = number of texts.

Period 1450–1500

Genre	-*ous*	/1,000
Acts	12	0.4
instruction	157	3.1
Total (N = 10)	169	1.8

Period 1500–1570

Genre	-*ous*	/1,000
Acts	16	0.5
local record	12	0.3
instruction	10	1.0
trial	9	0.4
pamphlet	44	1.5
history	72	3.3
official letter	32	0.9
Total	195	1.0

Period 1570–1640

Genre	-*ous*	/1,000
Acts	51	1.0
local record	10	0.5
handbook	2	0.3
science	40	4.5
instruction	61	3.1
sermon	33	2.1
trial	19	0.6
pamphlet	119	5.6
history	31	1.0
travelogue	78	5.6
diary	42	0.9
biography	8	0.9
private letter	6	0.4
official letter	29	2.6
Total	529	1.7

Period 1640–1700

Genre	-ous	/1,000
Acts	43	1.1
local record	33	1.2
handbook	17	1.4
science	12	0.8
narrative	9	1.1
sermon	1	0.2
trial	19	2.3
pamphlet	71	8.4
history	26	1.7
travelogue	48	3.7
diary	32	0.7
biography	39	2.6
private letter	17	0.9
official letter	17	2.3
Total	384	1.6

TOWARDS RECONSTRUCTING SCOTS

The perspective frequently adopted in earlier research of the so-called regional varieties such as Scots tends to be biased in three different ways. There is a tendency to objectify or reify regional varieties assuming they form relatively homogeneous – perhaps even relatively self-contained – entities or systems (Milroy 1999: 17; cf. also Benson 2001: 21); a tendency to historicise stressing socio-political rather than linguistic factors as legitimising the naming and describing of regional varieties in a certain way (Milroy 1999: 28); and a tendency to hierarchicise leading to the analysis of a regional variety exclusively in rerference to a standardised variety. In my view, these three tendencies may sometimes have negatively influenced the approach to the study of Scots (Meurman-Solin forthcoming c). The negative consequences of reification, historicisation and hierarchicisation can be avoided by significantly improving both the quantity and quality of text corpora containing digitised and preferably tagged data produced by as wide a range of text and discourse communities as possible.

In recent years there has been a notable intensification in efforts to map the languages of Scotland and their history by compiling diachronically, diatopically and diastratically representative electronic databases. This process has been accompanied by the development of software tailored for searching even in language varieties where a great degree of spelling variation requires the use of quite sophisticated tools and methods such as Older Scots. The continuing descriptive work based on these databases and tools will allow us to produce a comprehensive account of Older Scots grammar and lexis.

NOTES

1. Kroch et al. (2000, as summarised by Herring et al. 2000: 22) suggest that the difference in the way the northern and southern dialects of Middle English implemented the verb-second (V2) constraint common to the Germanic languages 'was a syntactic consequence of contact-induced simplification in the verbal agreement paradigm of the northern dialect'.
2. NAS: National Archives of Scotland. In the examples, the expansion of a contracted form is given in italics.
3. In the ICAME corpus collection, both the HCOS and the Helsinki Corpus of English Texts are provided with the WordCruncher search engine.
4. Notice that a number of the texts in the HCOS are based on early prints (Meurman-Solin 1993: 137–48). Instead of reflecting the linguistic preferences of their writers, the language in these may have been influenced by the practices adopted by their printers.

CHAPTER 9

The Language of Older Scots Poetry

Jeremy J. Smith

THE LANGUAGE POETS FIND

It is sometimes claimed by the linguistically innocent and nationally prejudiced that particular languages have particular virtues or vices, correlating with certain perceived virtues and vices in national character. French, we are often told, is a logical language, and post-structuralist literary theorists have been known to claim that they cannot express themselves coherently in lesser tongues; Italian and Spanish are naturally musical, perfectly designed for the opera, or for guitar-accompaniment; Gaelic is a poetic, dreamy language; German is an earthy language with a fiddly, philosophical side indicated by its relegation of verbs to the end of its subordinate clauses; Russian is a soulful language, ideal for use in cherry orchards; true mastery of Chinese is impossible for the foreigner who does not wish to become Chinese; Zulu has 'natural rhythm'; and the evildoers in Hollywood films, these days, of course habitually speak Southern British English.

What kind of views are taken of Scots? Here is a selection: Glaswegian Scots has the 'ugliest accent imaginable' – the opinion of an anonymous university lecturer, quoted in R. K. S. Macaulay's classic sociolinguistic survey from the 1970s (Macaulay 1977: 94). Scots is a violent language; Scots is the perfect language for lovers. Scots is a dying language, inferior to English in its range of expressive possibilities. Scots is a vibrant language, superior to English in its capacity for the expression of human warmth. Scots is a national treasure, under threat from English. Scots is not a language at all, but a dialect of English. Though rural Scots may be dying out, urban Scots is a living language: the language of the people. Scots is 'more genuine' than English. Scots is an aspect of 'tartanry', and thus a fake. Scots is a Scandinavian language, quite different from English (John Jamieson's view, expressed in his *Etymological Dictionary of the Scottish Language* in 1808, and arguably not quite so deluded as it is generally considered). And – the main starting-point for this chapter – the vigour of Scots, 'a language in its string vest', as a distinguished cultural commentator (who will remain anonymous) once called it, makes it perfect for literary expression, whether in novels or in poetry. It is of course quite unscholarly not to cite sources for all these views, but no observer of the cultural scene in present-day Scotland will fail to recognise their currency.

Now no modern linguist could accept any of the views just expressed without careful and substantial qualification. It is an axiom of descriptive linguistics that no language is superior to any other: all languages can express whatever their users need to express. To argue that certain languages are 'naturally' more capable of doing one thing rather than another is quite extraordinarily patronising. It is even potentially racist, in the same way as suggesting that some races are 'better' at dancing or singing or painting – or, for that matter, leading.

But it is true to say that Scots, during the last 600 years, has been fortunate in its poets; and it is also true that, although poets may be inspired by that unfashionable faculty, genius, their idiom derives from the language around them. 'No poet makes his own language,' said Glasgow professor Sir Walter Raleigh; poetry, it may be argued, is a 'found art', comparable (*mutatis mutandis*) with that splendid bull's head which Pablo Picasso created from a bicycle saddle and handlebars. Thus – to move at last to the central concern of this chapter – Older Scots poets wrote as they wrote because they wrote when and where they wrote. If they had written in another time, at another place, they would have written differently about different things.

SOUND-PATTERNS IN OLDER SCOTS VERSE

The verse of Robert Henryson may be analysed to demonstrate this point, as a good example of Scots in the second half of the fifteenth century, that is Early Middle Scots (c.1450–1550). Here is a passage from one of his *Morall Fabillis: The Preaching of the Swallow*:

Thir small birdis, for hunger famischit neir,
Full besie scrapand for to seik thair fude,
The counsall off the swallow wald not heir,
Suppois [although] thair laubour dyd thame lytill gude.
Quhen scho thair fulische hartis vnderstude
Sa indurate, vp in ane tre scho flew –
With that this churll ouer thame his nettis drew.
Allace, it wes grit hart sair for to se
That bludie bowcheour beit thay birdis doun,
And for till heir, quhen thay wist weill to de,
Thair cairfull sang and lamentatioun.

Sum with ane staf he straik to eirth on swoun,
Off sum the heid, off sum he brak the crag [neck],
Sum half on lyfe he stoppit [stuffed] in his bag.
(Fox 1987: 72–3, lines 1867–80)

These stanzas illustrate many of the major characteristics of Scots in about 1500. The spellings *sa* 'so' and *sair* 'sore', *gude* 'good' and *bludie* 'bloody' correlate with the fronting of the Old English/Old Norse back vowels *ā* and *ō* characteristic of Scots and northern Middle English, cf. midland and southern Middle English *so(o)*, *god(e)*, *blody*; the characteristic use of <i> to indicate a long vowel may be noted in *heid* 'head', *seik* 'seek', *cairfull* (cf. Present-Day English 'careful'), *straik* 'struck'. Also characteristic of Scots in combination with other forms is the <quh-> spelling (cf. Present-Day English <wh->) in *quhen* 'when'. In grammar, the characteristic Scots system of pronouns and determiners – *thir* 'these', *thay* 'those', *thair* 'their', *thame* 'them', *scho* 'she', *ane* 'a' even before consonants – may be noted, as may the verb-endings <-it> (past participle and preterite, cf. Present-Day English <-ed>) in *famischit*, *stoppit*, and <-and> (present participle, cf. Present-Day English <-ing>) in *scrapand*. Adjectival inflexion in <-e>, characteristic of southern English in the time of Chaucer, is not found in Middle Scots, for example *Thir small birdis* (cf. Chaucerian *the smale briddes*). 'Verb-final' constructions in the manner of present-day German are still widely used in Middle Scots: *With that this churll ouer thame his nettis drew*. The vocabulary of the passage derives from various sources: from Old English (*besie*, *seik*, *fude* and so on), from Old Norse (*thair* and so on), and from French (*counsall*, *laubour*, *lamentation*).

Philological analysis of the passage, in the way that has just been offered, proceeds logically, by levels of language: sounds and spellings, grammar, vocabulary. However, such analysis is only part of the story, for the meaning of a text derives from its context, and the verse-context of this philological material still remains to be examined. To exemplify this point, we might take the following lines from the passage:

Allace, it wes grit hart sair for to se
That bludie bowcheour beit thay birdis doun,
And for till heir, quhen thay wist wcill to de,
Thair cairfull sang and lamentatioun.

Henryson's use of sound-patterning, both metrical-rhythmical and phonaes-thetic, is well illustrated by these lines. The metre of *The Preaching of the Swallow* is of course 'iambic pentameter', consisting of five sets of the cluster x/ (the 'iamb'), where x is an unstressed and / is a stressed syllable. However, it is equally obvious that the rhythm of these lines does not follow a regular x/ x/ x/ x/ x/

pattern. Such effects are monotonous if sustained without modulation, and most metrists are agreed that poems 'work' by varying rhythmical effects against metrical norms for the purposes of foregrounding. In other words, the natural stresses demanded by speech-rhythm – whereby prominence is assigned to key syllables in lexical words – contrasts with metre, whereby stress is expected at regular intervals, whether the word be lexical or not. The failure to encounter the regular stress predicted by the metrical norm is a major source of poetic foregrounding. Thus, in the following line:

Allace, it wes grit hart sair for to se

the expected metre (x/ x/ x/ x/ x/) contrasts with the the the actual rhythm (x/ xx // /x x/). In place of the second iamb, a pyrhhic (xx) appears; in place of the third, a spondee (//); in place of the fourth, a trochee (/x). The effect is to throw emphasis onto the grammatical complement *grit hert sair* – an emphasis which is entirely appropriate at this sad moment in the poem. The s-alliteration on *sair . . . se* draws a link between feeling and perception. Of course, we do not need to know the technical terminology of metrical theory to appreciate the effect achieved.[1]

Another interesting effect is demonstrated by the following line:

That bludie bowcheour beit thay birdis doun

Here there is no deviation in rhythm from the metrical norm, and rhythm and metre correspond: x/ x/ x/ x/ x/. The stresses come with the regularity of hammer-blows; there is an obvious enactment of the sense of the line. And, just in case readers/listeners miss the point, Henryson chooses a lexis which has a very distinct phonaesthetic effect: each stressed syllable begins with the voiced bilabial plosive, [b].

The technical term *phonaesthesia* may be unfamiliar to students of literature; it is certainly controversial for students of language. There is of course nothing intrinsically violent about voiced bilabial plosives, as witnessed by Present-Day English words such as *bless, bed, boring, bath*, none of which signifies a violent action or entity. But it is undeniable that a high proportion of lexical words with initial [b] have a semantic component signifying violence in Present-Day English, and the same situation seems to have obtained in Older Scots. In the *Concise Scots Dictionary*, for instance, the following words all signify violent or sudden action or temper, argument or insult, or weaponry of some kind or another *bang, bank* 'drum-beat', *bargle, barrat, bash, bastion, bat, batailúe, bate, batoun, battard, batter, bauch, bauchle* (verb), *bauld, beal, beff, bicker, birkie, birr, birst, bite, bittle, blaff, blast, blaud, blaw, blowder, bluiter* and so on (see Robinson 1985: *passim*).

The notion of phonaesthesia was first fully formulated by the linguist J. R. Firth who saw it as a matter of what he called 'phonetic habit' (Firth 1964: 184–5):

Consider the following English words: *slack, slouch, slush, slime, slosh, slash, sloppy, slug, sluggard, slattern, slut, slang, sly, slither, slow* . . . a group of words such as the above has a cumulative suggestive value that cannot be overlooked in any consideration of our habits of speech. All the above words are in varying degrees pejorative. There is nothing inherently pejorative in the sounds . . . It so happens that we hear and learn to make these sounds at present in what we may describe as pejorative contexts of experience. The more consistently similar sounds function in situations having a similar affective aspect, the clearer their function. In this way, then *sl* can be said to be a pejorative phonetic habit.

In other words, there is nothing intrinsic about the meaning of a sub-lexemic item such as sl- (or b-) but there are 'phonetic habits' which associate particular meanings, inconsistently but persistently, with particular sounds or clusters of sounds.

Phonaesthetic phenomena have long been exploited by poets. It seems no coincidence that Grendel, the monstrous villain of the Anglo-Saxon epic poem *Beowulf*, has a name whose initial phonaestheme, in Old English, clustered with words such as *gram* 'angry', *grennian* 'gnash', *grimm* 'grim', *grindan* 'grind', *gryre* 'horror'. The alliterative patterning of Old English verse encouraged the development of such habits, habits that continued into the alliterative verse of the Middle English and Older Scots periods. Although Henryson does not write in alliterative verse, his contemporaries still did; Henryson was well aware of the phonaesthetic advantages of alliterative patterning, and this would have been salient for him from a reading of contemporary Scots verse.[2]

Henryson's contemporary, William Dunbar, who wrote both in alliterative and in rhyming modes, was a master of such effects. His poem *On the Resurrection*, dominated by plosives, is a good example of phonaesthesia in action:

Done is a battell on the dragon blak;
Our campioun Chryst confoundit hes his force:
The úettis of hell ar brokin with a rak,
The signe triumphall rasit is of the croce,
The divillis trymmillis with hiddous voce,
The saulis ar borrowit and to the bliss can go,
Chryst with his blud our ransonis dois indoce:
Surrexit Dominus de sepulchro.
                  (Kinsley 1979: 11, 4.1–8)

The lines are linked by rhyme, but they draw on ancient traditions of alliterative verse. The poem is concerned with the Harrowing of Hell, that apocryphal, violent act whereby Christ, between Good Friday and Easter Sunday, descended into Hell and released the patriarchs and prophets of the Old Testament. And, of course, like so many of Dunbar's works, the poem has cognate expressions in contemporary iconography, for Dunbar is the great word-painter of Middle Scots poetry.

The lines from *The Preaching of the Swallow* just quoted, therefore, can be analysed not just as a good example of Middle Scots but as a good example of the kind of poetry which could be achieved with Middle Scots, drawing upon available literary traditions. Moreover, the interpretation offered would seem to fit rather well with traditional views on the working of verse.

From an eighteenth-century perspective, Pope puts the matter explicitly in his *Essay on Criticism*:

> True Ease in Writing comes from Art, not Chance,
> As those move easiest who have learn'd to dance.
> 'Tis not enough no Harshness gives Offence,
> The *Sound* must seem an *Eccho* to the *Sense*.
> *Soft* is the Strain when *Zephyr* gently blows,
> And the *smooth Stream* in *smoother Numbers* flows;
> But when loud Surges lash the sounding Shore,
> The *hoarse, rough Verse* shou'd like the *Torrent* roar.
> (Butt 1963: 155, *Essay on Criticism* 362–9)

Pope, an expert metrist, correlates meaning, metre and phonaesthetic effect in this passage in an extraordinarily subtle way; but it is quite possible to see something similar operating in much more ancient forms of verse.

Thus, when we turn to the Old English epic poem *Beowulf*, there is a similarly obvious correlation between emphasis and metrical deviation. As is well known, Old English grammar was more 'synthetic' than that of Present-Day English. Inflexions were characteristically used in preference to prepositions – which were closer in function to adverbs – and determiners had a more deictic role distinct from that played by their present-day equivalents. As a result, the dominant metrical unit in Old English is the trochee/dactyl, with stress falling on the initial syllable within the foot. In Old English verse, there are prototypically two such feet within each 'half-line', the main metrical unit; we thus find half-lines such as *Beowulf mapelode* (Beowulf spoke), *wine Scyldinga* (Lord of the Scyldings), *wīsa fengel* (wise prince) and so on. Such units demand no particular emphasis in terms of the narrative, and therefore a trochaic/dactylic measure is chosen; by far the majority of such Old English 'half-lines' are trochaic/dactylic. Thus we might scan a half-line such as *wine Scyldinga* as follows:

```
 / x      / x x
wine     Scyldinga
```

that is a trochee followed by a dactyl. However, we might compare such 'norm' half-lines with the following,

Wæs se grimma gæst   Grendel hāten,
The evil spirit was   called Grendel
(Klaeber 1950: 5, line 102)

In this pair of half-lines there is a combination of phonaesthetic effect (already discussed) and metrical deviation; the first half-line might be scanned as an anapaest followed by an iamb, thus:

x   x / x /
Wæs se grimma gǣst

According to Eduard Sievers, who first offered a convincing classification of Old English metrical patterns, half-lines of the *Wæs se grimma gǣst* type (Sievers 'B') may be considered 'rousing, exclamatory' as opposed to the 'steady progress' of *wine Scyldinga* type (Sievers 'A'); in modern terms, these somewhat impressionistic descriptions can be expressed as 'foregrounded' and 'norm' respectively (see Klaeber 1950: lxix, and references there cited).

There is thus a clear correlation between sound-pattern (including metre) and meaning in verse; to repeat Pope's axiom, 'The *Sound* must seem an *Eccho* to the *Sense*'. This view has been expatiated in a rather more explicit fashion by George Kane, the editor of William Langland's fourteenth-century Middle English alliterative poem *Piers Plowman*, who points out (1981: 46) that a poet's success derives from the way in which

> his versification exists as part of the meaning of his poetic statements,
> not merely because the verse is effective in making that meaning more
> emphatic, clearer, more evidently interrelated, but also because it will
> engage the reader's auditory interest and confer the combination of
> physical and intellectual pleasure experienced when pattern and meaning
> are simultaneously apprehended.

This description, albeit written to describe the practices of a quite distinct verse-form (alliterative verse), fits rather well with the kind of analysis already offered of Henryson's poetry, as evidenced by the passage from *The Preaching of the Swallow*.

PATTERNS OF GRAMMAR AND VOCABULARY

So far, this chapter has concentrated on sound-patterns, and indeed it is crucial – especially in any analysis of poetry from the Middle Ages, designed for a culture nearer the oral pole of the oral-literate cline than our own – to emphasise the importance of such effects. However, truly satisfying poetry, such as that of Henryson and Dunbar, has to link sound-effect to an underpinning philosophy. As Wordsworth put it in his Preface to the *Lyrical Ballads* of 1798,

> Poems to which any value can be attached were never produced on any variety of subjects but by a man who, being possessed of more than usual organic sensibility, had also thought long and deeply.
>   (Hutchinson/de Selincourt 1969: 735)

To demonstrate this point, another passage might be analysed: the opening lines from *The Preaching of the Swallow*.

The hie prudence and wirking meruelous,
The profound wit off God omnipotent,
Is sa perfyte and sa ingenious,
Excellent [*excelling*] far all mannis iugement;
For quhy to him all thing is ay present,
Rycht as it is or ony tyme sall be,
Befoir the sicht off his diuinitie.

Thairfoir our saul with sensualitie
So fetterit is in presoun corporall,
We may not cleirlie vnderstand nor se
God as he is, not thingis celestiall;
Our mirk and deidlie corps materiale
Blindis the spirituall operatioun,
Lyke as ane man wer bundin in presoun.

In *Metaphisik* Aristotell sayis
That mannis saull is lyke ane bakkis ee,
Quhilk lurkis still, als lang as licht off day is,
And in the gloming cummis furth to fle;
Hir ene ar waik, the sone scho may not se:
Sa is our saull with fantasie opprest.
To knaw the thingis in nature manifest.

For God is in his power infinite,
And mannis saull is febill and ouer small,
Off vnderstanding waik and vnperfite
To comprehend him that contenis al;
Nane suld presume be ressoun naturall

To seirche the secreitis off the Trinitie,
Bot trow fermelie and lat all ressoun be.
        (Fox 1987: 64–5, lines 1622–49)

As with the previous passage, it is possible to offer a philological analysis of these lines. Old English *ā* is reflected as < a > in *sa* 'so', *knaw* 'know', *lang* 'long'; the characteristically Scots spelling < quh- > as the reflex of Present-Day English < wh- > appears in *quhy* 'why'. Scots pronouns and determiners again appear: *scho* 'she', *ane* 'a/an'. The northern pattern of verb-inflexion is exemplified in *cummis* 'comes', *lurkis* 'lurks'; cf. southern Late Middle English < -eth >; the Old English weak noun-inflexion is retained in *ene* 'eyes'. The passage also contains the distinctive Scots/northern Middle English *sall/suld* 'shall/should'; the Scots form, not the English, is of course in West Germanic terms the non-deviant form (cf. German *sollen*). So far, we are noticing the same sort of thing as in the earlier passage.

But there are also some other features of vocabulary and grammar that are more salient than in the first passage analysed. Some words obviously have meanings which differ from those in Present-Day English: *wit*, for instance, has a much stronger meaning in Older Scots, referring to the 'part intellectiue' of the human psyche which Henryson – following Boethius – identified in *Orpheus and Erudices*, and which he contrasts with *wil*, that is *affection* which *to the flesch settis the appetite* (see Fox 1987: 146–7, lines 428–34). Above all, the passage is full of words derived from French: *prudence, meruelous, profound, omnipotent, perfyte, ingenious, excellent, iugement, present, diuinitie, sensualitie, presoun, corporall, celestiall, corps, materiale, spirituall, operatioun* and so on. There is even a marked tendency to adopt the characteristically French post-modifying adjective construction, even when a Germanic word is used as the headword: *wirking meruelous, God omnipotent, presoun corporall, thingis celes-tiall, corps materiale, power infinite, ressoun naturall*. These French grammatical constructions are accompanied by a complex syntax, flagged by subordinating conjunctions and non-finite verb phrases acting as the predicators of sub-ordinate clauses.

However, simply listing words and constructions derived from French in a passage such as this is not sufficient, if we wish to understand what Henryson is trying to achieve; we need to know how these words functioned in the wider context of Older Scots. As in the analysis of sound-patterns in the section above, it is important to move beyond straightforward philological analysis to identify the function of these forms in the wider context of Scots at the time. And of course there is something in this passage which Henryson shares with present-day 'high style' English: French-derived vocabulary even now in Present-Day English is associated with complex philosophical discourse and high-status expression, as is evidenced by the semantics of 'regard', 'commence' beside neutral 'look at', 'begin' (the French words *regarder*, *commencer* share denotations but do not have the same heightened, formal connotations as their English derivatives).

In sum, Henryson is here attempting to express a complex set of philosophical notions, and has chosen to adopt a variety of Scots – a register of vocabulary and grammar – appropriate for such high-flown subjects. Fascinatingly, in the last stanza quoted he sums up his argument by referring to the limits of *ressoun* – yet he couches his argument using a complex, high-style scholastic mode of discourse derived, explicitly, from Aristotle. It is possible to detect some subtlety here which it would be too crude to characterise as ironic; *mannis saull*, we are told, is *Off vnderstanding waik and vnperfite*, yet our status as fallen angels allows us some apprehension of the divine; as Henryson goes on to say (Fox 1987: 65, lines 1650– 51), *neuertheles we may haif knawlegeing/Of God almychtie be his creatouris*. In other words, our abilities in reasoning make it possible for us to read the signs God has left for us in his creation.

It may be noted that reference has just been made to 'a variety of Scots'; much of the vocabulary in the passage may be derived from French, but the use of these loanwords in Scots has changed their semantics, just as happened to 'regard' and 'commence', and the words have become part of the Scots language, just as 'bungalow' and 'chocolate' are part of Present-Day English though (ultimately) from Bengali and Nahuatl respectively. Indeed, 'loanwords' is perhaps an unfortunate term; languages steal from each other ruthlessly, and put the words they steal to different uses than their original owners.

We may be sure that Henryson's first readers and listeners would have been aware of what the poet was trying to do. Art historians have shown us that the characteristic blue garment worn by the Virgin Mary derives from the expensive nature of the pigment in the late Middle Ages, powdered lapis lazuli; to use this kind of blue in paintings, as frequently stipulated by medieval patrons, is therefore a stylistic decision which contemporaries would have appreciated but which is generally lost on us now without special knowledge. Similarly, the choice of French-derived vocabulary, irrespective of its etymology, and of complex syntax, was foregrounded for Henryson's contemporaries. If we want to understand what Older Scots poets were trying to achieve, we need to grasp this characteristic. That they were able to write in this way, of course, related to the elaborated status of Scots at the end of the fifteenth century, and it is to such matters that this chapter now turns.

THE STATUS OF OLDER SCOTS

At the end of the previous section, the term *elaborated* was used. This term derives from the terminology of standardisation first distinguished by the linguist Einar Haugen:

- A usage can be *selected* for some reason
- A usage may be *codified* and thus fixed (for example by an Academy, as in seventeenth-century France, or simply by means of an educational system)
- A usage may be *elaborated*, in that it becomes the usage available for every linguistic function
- A usage may be ultimately *accepted*, as the only usage acceptable in the usage of powerful members of the society in question.

(Haugen 1966, cited most accessibly in Hudson 1980: 33)

This terminology is useful when we attempt to place Older Scots poets in their linguistic context. Early Middle Scots – that is, the Anglo-Saxon-derived language spoken north of the border in the fifteenth century – seems to have developed by the end of the fifteenth century as an elaborated language. As Scots became elaborated, it underwent certain formal changes also found in Middle English. Thus dialectal diversity in the written mode, a feature of earlier Scots, became muted as the Middle Scots period progressed. Scots was also used with an increasingly wide range of functions, in a variety of settings; the poetry of Dunbar and of Henryson, therefore, is appropriate for court and cloister as well as street and farmyard.

Thus far there is a parallel with English developments; in England, a variety focused on London usage – sometimes called 'Chancery English' but perhaps better 'King's English' – was selected and became accepted as the norm for elaboration. Such a development could occur only if English itself had 'triumphed' as having the possibility of elaboration; in the Early Middle English period, when England was a multi-lingual nation, English had occupied a restricted, local currency in comparison with the national languages of record and culture, Latin and French (see further Benskin 1992).

Something similar seems to have been happening to Scots in the late fifteenth century. However, whereas standardised written English subsequently became, in England, the written norm, political and cultural events supervened in Scotland to prevent 'standardised' Scots – even in its incipient form – following the same path. There were two connected historical reasons why this variety did not succeed in the same way that King's English did, that is, develop into a prestigious norm not restricted to its place of origin:

(i) On the one hand, Middle Scots evidently had an uneasy relationship with English south of the Border. Up until the late fifteenth century, the term used for the Old-English-derived language spoken in the south of Scotland was *Inglis* (the term *Scottis*, up to the same date, was reserved for Gaelic). That there was intimate cultural contact between English and *Inglis* is illustrated by the close connection between the flowering of Scottish vernacular literature, associated with the poets Robert Henryson and William Dunbar, and the slightly earlier English pantheon of Chaucer, John Gower and John Lydgate. The strength of these cultural connections is demonstrated by the curiously English-Scots blend-language of texts such as *Lancelot of the Laik* in MS Cambridge, University Library, Kk.I.5, or the odd, quasi-anglicised spellings which appear in the early prints of, for instance, Dunbar's 'high-style' verse, such as *quho* 'who' in place of the expected Older Scots *quha*; cf. Southern Middle English – and Present-Day English – 'who'.

(ii) The second (and probably stronger) reason why written Older Scots did not develop a fixed standard variety in the written mode was the collapse of real Scottish political autonomy in the wake of the disaster of the battle of Flodden (1513), followed quite soon afterwards by the Reformation and the adoption of English written norms through the adoption of the vernacular Bible. It is no coincidence that anglicisation of writing appears first in Scottish texts concerned with religion. The Union of the Crowns in 1603 meant a decisive shift south in the centre of Scotland's political gravity. By 1700, written Scots was confined to material with a local or private currency, such as letters between family-members, although it developed as a significant poetic medium – often with a 'closet-Jacobite' connotation – once again in the eighteenth century, and as a sentimental discourse in the nineteenth. The potential for diversity bequeathed to modern Scots writers is pursued by McClure (this volume).

IMPLICATIONS

What are the implications of this historical narrative for our understanding of Older Scots poetry? The evidence is, both from the texts themselves and from the contexts which have been described, that Scots in the time of Henryson and Dunbar was hardly 'a language in its string vest'. Rather, Older Scots was a highly flexible social instrument, capable of being used across a whole range of registers, and allowing the expression of philosophical notions of considerable subtlety. In other words, the language provided poets with numerous choices and opportunities for modulation.

It remains an important task for students of Older Scots verse to investigate how these choices were made; the purpose of this chapter has been to flag how such a task might be pursued. In doing so it seems to the present author to be crucial to harness both literary and linguistic approaches; the two have diverged markedly in recent years, so much so that there is sometimes active scholarly antagonism between them, but it is time for a rapprochement.

Henryson and Dunbar of course seized the opportunities offered by the language of their time, and this act of seizure, in a way, lies at the heart of that odd notion referred to at the beginning of this chapter, namely, genius. The term 'genius', of course, originally referred to what Jonathan Bate has formulated as 'the particular combination of astral influences represented in a person's horoscope' (Bate 1997: 5). We do not need to accept the principles of astrology to accept that the idiom adopted by a genius depends on when that genius was born. We might recall the axiom with which this chapter began: Robert Henryson and William Dunbar – like other poets – wrote as they wrote because they wrote when and where they wrote. If they had written in another time, at another place, they would have written differently about different things.

NOTES

1. A parallel is often made between poetry and music. A piece of music may be composed 'in the key of A', but the music itself does not consist of a series of A-scales. Thus all music is, in a sense, a set of variations. (See further Leech 1969: chapter 7; see also Fraser 1970 and Davies Roberts 1986 for an initial statement and Attridge 1982 for a more advanced discussion.) It is worth recalling that music can be enjoyed by those who know nothing about musical theory.
2. For further discussion of phonaesthesia in medieval verse, with references, see Smith 2000, especially p. 95 n. 26.

CHAPTER 10

The Language of Modern Scots Poetry

J. Derrick McClure

INTRODUCTION

A language, particularly a mature literary language, is never a uniform entity. Even languages with tiny numbers of speakers often show remarkable degrees of dialectal variation within their domains (a case in point is Gaelic); and languages which have existed in written form for any length of time are certain to show changes from one century to another. If the speakers in a given language community are influenced, for whatever cultural or political reason, by those of another, the language itself will be affected; but to different degrees among different groups of speakers, giving rise to social as well as geographical variations. In a language with a well-developed literary tradition, great individual writers who use their mother tongue in adventurous and innovative ways will play a part in its development, enlarging its expressive scope and widening the range of linguistic effects available to their successors. And since any language, in the last analysis, exists primarily as a means of communication and self-expression by individuals, every speaker – if the argument is applied *in extremis*, every *utterance* by every speaker – is to some extent linguistically unique.

Languages can pass through periods of brilliant efflorescence, during which their vocabulary grows and their resources in idiom and modes of expression enjoy a burgeoning expansion. For readers of the present book the best-known example will be the case of English in the Elizabethan period: French at the same time was likewise undergoing a remarkable development, perhaps less spectacular but also longer-lasting; and the turn of German came in the eighteenth century. Examples abound of the well-known pattern in cultural history whereby a language, and the literature for which it is the medium, display cyclical phases of expansion and stasis or decline. Furthermore, a language is not only the medium for conversation and writing but an intimate reflection, indeed an integral part, of the entire life of a community, including its self-perception and its status in the eyes of the world, from which it follows that a change in the way a speech-community evaluates itself will be accompanied by and reflected in some changes in its language.

THE CASE OF SCOTS

These considerations may serve to introduce our examination of literary Scots in the later twentieth century. The briefest glance at the corpus of poetry produced from – to select two almost arbitrarily chosen landmarks – Charles Murray's *Hamewith* (1900) to the Scots pieces in the anthology of work by young contemporary poets *Dream State* (1994, 2002) reveals a literary medium of extraordinary diversity. The many traditional dialects heard in different parts of the kingdom are all exploited by local writers: two of the most distinguished from the beginning and the end of the century, Violet Jacob and Sheena Blackhall, made of the Eastern and North-Eastern folk-tongues media for poetry of outstanding quality; and other dialectally well-marked regions such as Ayrshire, Fife, the Borders and the Northern Isles have likewise produced creditable poetry in their local speech-forms. A form of Scots both linguistically and socially very unlike the dialects which have survived from (and still, in their traditional vocabulary and idiom, show their origins in) the rural life of pre-industrial Scotland, the modern argot of the Glasgow conurbation, has become the medium of poetry of a more radical type, challenging the social and political, as well as literary, assumptions of its readers. Besides written forms based firmly on Scotland's actual spoken dialects and sociolects, the poetic medium established during the Vernacular Revival of the eighteenth century, namely a common-core Scots eschewing the most strongly marked features (in vocabulary and phonology) of regional dialects, remains a staple. And in increasingly marked contrast to this, poets of an experimental bent have used, and continue to use, forms of Scots containing rare and obscure words, some markedly local or archaic, others outright inventions: a procedure which has had the result that the medium of some Scots poetry bears only the most tenuous relationship to any spoken vernacular currently, or ever, used in Scotland.

A *prima facie* surprising fact is that concurrently with this astonishing efflorescence of Scots as a poetic medium, the *spoken* language has suffered an undeniable decline. That Scots, in its various dialects and sociolects, still exists as the mother tongue and preferred conversational medium of many people (defying the predictions of its imminent disappearance which have been made for well over two hundred years) is a matter of ready observation; but the stable and cohesive communities of Scots-speakers, in which the language was passed from one generation to the next as a normal and integral feature of family and social life, have vanished beyond recall – casualties of the revolutionary social and economic changes of the twentieth century; and lacking this social underpinning the language has become far more vulnerable than before to pressures of anglocentric education and the mass media. Recent efforts to promote the language as a field of study at all levels in education and to enhance the respect accorded to it as a spoken tongue have undeniably had some effect; but it cannot be suggested that they have (as yet) restored Scots to a central place in the life of the nation. Yet the seemingly paradoxical coincidence of a decline in the range and status of spoken Scots and an expansion of its expressive powers in the literary field is less remarkable than might be thought. R. L. Stevenson, not only a forerunner of but a seminal contributor to the twentieth-century revival of poetry in Scots, associated the expected demise of Scots with a new freedom to experiment:[1] since the language would shortly no longer reflect current spoken usages, the entire collective wealth of all its dialects of the recent past could be exploited in a composite medium. This, in effect, is what has happened to Scots in the hands of its twentieth-century writers; and though several different literary and ideological justifications for this practice have been propounded in the course of the century, its pragmatic usefulness is visible to all.

THE SCOTS RENAISSANCE: THE BACKGROUND

The present chapter will concentrate on developments in the language of Scots poetry in the last quarter of the twentieth century; but a brief overview of the Scots Renaissance in its linguistic aspect may help to set the scene. For much of the nineteenth century, the standard of poetry written in Scots was distressingly low: a critical commonplace which no amount of revisionist thought, or attempts to relieve the overall impression of gloom by pointing to the occasional talented poet who temporarily enlivened the literary world, is likely to overturn. The weakness did not lie in the language itself. As a spoken tongue, Scots continued as the everyday means of communication among all classes of society; and the traditional vocabulary, phonology and idioms of Scots are as readily visible in the pages of *Whistle-Binkie* as in the poetry of Fergusson or Burns. Rather, it took the form of a loss of ambition, or a failure of nerve: the tongue that in the eighteenth century had been used for intellectually challenging poetry, questioning and subverting the social, political and ideological orthodoxies of the day, became domesticated, restricted by its writers to humorous and nostalgic trivia. Explanations for this can be sought in a variety of social, educational, economic and political factors; but a fundamental and unmistakable cause is a loss of confidence in the Scots tongue; itself symptomatic of a profound psychological malaise regarding the Scottish national identity. During a period when the face of Scotland was being transformed by the growth of industrialisation, with its twin corollaries of enormous increases in material prosperity and the unrestrained growth of appalling urban slums; when

Glasgow was developing as the world's leading centre for shipbuilding, when the nation's trading and commercial connections were being expanded world-wide, and when individual Scots were making a contribution out of all proportion to their numbers to the administration and development of the British Empire, writers in the Scots language failed totally to reflect those vast social changes in the works they were producing: though Scots was the language of one of the commercial and technical power-centres of the world, its status as the medium of one of Europe's great national literatures was shamefully betrayed – there is no denying the appropriateness of that expression – by the narrowness and triviality of the period's poetic achievement. Some of the most impressive Scots works of the mid and later nineteenth century are not in poetry but prose, and sometimes of an unexpected nature: the remarkable school of local journalism which flourished, most notably in the north-east but in other parts of Scotland as well, produced at least one writer of outstanding ability in William Alexander, whose masterwork, the serially printed novel *Johnny Gibb of Gushetneuk*, depicts members of the north-east farming community discussing, with knowledge, understanding, passionate commitment and complete linguistic fluency in unadulterated Doric, the social, political and religious issues surrounding the Disruption.[2]

As the nineteenth century closed and the twentieth opened, however, a revival gradually took shape. Signs of recovery came from several directions: Robert Louis Stevenson in *Underwoods* produced a collection of Scots poems which, though small in bulk, far surpassed in quality anything produced since the death of Burns; a sudden efflorescence of poetry in north-east Doric was initiated by Charles Murray and Mary Symon and soon imitated in other parts of the country; Lewis Spence found inspiration for some attractive poems with quasi-medieval themes and poetic forms expressed in pastiche Middle Scots; poetry in traditional modes was given new life by gifted writers such as Marion Angus and Violet Jacob. Although the 'Scots Renaissance' is inseparably associated with the portentous figure of Hugh MacDiarmid, the revivification of the Scottish poetic scene was gathering strength well before the publication of *Sangschaw*, Mac-Diarmid's first volume of poems in Scots, startled the literary world.

THE LINGUISTIC ASPECT OF THE RENAISSANCE

MacDiarmid's extensive quarrying of linguistic reference books, of which John Jamieson's *An Etymological Dictionary of the Scottish Language* was by far the most important, for interesting words and phrases to enrich his poetic vocabulary was from the outset an integral and clearly stated part of his technique. And though MacDiarmid's Scots, this lexical aggrandisement notwithstanding, rarely lost contact with either the spoken dialect of the Borders in which he had been brought up or the literary Scots of the Burns tradition, his exuberant delight in linguistic experimentation was indulged to an even greater degree by some of his successors, resulting in a series of distinctive and brilliant literary idiolects utilising a Scots which, though self-justifying in its success as a literary medium, bore little or no relation to any *spoken* form used, then or ever, within the bounds of Scotland. It was to some extent in reaction to this – not only to the artificiality of the language, but to the patent fact that it was constructed by men of wide-ranging erudition and culture – that the speech of the Glasgow tenements was drafted into service, in the 1960s, as a poetic medium revolutionary not only in its results but in its socio-political implications. And as both those startlingly contrasting registers persisted and developed, so too did both traditional literary Scots and the various rural dialects, most notably those of the north-east and, somewhat later, the Northern Isles.

What emerges from this is that 'Scots' is a remarkably flexible term, covering a great diversity of styles, registers, dialects and sociolects. This fact is often misunderstood by critics who appear, in discussing the language of a particular Scots poem, to be measuring their chosen text against an assumed 'norm' for Scots. Hugh MacDiarmid was guilty of this when he attacked Charles Murray for writing in Aberdeenshire dialect: 'Anything further from the conceivable norm – anything more corrupt – it would be difficult to find in any dialect of any tongue';[3] and MacDiarmid's own Scots has been criticised from its first appearance for its alleged artificiality. It must be admitted that he invited this by his concoction and frequent use of the unfortunate term 'synthetic Scots'. But the presupposition that there exists a single, identifiable form which is simply 'Scots', from which other forms are more or less legitimate deviations, is not tenable with reference to either observable linguistic facts or established literary practice. There are, of course, numerous different dialects spoken in different parts of Scotland (MacDiarmid's native Border dialect, traces of which emerge very clearly in his poetry, being fully as much a regionally marked form as Murray's Aberdeenshire), and there are no grounds for arguing against the right of local poets to exploit the resources of their local tongues. From another point of view, not only Scots but all European languages, in the modern period, have been the medium of imaginative and sometimes extravagant linguistic experimentation.

> No, but it was not these.
> The jading and jar of the cart,
> Time's tasking, it is fathers that asking for ease
> Of the sodden-with-its-sorrowing heart,
> Not danger, electrical horror; then further it finds
> The appealing of Passion is tenderer in prayer apart:
> Other, I gather, in measure her mind's
> Burden, in wind's burly and beat of endragonèd seas.
> (Gerard Manley Hopkins, *The Wreck of the Deutschland* (extract); *Poems*,
> ed. Robert Bridges, Oxford 1930 (1940 reprint), p. 20)

This verse (composed in 1876) is obviously in very peculiar English; but no one would deny that it *is* in English; and by the same token a passage like the following:

> A dour dark burn that has its ain wild say
> Thro' a' the thrang bricht babble o' Earth's flood.
> Behold, thwart my ramballiach life again,
> What thrawn and roothewn dreams, royat and rude,
> Reek forth – a foray dowless hearts condemn –
> While chance wi' rungs o' sang or silence renshels them.
> (Hugh MacDiarmid, *Gairmscoile* (extract); *Collected Poems*,
> London and New York (Macmillan) 1967, p. 57)

is incontrovertibly in Scots, even if not a Scots which can be heard in any street or pub. Indeed, the reluctance of many readers to acknowledge the right of recent poems in experimental language to be classed as 'Scots' could be said to betray a reluctance to accept the maturity of Scots as a literary medium, capable of being used like any fully developed national language in a variety of styles and registers limited only by the inventiveness of individual writers.

EXPERIMENTATION WITH SCOTS VOCABULARY

This argument must not be taken as implying that 'anything goes' in the writing of modern Scots poetry. Linguistic and literary experiments may be successful or unsuccessful; and the issue of poetic merit is distinct from, though of course not unrelated to, that of linguistic credibility. MacDiarmid established the practice of weaving poems around interesting and evocative words and phrases, and many of his early lyrics contain words or expressions which, though obscure probably to most readers at first sight, prove on examination to have been selected with unerring aptness to contribute to the emotive and imaginative effect which the poet intended. This may be illustrated by one of the best-known lyrics in twentieth-century Scottish literature.

> I' the how-dumb-deid o' the cauld hairst nicht
> The warl' like an eemis stane
> Wags i' the lift;
> An' my eerie memories fa'
> Like a yowdendrift.
>
> Like a yowdendrift so's I couldna read
> The words cut oot i' the stane
> Had the fug o' fame
> An' history's hazelraw
> No' yirdit thaim.
> (*The Eemis Stane*, ibid., p. 17)

How-dumb-deid 'dead of night', *eemis-stane* 'insecurely balanced stone', *yowden-drift* 'snow driven by the wind' and *hazelraw* 'a kind of lichen' are certainly not part of many people's active vocabulary; but once their meaning has been ascertained, the images suggested fit together with complete coherence into a haunting and disturbing vision. Not only their semantic force but their sound structure contributes to the effectiveness of the poem: the balancing of three heavy syllables in *how-dumb-deid* and *cauld hairst nicht*, the linking of the initial vowels in *eemis* and *eerie*, the pattern [ʌu] – [d] – [d] in *yowdendrift* echoing and recalling *how-dumb-deid*, the alliteration of *history's hazelraw* and the rhyme of the latter word with *fa'* at the corresponding point in the previous verse, combine in an intricate and delicate patterning of sound-embroidery. By all literary criteria, this is an excellent poem in which the resources of Scots are utilised with masterly skill. Experimental use of Scots vocabulary can, unfortunately, just as readily result in unsuccessful poetry, such as the following:

> Yince auld mithir Lirklips
> hoolocht owre thi land
> inna cauld sea's grouse an grue,
> an doon thi sealblack deeps,
> the weelthrainit steps;
>
> nae camera cud recaa
> hoo dumbfounert aa 'ur weans
> did stare aboot lyk hotties, then,
> did thirsty raise
> a renaissance o sang!
> (William Herbert, *The Renaissance of Song*, in *Dream State: the New Scottish Poets*, ed. Daniel O'Rourke, Edinburgh (Polygon) 1994, p. 148)

Here, the poet has exercised both learning and ingenuity in his choice of vocabulary, and there is real interest in the individual words. *Lirklips* is derived from *lirk* 'wrinkle', *hooloch* is a rare and local onomatope for the noise of a rockslide or avalanche, which the author has transformed into a verb and given the meaning 'roll like a rockslide', *weelthrainit* is a concoction based on *thrain*, which can mean both a dirge or lamentation or the act of harping constantly on the same theme, and is glossed by the poet as 'worn by constant use, like a familiar tune', and *hotties* is an old term from Edinburgh High School for people who, unknown to them, have had a message pinned to their backs. On the other hand, the words and images do not combine to express any intelligible thought. Who or what 'old mother Wrinkle-lips' is and who or what her weans are, what kind of human action is suggested by the metaphor of a rockslide, what colour 'sealblack' is (seals are grey), why, if the steps are 'weelthrainit', one more person's going down them should make any difference to anything, why a woman's descent into the sea – or whatever other action or event that image is supposed to symbolise – should prompt 'a renaissance o sang', why a 'camera' and why 'thirsty': without at least some credible answers to these questions, the poem does not make sense. Nor is it distinguished by such musical effects of sound and rhythm as are illustrated by MacDiarmid's lyric. The moral of this is that a selection of recondite words, however interesting in themselves, no more make a poem good than they make it bad; and a poem in Scots, whether traditional or experimental, must be judged by the same criteria as one in any other language. It is by no means sufficient, in assessing a Scots poem, simply to determine what the Scots words mean; that is only the beginning of the task of literary criticism.

BOUNDARY BETWEEN SCOTS AND ENGLISH

A further difficulty in determining the referential boundaries of the term 'Scots' lies in the relationship of Scots to English. One of the most common, yet most fundamental, errors made in discussing Scots as a literary language is the notion that the terms 'Scots' and 'English' refer to mutually exclusive language forms, like French and German. And since any passage in Scots will certainly include words which would be identical were it written in English, the assumption is all too frequently held that such words are not Scots and do not belong to the Scots language; hence, that 'Scots' consists *only* of the words which are different from standard literary English of the present day, and which do not occur in the conversation of monolingual anglophones. On this assumption, the first of the two following poems would be *less* Scots than the second, since a reader unused to Scots would require to consult a glossary only rarely for one and much more frequently for the other:

1. Frae here
   it's a ferlie,
   a milky way
   o city lichts.

   But I hae been
   whaur tenements rot,
   whaur fowk yet bide
   as if forgot

   and I hae been
   whaur Setterday nichts
   grat blood
   alow yon heich lichts.

The closer you come whiles
the darker you see,
or there's nocht left ava
but misery.
(Raymond Vettese, *The Closer you Come*, in *Four Scottish Poets*, Garron
Publications 1983, pp. 60–1.)

2. Frae the blek lift
   the rain teims doun,
   stottin af stanes,
   lounderin itsell
   sair on the caussie
   whan the wund lowdens.
   Droukit guidwyfes
   hoys hame wi prams
   an plowterin bairns,
   ablo the blash
   frae dreipin rones.
   Im A no gled bi the bricht ingil
   A'm inby the-day
   an canna gang
   out for ti play,
   whyle the rain raens on
   at me aw day?
   (David Purves, *Haill Wattir*, in *Hert's Bluid*, Edinburgh (Chapman)
   1995, p. 51)

But the truth is that Scots and English are *not* mutually exclusive: a fact which
does not in any respect counter the perfectly tenable view that Scots is a
language in its own right. The case is frequently encountered of two (or more)
speech forms which diverged only in relatively recent times from a common
ancestor, and which therefore have much or even most of their vocabularies and
grammatical structures in common; and in many such cases the speech forms in
question have for political or cultural reasons acquired the status of distinct
languages: Scottish and Irish Gaelic, Norwegian and Danish, Czech and Slovak,
Finnish and Estonian are ready examples. Scots has words which have never
existed in English (such as *brae, clachan, fasherie, groset, redd*), words formerly
common to both countries but which happen not to have survived in English,
thus becoming Scots by default (such as *bairn, bide, deave, dree, thole*), words
which differ from their English counterparts through divergent phonological
developments in the two languages (such as *hous, stane, muin, licht, siller*), and
words which in their appearance, though not necessarily in every detail of their

range of use, are simply part of the word-stock shared by all speech-forms descended from Anglo-Saxon. And it is essential to appreciate that such words are fully as integral to the Scots tongue as the more distinctive sections of its vocabulary. The practice of some recent writers of attempting to naturalise them by arbitrary and unhistorical alterations of the spellings, such as Herbert's *thi* for 'the' or Purves's *im A* for 'am I', is unhelpful and misguided, and achieves nothing except to distract Scots and non-Scots alike from the meaning of their writings. There is no difference in degree of Scotsness (so to speak) between Vettese's poem and Purves, because *city, tenements, closer, misery* and the like are just as much part of the Scots vocabulary as *stottin, lounderin, droukit* or *plowterin*. Even when, as frequently, a distinctively Scots word is close or identical in meaning to a familiar word in the common English vocabulary, a poet who chooses the latter instead of the former may have sound literary reasons for doing so (for example, 'misery' in Vettese's poem quoted above is more effective in its context, for obvious metrical reasons, than (say) *teen, dule* or *grame*); and is no more necessarily guilty of any lack of linguistic patriotism than an English-writing poet using a French-derived term like *liberty* or *assist* instead of a native one like *freedom* or *help*. Allan Ramsay in the preface to his first volume of poems, published in 1721, remarked on the usefulness of the shared vocabulary to Scots writers: 'I can say, an empty House, a toom Barrel, a boss Head and a hollow Heart';[4] and his poetic successors to the present have likewise availed themselves of the double store of wealth in the uniquely Scottish and the common-core international English words which the Scots tongue contains. One reservation applies to the general principle that the use of words shared with English does not necessarily undercut the linguistic integrity of a Scots text. This is the practice nicknamed 'border-lowpin', of using an English instead of a Scots phonological form in a passage otherwise consistently in Scots for no other purpose than to secure a rhyme.

> The wanderin' bee it seeks the rose,
> Tae the lochan's bosom the burnie goes;
> The grey bird cries at evenin's fa':
> 'My luve, my fair ane, come awa'.'
> (Marion Angus, *Mary's Song* (extract), in *The Tinker's Road, and Other Verses*, London (Gowans & Gray), 1924)

This verse, and the poem to which it belongs, are in Scots, most of the vocabulary being drawn from the section shared with English: the form *goes*, however, is not in *any* respect Scots but an English word used instead of *gaes* or *gangs* for the sake of the rhyme. Marion Angus is one of the greatest lyric poets of the twentieth century; but this is a flaw, if a very minor one, in an exquisite poem.

ILLUSTRATIONS OF DIFFERENT FORMS OF SCOTS

The diversity of Scots in modern poetry will now be illustrated by an examination of a number of extracts showing some of the different linguistic forms which can come under the blanket heading of 'Scots'.

> ### A. A modern dialect (Fife)
> A cauld, sleety wind angles down the High Street.
> It blaws aff the Forth and ower the Links,
> Past the butcher's, the bookies, the pub and the Store.
> It rattles the lichts on the toun Christmas tree,
> It birls the newsagent's sign aroond,
> It blaws like a wild Blake picter
> On this mirkfu januar efternin.
> The Siberian wind kyths fae an airt lang held in ice
> And has blawn whaur a biggin-wa's ca'd doon.
> It has blawn whaur a playwricht's heezed up president,
> It has blawn ower a tyrant's bluidy heid,
> Through a year o revolutions.
> It blaws fae the Kremlin ower the Lammerlaws
> And through the tuim heids o Burntisland fowk
> On its road ti Glesgi. Syne we craw
> At the deith o Socialism and nivir speir oor thirldom.
> We blaw o oor culture capital – hot air.
> The cauld wind o reality yowls sairly past the Labour Club
> Singan that in Prague, Berlin and Bucharest
> Are the fowk wi a speerit and smeddum.
> (William Hershaw, *Januar Winds o Revolution*, in *The New Makars*,
> ed. Tom Hubbard, Edinburgh (Mercat Press) 1991, p. 169)

The first selection illustrates what is linguistically a register of Scots suggestive of the language as it survives in communities, such as Hershaw's Fife, where traditional dialects survived more or less unchanged until within living memory, though now their vocabulary at least is being homogenised to fit the common Anglophone culture. Many words are marked as Scots by spellings which convey the native pronunciation: *cauld, blaw, doon, toun* (Hershaw's spelling of this sound is inconsistent), *ower, licht, sair* and so on; and several distinctively Scots lexical items are easily identifiable: *birl* 'spin', *mirkfu* ('dark': the simple form *mirk* is actually more common, as adjective as well as noun), *kyth* 'appear', *airt* 'direction', *biggin* 'building', *heeze* 'raise', *tuim* 'empty', *smeddum* 'force of character'. On the other hand, all those words either belong to a fairly basic level of the vocabulary or are well-known from familiar passages in literature, folksay or popular entertainment.

Several instances occur of words for which a distinctively Scots equivalent could have been found without too much searching ('angles' could have been, say, *sklents*, 'butcher's' *flesher's*, 'pub' *howff*, 'rattles' *tirls*); but the Scots of this poem is, for the most part, such as might be expected to come naturally to contemporary speakers and hearers; and those more markedly Scots words are probably now recessive and out of keeping with the overall register. Only one word, *thirldom*, is really unlikely to belong to the active vocabulary of any living idiolect: it is chosen for its potent literary associations, recalling to educated readers Barbour's reference in his *Brus* to 'foule thirldome', describing the state of Scotland under English occupation. (The poem's title, too, *Januar Winds o Revolution*, recalls Burns, who in the song *There was a Lad* associated 'a blast o' Janwar win'' with his own birth; and who was seen in his time as a dangerous radical and revolutionary.) Nor is there anything in the language by which it can be identified with any specific part of Scotland (though this is, incidentally, achieved by a different method, namely the use of geographical markers: the Forth, Burntisland, the Lammerlaws): it is simply Scots in a typical modern form.

This realistic, unexaggerated Scots is used by Hershaw for a strongly expressed poetic statement relating to the contemporary world in which, appropriately, the dismal state of Scotland is mirrored by the plainness of the language. (It may be significant, however, that the only line in the poem with no Scots features of any kind, line 3, is a list of institutions which might be taken as typifying the unambitious, unimaginative, uninspired everyday life of most Scots.) The poet's aim is to present a scathing criticism of Scotland and the 'tuim heids' of its citizens, content with tokens such as the nomination of Glasgow as European City of Culture[5] while other countries are liberating themselves from far more oppressive and tyrannical regimes. The pervasive evocation of a freezing wind reinforces the harshness of the poet's judgement on the condition to which Scotland has been reduced by the apathy of the Scots. 'In Prague, Berlin and Bucharest' – the implication is clearly 'but no here' – 'are the fowk wi a speerit an smeddum': the last word is stereotypically held to designate a quality character-istic of the Scots as a race, but the bitter conclusion is that we are the people who do *not* possess it. The poem, in accordance with the ideals of the Scots Renaissance, is cosmopolitan in scope, with its references to momentous political events in Eastern Europe:[6] the first lesson to be learned from it is that any association of Scots with the 'kailyaird' – with a naively complacent acquiescence in a constructed world from which serious issues are firmly banished – is gone, beyond any fear of its revival.

> B. *A highly differentiated literary register*
>   Yonner awa, faur owre Clauchrie Tap
>   the smirrin clouds o the gloamin fa
>   in murnin reebans doun in ilka glack

tae thowe the shairds o the winter snaw.
Ma thochts are gruppit wi a skeer mindin
o a biggin faur owre the muir awa . . .
the brawest airt o ma halflin bydin
whaur ma hert raise up wi the daylicht's daw.

The Makkars say whit the hert lacks
is skailt abreid in the licht o Mey . . .
the morn it micht be that the suin braks
tae pent the hulls wi the wairtid's blae;
but thare's nae saw for whit canna hale . . .
a greinin efter a santit day.
Thare's nae licht in onie lift kin steal
the lang ladin o a lastie wae.

(William Neill, *Yonner Awa*, in *Selected Poems 1969–1992*, Edinburgh
(Canongate) 1994, p. 124)

The most immediately obvious feature of Neill's poem, to most readers, will be
the density of the Scots vocabulary:[7] nearly every word is distinctively Scots.
Many of the words are common literary currency and some could still be heard in
speech: *smirrin* 'drizzling', *gloamin* 'twilight', *halflin* 'boy, youth', *biggin* 'building', *airt* 'place', *skailt* 'scattered', *lift* 'sky'; others are more local, such as *glack*
'cleft between hills' which is mainly Eastern and North-Eastern, or likely to be
familiar, if at all, mainly from literature: *skeer* 'bright', *saw* 'salve', *greinin*
'longing', *lastie* 'enduring', *santit* 'blessed'; and one, *wairtid* 'time of change in
weather', is very rare. Words which are not exclusive to the lexis of Scots appear
in forms conditioned by the language's phonological history: *faur, owre, tap, fa,
doun,* etc. By its immediate appearance, that is, the language is near to what
Aitken has called 'Ideal Scots'[9]: a very different register from the contemporary
realism of Hershaw's language. Neill uses this register for a carefully worked
poetic statement.

The poem is written to a regular pattern: two eight-line stanzas rhyming
ABABCBCB (though some of the rhymes, such as 'Tap' – 'glack', are only
approximate). The rhythm cannot be consistently described in terms of iambics,
trochaics or the like; but a consistent pattern is maintained of five-beat lines in the
first stanza and (until the last two lines) four-beat in the second. A frequent
rhythmic device of juxtaposing two stressed syllables ('[a]wa faur', 'hert raise',
'nae saw' and so on) helps both to maintain a slow pace, appropriate to the
reflective tone of the poem, and sometimes to underline important words (such as
'skeer') or collocations (such as 'lang ladin'). The sound-music of the opening line
is immediately arresting: in all forms of Scots the words 'awa', 'faur' and
'Clauchrie', and in some at least 'yonner' too, have the same vowel sound.

The rhythm of 'Yonner awa', its suggestion of a dramatically emphasised gesture towards a distant view (underlined by the word 'faur'), and the use of a name strongly Scottish in its sound and obviously referring to a hill or mountain, add to the powerful impression of the line. Another instance of sound patterning occurs in the last lines, with the extended alliteration on [l], the vowel harmony in 'licht' – 'lift', and the alternating [a] – [e] – [a] – [e] in 'the lang ladin o a lastie wae'. (Possibly it was for the sake of this pattern that Neill used the form 'lastie' instead of the more common 'lestie'.) 'Murnan reebans' is a splendidly apt comparison for the dark vertical streaks of falling rain seen from a distance; and after the images of gloomy, forbidding weather, reinforced by the melancholy suggestions of the simile, the word 'skeer' effectively introduces a dramatic change of imagery and of mood. And the inherent emotive force of the Scots words is sometimes strengthened by the juxtaposition of two words of related or strongly contrasting meanings in the same line: 'smirrin' – 'gloamin', 'greinin' – 'santit'. This poem, with its highly charged and skilfully manipulated language, demonstrates that a maximally distinctive form of Scots (though one still closely related to traditional literary registers and spoken dialects) can be a potent medium for vividly descriptive and emotive poetry.

C. Contemporary urban colloquial

Ah'm shy. Aye, ah am. Canny look naebody in the eye.
Ah've seen me go in a shoap an jist hoap naebody wid talk tae me.
Things that happen, likesae – yer oot fur a walk
an some bloke whits never even spoke afore goes by
an he's givin ye the eye. See me, ah jist want tae die.
Ah go rid tae the roots o ma hair. Weel it's no fair, is it?
Feel a right twit. See ma Ma. She says it'll pass.
'Ye'll grow oot o it hen.' Aye, aw right. But when.
Ye kin get awfy fed up bein the local beetroot.
So last time ah went oot – tae the disco,
ah bought this white make-up. White lightning it said.
Ah thought nae beamers the night, this stuff'll see me aw right.
Onywey, there ah wis, actin it. Daen ma pale an intrestin bit.
White lightning. See unner them flashin lights.
it was quite frightnin. Cause ma face looked aw blue.
See, when ah think o it noo, it was mortifyin.
Cause they aw thought ah wis dyin, an they dialled 999.
(Janet Paisley, extract from *Sharleen: Ah'm Shy*, from *Ye Canna Win: Monologues*, Edinburgh (Chapman), 2000)

This extract illustrates an unmistakably different form of Scots: an accurate rendering of contemporary urban vernacular speech. Unlike Neill's densely Scots vocabulary, this passage contains almost no lexical items not to be found in a pocket-sized English dictionary: the exception is *beamer*, and that is not classical Scots but contemporary slang for a blush. In this, Janet Paisley is entirely realistic: the vocabulary associated with conservative rural dialects and literature in the mainstream Scots tradition is attenuated almost to vanishing in modern urban vernaculars (the process, that is, has advanced much further than in dialects of small towns and rural communities such as that used by Hershaw); but they have maintained a considerable measure of lexical distinctiveness by an inventive and colourful lexis of slang. The orthography, too, is not traditional (English or Scots) but is a quasi-phonetic spelling representing familiar pronunciation features of the dialect. Included are not only spellings representing anciently established sound developments exemplified in many words and in all forms of Scots, such as *naebody, tae, unner*, but also forms which are popularly – though with doubtful historical justification – associated with low-prestige urban sociolects, such as *ah* 'I', *ma* 'my', *fur* 'for', *shoap* 'shop', *rid* 'red'; spellings representing the reduced pronunciation of unstressed syllables such as *kin* 'can', and mis-spellings with no purpose except, perhaps, to contribute to the impression given of a lack of education on the part of the supposed speaker, such as *hoap* 'hope'.[10] A quasi-phonetic *canny* is used instead of the traditional *cannae*, the characteristically Scots vowel in *oot, noo* and the like is represented by the inauthentic, but unambiguous, < oo > instead of the < ou > favoured by writers in a more classical vein. This emphasis on the actual sounds, a notable feature of writing in this register, suggests an authorial intention of helping the reader to imagine with maximal accuracy and clarity the voice of the poem's supposed speaker.[11] The impression is reinforced by equally well-observed and realistically presented grammatical features, neither standard English nor traditional literary Scots but characteristic of the spoken register: the use of *see* to introduce a topic, the double negative 'canny look naebody . . .', the colloquial use of the second person pronoun for general statements, elision of the subject pronoun in 'Feel a right twit'; and by informal expressions like 'givin ye the eye', 'see me aw right', 'daen ma . . . bit' (in the sense of 'putting on my act': *daen* 'doing' is Scots *daein* but with a spelling suggesting the slurring of the second syllable). In this ostentatiously colloquial register, the presence of rhymes, occurring irregularly (and rarely at the ends of lines) and unobtrusively, but pervasively throughout the poem, adds a note of humorous irony. This language is used appropriately for a monologue in which the speaker, with some measure of ironic self-reflection, narrates a credible, though ludicrous, incident.

The function of this register, with its emphasis on realistic evocation of the phonology, grammar and idiom of contemporary speech, is to locate the supposed action of the poem firmly within a living and easily recognisable contemporary world. The expectation aroused by such a register would be of poetry in a realistic vein; though of course this could be ironically subverted.

D. Pseudo-medieval Scots

Bot see, Roberte, hou this selvin I yestreen
Stuid stracht and chauntitt oot the melodie
Aroon the quhilk thrie uthir vocis wyved
Your ornaments, your dansand, lowpand rinns
That mak repone until the auld firm tunes,
Quhill aa the pairts thegither mell tae mak
Your harmonie – and sae aa fower o us, throu you,
O lang-deid fere, stuid singand furth the Sooth:
Life's quhy, tyme's fullness, and the joie o treuth –

Amid the mirkness o December's drumlie licht
He coms, Mariae Filius, he coms in nomine
O Him quhase praise is peace, Creator omnium:
And wi this Co-eternal Bairn, we pray Thee com
Thou Consolator Spreit, et nobis tribue
Tae see this winter warld reborn spring-bricht,
And in oor herts tae hear, als I daed dae yestreen,
The soondand colours o Eternitie. Amen.

(James Reid-Baxter, *Domino Roberto Carwor Canonico de Scona*
(extract), in *The New Makars*, op. cit, p. 163)

This extract may be cited as a recent example of writing in a quasi-archaic register. This literary device has proved attractive to many twentieth-century poets, a major reason being its associations with the period when the Scots tongue was at its peak of development as a literary language and Scotland itself was an independent and active player on the European political, military and cultural stage. This poem is inspired by one of the great figures of the Stewart period, the composer Robert Carver[12] (the title means 'For Master Robert Carver, Canon of Scone'), who at one point is addressed as 'O lang-deid fere'; and refers to a performance of his Mass for Four Voices in which the poet (an authority on the Scottish musical tradition) took part. Latin phrases from the Mass are incorporated in the final section, and the composer is apostrophised using the Latin vocative 'Roberte'. The language suggests that Carver is being addressed in the Scots of his own time. Numerous orthographic and grammatical features of the pre-Union period are included: the spellings *uthir* and *com*, initial < quh- > corresponding to < wh- > in the modern language; < -is > for the plural ending (*vocis*), < -itt > (though the more usual spelling was < –it >) for the past tense (*chauntitt*) and < –and > for the present participle (*dansand* and so on);[13] the adjective ending of *selvin* (the same word as 'self' but meaning 'same' here: the expression *sel an same*, that is 'identical', can still be found in contemporary Scots speech); the relative pronoun form *the quhilk*, the obsolete conjunction *als* 'as' and noun *repone* 'reply'. This careful reconstruction of the Scots of an earlier age is used for a meditation in regular iambic rhythm, evoking not only Carver and his intricate and beautiful music (the phrase 'auld firm tunes' is a reference to the *cantus firmus* or principal melodic line) but the King's College Chapel of Aberdeen, built during Carver's lifetime and still retaining much of its original fabric. The associations of December and the Christian hope of rebirth, though familiar from countless songs and poems, are impressively and movingly revived: the contribution of the archaic language is to emphasise not only the formal and dignified tone, but the timelessness of the Christmas message. Whereas in the past, however, such re-affirmations of faith were often made for public performance (Carver's Mass itself, of course, being a case in point), Baxter's poem is intensely personal. This imparts, at least superficially, an element of paradox to the writing: a twentieth-century man is apparently presenting himself as talking in sixteenth-century Scots. The effect of this is to emphasise the intimate nature of his response to Carver's music, and by extension his imagined spiritual closeness to Carver himself:

> . . . aa fowr o us [i.e. the singers] *throu you*,
> O lang-deid fere, stuid singand furth the Sooth . . .

Sooth is 'truth'. The literary use of an archaic register is by now much rarer than in earlier stages of the Scots Renaissance; but Baxter's highly individual application of the device demonstrates clearly that it is still potentially a medium for impressive poetic statements.

E. A traditional dialect (Shetland)

> Veeve can I mind dat lang traik trowe da hill,
> Whin me feet felt laek lead, but left hardly a mett
> Idda boannie green moss at lay tick idda gyill.
> An I grett.
>
> Nae mair wid I waander alang da banks broo,
> Help wi da hirdin, or dell idda voar,
> Or waatch da froad rise as I mylkit da coo
> At da door.
>
> Nae mair wid I sit doon wi idders ta dine,
> Or cradle a peerie ting up i me bight,
> Fin waarm freendly fingers at clespit ower mine,
> An höld tight.
>
> Noo me böl wid be lonnly an caald o a night,
> An me days wid drag on athin lang idle-sit.

An me sweein een waatched da men right oota sight,
Help me flit.

I tink at da böst be a braa start sin syne.
A'm seen twa simmers here, or mebbe hit's tree.
Bit I weel mind da winters – dey wirna sae fine,
Tryin me . . .
(Rhoda Bulter, *Da Spilt Wife's Tale* (extract), in *The New Makars*,
op. cit, pp. 70–1)

Since the emergence of north-east Doric poetry at the turn of the century, a conspicuous thread in the tapestry of Scots literature has been local dialect poetry: verses written in a medium representing the phonology, grammar and vocabulary of a form of Scots spoken in a specific area. The north-east has always maintained a foremost place in this movement, with several writers (Sheena Blackhall being the finest contemporary example) transcending local status to acquire a national reputation; this region has the advantage of a highly differentiated set of dialects, actively supported by local patriotic pride. Other regions too, such as Fife and the Borders, have their dialect poetry. The present extract is taken from a part of Scotland[14] even more distinctive, linguistically and culturally, than the north-east, namely Shetland. The word 'Shetlandic' has recently come into use as a term for the dialects of the Shetland Isles, though it should be noted that by no means all Shetlanders approve of the term: whether so designated or not, it is a form of Scots with extensive Scandinavian influence. Many features of the dialect are visible at first glance in the passage, notably the front rounded vowel (like French *eu* in *peu*) represented by the spelling < ö >: *höld* is simply the dialect form of 'hold', *böst* a form of Scots *bude*, itself related to English *behove*, and means 'must'; *böl* is a noun meaning the lair or resting place of an animal (but here, touchingly, of the woman). Spellings such as *da* and *dat* for 'the' and 'that' (*idda* is 'in the'), and *trowe*, *tick* and *froad* for 'through', 'thick' and 'froth', show the absence of the fricative 'th' (that is [θ] and [ð]) sounds in Shetlandic. Other individual spellings representing a distinctive local pronunciation (as contrasted with the common Scots sounds of *broo*, *waatch*, *freendly* and so on) include *laek* 'like', *lonnly* 'lonely', *gyill* 'gill, that is, steep-sided valley'. 'My' unstressed is *me*; in other dialects the actual pronunciation is generally *ma*, though this is not always represented in the spelling. A characteristic grammatical feature of the dialect is the use of *be* instead of 'have' to form the perfect aspect: *A'm seen* for 'I've seen'. The distinctive Shetland vocabulary is represented by *mett* 'footprint', *voar* 'spring', *peerie* 'little'; and from other verses of the poem *aarl* 'walk feebly', *badd* 'garment', *dim-riv* 'daybreak', *hömin* 'twilight'.

A strongly regional language in poetry is often associated with equally localised subject matter: this is notably true of much of the large body of north-eastern poetry, inspired by, and deliberately conceived as a memorial to, the distinctive farming culture which survived well into living memory. This is not true of Rhoda Bulter's poem: the setting cannot be identified as Shetland, only as a general rural scene. The period also is indeterminate, though it is not the present or recent past: *spilt* in the title means 'ruined', but *spilt wife* is a specific euphemism for 'leper woman'. And the vivid and moving evocation of the woman's bravely endured suffering is presented by focusing on the daily tasks and social interactions that constitute the unvarying basis of life in rural communities, from which she is excluded. To that extent, the function of the Shetland language is not to locate the action of the poem, for nothing depends on the actual place. It is not merely incidental, however, nor lacking in any significance beyond the contingent choice of the author: by emphasising the individual humanity of the speaker it makes it impossible for readers to see her as simply an abstract specimen, thereby inviting them to empathise more closely with her plight. Dialect writing within Scots is no more necessarily a constraint on the range on the poet's creative expression than is the use of Scots itself, and Rhoda Bulter is one of several local dialect poets who have demonstrated this.

F. Experimental language
A freen is whiloms widder-gleam,
whiloms watter.
Lat gang thi dounmaist souch
o' August; a body

isna ae the ben o' an auch,
nakit licht, o' burd –
bouky birks,
summer-cloks i' thi snood;

it's i' the daurk fullyerie o' sleep
that lytach flesh
sheens,
thi fykie lempit-ebb o' thi tongue.

Whit is rale is thi wurd.
Na, it's no yit thi fykie
licht o' Mairch
at the neb o' a smirk,
nor thi greeshoch speil o' thi bere,

a shot-star o' swalla
showerickie

at a nakit shouder,
a smaa lane burn nid-noddy
i' its thrapple;

na, nor the guid, tairt guff
o' thi body, eftir luve,
snaikin doun-by tae the tide,
or thi doukin lown

o' thi peerie yaird,
lik a yawl wi a smirk at its neb;

na, it's jist a blink.
(David Kinloch, *Eftir Eugenio de Andrade* in *The New Makars*, op. cit,
pp. 176–7)

Finally, Kinloch's poem (based on a work by a contemporary Portuguese poet)
demonstrates the adaptability of Scots for modernist, experimental poetry. The
vocabulary is densely Scots, like Neill's poem; but unlike it, a reader cannot arrive
at the meaning of the poem simply by ascertaining the meanings of any unfamiliar
words. Most of the words are authentic Scots and have meanings which *can*
readily be ascertained. Many are relatively familiar from literature and can still be
heard in speech: *souch* 'sigh', *snood* 'hair-ribbon', *fykie* 'fussy, fidgety', *neb* 'nose'
or 'tip, point', *bere* 'barley', *guff* 'smell', *lown* 'calm, peace'. Some have an archaic
ring: *whiloms* 'sometimes', *fullyerie* 'foliage'; some are of local currency: *greeshoch*
'glowing embers' and the pronunciation *widder-gleam* ('weather-gleam' means
'band of clear sky on the horizon at twilight') suggest North-Eastern usages, *auch*
(glossed by Kinloch as 'fearful') is a rare North-Eastern form of *ergh*, itself not a
particularly common word; *simmer-clok* 'shimmering of sunbeams in the air' and
lempit-ebb (the shore between high and low tide: *lempit* is 'limpet') are attested
only in Shetland texts; and *shot-star* 'meteor' and *lytach* ('a large mass of wet
substance'; 'speech in an unknown tongue' or 'awkward, confused'), though
authentic, are decidedly unusual. Besides the obscurities of the vocabulary, some
avoidable irritations are presented by the poet's idiosyncratic spellings: *thi*, the
long-discredited apostrophes in *o'* and *i'*, the inexplicable *ae* in the fifth line.[15]
However, though the Scots is undeniably daunting in itself, the difficulty in
interpreting the poem inheres not principally in this but in the absence of any
obvious relationship among the images, or between them and anything they could
be taken as representing. 'A freen is whiloms widder-gleam, whiloms watter':
readers must interpret that as they will, and they will be no nearer to making sense
of it for learning that its English translation is 'A friend is sometimes a band of
clear sky on the horizon, sometimes water' – though they will certainly recognise

that the Scots at least reads better. Indeed, sound-patterns and rhythmic cadences are manoeuvred to attractive effect in the poem; and to that extent the use of Scots is a definite poetic asset. The general conclusion to be drawn here is that Scots can be used, without straining the boundaries of its vocabulary and grammar beyond the limits of credibility,[16] for poetry in an aggressively modernist vein, of which deliberate obscurity of thoughts and images is an integral part.

SUMMARY AND CONCLUSION

To summarise, then: the task of analysing, interpreting and evaluating a poem in Scots has many layers. First and most obviously, it behoves a reader to make sure he or she understands the *words* correctly. There is no difficulty in this: most published collections of Scots poetry include glossaries (a tradition which goes back to Allan Ramsay and includes, in his glossaries, those of Burns, and several others, some exceptionally interesting contributions to the study of Scots); and the language is splendidly provided with dictionaries and other reference works of the highest academic standards. This first stage may reveal subtleties beyond the surface meanings of the words: a very common device in modern Scots poetry (and by no means unique to it) is to include words or phrases which intentionally recall specific passages from earlier literature, making the context of *those* passages an integral part of a reader's response to the more recent poem. The *Scottish National Dictionary*, which gives quotations illustrating the uses of words throughout the eighteenth, nineteenth and twentieth centuries, can be highly revealing here. Next, the *particular form of Scots* being used should be identified: is it a traditional Scots, a strongly marked regional dialect such as that of Aberdeenshire or Shetland, a modern urban sociolect, a reconstructed archaic form? The spelling will certainly provide clues here: are uniquely Scots words written to suggest a general or a strongly local pronunciation (*stane* or *steen*); are international words written with the standard spelling or with something intended to suggest a locally or socially marked pronunciation (*am I* or *umma*)? If the language chosen carries overtones of a specific social or geographical setting, is this merely incidental, or has it a definite relevance to the overall impression given? What of the *verse*: does the poet use a metre reminiscent of ballads or bairnsangs, or one of the emphatically Scottish stanza forms known as the Habbie stanza, the Christ's Kirk stanza and the Helicon stanza[17]; and if so, why? To emphasise his membership in a continuous literary tradition dating back to Burns and beyond or – as not infrequently in modern literature – to suggest an ironic, subversive contrast between the traditional associations of the verse and an aggressively modern theme? Conversely, if he uses free verse, associated with writing of recent periods, does he make it coincide with a modern register of the language, such as an urban argot?

To any critic who imagines that it is sufficient to identify the language of a poem as 'Scots', the deserved response is MacDiarmid's line:

Nothing but heather! How marvellously descriptive! And incomplete!

NOTES

1. In the preface to the Scots section of *Underwoods*, his first collection of poems, first published in 1887.
2. A split in the Church of Scotland, arising from a dispute on the question of whether the appointment of ministers should be entirely the responsibility of the Church or within the jurisdiction of secular authorities. The dispute, which aroused passionate feelings, culminated in 1843 when a group of ministers walked out of the General Assembly to form the Free Kirk.
3. In *Contemporary Scottish Studies*, *Scottish Educational Journal* 10 July, 1925. This series of articles by Grieve, with the associated correspondence and a new introduction, was published by the *Scottish Educational Journal* in 1976; the reference to Murray is on p. 7 of this edition.
4. *The Works of Allan Ramsay Vol. 1*, eds B. Martin and J. W. Oliver, Scottish Text Society Third Series 19, Edinburgh and London (Blackwood) 1945, p. xix.
5. In the event, Glasgow rose splendidly to this opportunity, despite initial misgivings, and the year was a major success; but carpings on various political, ideological and pragmatic grounds were heard from several quarters throughout the period.
6. The collapse of the Berlin Wall; the election of the distinguished revolutionary dramatist Vaclav Havel to the presidency of Czechoslovakia; the downfall of the Romanian dictator Ceaucescu, all of which took place in 1986.
7. For convenience I will use the familiar expressions 'Scots words' or 'Scots vocabulary' to refer to *exclusively* Scots words; but the caution given against failing to recognise words which are similar or identical to their English cognates as being equally Scots may as well be repeated here for safety.
8. This is Neill's gloss; but the word can also mean 'spirited away', which would also make good sense in the context. In the work of as literary a writer as Neill, this double meaning was surely intentional.
9. See 'The Good Old Scots Tongue: does Scots have an Identity?', by A. J. Aitken, in *Minority Languages Today*, eds E. Haugen, J. D. McClure and D. S. Thomson, Edinburgh (EUP) 1981, pp. 72–90. I use the term here without Aitken's ironic overtones.
10. This detail could be seen as an authorial misjudgement, since it invites a patronising attitude to the persona. Orthographic idiosyncrasies which actually convey a definite and distinctive pronunciation are presumably intended to evoke the sound of the speaker's voice, leaving the reader to form his or her own impression of (in this case) her character and human worth; but since *hoap* has precisely the same sound-implication as *hope*, the implication is pointedly something like 'look how ignorant this girl is – can't even spell!'
11. A device which would only work, of course, for readers familiar with the sound of the accent represented.

12. On Carver see 'Scotland's Greatest Composer: an Introduction to Robert Carver (1487–1566)' by Richard Turbett, in *Bryght Lanternis: Essays on the Language and Literature of Mediaeval and Renaissance Scotland*, eds J. D. McClure and M. R. G. Spiller, Aberdeen University Press 1989, pp. 48–54.

13. In the middle decades of the century many poets made a consistent distinction between < –an > for the present participle and < –in > for the verbal noun, following the MSc distinction of < –and > and < –ing > : a somewhat pedantic procedure since the distinction had long vanished from most forms of spoken Scots. Baxter's use of the MSc ending in its full original form, unlike this practice, is a deliberate archaism.

14. Politically and administratively this is true, just as it is true that Scotland is part of the United Kingdom. It is equally true that many Shetlanders do not consider themselves to be Scots, just as many Scots do not consider themselves to be British.

15. Conceivably this means 'in': when unstressed, and with the frequent Scots elision of the 'n', the pronunciation would be indistinguishable from an unstressed 'ae'. But as the poet writes 'in', conventionally, as 'i' elsewhere, there is no obvious reason for this idiosyncratic spelling to be used here.

16. W. N. Herbert, as we have seen, is notoriously guilty of that; another contemporary example is Robert Crawford.

17. For examples of these see Burns' poems *To a Mouse, Holy Fair* and *Epistle to Davie, a Brother Poet*. All can be illustrated from recent Scots poetry, though no examples have been discussed in the present chapter.

CHAPTER 11

The Scots Language Abroad

Michael Montgomery

If it is true that those who migrate to a new land always carry linguistic bags along, it often remains difficult to identify the contents of those bags – either specific speech patterns or, in the case of the many leaving Scotland, what language(s) they spoke.[1] Gaelic, English and Scots, as well as varieties intermediate between the last two and regional varieties of each, have departed Caledonia's shores since the late fourteenth century for Ireland or more distant lands. Estimating the speakers of each within the diaspora is a matter of considerable guesswork, as records from which their speech can be discerned have varied greatly in time and place and often offer only fragments or suggestions. Most evidence before the twentieth century is indirect, anecdotal or clothed in a written form that disguises it to one degree or another. Some of the richest survivals of Scots date from the early seventeenth century in Ulster, the northern province of Ireland, in less-monitored documents like correspondence or in legal documents that preserve conventionalised forms from the previous century, the high point in the development of Lowland Scots.[2] Many emigrants spoke both Scots and English, Gaelic and English, or Scots and Gaelic. Whatever English they spoke was often scotticised to one degree or another.

Gaelic went to north-east Ulster between the fourteenth and seventeenth centuries, to eastern North Carolina in the Argyll Colony beginning in 1739, and to Nova Scotia, Newfoundland and Australia in the nineteenth century. It remains a living language only in eastern Canada (Shaw 1997). It persisted for a century in North Carolina, where remnants were recalled into the twentieth century (MacDonald 1993), but left little if any imprint on the English there.

Varieties of English also left Scotland, including Scottish Standard English and Highland and Island English.[3] These varieties are dated from at least the late seventeenth century (Aitken 1992a, b). A fascinating letter in Highland English from a Highland emigrant in Maryland to his Inverness-shire father around 1710 was possibly the work of an untutored individual. It has been published as a rhetorical set-piece since the late eighteenth century and is more likely a 'pseudo-dialect', stylised document self-consciously composed, as hardly a word has escaped modified spelling (for example, 'Dis is te lat ye ken, dat I am in quid healt, plessed be Got for dat, . . .') and its punctuation is standard. Its importance to linguistic historians lies in its implication that some early emigrants to North America spoke Scots or English heavily influenced by Gaelic, especially in phonology (McPherson c.1710; Millar 1996). The colonists to North Carolina usually had Gaelic as their first language, but the writing they left was in an English also influenced by Lowland Scots (Montgomery 1997a), implying either an English-Scots continuum in parts of Argyll or the existence of Highland Scots. Meyer (1961: 112–19) outlines the history of Gaelic in North Carolina, but says nothing about Highlanders using Scots or English.

This chapter overviews distinctive features of Scots and Scottish English that can be traced from Scotland to Ulster or farther abroad. Reconstructing the migration of Scots overseas might seem dubious at best, given the assessment of a prominent recent work sketching the history of the language:

> Scots, by contrast [with English], is a language spoken nowhere else in
> the world . . . But despite the vast number of Scots who have
> emigrated in the past two centuries, there appears to be no clear case of
> Scots surviving outwith Scotland as a community language, as Gaelic
> survived until recently in Argentina and has endured to the present day,
> in some cases through an astonishing seven generations, in Nova Scotia:
> all that remains of a Scots linguistic presence overseas is a handful of
> dialect words in the folk-speech of some regions of eastern North
> America and New Zealand. (McClure 1997: 56)

If this statement represented a full and accurate profile of the migration and influence of Scots abroad, this chapter would be a short one indeed.[4] It overlooks the large, still thriving areas of Scots spoken for 400 years in Ulster, the only area beyond Scotland where broad Scots (sometimes still called 'braid Scotch' in the countryside) remains a medium of daily life.[5] And it does not take into account the significant scholarly literature produced in the past decade or so, especially in the United States and New Zealand. This chapter will survey and assess this scholarship and where possible discuss earlier work. Much of this is little known outside Scotland.

At the time that English replaced it as the language of established and professional classes, first in writing in the late sixteenth century and in speech a century or more later, Scots began to be taken beyond the bounds of Scotland. Because it remained the everyday spoken tongue for most in the Lowlands and those who emigrated were overwhelmingly from the working classes, first from rural areas but by the nineteenth century also from cities, there can be no doubt that the Scots language frequently arrived on foreign shores, whatever its ultimate fate there might have been. Across the Irish Sea it took root as Ulster Scots, and in locales beyond Ulster it continued to be used by first- and possibly many second-generation emigrants. Expatriates and in some cases their children wrote in Scots in the United States in the eighteenth century, Australia in the nineteenth, and perhaps elsewhere. Beyond Ireland Scots is traceable in specific lexical, grammatical and phonological features. In general the influence is most detectable in grammar and least in pronunciation.

The *Scottish National Dictionary* (Grant and Murison 1931–76) more than any other resource has made comparative work on Scots possible. Before its publication scholars were dependent on the *OED* and *EDD*. Neither of these minimises the Scottish component, but neither rivals the coverage of the ten–volume *SND*. For a long time scholars working on Scots or Scottish linguistic elements abroad have worked in isolation and have, especially in Ulster[6], produced bodies of research often local and little known to their counterparts. The North American literature, with the exception of one or two writers, rarely uses the designation *Scots*, recognises a distinction between Scots and Scottish English or employs the *SND* or other standard resources from Scotland. This chapter seeks not only to bring cohesion to the disparate scholarship, but to bridge the many barriers in the field.

ULSTER

Coastal areas of Ulster are more accessible to much of western and south-western Scotland than to the rest of Ireland. From Fair Head in north-east County Antrim across the Irish Channel to the Mull of Kintyre is only 12.6 miles, from Donaghadee in County Down to Portpatrick on the Mull of Galloway only twenty-two. Across these narrow sea-bridges peoples have crossed for millennia and intertwined their linguistic histories. Given all this, one might question whether Ulster is truly 'abroad'.[7] Events of the seventeenth century, especially the Plantation of Ulster (1610–25), had the profoundest effect and a lasting one on the linguistic geography and cultural politics of Ireland to the present day. Since that time many have returned to Scotland to escape political or other hardship or to seek tertiary education, continuing to tie the two together. Gallowglasses in the fourteenth century and other early settlers in Ulster were Gaelic speakers mainly from Argyll and the Hebrides, but Scots was planted permanently by the end of the sixteenth. The earliest known document from Ulster written in Scots is a letter to Elizabeth I written in March 1571 by Agnes Campbell, a member of the house of Argyll and native of Kintyre, on behalf of her husband Turlough O'Neil and addressed from County Tyrone. It begins:

It will ples your maiestie knaw yat I your ma[ties] suitore Agnes
Campbell Lady of Cantire in Scotland hes happynit threw my chance
and portoun to cum heir in Irland in yo[r] maiesties realm and is marreid
uponn Oneill quha is yo[r] maiesties trew subject . . . I am maist
desyrous of any erthlie thing that zour grace will accept and recive my
said husband Oneill in zour hienes service and subiectioun quha is
verrie earnestlie bent th[r] unto . . . (Hayes-McCoy 1937: 116)

Herein we find numerous forms having Scottish orthography (*zeirlie, uthris, quha*), pronunciation (*maist, quha*) and morphology (*happynit*). Perhaps the most diagnostic feature in this and many other texts and varieties is the concord between subjects and verbs. This follows the traditional Scottish pattern of marking any present-tense verb with *-s* (or by analogy, using *is* or *has*) if its subject is not an adjacent personal pronoun (Murray 1873: 211–13; Montgomery 1994). (The pattern is called, *inter alia*, the 'Northern concord rule' and the 'Northern present-tense rule', as historically it has also characterised the English north of the Humber.) Lowland Scots and English thus have two different concord paradigms, one depending on the proximity between a subject and its verb and on the type of subject (noun vs. pronoun), the other on the number and person of the subject. The excerpt from the Campbell letter has three contexts, all adhering to the Scottish rule: *I . . . hes happynit, I . . . is marreid* and *I am maist desyrous*. In Ulster Scots and more particularly for varieties of English overseas, the presence or absence of this concord pattern is an index to Scottish influence. It occurs widely – in the United States (Montgomery 1997b), in Nova Scotia (Kinloch 1985), in Australia (Tulloch 1997b) – and found its way even into African American English (Montgomery et al. 1993).

Following the death of Elizabeth I in 1603 and a series of largely ineffective attempts at English plantations (that is, permanent settlements) in Ireland, her successor James I initiated a joint English and Scottish colonial venture for the province in 1610. The Plantation of Ulster was a large-scale programme that followed the lead of Scottish noblemen James Hamilton and Hugh Montgomery, who had acquired lands in County Down in 1605. It involved the settlement of English and Scottish 'undertakers' and 'servitors' (now generally referred to as 'planters', a modern term) in six of Ulster's nine counties west of the River Bann: Armagh, Cavan, Coleraine, Donegal, Fermanagh and Tyrone. Scottish settlers came mainly from the south-west Lowlands from Renfrewshire to Wigtonshire, with not insignificant numbers from the central Lowlands and south-west Highlands. English settlers were largely from the north-west Midlands and London. Progress was to be monitored by the Crown, with the English to settle in some areas and Lowland Scots in others (Perceval-Maxwell 1973; Robinson 1984). The result was 'one of the most politically significant mass migrations to have taken place in western Europe since medieval times' (Robinson 1984: 1).[8]

Linguists have noted that when Lowland Scots was brought to Ulster at the beginning of the seventeenth century, this was when 'it displayed the greatest difference from English' (Barry 1996: xi). Though this assessment pertains to speech, it can also be surmised from surviving documents, as in an assignment of land from Robert McClelland to David Cunningham, dated 1614:

I Sir Robert McClellane of Bomby knight be thir presentis does faithfullie promeiss to my gud freynd David Cunynghame of Heurt his airis and assignayis to set to thame ane sufficient Laice of twell scoir aikeris of land that I haif of the Happerdaschers portion of Londary and that for the space of one and fiftie yeirs lyand within the Countie of Culraine in ony pairt of the said Happerdaschers proportioun now perteyning to me exceptand and reservand the stone hous and mannis . . .[9]

This short passage contains numerous Scottish forms, including the plural demonstrative adjective *thir*, noun plurals in *-is* (*presentis, airis, aikeris*), a non-adjacent verb marked with *-s* (*I Sir Robert McClellane . . . does*), the indefinite article *ane* before a consonant, present participle forms in *-and* (*lyand, reservand*) and such variants as *twell* 'twelve' and *haif* 'have'.

In Antrim and Down a private plantation took place involving Scots largely to the exclusion of English colonists. Scots established demographic dominance over the English in much of seventeenth-century Ulster. According to Braidwood:

[even] in what might well have been a purely English plantation the Scots intruded early and increasingly, till they eventually became predominant, encroaching at first across the Bann from Scots-settled Antrim, and in the later seventeenth century direct from Scotland through Derry city, a natural port for Scots immigrants. (1964: 31)

The ratio of Scots to English during the century has often been put at five or six to one (Adams 1977: 57). This would have been higher in Antrim and north Down, but more evenly balanced in the six escheated counties, where the native Irish were still in the majority in most Ulster parishes, according to the 1659 hearth money rolls. One calculation cited by Braidwood (1964: 6) 'reckons there were 100,000 Scots and 20,000 English in Ulster' at the time of the 1641 uprising by the Irish. Demographic patterns resulting from plantation settlements ensured that there were two, and sometimes three, cultural traditions in contact in much of the province.

The features of Scots used in the receipts, leases, promissory notes and other documents among McClelland's papers are conservative ones, but documents dating from the 1620s already began shifting markedly toward English counterparts of the forms cited above. After the Plantation generation Scots declined as a written medium in Ulster if anything more rapidly than on the Scottish mainland (Montgomery 1992a), in the process usually termed 'anglicisation'. Only traces can be found after 1630, in church records and letterbooks (Montgomery and Gregg 1997: 589–90).

However, Ulster Scots found voice anew in following centuries in vernacular literature (see Montgomery and Gregg 1997) for a detailed account). Three principal periods of expression can be identified. One lasted from the 1780s through the mid-1850s and involved the 'Weaver' poets, a school of popular versifiers who wove linen by trade. Many assumed the stance of community spokesmen and were given nicknames signifying this; James Orr (1770–1816), perhaps the most notable, was known as the 'Bard of Ballycarry' and wrote in 'The Dying Mason' c.1790:

Nae mair shall I gang, while in this side o' time . . .
Nae mair, while ilk mouth's clos'd, an' fast the door bar'd,
Initiate the novice, baith curious and scaur'd;
Nae mair join wi' scores in the grand chorus saft . . .
Nor fandly toast 'Airlan' – and peace to the craft';
I aye cud been wi' ye, but now I maun stay
Confin'd in my lang hame – the cauld house o' clay.

This poetic movement drew from local themes and was by no means a mere imitation or derivation from Robert Burns' work. A definitive account appears in Hewitt (1974).

A later stage of Ulster Scots literature extended from the 1850s well past 1900. It consisted of popular sketches, commentaries and stories in local newspapers in Antrim and Down. These were typically couched in a folksy first-person style and addressed a range of social and political topics and issues, the authors (often pseudonymous) seeing themselves as voices of the people. Most recently a literary revival has once again taken place in Northern Ireland, symbolised by the founding of the Ulster-Scots Language Society in 1992 and the advent of its magazine *Ullans*, which regularly features new writing in Ulster Scots (Montgomery 1997c).

Scottish works on emigration to North America are numerous (Graham 1956; Adams and Somerville 1993; Dobson 1994 and so on). But despite considerable literature on the migration of Scots to Ulster produced on the other side of the 'Sheugh' (Hill 1873; Perceval-Maxwell 1973; Robinson 1984), references in Scotland to its people making the much shorter journey across the Irish Sea in the seventeenth century are remarkably difficult to find. The continuing national amnesia about those who left for Ulster is seen in that the only connection between Scotland and Ulster identified by the newly expanded

National Museum of Scotland's 'Scotland and the World' exhibit is migration from the other direction – the arrival of thousands from Ulster and the rest of Ireland since the nineteenth century.

The extension of the Scots language to Ulster has rarely merited a passing note by Scottish scholars (Aitken 1998 is one exception), and outside one or two major sources (such as Patterson's *Glossary of Words in Use in the Counties of Antrim and Down*, 1880)[10], the literature on Ulster Scots seems virtually unknown in Scotland. But connections with Ulster were recognised from the beginning by the *SND*, which refers to 'Ulster Scots' as primarily a 'variant of West-Mid Scots' from Ayrshire and Renfrewshire (Grant 1931: xli), and by the *Linguistic Atlas of Scotland* (Mather and Speitel 1975–86), which collected 116 questionnaires in seven Ulster counties.[11] Perhaps because of their preoccupation with such issues as the literary status of Lowland Scots or its relations with English, scholars have hardly begun to compare varieties, developments or individual features across the channel (but note Milroy 1981 and Macafee 2001a and forthcoming a).

To be fair, most literature on Ulster Scots has until recently been produced by Ulster-based scholars or had only local dissemination. Milestones include Patterson's glossary, Marshall's *Ulster Speaks* (1936), Gregg's 'The Scotch-Irish dialect boundaries in Ulster' (1972), Macafee's *Concise Ulster Dictionary* (1996), Fenton's *The Hamely Tongue* (1995/2000) and Robinson's *Ulster-Scots* (1997). And to be sure, scholars in Ireland have too often displayed a comparable blind spot by approaching all differences between Irish English and Standard British English as based on a Gaelic substratum in one way or another. For example, the *Dictionary of Hiberno-English* (Dolan 1998) cross-references many items to the *OED*, but makes no use of the *SND* or *DOST*. The bias affects studies of grammatical features especially. For example, in referring to the Scottish verbal concord pattern outlined earlier, which has spread throughout the north of Ireland, Todd (1971: 37–8) states that 'a factor which probably contributed to its widespread use is the fact that, in Gaelic there is no agreement between NP and the VP', here and elsewhere attempting to associate grammatical features in Ulster English with a Gaelic source but never a Scottish one.

Through Ulster Scots the linguistic influence from Scots pervaded Mid-Ulster English (spoken in Armagh, Fermanagh, most of Down and Tyrone, and other areas settled in the seventeenth century mainly by the English). This is most salient in vocabulary, but present as well in pronunciation and grammar. Ulster is the only place where the Scottish Vowel-Length Rule (by which vowels are lengthened before /r/, voiced fricatives or a morpheme boundary; Aitken 1981) survives, in both the Ulster Scots and Mid-Ulster English territory (Harris 1984, 1985). The extent of its operation is a prominent feature distinguishing the two speech areas. 'Punctual *whenever*' to indicate an event that happened only once in the past is ubiquitous in both and in some American varieties, but came originally from Scotland (Montgomery and Kirk 2001).

In reconstructing the input of English and Scots to North America in the eighteenth century, scholars must avoid simplistic correlations of regions on each side of the Atlantic. It is easy to rely falsely on extrapolations from modern data based on assumptions (as in Tagliamonte and Smith 2000) that regions have been static over the past two or more centuries. Most linguistic influence from Ulster came ultimately from Lowland Scotland, but some can be traced to England or to indigenous developments (as adverbial positive *anymore* 'nowadays'). Events of the seventeenth century, in bringing thousands of Scots and English to the province, made Ulster a complex linguistic bridge across the North Atlantic between Britain and North America (Montgomery and Robinson 2000).

Thus, Ulster has represented a dynamic situation of language and dialect contact, perhaps the most dynamic in the British Isles over the past half-millennium. In Scotland, Scots had already been in contact with Scottish Gaelic and English in the late-medieval/early-modern period. In Ulster it came into contact with Irish Gaelic and types of English, in North America with several other types of English, as well as German and other European languages, especially in Pennsylvania. In each of these locales the contact was usually long-term. When we move farther abroad, it is both Scots and Ulster Scots which formed input varieties. In many places, especially in the United States, there are reasons to believe that Ulster Scots was the more prominent of the two.

NORTH AMERICA

Beyond Ulster our attention will focus mainly on the United States. Historical research on its varieties is the farthest advanced and has found that Scots played a significant role in the formation of American English. Donaldson (1980: 908) estimates that as many as one and a half million people have emigrated from Scotland to the United States since the seventeenth century. Though forming a considerable number, their settlement was rather dispersed in time, somewhat less so in areas of settlement. Migration from Scots-speaking parts of Ulster was more concentrated and had a greater linguistic impact, but Lowland Scots and Ulster Scots were varieties that differed little and must have coalesced in some places. Estimates of emigrants from Ulster to North America between 1717 and 1775 range between 50,000 and 250,000.[12] Most were Presbyterians of Scottish ancestry, and many accounts assume that the numerical superiority of the Scottish population in Ulster meant that people of either English or Irish background had become culturally if not linguistically Scottish by their departure for North America. Hence the inclusive term *Scotch-Irish* employed over the past three centuries first mainly by outsiders but by the nineteenth century generally by Americans of Irish Protestant background.[13] Lowland Scots/Ulster Scots formed a linguistic continuum with English that allowed emigrants to shift easily

to the latter (and back) in their new environments. This eroded awareness of
Scottish linguistic identity within a short time of arrival. It was responsible for the
loss of many salient Scottish features and the survival of others in regional
varieties or as covert recesses.

While Lowlanders settled in most colonies, Ulster Scots generally landed in
Delaware or Pennsylvania and headed to the frontier, reaching Virginia by the
1730s and the Carolinas by the 1750s. As a plurality of those populating the
interior in the latter half of the eighteenth century, the Ulster Scots/Scotch-Irish
and their descendants became culturally influential in much of Appalachia
(Tennessee, Kentucky, North Carolina and so on). There and in Pennsylvania
the most profound linguistic connections can be detected.

Ulster may be only the location outwith Scotland where Scots *per se* is spoken
today, but evidence indicates that it was used in America in the eighteenth
century. It was a vehicle for both poetry and for dialogue in drama and fiction in
colonial and early American literature. The best-known work using Scots is
Modern Chivalry (4 volumes, 1792–1815), a picaresque novel by Hugh Henry
Brackenridge, who came from Kintyre as a child to Pennsylvania. Brackenridge
satirised excesses of democracy in the new republic through stock characters such
as Duncan Ferguson, a servant of his protagonist, Captain John Farrago.
Ferguson's speech is lexically and phonologically Scots:

'Captain,' said Duncan, 'it canna be, but ye ken right weel what I
mean. It is na the denomination o' your temporal capacity, that I wad
be at; but of your religion, and to what persuasion ye belong; whether
o' the Covenant, or of the Seceders, or the high kirk o' Scotland.'
(1965: 269)

Brackenridge was representing speech he knew well, but also exploiting established conventions. Research by Cooley (c.1995) has identified ten stock characters in eighteenth-century American literature, including Irish, German,
French, Scottish, African-American, Quaker, Yankee, Amerindian, Yiddish
and Fops, for some of which a standard set of linguistic features was employed.
Eight authors, beginning with Arthur Murphey in *The Apprentice* (1756), use
Scots features, eleven of pronunciation (*guid, mony*), eight of grammar (*maun,*
preterites in *-it*) and seven of lexicon (*muckle, bairn*). Such inventories no doubt
had a basis in real-life models, but also indicate that portrayals of ethnic and social
character types, especially on the dramatic stage, had taken a life of their own by
the time of the American Revolution.

Two Ulster-born poets who used Scots in America have come to light
(Montgomery 2000). It is clear that individual emigrants like these men, and
sometimes their descendants, maintained it as a resource for certain purposes.
This is evident from ephemeral literature in areas where Ulster emigrants

predominated in the eighteenth century (such as parts of Pennsylvania and south-eastern New Hampshire) and left their stamp through place names of Ulster provenance (*Londonderry*, *Donegal*). Since most poetry in Scots appeared first in newspapers, it must have been accessible to a general public. Its publication over a course of years suggests a continuing vernacular tradition that had roots in the British Isles.

The more notable of the two poets was David Bruce (c.1760–1830), who wrote twenty-two poems and songs in Scots under the name 'the Scots-Irishman' (Newlin 1928). His 1801 collection, *Poems Chiefly in the Scottish Dialect, Originally Written under the Signature of the Scots-Irishman*, embodies the conviction that the Scots language was an entirely fit and effective medium for literary expression. Bruce's support for a local insurrection opposing a federal tax on the private production of whiskey prompted his first poem in Scots, 'To Whiskey', in 1794. It begins:

I wat ye are a cunning chiel,
O' a' your tricks I ken fu' weel,
For aft ye hae gien me a heel,
And thrown me down,
When I shook hands wi' heart so leel,
Ye wily loun.

Robert Dinsmoor (1757–1836) was the great-grandson of an emigrant from County Antrim in 1723 who was an early settler in Londonderry, New Hampshire. He employed 'Scotch' in poetry about daily and personal events, usually with little view to publication (Dinsmoor 1828). Such locally known, topical literature in the late eighteenth and early nineteenth centuries implies more extensive material that has not survived. We know of Bruce and Dinsmoor primarily because their collective poetry was reprinted towards the end of the lives through the initiative of others. The work of each indicates that many fellow citizens were either fluent in Scots or familiar with the tradition of writing poetry in the common language of Lowland Scotland and parts of Ulster in the eighteenth century.

Other eighteenth-century documents written in Scots include a 1737 'pseudo-dialect' letter from an Ulster emigrant in New York (Montgomery 2001b) and a 'Petition and Remonstrance to the President and Congress of the United States' (1794), an extended verse by an anonymous North Carolina Planter protesting the same tax that David Bruce of Pennsylvania opposed.

From the lack of discussion of scotticisms in synoptic treatments of American English such as Krapp (1925) and Marckwardt (1958), it would seem that the Scots were the largest colonial emigrant group not to have had a linguistic impact on American English. While the Scottish contribution has been slow to be recognised, this is in part due to the lack of American resources comparable to the *SND*. The topic has been revolutionised by the *Dictionary of American Regional English* (Cassidy et al. 1985–). Analysis of materials in *DARE* can be undertaken along many lines, including etymology, regional labels and parts of speech. Hamilton (1998a, 1998b) has made a significant start in exploring the linguistic legacy of Scottish settlers in the US, citing principal trends for 365 items identified as Scottish (usually this means attested in the *SND* and other works of Scottish lexicography) in the first two volumes of *DARE* (letters A–H).[14] For the same letters the *American Dialect Dictionary* (Wentworth 1944) identified sixty-one items as Scottish, extracted from *Webster's Second International Dictionary* (1934), which apparently relied on labels from the *OED*.

Hamilton extrapolates that *DARE* as a whole will contain one thousand Scottish items that made their way into regional American English. This number is not only respectable, but rather surprisingly, it outranks the contribution of French, German or Spanish (this last includes Peninsular, American, Cuban and Mexican varieties).[15] Macafee (forthcoming b) states that it is 'striking . . . what a small proportion' of Scottish items has survived in overseas varieties of English, estimating that for the United States they represent only about two per cent of the material in the *SND*. She is puzzled that Scottish terms for body parts and other common vocabulary are absent in the *DARE* record, but these would almost certainly have eroded early under the massive levelling processes in the United States. Scottish items in *DARE* represent forty semantic categories, but most often surviving are ones that involve cultural elements and practices such as foodways (*clary*, *dropped egg*), seasonal customs (*first-footer*) and children's games (*horns*, *hy spy*). According to Hamilton (1998a: 116), the largest number of items was documented for Pennsylvania (77), North Carolina (76) and Virginia (70).[16]

Even so, this quantification is deceptive in two ways. Whereas other sources in the US fail to acknowledge or else underestimate the influence of Scots on American English, *DARE* overestimates it in not indicating that many items cited as having Scottish etymologies probably came from Ulster. This is rather understandable in that the dictionary for its early volumes did not have resources for Ulster Scots such as Macafee (1996) and Fenton (1995/2000) to consult. More importantly, the quantification pertains overwhelmingly to lexical items, reflecting *DARE*'s reliance on sources that are themselves compilations of lexical material. Despite reasons why lexical items would be most expected to survive in language contact situations, thorough investigation finds that not only has a much larger portion of Scottish grammatical patterns been maintained, but that these are less likely to be relics than their lexical counterparts.[17]

The grammatical influence of Scots on American English has been most profound in Appalachia and in the Midland region, which derived from Pennsylvania through eighteenth-century migration.[18] Among the respective features we can identify three broad types:

First are features clearly traceable to Scots, though in only a few cases have these remained the same in distribution or function in American English. In addition to verbal concord (outlined earlier), these include:

1. the combination of modal auxiliary verbs (usually an epistemic and a root modal, as *might could*, *might would*) has been documented in the modern day in Scotland (Miller and Brown 1982), Ulster and northern England on the one hand and the American Midland and South on the other (Montgomery and Nagle 1994; Mishoe and Montgomery 1994). More combinations and different pragmatic functions are found in the US, where *will can*, the most common combination in Scotland and Ulster, is unknown.
2. *have* deleted before past participles (note Orr's verse cited earlier: 'I aye cud been wi' ye . . .').
3. *need* + past participle, as 'that table needs cleaned'.
4. *want* + preposition (that is ellipsis of infinitive *to go/to come*), as 'the dog doesn't know whether he wants in or out'.
5. *till* 'to' (now in the US only to express time before the hour), as 'he'll be here about quarter till eight'.
6. the tendency to attach *yin* (in Scotland) and *one* (in the US, where it is often reduced *'un*, as *big 'un*) to adjectives and pronouns. The form *you 'uns* is attested in Scots (*SND*, s.v. *ane¹/yin* III 2), but apparently as a phrase. In the US it became a second-person-plural pronoun. Often written *yinz* or *yunz* to indicate its monosyllabic pronunciation, it has currency in Appalachia and the Upper Ohio Valley as far north as Pittsburgh. The equivalent form *yous* is now common in vernacular Scots (especially in the south-west) and Ulster (where the hybrid *yuz yins* is also in Ulster Scots).

Second are features reinforced by Scots and Standard Scottish English, as seen in quantitative preference of one form over another: *that* as a relativiser rather than *who/which*; *wait on* rather than *wait for*, contraction of an auxiliary with the subject rather than with *not* ('He's not' vs. 'He isn't'). Others involve contextual details, such as use of modal *will* in questions ('Will I take your coat?').

Third are covert or disguised features that involve collocations or functions not recognised because they appear to be general English. Examples include the combination of *all* with interrogative pronouns (as 'Who all is coming?', 'What all did he say?')[19] and 'punctual *whenever*' 'at the time that' (for a single event in the past, 'He wasn't born whenever we moved off') or 'as soon as' ('Whenever I heard about it, I signed up right away'; Montgomery and Kirk 2001).

The Scottish contribution to American pronunciation appears to be modest and consists of contributing factors rather than fundamental ones, but to date the question has not been explored comprehensively. The main American resource is Kurath and McDavid's *Pronunciation of English in the Atlantic States* (1961), based on interviews conducted by the Linguistic Atlas of the United States and Canada project with older speakers from 1931 to the early 1950s. According to *PEAS*, specific American pronunciations (mainly in Pennsylvania) that reflect ancestry from Scotland or Ulster include *calm* with vowel /a/ or /æ/ (142), *food* with /ʊ/ (156), *yolk* /jok/ (160), and *drought/drouth* with /u/ (167).

According to Lass, the vowel systems of all American and overseas dialects of English are essentially that of southern, especially south-eastern, England – and any 'non-southern features that do occur are generally unabsorbed relics' (1987: 275). Completely lacking in American English are most northern British patterns that must have been brought by many Scottish and Ulster emigrants, such as the non-shifting of /u/ to a diphthong in *house* (except in *drouth*, mentioned above) and the non-lowering of /ʊ/ in *but*. Possible exceptions to Lass' general statement are the merger of the vowels of *caught* and *cot*, maintenance of post-vocalic /r/ and centralised diphthongs before voiceless consonants. In these cases the speech of Ulster Scots and possibly Lowland Scots settlers reinforced or served as the basis for a similar pattern in American English.

The merger of low vowels /a/ and /ɔ/ involves the fronting and sometimes unrounding of Middle English 'short *o*' in *caught* and *dawn*. Now spreading rapidly in urban America, this was once a geographically based phenomenon confined mainly to western Pennsylvania and a band of territory widening from there through the Ohio Valley and encompassing most of the western half of the country (Kurath and McDavid 1961: 17; Labov, Ash and Boberg 1997: 34). According to Lass, 'despite its recent spread into new areas, the merger itself is clearly an old one and ties in well with settlement geography. The most likely source is Ulster Scots' (1990: 273). Two matters complicate this scenario. The merger is to a different vowel in American English (/a/ or /ɒ/) and in Scotland and Ulster today (/ɔ/), and evidence is lacking that the merger spread into the Upper South, as did many other Pennsylvania features (Labov, Ash and Boberg 1997 find it only as far south as West Virginia and Northern Kentucky).

The maintenance of post-vocalic /r/ in words like *board* and *here* in colonial Pennsylvania (and its subsequent extension to most of the country) has been attributed to the relative lack of contact of Philadelphia, where the loss of /r/ was becoming prestigious, with London and to reinforcement by *r*-ful Ulster Scots speakers in the middle colonies. Lass (1990: 279) is one commentator to advance this explanation for American English remaining *r*-ful by and large. But this possible connection is complicated by facts on the ground. It does not work, for instance, for Canadian English, where influence from Britain in the nineteenth century would have been expected. A third pattern, involving the modern reflexes of Middle English 'long *i*' and 'long *u*', is discussed in the next section.

Braidwood (1975: 31–2) was apparently the first scholar to compile a list of American linguistic connections to Ulster, most of which derive from Scotland (*hap* 'quilt', *mooley* 'hornless cow'). Crozier (1984) documents the Ulster ancestry of thirty-three items (including *piece* 'short distance', *fireboard* 'mantle' and *redd up* 'to prepare, tidy up') in Pennsylvania, where the Scotch-Irish influence was strong. After the American Revolution, newspapers around Pittsburgh featured poetry in Scots on local political topics, such as that of David Bruce cited earlier. Today the speech of Pittsburgh (locally known as 'Pittsburghese') is noted for such usages as *nebby* 'nosey', *you' uns/yinz* 'you (plural)' and *need* + past participle, all ultimately from Scotland.

In Pennsylvania Lowland Scots and Ulster Scots emigrants often found themselves settled near Germans. They influenced both Pennsylvania German, which adopted pronunciations and vocabulary from Ulster-born neighbours (such as *hap* 'quilt'; Reed 1953), and the English of speakers having German heritage (*need* + past participle; Tucker 1934). The latter process must have happened across a broad territory as German and Scotch-Irish settlers moved into Virginia and beyond. Little direct influence from German has turned up in language beyond Pennsylvania (though it can be seen in foodways, vernacular architecture and so on), but by the early nineteenth century the children and grandchildren of German settlers were acquiring a type of English with many Scotch-Irish features such as the Northern concord rule. A factor promoting survival of a Scottish pattern was structural congruence with another language, such as German. Patterns in the two languages reinforced one another in some cases, as with *leave* 'let' (as 'leave me be') and *want* + preposition (as *want in* 'want to go/come in'; Marckwardt 1948; Adams 2000).

CANADA

Two specific locales in Canada have been identified as having Scottish linguistic influence, the Ottawa Valley of Ontario (Pringle and Padofsky 1981, 1983) and the Red River Valley of Manitoba (Blain 1987). Scottish (and Ulster) speakers may have contributed what has become the most signal feature of Canadian English – 'Canadian raising'. Coined by Chambers (1973; see also Chambers 1979), the term refers to a phenomenon noted anecdotally by earlier scholars who related it to an intermediate stage of the Great Vowel Shift (and thus saw it as conditioned non-lowering of the diphthong). It involves the pronunciation of Middle English 'long *i*' and 'long *u*' with a central, somewhat reduced onset of the diphthong to produce [əi] and [əu] before voiceless consonants). Gregg (1973) examines diachronic and synchronic data from Scotland and Ulster and suggests reinforcement of the Canadian process rather than direct input, but a historical basis in the Scottish Vowel-Length Rule is quite possible. Any account needs to recognise that the same process occurs in such conservative speech regions of the US as eastern Virginia, coastal South Carolina and nearby areas (Kurath and McDavid 1961: 109–11), where it would not seem attributable to Scots-speaking settlers. A good synopsis of the relevant issues for Canada can be found in Bailey (1982: 153–4).

The lexicography of Canadian English is well developed, but from its publications scholars have yet to assess the Scottish element on the whole or on regional varieties. For example, the *Dictionary of Prince Edward Island English* cross-references items (*puckle* 'small quantity or amount', *slippy* 'slippery') to the *SND* (Pratt 1988). Lexical items having more general usage are *dunch* 'push out of the way', *slouster* 'mess' and *drunniel* 'heavy burden' (McConnell 1979: 182–3).

AUSTRALASIA

In the nineteenth century speakers of Scots took the language to Australia and New Zealand from Scotland and Ulster. Kiesling (forthcoming) finds no Scottish trace in Australian speech today and (following Robson 1965) attributes this to the principal early input varieties to the Australian colony in the late eighteenth/early nineteenth century, namely London English and Irish English. Though later-arriving Scots were less concentrated or recognised as a constituent group in Australia, recent scholarship indicates they maintained a voice in both popular and more literary writing. Cardell and Cumming (1992–3) find extensive use of Scots in the 1860s/1870s in the newspapers of Hamilton, Victoria. Tulloch (1997a, 1997b) shows that from the 1850s until well into the twentieth century Scots was an 'alternative literary language' to English, especially in fiction. It also contributed vocabulary (*darg* 'allotment of work', *slater* 'woodlouse') to Australian English.

In New Zealand Lowland Scots settled most often in Otago and Southland on South Island. Bartlett (1992) and Bauer (1994: 400–7) identify many grammatical elements of Southland speech that reflect Scottish influence, including the preference of *will* over *shall* (in interrogatives, as 'Will I close the door?'), *ones* compounded after pronouns (*my ones*), *all* after interrogatives (*what all*, *who all*) and ellipsis of an infinitive after *need* and *want* (*want washed*). The lexical component is also significant (*byre* 'cow shed', *ashet* 'platter'); Bauer (1997) reports finding 130 words probably contributed by Scottish emigrants, but emphasises that Ulster Scots may also have had a role in this. Bauer (1997) and Trudgill et al. (forthcoming) survey possible phonological connections.

CONCLUSION

McClure's assessment notwithstanding, that spoken Scots reached foreign shores and left substantial imprints is now in no doubt. It took firm root in Ulster. Farther afield, Scots and Ulster Scots not only played major roles in the formation of new colonial and regional varieties of English. Its contribution to American

English was considerable, though it is not possible to measure with precision, given that surviving records are almost all in Standard English. Because so many speakers knew both Scots and English, their Scots covertly influenced the English that their children, communities and even neighbours acquired. Paradoxically, it is the closeness of the two that led to a greater influence of the former on the latter abroad than was experienced by few other European tongues.

Lowland Scots and Ulster Scots were the language of expatriate communities for one or more generations. In part this was an extension from the Scottish mainland, where Scots has been the medium of a literary tradition with which speakers of Scots elsewhere maintained familiarity. Poets have often been inspired by Burns, but only when this inspiration has concerned speakers of Scots have they been derided as 'Burns imitators'. The manifestation of literature in Scots was particularly significant in Ulster, where it flourished before and after Burns and took a life of its own as an instrument of occasional and other social commentary. Perhaps most revealingly, much of the evidence for literature written in Scots elsewhere, especially beyond Ulster, has come to light only in the past decade because it appeared in ephemeral outlets, such as newspapers, that were lost or buried. As a result, Scots can be seen to have had a much more vigorous, though often submerged, life as a spoken language that surfaced only intermittently. It is time for histories of Scottish literature to take the international record of literature in Scots, especially that in Ulster, fully into account.

The transplantation of Scots to Ireland and its use there in parts of what have become Northern Ireland and the Republic of Ireland means that, like many other European tongues, Scots is an international language, a fact that even authorities in Scotland (such as Aitken 1998) have recently begun to recognise. Nor was Scottish linguistic influence taken abroad centuries ago only to recede inexorably or be smothered under the domination of English. Rather, Scots has continued to enrich English, even in areas where the latter spread overseas long before. Only a half-century ago, for instance, few Americans would have recognised *sporran*, *kilt*, *caber* and *haggis*. Today, due undoubtedly to the popularity and marketing of Highland Games and Burns Clubs in the twentieth century, such terms increasingly are everyday vocabulary and have become part of the fabric of international English.

NOTES

1. The author is grateful to Sandra Clarke, Scott Philyaw and Caroline Macafee for suggested references and advice. In her forthcoming essay 'Scots and Scottish English', Macafee covers some of the same ground as this chapter, though her exposition deals primarily with the historical phonology of Scots.
2. The historic province of Ulster containing nine counties contrasts with the present-

day province of Northern Ireland, which has six. The remaining three (Cavan, Donegal, Monaghan) are now in the Republic of Ireland.

3. The finer linguistic differences between Highland English, a first-language variety, and Island English, one employed by Gaelic-language natives, are not germane to our discussion. The distinction was first made by Catford (1957).

4. McClure (personal communication) informs the author that he would revise this discussion in a further edition of his book, especially given recent developments for Ulster Scots, for a discussion of which, see Montgomery (1997c, 1999).

5. Adams (1968) estimated the number of speakers of Ulster Scots to be 100,000.

6. See Erskine (forthcoming) for an annotated bibliography of Ulster Scots language and literature.

7. Among recent books examining historical connections between Scotland and Ulster is Wood (1994).

8. Robinson maps the settlement of Scots in seventeenth-century Ulster using two period features (surnames of settlers and sites of Presbyterian churches) and one modern-day one (dialect boundaries as established by Gregg 1972).

9. The McClelland of Bombay legal documents are deposited in collection T640 of the Public Record Office of Northern Ireland in Belfast.

10. This glossary was not only the principal source of Ulster Scots material in the *English Dialect Dictionary*, but was incorporated without attribution into many subsequent compilations of Ulster dialect.

11. Totals by county were as follows: thirty in Down, sixteen in Tyrone, thirty-five in Antrim, seven in Londonderry, ten in Fermanagh, six in Armagh and twelve in Donegal. Lexical data collected on behalf of the Linguistic Survey of Scotland enabled Adams (1954) to draw the first maps of Scottish forms in Ulster. In the early 1950s Angus McIntosh of Edinburgh University approached Adams to distribute the Scots section of the LSS lexical questionnaire in parts of Ulster, a task that Adams undertook through the Belfast Naturalists' Field Club. He mapped responses to four items, including terms for *earwig* and forms of *one*, and found that *gellick* and *yann*, the Scottish variants, 'occupy the Northeastern or Coastal Crescent' (1956: 7) of Ulster. In so doing, he carefully related both Scottish and non-Scottish responses to cultural geography and demographic history, proposing general principles for the diffusion of linguistic forms in the north of Ireland.

12. Conventional estimates of pre-Revolutionary emigrants from Ulster are in the range of a quarter of a million. Research based on more recent scrutiny of records suggests a figure perhaps as low as fifty thousand (Wokeck 1999).

13. *Scotch-Irish* is the term traditionally used in the United States for Ulster emigrants primarily of Presbyterian heritage. It remains the most widely used term by Americans of that heritage, though in recent years *Scots-Irish* has begun to compete with it. Leyburn (1963), Ickringill (1994–95) and Montgomery (2001a) document its somewhat problematic, controversial history.

14. It is important to remember that in their etymologies neither *DARE* nor other American dictionaries derive American items from Scottish ones in a strict historical sense. Rather, they cross-reference items from their dictionary to others. Citations of the Scottish counterpart to an American form, much less the regional distribution of that counterpart in Britain, are rarely dated to the time of emigration.

15. Following Hamilton, this assessment is based on items labelled in the first two volumes of the dictionary, which cover A–H (*An Index*, 1993).

16. Shoemaker (1930), a glossary of old-fashioned Pennsylvania usage, is especially rich in

items traceable to Scots and Gaelic; a selection of its material has recently been edited and analysed by Gilmore (1999).

17. There has been no such computation for Scots *per se*, but a survey of features of Ulster ancestry (most of which are traceable to Scots) in the English of the Appalachian region of the United States (and the larger Midland of which it is a part) has found a broad and deep continuity. See Montgomery (1997d, forthcoming).

18. This subject is dealt with more extensively in Montgomery (forthcoming).

19. The combination of *you* with *all* (more precisely, their variants *ye* and *aw*) is a likely source for *y'all*, a well-known pronominal form in the American South (Montgomery 1992b), where today it expresses plurality by association, collective reference and so on (Montgomery 1996).

CHAPTER 12

Language Planning and Modern Scots

John Corbett

INTRODUCTION

The field of language planning encompasses the influence brought to bear upon a speech community, either by state institutions or pressure groups, in order to change the way its members use language. Cooper (1989: 45) defines it thus:

> Language planning refers to deliberate efforts to influence the behaviour of others with respect to the acquisition, structure, or functional allocation of their language codes.

Few major languages in the world escape such pressures. Some are inspired by government, for example the decision in 1917 by the newly instated Bolshevik regime to reform Russian spelling, while some derive from groups such as those in Britain that promote the use of 'plain English' in official documents (cf. Cameron 1995). In Scotland, the study of language planning in general could conceivably focus on the relationship between English, Gaelic, Scots and newer 'Community' languages, such as Urdu or Chinese, as they are used in and across the various speech communities that make up the nation. In fact, most attention has been paid to language planning in Gaelic (see for example, MacPherson 2000; Mackinnon 2001) and Scots, the focus of this chapter.

Of the three 'heritage languages' in Scotland, it is English that has the most highly developed written standard variety, characterised by a long-established spelling system, prescribed grammar, and a continually extending vocabulary that can articulate the concepts we associate with modern life. Scottish Standard English is widely recognised as the 'normal' medium of education in Scotland, as well as the variety used in public life and other formal discourse. This state of affairs, of course, is not the result simply of 'natural' linguistic evolution; it, too, represents overt and covert 'language engineering' in which standard varieties of

English have, for generations, been mythologised as the 'correct' forms for most public and many private communicative functions (cf. Crowley 1989; Joseph 1987; Milroy and Milroy 1991). Standard English has become the dominant global language, threatening less powerful languages by encroaching into communicative functions in which they previously held sway (Crystal 2000; Graddol 1996; Nettle and Romaine 2000). It should not therefore be surprising that Gaelic and Broad Scots have long been under threat from English in Scotland. The process of 'language shift' (Fishman 1991, 2001) from Broad Scots and Gaelic to Scottish English started in the Middle Ages and is still ongoing. Research into language planning with respect to Scots (that is, a much broader form of Scots than is represented by Scottish Standard English) can therefore focus on two general topics:

- what are the historical causes of language shift?
- how can it be reversed?

One key battleground in the historical process of language shift is education. Parish schools were established in Scotland by an Act of Parliament in 1696, supervised by the church and financed in part by local landowners. In these parish schools, as recently as the early 1700s, the terms 'Scots' and 'English' seemed to have been used interchangeably to refer to vernacular education (Aitken 1992c: 894). However, by the mid eighteenth century, throughout Britain, a 'fixed' form of standard English had become the mark of an 'educated' writer, no matter which variety he or she spoke. At the same time, social pressure began to be exerted on upper- and middle-class Scots to speak in a more anglicised manner (Jones, 1996). The attitude of 'genteel' Scots at the time can be illustrated from the case of James Boswell, who sent his daughters, Veronica and Euphemia, to be schooled by a certain Mrs Billingsley in Edinburgh, 'to correct the Scotch accent' (Lustig and Pottle 1981: 34n). In 1872 the Education (Scotland) Act made it compulsory for every child between the ages of five and thirteen to receive education, and the Scotch Code of 1878 set examination standards in reading and writing in English, with particular attention being paid to spelling, grammar, handwriting, and the forms of composition. In some contexts, such as literature and music classes, there is some evidence that forms of Broad Scots were encouraged and maintained through poetry and song, when they were proscribed and even punished in everyday classroom talk. Among the songs presented to schools inspectors in one parish school in Lanarkshire in 1875 were several by Robert Burns and one entitled 'Nae Luck About the House' (Cooper 1973: 60–1).

Although there are instances in which Scots did appear in educational curricula, schools nevertheless reinforced the notion that Scots was only appropriate in affectively powerful but instrumentally limited arenas, such as literary expression, comic narrative and song. Fishman (1991, 2001) argues that, to survive, threatened languages must sustain and possibly even enlarge the number of communicative functions in which they are employed by their speech community. That is, only by planning and implementing policies that ensure that Scots is used in what Fishman calls 'powerful' and 'non-powerful' contexts can the historical process of language shift be reversed, and the future of the language ensured.

REVERSING LANGUAGE SHIFT

Since the early twentieth century there has been a series of attempts in both Scotland and, more recently, in Northern Ireland to develop Scots to the point where it can either function alongside or replace Standard English as the language variety used in a range of communicative functions, particularly formal or powerful ones. Research into language planning could consider a range of issues, such as:

- the reasons for language planning in Scotland and Northern Ireland
- the initiatives hitherto taken to standardise and raise the status of Scots
- the priorities for research in this controversial but under-investigated field.

Studies of language planning in Scotland have often been undertaken by those advocating a change of status for Scots, and therefore the studies actively seek to justify such a change. Few studies have sought disinterestedly to chart the effect, or lack of it, of educational and other initiatives intended to alter linguistic attitudes and usage (though see Macafee and McGarrity 1999).

The partisan nature of much writing on this subject no doubt stems from the fact that the purpose of language planning is seldom to facilitate more effective communication (cf. Cooper 1989: 79–87; Fishman 2001: 6–8). The two main reasons usually given for raising the status of a marginalised language variety are to improve the self-esteem of the users, and to bind the marginalised speech community together as a homogenous political entity. Lorvik (1995: 55) stresses the former of these aims:

Children very soon sense what is, and is not, acceptable in their
environment. If they encounter negative reactions to their natural speech
at an early stage in their education, it is hardly surprising if within the
confines of the classroom their lips and minds are firmly sealed. This
linguistic insecurity may well remain with them for the rest of their lives.

Lorvik supports the establishment of a 'maintenance' form of bilingualism whereby instruction in Scots would be sustained through the pupil's life, to foster the linguistic security of the child. This is opposed to the 'transitional' form of bilingualism, which has been the norm in British schools, whereby a second language is supported, if at all, only to the point where the pupil can function adequately in English. As Crystal (1987: 366) notes, there are strong social pressures against language maintenance:

> it is pointed out that a permanent dual-language policy may foster social divisions and narrowness of outlook (through ethnocentric churches, media, schools, etc.); the children may become 'trapped' in their mother tongue, and fail to achieve the majority language, thus reducing their access to prosperity; and where there is inadequate teacher preparation, timetabling and materials, they may fail to achieve in their mother tongue also.

From a political rather than an individual perspective, McClure (1980: 38) explicitly links raising the status of Scots to the establishment of an independent Scottish parliament and 'an awareness of Scottish nationhood and its roots'. For McClure, a linguistic and political revival must go hand in hand with cultural rediscovery, though his relatively inclusive vision is of a pluralist nation in which Gaelic, English and Scots have equal places. At this level, support for a change in status for Scots depends on individuals sharing a particular political and cultural outlook, however broadly conceived.

Support for institutional language planning in support of Scots, then, tends to accentuate:

- the benefits for children in self-esteem, linguistic security and enhanced linguistic facility if they have access to a greater range of socially accepted varieties
- the benefits to the nation in a greater sense of pride and belonging that would presumably derive from the development of a linguistic medium that would distinguish us from other nations and associate current generations with those who have gone before.

What little research has been done on language planning in Scotland tends to focus on the possibilities and processes of developing a Standard Scots that could function alongside English, in at least some powerful social and cultural contexts. Little has been done directly to test the benefits to individuals or to the nation of having such a linguistic medium available, although parallel developments in the promotion of Gaelic and of minority languages in other countries are sometimes alluded to (in, for example, Haugen, McClure and Thomson 1981; Lorvick 1995: 10–12, 14–16; Johnstone et al. 1999; Johnstone 2001). This area is another aspect of language planning that requires extensive investigation.

In contrast, the stages that a minority language undergoes if it is to be raised to the level of national language are well established in the research literature: status planning, corpus planning and acquisition planning. Scots is more advanced in some of these stages than others.

STATUS PLANNING

Status planning refers to the functions to which a language is allocated, that is, the range of purposes for which speakers use the languages. A number of scholars see the question of functional range as criterial in the definition of a 'full' language (cf. Görlach 2000: 21). As far as can be gathered from the evidence available, Broad Scots today is largely the spoken language of the domestic sphere, and the spoken medium of manual labour and traditional industries, such as farming and fishing; while Scottish Standard English is largely the language of public life, education and official documentation and pronouncements. Language planning for Broad Scots can focus on strengthening the functions where it still survives, or on recapturing the functions that have been transferred to Scottish Standard English (cf. Fishman 2001). Much language activism in Scots addresses the latter, more difficult task (cf. Purves 1997b; Horsbroch 2001).

Language activists argue that if broad Scots is to be revived as a public standard, then its functions have to be extended beyond the domestic and traditional spheres. What kind of targets are appropriate to a 'full' national language? Stewart (1968; cited in Cooper 1989: 99–118) advocates the following list:

1. *Official*   is the language the legally appropriate language for all political and culturally representative purposes on a nationwide basis? is the language used symbolically and/or as a working language by the governing authorities?

2. *Provincial*   is the language used as an official language, as above, for part of the nation only?

3. *Lingua franca* is the language used for wider communication amongst different speech communities in the nation?

4. *International* is the language used for communication in the spheres of diplomatic relations, foreign trade, tourism and so on?

5. *Capital*   is the language the major medium of communication in the vicinity of the capital city, in this case, Edinburgh?

6. *Group*   is the language the normal medium of communication among the members of a single cultural or ethnic group?

7. *Education*   is the language the medium of communication in primary, secondary and/or higher education?

8. *School*   is the language studied as part of the curriculum in primary, secondary and/or higher education?

9. *Literary*   is the language used for literary or scholarly purposes?

10. *Religious*   is the language used in the rituals of a particular religion?

It is clear that, in past centuries, Scots fulfilled virtually all of these language functions; during the sixteenth century, the language variety of east central Scotland was used for official purposes and written state documentation, used in education and for literary and religious purposes. Now, however, Scottish Standard English has replaced Scots in most functions, save the literary. If nowhere else, literary Scots is alive on the pages of *Lallans* and occasionally in other literary magazines such as *Chapman* and anthologies such as *Mak it New* (McCallum and Purves 1995). But, as Cooper (1989: 115) argues:

> The promotion of vernaculars for literary and scholarly purposes is a common feature of nationalist movements, perhaps because such development may serve to raise the national consciousness of the masses or at least of the intellectuals. Also some nationalists may believe that the literary development of a national language buttresses the legitimacy of claims for national autonomy. Nonetheless it is likely that it is not *belles lettres* but the less glamorous non narrative prose, 'the realm of information, not of imagination,' that lends prestige to vernacular languages (Kloss 1967: 33).

It would be wrong to suggest that Scots is entirely absent from the other domains that Cooper notes. There is, for example, some degree of presence in official documents, education and religion. For a number of years, at the annual convention of the Scottish National Party, the party leader has had open letters to activists recast in Scots as well as in Gaelic (see below). This is a perfect example of a political party affirming the symbolic significance of a language, although it is unlikely that the SNP policy-makers actually use such a broad variety of Scots as an everyday working language. Falconer (2001) reports on the use of Scots in debates in the early days of the devolved Scottish Parliament and Northern Ireland Assembly. Scots also appears as the medium of the minutes of meetings of the Scots Language Society, and, more recently, of the Cross-Party Group on the Scots Language, established in the wake of the devolved Scottish Parliament to inform and influence official policy on Scots. The Cross-Party Group is currently forming working groups to shape opinion in the media, politics, education and public and private organisations. It has also been involved in drafting a statement of principles, based on the Universal Declaration of Linguistic Rights, formulated by the European Bureau of Lesser-Used Languages, asserting the right of the Scottish people to communicate in Scots at all levels of society (Cross-Party Group on the Scots Language, 2003). After some debate in the Group, these principles were cast in Scots by working party, with the following results:

Thirteen Principles for the Scots Language
1. Scots is a language.
2. Action maun be taen tae pit an end tae aw prejudice an discrimination agin the Scots Language.
3. The Scots Language is integral an essential tae cultural an personal identity in Scotland.
4. A knowledge o Scots is vital tae a knowledge o Scotland.
5. Action maun be taen tae gie the Scots Language whitiver means is needed tae mak siccar its transmission an continuity.
6. Scots shuid be an essential pairt o the educational curriculum in Scotland at aw levels.
7. Naebody shuid be penalised or pitten doun for speakin Scots.
8. Scots proper names an place names shuid be valued an safegairded.
9. Speakers an writers o Scots shuid hae scowth tae develop an active role an presence for the Scots Language in aw pairts o the communications media.
10. Ongaun study an documentation o the language maun be gien ful resourcin.
11. Initiatives shuid be sterted tae mainteen an uphaud Scots terms an uisage specific tae sindry trades an occupations.
12. The Scots Language shuid be uised in adverts, in signs, in signpostin, an in the presentation o an accurate image o Scotland.
13. The people o Scotland has the ability an responsibility tae uphaud the Scots Language an tae gar Pairliament uise its pouer an authority tae realise the foregaun principles an statements o intent.

In Northern Ireland, the Boord o Ulstèr-Scotch has also produced a corporate plan, or *heich ploy* (The Boord o Ulstèr-Scotch/Ulster-Scots Agency 2000) and a list of human rights, or *a leit o richts for Norlin Airland* has also been produced (Norlin Airland Commeission o Fowkrichts 2001), both in formal written Scots. The former document sets out the mission of the Ulster-Scots Agency (2000: 3):

> The Boord o Ulstèr-Scotch bis gart unnèr tha laa guide tha 'forderin o
> mair forstannin an uise o tha Ulstèr-Scotch leid an o Ulstèr-Scotch
> fowkgate daeins, baith ben Norlin Airlann an athort tha islann.'
> The legislative remit of the Ulster-Scots Agency is 'the promotion of
> greater awareness and the use of Ullans and of Ulster-Scots cultural
> issues, both within Northern Ireland and throughout the island'.

The recent spurt of interest in Scots in Northern Ireland, documented in Kirk and Ó Baoill, eds (2000, 2001a, 2001b) is indicative of the close relationship between language planning and politics. Substantial communities of Scots speakers settled in Northern Ireland in the seventeenth century, as part of James VI's policy of diluting Catholic influence in Ireland by encouraging Protestant 'plantations'. The result was a variety of Scots spoken in the counties of Antrim, Derry, Donegal and Down, and influencing the speech spoken elsewhere in both Northern Ireland and the Irish Republic. Later, the language of the 'Scotch-Irish' was to migrate across the Atlantic and have a profound influence on American English (see Robinson 1997; Montgomery and Gregg 1997; and Montgomery this volume). Since the eighteenth century, Ulster Scots has had its own literary tradition, surviving down to the present day. In the wake of the Good Friday Agreement of 1998, political initiatives designed to protect minority rights led to the establishment of a North/South Language Implementation Body *(An Bord Teanga/Tha Boord o Leid)* to promote Irish Gaelic and Ulster Scots. The sensitivity to minority rights in Northern Ireland has, ironically, led to more public funding being made available there than in Scotland to language planning bodies. Some of the output of these bodies is available on the web (www.ulsterscotsagency.com and www.nihrc.org).

The difficulties in gaining acceptance for a formal written Scots, which inevitably departs from spoken usage in as many respects as formal Standard English does, is clear from the mixed public response, particularly in Northern Ireland, to the few documents that have appeared. Even a review of the Ulster-Scots Agency's website in *Lallans* complains of its obscurity: 'unless ye'v etten a Scots dictionar an duin a coorse in cryptography ye micht find the English version a bittie mair eith tae lift' (Eagle 2002: 111). Part of the problem for supporters of formal Scots, of course, is that it does not figure largely in the Scottish or Northern Irish education systems. It seems neither to be much used nor studied in schools, though information on this is sketchy (Niven 2002). Although Scots is not the main medium of communication in Scottish or Northern Irish schools, Scots has recently made some inroads as a subject of study in the Scottish and Irish primary and secondary curricula. Again, here, the situation is patchy (see further the section on acquisition planning below).

Scots might make occasional forays into the world of religious ritual, most recently thanks to Lorimer's *New Testament in Scots* (1983), the most celebrated of a number of biblical translations into Scots (Tulloch 1989). Historically, biblical translation is heavy with significance, given that the decline in the use of Scots for official purposes is often associated with the adoption of the Geneva Bible in English by the reformed church in Scotland, a decline accelerated by the adoption of the King James Authorised Version in the early 1600s. Lorimer's *New Testament in Scots* was written as a deliberative corrective to the anglicising tradition of 'authorised' Bible translations in Scotland; however, its linguistic impact in the late twentieth century could not be as profound as that occasioned by the publication of the Geneva and King James Bibles in the sixteenth and seventeenth centuries.

The criterion of *Group use* is interesting, if only because it raises the question of which variety of Scots standardisers should adopt. If Scottish Standard English and Broad Scots are imagined as forming a continuum, then the Broad Scots end of that continuum is frayed; the communities that speak Broad Scots in the south-west, the Borders, the north-east and in Orkney and Shetland certainly share some linguistic features, but they are also distinctive in vocabulary, grammar and accent. The spelling of those who write in these regional forms usually also reflects regional characteristics. The adoption of one robust variety of Scots – let us say north-eastern Scots, or 'Doric' – as the normative or standard variety for all Scots obviously privileges native speakers of that form and disadvantages all other Scots, who must then learn the standard variety. An alternative approach is to create a standard variety of Scots that is not tied to any one regional or social group, but which extends the 'core' lexical and grammatical features shared by most. Such a variety could be extended in a number of ways, for example by reviving archaic words and extending their meanings, coining new terms, and borrowing and adapting from other languages, particularly cognate ones like German and the Scandinavian languages. Such a 'synthetic' Scots is sometimes called *Lallans* 'Lowlands', a term taken from Robert Burns, who, for instance, refers to 'a Lallan tongue' in 'Address to the Deil'. Lallans was popularised by the school of poets who followed the example of Hugh MacDiarmid in the twentieth century; however, the term has not been universally popular, even amongst Scots writers and activists. For instance, the Lallans Society, formed in 1972 to promote the use of Scots, decided after a few years to change its name to the Scots Language Society, although its main publication retained the name *Lallans*. The main advantage of Lallans, or 'synthetic Scots', as a revived standard is that it does not privilege any one regional or social group. Another way of looking at it is that Lallans disadvantages everyone equally. Here one might compare the situation in Scotland with the case of India, which in its post-colonial history has kept English as an official state language, primarily because, shorn of its imperialist trappings, English has become a neutral language, and so none of India's many and various language groups has then been privileged above the others in the independent state. English remains the official language in Scotland, at least partly because no variety of Scots – regional, social or synthetic – immediately presents itself as an alternative that could gather wide support from the various communities that make up the nation. The question of which form of Scots could in principle become the basis of a formal, written variety leads us to the topic of corpus planning. In this sense, 'corpus' does not refer to an electronic archive of the language (cf. Meurman-Solin, this volume), but to the compilation of a body of texts that represents the standard variety of the language.

CORPUS PLANNING

What happens when a language develops a standard variety? In brief, one variety of a language comes to be accepted as normative and even sometimes as the only 'correct' variety. As it becomes normative, the language variety is codified; in other words, dictionaries and grammars are written that 'fix' its lexical resources, its spelling, its morphology and its syntactical constraints. It is accepted as an official language and is disseminated through the education system. It is the general written form of the language, although it does not necessarily have to correspond directly to the spoken forms. The standard language obviously has to be used for a whole range of language functions, and so it should be able to deal with the scientific, technical, economic and political domains of modern life.

The lexical resources of Scots have been extensively recorded, particularly in the two great dictionary projects of the twentieth century, the *Scottish National Dictionary* and the *Dictionary of the Older Scottish Tongue*. Since the completion of *DOST* in 2002, a new company, Scottish Language Dictionaries, has been formed to continue the lexicographical tradition these two major projects represent. More influential, perhaps, are the one-volume *Concise Scots Dictionary*, its pocket editions, and the English-Scots/Scots-English *Schools Dictionary*. A significant by-product of the smaller dictionaries is a move towards the regulation of the spelling system of Scots – *CSD* still offers alternative spellings of words, but the pocket and school editions rationalise these, and for the first time ever, a standard Scots spelling system is emerging, to the point where a spellcheck program *CannieSpell* has been devised and marketed. This system is not always to the liking of all supporters of a revived Scots, some of whom have long advocated their own orthographies.

Devising a normative orthography for Scots has been one of the great linguistic hobbies of the past century. In 1947, a group of Lallans poets, 'The Makkar's Club', led by A. D. Mackie and Douglas Young, devised 'The Scots Style Sheet', a single side of paper whose purpose was to give guidance to the various writers who were experimenting with Scots as a literary medium. David Purves, a writer and editor, published further proposals in 1979, and the Scots Language Society printed a revised and expanded form of the Scots Style Sheet in 1985. McClure (1985) summarises the debate to that point, and Purves (1997a: 57–68; 2002: 109–18) reviews the Scots Language Society's contribution. Debates on 'maximalist' and 'minimalist' approaches to spelling reform are recorded in McArthur (1998). A different tack was taken by Angus Stirling (1994) and George Philp (1997), and yet further views on Scots orthography were aired in a Scots Spellin Comatee, established in 1996, whose work was reported on and argued over in two consecutive editions of Lallans magazine (issues 56 and 57, 2000; see also www.pkc.gov.uk.slrc). Tom Leonard has satirised spelling reform in a cartoon advertisement for the 'Makars' Society' that invites viewers to a 'gran' meetin' the nicht tae decide the spellin' o this poster' (Leonard 1984: 53). Scots spelling generates righteous fervour amongst those who participate in the debate. Ultimately, however, the orthography of Scots will only be fully standardised if there is social pressure on all writers to conform to a fixed set of norms. This pressure is not likely to be felt if Scots is used for literary purposes alone: literature is by its very nature experimental, and its departures from homogeneous norms are often deliberately intended to give a sense of the regional or social specificity of a character or text. It follows that Scots orthography will only be standardised if Scots were to be used more widely in functions beyond the literary, and if a standard Scots spelling system were to be taught in schools so that writers could perform these functions adequately. At the present moment, despite the initiatives of pressure groups like the Scots Language Society and the Cross-Party Group on the Scots Language and agencies like the Boord o Ulstèr-Scotch, there seems little prospect of this happening. However, thanks to the style sheets and the dictionaries, more than at any time in the history of the language, the possibility of training oneself in a more 'focused' Scots spelling is available to committed writers who wish to conform to a normative set of practices.

Descriptions of Scots grammar are also emerging. Caroline Macafee has produced a short grammar of Older Scots, based on materials in *DOST* (Macafee 1992/3), and Jim Miller has produced a short grammar of modern 'Scottish English' (Miller 1993; see also his chapter in this volume). These grammars are ostensibly descriptive rather than prescriptive; that is, they aim to describe what people did or do, rather than to tell them what they ought to have done or should be doing. Purves (1997a; revised and expanded 2002) has, however, produced a short prescriptive grammar of modern literary Scots, inspired by an earlier guide to Shetlandic usage (Robertson and Graham 1952; reprinted 1991). Robinson (1997) has also produced a detailed guide to usage for Ulster Scots, and Rennie and Fitt (2000) have published a guide to grammatical characteristics of Scottish speech, aimed at children. Although linguists tend to insist on the descriptive/prescriptive distinction because they like to present themselves as scientific scholars, objectively describing data without making evaluations, descriptive grammars can be used prescriptively by educationalists. The boundaries are not entirely clear-cut. For example, the observation that many Scots use 'how?' to ask about reasons (in Chapter 5 of this volume, Miller cites, 'how did you not apply?') can easily be turned into a rule of Scots grammar that we *should* use 'how' in such contexts. Nevertheless, problems arise when prescriptivists take exception to perfectly rule-governed but highly stigmatised features of common usage, such as 'I should have went'. Aitken (1982) observes that judgements about what becomes 'standard' and 'non-standard' in any language depends more on social than linguistic criteria, although even observations like this raise the hackles of activists like Purves (1997b: 14):

It is not very helpful to the disadvantaged linguistic situation of the Scottish, urban, slum-dwelling speakers of what Aitken would agree is normally called 'Bad Scots' to be told that there is no such thing as 'Bad Scots' or 'Good Scots'.

A difficulty, then, of defining the rules of a 'Standard Scots' in the twenty-first century is establishing which regional or social variety or varieties should become the basis of the prestigious dialect, and by what authority the norms should be legitimised. Although many Scottish people speak a language variety that is distinctive, few speak a single, homogeneous variety that Scots language supporters would happily accept as 'Good Scots'. Purves' solution is to gather features from the literary tradition, from the ballads down to, say, Robert Garioch, but precisely because this literary tradition is associated less and less with everyday speech, the texts that result tend to be rejected as 'artificial'. This rejection may be misplaced, since all written standard languages are 'artificial' insofar as they are social constructs, developed primarily to serve administrative and other pragmatic communicative functions. However, we have become socialised into considering Scottish Standard English as 'natural' for fulfilling these pragmatic functions, and the use of Broad Scots would be likely to seem 'unnatural', as well as unnecessary, to many people who are currently uninvolved with the debate.

Even so, the grammar of Scots, like its spelling, could in principle be codified and standardised forms could be imposed through the educational system – but for corpus planning a final stage is needed. Scots would need to be modernised to cope with the demands of contemporary life, and that largely means adapting its lexical resources to allow it to express everyday concepts, such as those in science, engineering and computer technology. Only then could the full range of communicative functions be recaptured. Once again, in principle, there are strategies for modernisation that are long established and could be extended. McClure (1981b) identifies key strategies used by the literary 'synthesisers' of Scots:

- translation
- using dictionaries and reviving archaisms
- coining neologisms.

Literary translation has a part in both status raising and corpus planning (Corbett 1999). By showing that Scots can deal with a wide range of 'classic' texts, the status of the language is raised. Although Scots is still confined to literary functions, such translations normally demand that the lexical resources of the language are stretched, and so borrowings and adaptations enter Scots to fill lexical gaps. From at least the nineteenth century, Scots writers have departed from spoken varieties of Scots by employing more obscure Scots terms and archaisms. Hugh McDiarmid notoriously practised the former strategy, sometimes criticised as 'dictionary dredging'. For example, one passage in *A Drunk Man Looks at the Thistle* (lines 873–84) suggests strongly that he had Jamieson's Dictionary opened at 'M' and 'B' as he composed it. Archaisms in these ten lines include *mowse* 'joke', *munks* 'shrinks', *munkie* 'a small, looped rope', *biel* 'secure', and *belth* 'whirlpool'. Douglas Young (1946) argues in favour of extending written Scots by drawing upon vocabulary that would seldom now be heard in speech, observing that all written languages draw upon resources beyond everyday speech. In contrast, Youngson (1992) ridicules the use of archaic terms such as *aiblins* 'perhaps' in much Lallans writing. Youngson's article exemplifies an attitude that privileges the spoken language as somehow 'real', while written language is somehow 'unreal'. In the end, perhaps the issue can only be decided on the grounds of taste rather than objective linguistic criteria. Tastes change, and literature does not necessarily have to appeal to spoken language, as another Lallans poet, Sydney Goodsir Smith, observes, in the 'Epistle to John Guthrie', when he asks, 'wha the deil spoke like King Lear?'

The final strategy used by those extending the vocabulary of a language is to make up new words (neologisms). Although the introduction of new words is criticised as one of the 'artificial' characteristics of a synthetic Scots, coinages are continually being introduced in all languages, including standard varieties of English. Few would argue that such fairly recent words as 'modem' or 'cellphone' or 'skateboard' were 'artificial' when they were first coined. However, the Scottish Nationalist Party drew particular criticism at its 1993 Conference for using the word *unthirldom* in a letter in Broad Scots from the then Party Convener. This letter is reprinted below:

YEIRLIE NATIONAL CONVENE 1993
A Message frae the National Convener
The 1993 yeirlie Convene staunds at the hinner end o a spell o eftir election stievemakkin for the SNP an the oncome o twa vital walin campaigns for Scotland.

I the time sin the walin the SNP haes throcht a fair pairt o the rebiggin wi regaird til organisation an siller needfu ti allou us ti bear the gree agin our Unionist faes.

Wi hae, forby, cairriet on betterin our poleetical staundin as gaugit baith i pow counts an the outcome o Council walins, an aaready we hae, stellit an yokit til the campaign, maist o our foreseen Candidates for neist yeir's walin til the Paurliament o Europe.

The daeins o the Convene sall tak tent til the poleetical maitters that will be at the hert o that campaign, wi the wecht siccar on Unthirldom as the gait ti pittan richt aa the hairm an wrangs that Government frae Westminster haes gart Scotland dree.

The bygaen yeir haes brocht ti licht monie neu examples o the puirtith o London pouer gaen agley i Scotland – the Braer mishanter, the ongaun threit til Scotland's watter, the swick at Rosyth an the ettle tae fause-bounder our Councils.

The key maitter i the incomin yeir will be the forrit-luikin leet o cheynges that anerlie Unthirldom ben Europe can bring hame til the folk o Scotland.

Alex Salmond MP
National Convener
Scottis National Pairtie

The transitive verb *unthirl* has existed in the language since the late sixteenth century, at least in the form *unthirled* meaning 'unsubjugated', or, more narrowly, not bound by *thirlage* ('thrall' or 'bondage') to a particular mill (early eighteenth century). The neologism *unthirldom*, then, generalises the sense of 'bondage', and, by adding the prefix *un-* and the suffix *–dom*, creates the new sense of 'the state of being freed from bondage or subjugation'. Ironically, the new word is a distant relative of the current English word *unenthralled*, a term that captures the attitude expressed in the press coverage of the letter at the time.

New Scots words tend to be of four types (McClure 1981b):

- compounds such as *ayebydand* 'always-remaining' or *fause-bounder* literally 'false-boundary', that is, 'to gerrymander'
- figurative or metaphorical extensions of existing words, such as *pow count* 'head count', or 'opinion poll'
- words based on sound symbolism such as *flichterie-fleeterie* (which sounds like other words meaning light, quick activity, such as *flicht*, *flit*, *fleet*); cf. Smith on phonaesthesia, in Chapter 9
- calques, that is, words modelled on compounds or idioms in another language, preferably not English, but often German, such as *yearhunder* ('century', cf. German *jahrhundert*).

Some usages combine a number of these types, for example the SNP letter uses the word *walin* to mean 'political election', which extends the general Scots meaning, 'choice', in the direction of the German *walen* 'election'.

From the perspective of status raising and corpus planning, then, Scots is, at least superficially, going through several of the processes of standardisation. It is being codified; its status as a distinct minority language alongside Gaelic is recognised, for example by the European Bureau of Lesser Used Languages, and in literary Scots, at least, there are strategies in principle for the rebuilding of a fully functional corpus. There are attempts to reintroduce written Scots to public life beyond the domain of literature, in which, of course, there has been continuous activity since the Union of the Crowns. Where Scots yet has to make substantial inroads is in the realm of effective educational provision and acquisition planning.

EDUCATION AND ACQUISITION PLANNING

Cooper writes of acquisition planning (1989: 33):

> When planning is directed towards increasing a language's uses, it falls within the rubric of status planning. But when it is directed towards increasing the number of users – speakers, writers, listeners or readers – then a separate category for the focus of language planning seems to me to be justified.

The consideration of acquisition planning seems to be particularly justified in the case of Broad Scots, where speakers use different varieties, and most speakers would have to be taught *ab initio* how to write the language. While there is a widespread feeling that many Scottish people use some form of Scots in the streets and at home, there is still an issue about recognition of the language by parents and children, and anxiety that what is left of Scots is being lost, generation on generation.

Even calculating the number of speakers of Scots is a controversial issue. Following a pilot study by Murdoch (1995), the General Register Office for Scotland declined to include a question on Scots in the 2001 census, despite a vigorous campaign in its favour, and despite having completed its own test of possible question formats (Maté 1996; Horsburgh and Murdoch 1997; Macafee 1996, 2000a). Murdoch's figures suggest that over fifty per cent of Scots regard themselves as Scots speakers, while the GRO pilot figures suggest around thirty-three per cent. There are regional differences in the figures, and Macafee (2000a: 38) suggests that informants in west central Scotland often excluded themselves because they perceived their vernacular as slang, rather than as Scots. She observes that the imposition of a formal, written Standard Scots in schools would not necessarily raise the linguistic self-esteem of such speakers; rather they might feel doubly excluded as 'mixed language' speakers. The lack of definition of Scots led Murdoch and the GRO to test questions that allowed a relatively wide definition of Scots, for example (cf. Maté 1996: table 4):

Question	% age responses			Sample size
	Yes	No	Don't know	
Can you speak Scots or a dialect of Scots (e.g. Shetlandic, Glaswegian, Buchan)?	31	69	—	1022

The fact that present-day Scots exists in variety, and often unrecognised, across regions and social classes causes problems for those involved in acquisition planning. Clearly, a substantial proportion of Scots (one third upwards) identify themselves as Scots speakers. Equally clearly, the Scots that they identify involves differing densities of insular, rural and urban varieties, whose differences in, say, pronunciation and vocabulary will be as evident as their common characteristics. The situation is further complicated by the fact that, as noted above, the different varieties of Broad Scots all spread out in a continuum with Scottish Standard English, and most speakers will code-switch or style-drift according to current perceptions of the kind of speech behaviour that is 'appropriate' in formal and informal contexts.

Acquisition planners, therefore, are faced with a choice. They can opt for one of the following strategies:

- raise awareness of local regional and social varieties, in the hope that such awareness will broaden out to embrace other varieties, and that their common characteristics will be recognised implicitly or explicitly
- teach a 'Standard Scots', arrived by some form of consensus or authority (for example, by a committee of experts, drawn from past literature, or by other authoritative example).

Purves (1997b: 24) recommends the latter strategy, and voices concern about the former:

It is difficult to see how any of the surviving dialects of Scots could be effectively taught in schools. None of them has an extensive literature and none of them, except Shetlandic, has a contemporary published grammar which could be used as the basis for instruction. Furthermore, most teachers in Scotland are not native to the dialect area in which they teach. Scots cannot now be taught solely through the medium of its surviving regional dialects, which are now seriously eroded and infiltrated by English, to some extent as a result of earlier 'educational' policy.

In contrast, Macafee (2000a: 38) approves of the former strategy, although she recommends constant media exposure of children and adults to 'authentic examples' of Scots that would help focus their beliefs about what Scots is.

New resources for the teaching of Scots do occasionally come on the market, for example MacGillivrary, ed. (1997) contains position papers and exemplary materials for the use of Scots in the classroom, and *Scotspeak* is a guide to the pronunciations of Glasgow, Edinburgh, Dundee and Aberdeen, aimed at actors, students of drama and language, and school pupils (Robinson and Crawford 2001). However, the most comprehensive educational initiative of the past decade has been the publication of *The Kist* (Robertson, et al. 1996a), a selection of literary texts in different varieties of Scots, plus two Gaelic texts, with audio tapes, worksheets and a teacher's handbook. The resource is aimed at the 5–14 curriculum in Scotland, that is, primary to early secondary education, and its aim is to develop children's awareness of different kinds of literary Scots, as well as to develop their own spoken and written facility in Scots. Exploration of the language the children bring to school is privileged alongside the continuing development of Standard English. Advice given to teachers on writing in Scots is ambivalent about standardisation (Robertson et al. 1996b: 21; original emphasis):

> **A first word of warning** – ignore matters of spelling in the early stages of writing in Scots. But do try and head towards some sort of systematic policy on spelling, perhaps based on the variety of spelling found in your own area as revealed by the anthology's texts. At least initially, accept any form of phonetic spelling that pupils arrive at as long as you (and they!) can understand it.

However, teachers are then counselled to avoid apostrophes except in words like *Ah've*, a nod towards the Scots Style Sheets mentioned earlier.

Although the *Kist* resource was widely distributed in primary schools, and met with critical acclaim, there has been no systematic study of its use, or possibly neglect, in schools, or the extent of its impact. It certainly was introduced into an environment where attitudes towards Scots could be negative on the part of both teachers and pupils. Menzies (1991) reports an investigation into attitudes amongst Glasgow secondary schoolchildren, and concludes that they exhibited negative feelings towards their vernacular, even while they strongly identified with vernacular speakers; that is, Glasgow dialect was endowed with the 'covert prestige' that helps maintain stigmatised language varieties in the face of institutional denigration. Menzies also reports that her informants knew little literature in Scots and had negligible knowledge of the history of Scots, and she recommends teaching in Scots and about Scots as a remedy for the linguistic insecurity she found. Adaptations of Menzies' research with groups of children who had and had not been systematically exposed to *The Kist* would help ascertain whether the approach taken by its creators had the effect of raising linguistic self-esteem and self-identification with Scots.

Beyond the 5–14 curriculum, there has been little systematic attention given to Scots in school. The conservative attitudes of teachers, and their own linguistic insecurities, are often cited as reasons why Scots is avoided in the secondary curriculum (e.g. Gifford 1998); however, Lorvick's (1995: 56) survey of secondary teacher's attitudes found 'a considerable degree of support among the respondents for Scots in the classroom. The question is how that support can be exploited and extended in favour of the language.'

The upper school curriculum in Scotland has been subject to a swift succession of revisions over the past decade, and the situation has not yet stabilised. The 'Higher Still' curriculum was intended to replace gradually the previous 'Higher' examinations from 2001, and in the successive Intermediate, Higher and Advanced Higher examinations, space was to be found for Scots language beyond literature (Scottish Qualifications Authority 1999a–c, 2000). At Intermediate and Higher levels, a special subject option was devised to allow candidates to report on their investigations into language use in a local, vocational or personal sphere. At Advanced Higher, a new Scottish Language option was devised to encourage candidates to explore language variation in Scotland according to region, gender and social class, and to explore the use of Scots in literature and the media (cf. Hershaw 2002). However, the reform was to be short-lived, and take-up of the language options was to be minimal. By 2002, no schools and only one or two colleges of further education in Scotland had entered candidates for the language options at Intermediate and Higher level, and no candidates at all had been entered for the Advanced Higher in Scottish Language. From 2002, simplifications to the Intermediate and Higher examinations mean that the option of studying language as part of the English curriculum all but disappear, and unless there is evidence of interest, the Advanced Higher option in Scottish Language is also likely to wither away. This neglect of Scots in the 15–18 curriculum is not necessarily the result of hostility towards the language: the modifications to the Higher Still examinations were intended to simplify a complicated and so unpopular set of assessment instruments, and the language option seems to have been a casualty of that process. Since at the time of writing the education debate rumbles on unabated, even fairly recent position papers can seem dated, even if many of the issues in them are still unresolved (see, for example, MacGillivray ed. 1997; Niven and Jackson eds 1998). The only certainty is that there will be further curriculum revisions in the near future.

In higher education, the provision for Scots is also uneven – Glasgow, Edinburgh and Aberdeen Universities all offer courses that have components investigating Scots. Postgraduate students at Aberdeen University have been particularly productive in their research into language maintenance and planning (see, for example, Allan 1998; Hendry 1997; Horsburgh 1997; McGarrity 1998; Middleton 2001; Tsiona 1997). Aspects of modern and historical Scots are also studied in universities overseas, particularly in continental Europe. The first historical computer corpus of written Scots, covering the period from 1375 to 1700, was constructed at the University of Helsinki. Glasgow and Edinburgh Universities are currently undertaking a joint project to build a computer corpus of the languages currently used in Scotland, including Scots and Scottish English (www.scottishcorpus.ac.uk). Attempts to use Scots as a medium of scholarship are fewer, though lectures and talks have been given in Scots, and students have chosen to be examined in the medium, even at postgraduate level (see, for example, Allan 1998). Since its founding, *Lallans* has printed reviews in Scots, and some scholarly and polemical papers are also written in Scots, often but not always on the topic of language planning itself (see, for example, Allan 2000; Eagle 2001; Grant 2002; Hodgart 1997, 1998; Horsbroch 2001, 2002; Macafee 2000b, 2001b; McHardy 1998; Parsley 2001), but the most ambitious recent attempt to use Scots as a scholarly medium is *Cairn,* a journal of history articles that originated in Aberdeen amongst a group of students (Horsbroch 2001).

Despite the uneven nature of provision for Scots, support for the language has come a long way since the Scotch Code of 1878. Various pressure groups continue to influence educational policy in Scotland. Lo Bianco (2001) embeds Scots into an ambitious overall vision for Scottish education. In this vision, a role for Scots, alongside Gaelic, is central as a 'heritage language', and he cites Graddol (1997) to assert (Lo Bianco 2001: 33):

> The greater the force for English to fulfil international communications
> functions, the greater will be the force of the assertion of other
> languages as languages of identity, and solidarity, of affect and
> belonging, in reaction to English. And the greater will be the
> diversification of English itself.

In this vision of a multilingual Scotland in a world that communicates via global English, Scots and Gaelic are safeguarded as crucial to the sense of personal identity in relation to a more immediate community that is both contemporary and historical (cf. Joseph 1999). Fishman (2001) reports on ten years of research into reversing language shift against the grain of globalisation in communities across the world. One point he makes is that reversing language shift need not mean reclaiming wholly the ground lost to a powerful language – and no language currently is as powerful as English. Powerful languages such as English can easily encroach into those communicative functions, public or domestic, previously performed by threatened languages. However, it is difficult for threatened languages, such as Scots, to reclaim ground lost to English, and particularly difficult for them to move into the powerful arena of public discourse. Fishman (2001: 14) warns:

> Threatened languages cannot afford functionally diffuse or free floating efforts. Or, to put it another way, threatened languages must establish both (1) *a priority of functions*, and (2) *a priority of linkages between functions* in order to derive maximal benefit from their relatively weak resource base and unfavourable resource competitive setting. [Original emphasis]

Applied to Scots, Fishman's point is that sporadic efforts at reclaiming lost communicative functions – a political letter here, an academic article or even a spectacular translation there – cannot hope to stem the flow of anglicisation. Neither can recognition by European institutions, or the publishing of principles of linguistic rights – if they are isolated or 'free floating' efforts. If Scots is to maintain a significant presence in the communities where it is still used, its functions in these communities must be recorded, recognised, supported and gradually linked with other functions. So far, this process has hardly begun.

AVENUES FOR RESEARCH

Most of the little research that has been done on Scots language planning begins from the assumption that current provision is inadequate and that an enhanced role for Scots is necessary. As the educational and linguistic ground is continually shifting, systematic and objective research is needed in the following areas. The orthodox division into 'status planning', 'corpus planning' and 'acquisition planning' helps identify points of emphasis; however, the three processes are evidently interdependent.

Status planning

Scots language activists call for the use of Scots for a greater range of functions than is currently the case. In other words, they call for the use of Scots beyond the domestic and intimate domains of everyday speech, discourse associated with traditional occupations such as farming and fishing, and written literary expression. If Scots is to be used in official documentation, in formal spoken contexts (such as debates in the Scottish parliament), in advertising and in the media, there can be research into the reaction of the majority of the population to the *forms* in which Scots in these contexts should take. This might take the form of 'market testing' samples of formal and 'public domain' Scots with focus groups in different parts of the country. Such research can adapt the methodologies established by 'attitude surveys' such as those undertaken by Menzies (1991), Iacuaniello (1992/3), Lorvick (1995) and Macafee and McGarrity (1999). However, as Fishman (2001) demonstrates, status planning research must continue to monitor those areas of life in which Scots is currently perceived to be more or less acceptable or 'appropriate'. 'Appropriacy', as Fairclough (1995: 247ff.) observes, is a moveable feast, depending on a complex set of social relations of power and resistance. A revival of Scots, if such a process were to occur, would probably spread from domain to domain gradually, for example from casual conversation, to sports reporting in the media, to other genres of media journalism. Attitudes to the functions 'appropriate' to Scots is likely also to shift, according to the positive or negative image of Scots provided in education and the media, and this shifting of attitudes also requires monitoring.

Corpus planning

As noted above, research into corpus planning in Scots has hitherto been based largely on the strategies used by the 'Scots synthesisers' (McClure 1981b) to construct a 'plastic' or 'reintegrated' Scots for use in literature. As the use of Scots for other functions gradually increases, there is room for research into the processes used to extend the lexical, syntactic and discursive resources of the language in both speech and writing.

From a historical perspective, there is scope for a overview of corpus planning in literary Scots from the early eighteenth century to the present day. The Scots revivalists from Allan Ramsay onwards wrote in Broad Scots against a background of majority English usage amongst literate Scots. For the first time, their choice of Scots as a written medium, rather than English, was made deliberately, and their Scots was directed at a Scottish readership that was used mainly to English texts. Literary Scots was reinvented again by the Lallans school in the twentieth century, partly as a self-conscious reaction against the Scots of the eighteenth and nineteenth centuries, although the roots of a 'synthetic' Scots can be seen in the work of some writers of the early nineteenth century, particularly translators (Corbett 1999). Most written Scots since 1700 has been literary. However, the growing number of non-literary texts, their linguistic choices, the motivations of their authors and the response of their readers all deserve study. Much detailed work on the motivations governing the choice of lexis, grammar, orthography and discourse genres of the different generations of Scots writers remains undone.

Acquisition planning and educational provision

Education is at the heart of language planning. Particularly given the lurches in educational policy and practices over the past twenty years, Williamson's historical survey of Lowland Scots in education (1982/3) urgently needs to be updated and extended. On the contemporary front, as Lo Bianco (2001: 9) observes, we still need to know more about basic issues: 'The kinds of educational questions that need asking are: How is Scots represented in schooling? What pedagogy is used and what attitudes are exhibited towards it (in all its variety) by teachers and public administration?'

There is a woeful insufficiency of information about the effectiveness of educational initiatives to raise awareness of and sympathy with Scots in schools. In particular, as noted above, wide-scale research needs to be conducted on the positive or negative impact (if any) of ambitious projects such as the distribution of the *Kist* resource in primary schools. Notwithstanding Macafee's cautionary note about pupils in urban settings who perceive themselves speaking a slang deriving from two languages, it is often assumed that greater knowledge about Scots and its literary heritage will increase pupils' linguistic self-esteem. This, too, is an assumption sorely in need of empirical validation.

Language planning is sometimes perceived, with reason, to be at the margins of linguistic study. It is all too easy to ridicule the enthusiasts who regularly turn up with a new and 'authentic' way of spelling Scots, or the activists who disconcertingly code-switch into Lallans in the pub after a conference. However, the inescapable fact remains that public policy, whether *laissez-faire* or pro-active, does affect language use, change and maintenance. In a democratic society, individuals can seek to influence these processes, whether through the letters pages of newspapers, membership of pressure groups such as the Scots Language Society or forums such as the Cross-Party Group on the Scots Language. The way in which policy influences language use is therefore an important topic of study that merits on-going research.

NOTE

I am grateful to Fiona Douglas for reading and commenting on an earlier draft of this chapter.

Bibliography

An extensive on-line bibliography of material on Scots, compiled by Caroline Macafee and maintained by Marina Dossena, can be found at www.unibg.it/anglistica/slin/scot-bib.htm. Alternatively, a link to this bibliography can be found at www.scotslanguage.net/links.html or www.sldl.org.uk

Abercrombie, D. (1979), 'The accents of Standard English in Scotland', in Aitken and McArthur (eds), pp. 68–84.

Adams, G. B. (1964), 'Introduction', in G. B. Adams (ed.), *Ulster Dialects: An Introductory Symposium*, Holywood, Ulster Folk Museum, pp. 1–4. Originally published as 'Ulster dialects' in *Belfast in its Regional Setting*, 1952.

Adams, G. B. (c.1968), 'A brief guide to Ulster Scots', unpublished typescript.

Adams, G. B. (1977), 'The dialects of Ulster', in D. O'Muirithe (ed.) *The English Language in Ireland*, Cork: Mercier, pp. 56–69.

Adams, I. H. (1976), *Agrarian Landscape Terms: A Glossary for Historical Geography*, London: Institute of British Geographers.

Adams, I. and M. Somerville (eds) (1993), *Cargoes of Despair and Hope: Scottish Emigration to North America 1603–1803*, Edinburgh: John Donald.

Adams, M. (2000), 'Lexical Doppelgängers', *Journal of English Linguistics*, 28, pp. 295–310.

Agutter, A. and L. Cowan (1981), 'Changes in the vocabulary of Lowland Scots dialects', *Scottish Literary Journal*, Supplement 14, pp. 49–62.

Aitken, A. J. (1971), 'Variation and variety in written Middle Scots' in A. J. Aitken et al. (eds), *Edinburgh Studies in English and Scots*, London: Longman, pp. 177–209. [Summarised and revised in Macafee and Aitken (2002), pp. lxx–lxxv.]

Aitken, A. J. (1977), 'How to pronounce Older Scots' in A. J. Aitken, M. P. McDiarmid and D. S. Thomson (eds), *Bards and Makars: Scots Language and Literature, Medieval and Renaissance*, Glasgow: Glasgow University Press.

Aitken, A. J. (1979), 'Scottish Speech: a historical view, with special reference to the Standard English of Scotland' in Aitken and McArthur (eds), pp. 85–119.

Aitken, A. J. (1981a), 'The Good Old Scots Tongue: Does Scots Have an Identity?' in Haugen, McClure and Thomson (eds), pp. 72–90.

Aitken, A. J. (1981b), 'The Scottish vowel length rule', in M. Benskin and M. L. Samuels (eds), *So Meny People, Longages and Tonges: Philological Essays in Scots and Mediaeval*

English Presented to Angus McIntosh, Edinburgh: The Middle English Dialect Project, pp. 131–57.

Aitken, A. J. (1982), 'Bad Scots: Some Superstitions about Scots Speech', *Scottish Language* 1, pp. 30–44.

Aitken, A. J. (1983), 'The language of Older Scots poetry' in J. Derrick McClure (ed.), *Scotland and the Lowland Tongue: Studies in the Language and Literature of Lowland Scotland in Honour of David D. Murison*, Aberdeen: Aberdeen University Press, pp. 18–49. [Summarised in Macafee and Aitken (2002), pp. cxxxiii–cxli.]

Aitken, A. J. (1984a), 'Scottish accents and dialects' in Trudgill (ed.), pp. 94–114.

Aitken, A. J. (1984b), 'Scots and English in Scotland', in Trudgill (ed.), pp. 517–32.

Aitken, A. J. (1985), 'A History of Scots', in *The Concise Scots Dictionary*, M. Robinson (ed.), Aberdeen: Aberdeen University Press, pp. ix–xli.

Aitken, A. J. (1991), 'Progress in Older Scots Philology', *Studies in Scottish Literature*, vol. 26, pp. 19–37.

Aitken, A. J. (1992a), 'Highland English', in T. McArthur (ed.), pp. 469–70.

Aitken, A. J. (1992b), 'Scottish English', in T. McArthur (ed.), pp. 903–5.

Aitken, A. J. (1992c), 'Scots', in T. McArthur (ed.), pp. 893–9.

Aitken, A. J. (1996a), *The Pronunciation of Older Scots. Notes to Accompany the Audio Cassette (SSC 122), 'How to pronounce Older Scots'*, Glasgow: Scotsoun.

Aitken, A. J. (1996b), *How to pronounce Older Scots*, Audio Cassette (SSC 122), Glasgow: Scotstoun.

Aitken, A. J. (1998), 'Scots', in G. Price (ed.), *Encyclopedia of the Languages of Europe*, Oxford: Blackwell, pp. 409–17.

Aitken, A. J., posthumously ed. C. I. Macafee (2002), *The Older Scots Vowels: A History of the Stressed Vowels of Older Scots from the Beginnings to the Eighteenth Century*, Scottish Text Society.

Aitken, A. J. and T. McArthur (eds) (1979), *Languages of Scotland*, Edinburgh: Chambers.

Allan, A. (1998), 'New Founs fae Auld Larachs: Leid-Plannin for Scots', University of Aberdeen: unpublished PhD dissertation.

Allan, A. (2000), 'Language and Politics: A Perspective from Scotland' in Kirk and Ó Baoill (eds), pp. 127–32.

Anderson, R. D. (1995), *Education and the Scottish People 1750–1918*, Oxford: Clarendon Press.

Attridge, D. (1982), *The Rhythms of English Poetry*, Harlow: Longman.

Bailey, R. W. (1982), 'English in Canada', in R. W. Bailey and M. Görlach (eds), *English as a World Language*, Ann Arbor: University of Michigan Press, pp. 134–76.

Barrow, G. W. S. (ed.) (1960), *The Acts of Malcolm IV King of Scots 1153–1165: Together with Scottish Royal Acts Prior to 1153 not included in Sir Archibald Lawrie's 'Early Scottish Charters'*, Regesta Regum Scottorum, 1153–1424, vol. I, Edinburgh: Edinburgh University Press.

Barrow, G. W. S. (ed.) (1971), with the collaboration of W. W. Scott, *The Acts of William I King of Scots 1165–1214*, Regesta Regum Scottorum, 1153–1424, vol. II, Edinburgh: Edinburgh University Press.

Barrow, G. W. S. (1980), *The Anglo-Norman Era in Scottish History*, Oxford: Clarendon Press.

Barrow, G. W. S. (1981), *Kingship and Unity: Scotland 1000–1306*, London: Edward Arnold.

Barrow, G. W. S. (1998), 'The Uses of Place-names and Scottish History – Pointers and Pitfalls', in S. Taylor (ed.), *The Uses of Place-Names*, Edinburgh: Scottish Cultural Press, pp. 12–53.

Barry, M. V. (1996), 'Historical introduction to the dialects of Ulster', in C. I. Macafee (ed.), pp. ix–xii.

Bartlett, C. (1992), 'Regional variation in New Zealand English: The case of Southland', *New Zealand English Newsletter*, 6, pp. 5–15.

Bate, J. (1997), *The Genius of Shakespeare*, Basingstoke: Macmillan.

Bauer, L. (1994), 'English in New Zealand' in R. W. Burchfield (ed.), *Cambridge History of the English Language volume V: English in Britain and Overseas, Origins and Developments*, Cambridge: Cambridge University Press, pp. 382–429.

Bauer, L. (1997), 'Attempting to trace Scottish influence on New Zealand English', in E. W. Schneider (ed.), *Englishes around the World, vol. 2: Essays in Honour of Manfred Görlach*, Amsterdam and Philadelphia: Benjamins, pp. 257–72.

Bauer, L. (2000), 'The dialectal origins of New Zealand English', in A. Bell and K. Kuiper (eds), *New Zealand English*, Amsterdam and Philadelphia: Benjamins, pp. 40–52.

Beal, J. (1997), 'Syntax and morphology', in Jones (ed.), pp. 335–77.

Beale, P. (ed.) (1989), *A Concise Dictionary of Slang and Unconventional English*, London: Routledge.

Bennett, M. (1992), *Scottish Customs from the Cradle to the Grave*, Edinburgh: Polygon.

Benskin, M. (1992), 'Some new perspectives on the origins of standard written English', in J. A. van Leuvensteijn and J. B. Berns (eds), *Dialect and Standard Languages in the English, Dutch, German and Norwegian Language Areas*, Amsterdam: Royal Netherlands Academy of Arts and Sciences, pp. 71–105.

Benson, P. (2001), *Ethnocentrism and the English Dictionary*, London and New York: Routledge.

Bermúdez-Otero, R., D. Denison, R. M. Hogg and C. B. McCully (eds) (2000), *Generative Theory and Corpus Studies: A Dialogue from 10ICEHL*, Berlin: Mouton de Gruyter.

Biber, D. (1988), *Variation across Speech and Writing*, Cambridge: Cambridge University Press.

Biber, D. (1995), *Dimensions of register variation: a cross-linguistic comparison*, Cambridge: Cambridge University Press.

Biber, D., S. Condrad and R. Reppen (1998), *Corpus linguistics. Investigating language structure and use*, Cambridge: Cambridge University Press.

Biber, D. and E. Finegan (1988), 'Drift in Three English Genres from the 18th to the 20th Centuries: A Multi-dimensional approach', in M. Kytö, O. Ihalainen and M. Rissanen (eds), *Corpus Linguistics, Hard and Soft. Proceedings of the Eighth International Conference on English Language Research on Computerized Corpora* (Language and Computers: Studies in Practical Linguistics, 2), Amsterdam: Rodopi, pp. 83–101.

Biber, D. and E. Finegan (1992), 'The linguistic evolution of five written and speech-based English genres from the 17th to the 20th centuries', in M. Rissanen, O. Ihalainen, T. Nevalainen and I. Taavitsainen (eds), *History of Englishes: new methods and interpretations in historical linguistics*, Berlin: Mouton de Gruyter, pp. 688–704.

Black, G. F. (1946), *The Surnames of Scotland: Their Origin, Meaning, and History*, New York: New York Public Library; repr. 1996, Edinburgh: Birlinn.

Blain, E. (1987), 'Speech of the lower Red River settlement', in W. Cowan (ed.), *Papers of the Eighteenth Algonquian Conference*, Ottawa: Carleton University, pp. 7–16.

Boord o Ulstèr-Scotch/Ulster-Scots Agency (2000), *Corporate Plan/Heich Ploy 2000/1–2003/4*, Belfast.

Boswell, J. (1952), *Life of Samuel Johnson, LL.D*, Chicago: Encyclopaedia Britannica Great Books of the Western World.

Brackenridge, H. H. (1965), *Modern Chivalry*. Edited for the modern reader by L. Leary, Schenectady: New College and University Press. [Condensed from the original four volumes published 1792–1815.]

Braidwood, J. (1964), 'Ulster and Elizabethan English', in G. B. Adams (ed.), *Ulster Dialects: An Introductory Symposium*, Holywood: Ulster Folk Museum, pp. 5–109.

Braidwood, J. (1975), 'The Ulster dialect lexicon', Inaugural Lecture, Queen's University of Belfast, 23 April 1969.

Brinton, L. J. (2000), 'The Importance of Discourse Types in Grammaticalization: The Case of Anon', in Herring et al. (eds), pp. 139–62.

Brown, G., K. Currie and J. Kenworthy (1980), *Questions of intonation*, London: Croom Helm.

Brown, K. and J. Miller (1982), 'Aspects of Scottish English syntax', *English World-Wide*, 3:1, pp. 1–17.

Bruce, D. (1801), *Poems Chiefly in the Scottish Dialect, Originally Written under the Signature of the Scots-Irishman*, Washington, PA.

Buthlay, K. (1977), 'Shibboleths of the Scots in the poetry of Hugh MacDiarmid', *Akros*, 34/35, pp. 23–47.

Butler, C. S. (1985), *Statistics in Linguistics*, Oxford: Blackwell.

Butt, J. (ed.) (1963), *The Poems of Alexander Pope*, London: Methuen.

Buuren-Venenbos, C. van (ed.) (1982), *The Buke of the Sevyne Sagis*, Leiden: Leiden University Press.

Bybee, J. (2000), 'Lexicalization of sound change and alternating environments', in M. Broe and J. Pierrehumbert (eds), *Papers in Laboratory Phonology V, Acquisition and the Lexicon*, Cambridge: Cambridge University Press.

Caldwell, S. J. G. (1974), *The Relative Pronoun in Early Scots* (Mémoires de la Société Néophilologique, 42), Helsinki: Société Néophilologique.

Campbell, A. (1959; repr. 1997), *Old English Grammar*, Oxford: Clarendon Press.

Cameron, D. (1995), *Verbal Hygiene*, London: Routledge.

Cardell, K. and C. Cumming (1992–3), 'Scotland's three tongues in Australia: Colonial Hamilton in the 1860s and 1870s', *Scottish Studies*, 31, pp. 40–62.

Cassidy, F. G. et al. (eds) (1985–), *Dictionary of American Regional English*, Cambridge: Belknap Press of Harvard University.

Catford, J. C. (1957), 'The linguistic survey of Scotland', *Orbis*, 6, pp. 105–21.

Chafe, W. (1984), 'How people use relative clauses', in *Proceedings of the Tenth Annual Meeting of the Berkeley Linguistics Society*, C. Brugman and M. Macaulay (eds), Berkeley: Berkeley Linguistics Society, pp. 437–49.

Chambers, J. K. (1973), 'Canadian raising', *Canadian Journal of Linguistics*, 18, pp. 113–35.

Chambers, J. K. (1979), 'Canadian English', *The languages of Canada*, Montreal: Didier, pp. 168–204.

Chambers, J. K. (1992), 'Dialect acquisition', *Language*, 68, pp. 673–705.

Chambers, J. K. (1995), *Sociolinguistic theory: linguistic variation and its social significance*, *Language in Society*, 22, Oxford: Blackwell.

Chambers, J. K. and P. Trudgill (1980), *Dialectology*, Cambridge: Cambridge University Press.

Cheshire, J., V. Edwards, H. Munstermann, B. Weltens (eds) (1989), *Dialect and Education: Some European Perspectives*, Clevedon: Multilingual Matters.

Coates, R. (1987), 'Pragmatic sources of analogical reformation', *Journal of Linguistics*, 23, pp. 319–40.

Cooley, M. (c.1995), 'Sources for the study of 18th century literary dialect', 10 pp., unpublished typescript.

Cooper, R. L. (1989), *Language Planning and Social Change*, Cambridge: Cambridge University Press.

Cooper, S. (1973), *The 1872 Education Act in Lanarkshire*, Hamilton: Hamilton College of Education.

Corbett, J. (1997), *Language and Scottish Literature*, Edinburgh: Edinburgh University Press.

Corbett, J. (1999), *Written in the Language of the Scottish Nation: A History of Literary Translation into Scots*, Clevedon: Multilingual Matters.

Cottle, B. (1978), *The Penguin Dictionary of Surnames*, 2nd edn, London: Penguin.

Cox, R. (1999), *The Language of the Ogham Inscriptions of Scotland*, Aberdeen: Department of Celtic, University of Aberdeen.

Craigie, W. et al. (eds) (1937), *A Dictionary of the Older Scottish Tongue*, 12 vols, Chicago: University of Chicago Press; London: Oxford University Press; Aberdeen: Aberdeen University Press.

Crawford, B. (1987), *Scandinavian Scotland*, Leicester: Leicester University Press.

Cross Party Group on the Scots Language (2003), *Scots: A Statement of Principles*, Edinburgh.

Crowley, T. (1989), *The Politics of Discourse: The Standard Language Question in British Cultural Debates*, London: Macmillan.

Crozier, A. (1984), 'The Scotch-Irish influence on American English', *American Speech*, 59, pp. 310–31.

Crystal, D. (1987), *The Cambridge Encyclopedia of Language*, Cambridge: Cambridge University Press.

Crystal, D. (2000), *Language Death*, Cambridge: Cambridge University Press.

Darton, M. (1994), *The Dictionary of Place Names in Scotland*, Orpington: Eric Dobby.

Davies Roberts, P. (1986), *How Poetry Works*, Harmondsworth: Penguin.

Devitt, A. J. (1989), *Standardizing Written English: Diffusion in the Case of Scotland 1520–1659*, Cambridge: Cambridge University Press.

Dieth, E. (1932), *A Grammar of the Buchan Dialect*, Cambridge: Cambridge University Press.

Diller, H-J, and M. Görlach (eds) (2001), *Towards a History of English as a History of Genres*, Heidelberg: C. Winter.

Dinsmoor, R. (1828), *Incidental Poems Accompanied with Letters, and a Few Select Pieces, Mostly Original, for Their Illustration, Together with a Preface, and a Sketch of the Author's Life*, Haverhill: A. W. Thayer.

Dixon, N. (1947), *The Place-Names of Midlothian*, typescript PhD dissertation, Edinburgh University.

Docherty, G. and P. Foulkes (1999), 'Derby and Newcastle: Instrumental phonetics and variationist studies', in Foulkes and Docherty (eds), pp. 49–71.

Docherty, G. and P. Foulkes (2000), 'Speaker, speech and knowledge of sounds', in N. Burton-Roberts, P. Carr and G. Docherty (eds), *Phonological knowledge: Its nature and status*, Oxford: Oxford University Press, pp. 105–29.

Dobson, D. (1994), *Scottish Emigration to Colonial America 1607–1785*, Athens: University of Georgia Press.

Dolan, T. P. (ed.) (1998), *A Dictionary of Hiberno-English*, Dublin: Gill and Macmillan.

Donaldson, G. (1980), 'Scots', in S. Thernstrom (ed.), *Harvard Encyclopedia of American Ethnic Groups*, Cambridge: Harvard University Press, pp. 908–16.

Donaldson, W. (1989), *The Language of the People: Scots Prose from the Victorian Revival*, Aberdeen: Aberdeen University Press.

Dons, U. and L. Moessner (1999), 'The present participle in Middle Scots', *Scottish Language*, vol. 18, pp. 17–33.

Dorward, D. (1995a), *Scottish Surnames*, Glasgow: HarperCollins.

Dorward, D. (1995b), *Scotland's Place-names*, expanded edn, Edinburgh: Mercat Press.

Dorward, D. (1995–6), 'Scottish personal names', in E. Eichler et al. (eds), *Name Studies: An International Handbook of Onomastics*, 3 vols, Berlin: de Gruyter, vol. II, pp. 1284–9.

Dorward, D. (1998), 'Scottish *Mac* names', in W. F. H. Nicolaisen (ed.), *Proceedings of the XIXth International Congress of Onomastic Sciences, Aberdeen, August 4–11, 1996*, 3 vols, Aberdeen: Department of English, University of Aberdeen, vol. III, pp. 113–16.

Dorward, D. (1998–9), 'Scottish surnames in the context of Scottish culture, historical and contemporary', *Onoma*, 34, pp. 77–90.

Dossena, M. (2001a), 'Scotticisms in Johnson's Dictionary: A Lexicographer's Perceptions of a Sociolinguistic Change in Progress', *The History of English and the Dynamics of Power. Atti dell'8° Convegno Nazionale di Storia della Lingua Inglese*, a cura di E. Barisone, Alessandria: Dell'Orso.

Dossena, M. (2001b), 'The cruel slauchtyr that vas cruelly exsecutit: Intensification and Adverbial Modality in the Helsinki Corpus of Older Scots. A preliminary overview', *Neuphilologische Mitteilungen*, 102/3, pp. 287–302.

Dossena, M. (2001c), '*For the aduancement of the commoun weilth*: Hypotheses in Scots Scientific Discourse of the 16th–17th Centuries'. A Preliminary Investigation', *Scottish Language*, 20, pp. 47–65.

Dossena, M. (forthcoming), 'Modality and Argumentative Discourse in the Darien Pamphlets', *Proceedings of the International Conference on Late Modern English*, Edinburgh, 2001.

Douglas, F. (2000), 'The Role of Lexis in Scottish Newspapers', University of Glasgow: unpublished PhD dissertation.

Downie, A. (1983), 'The survival of the fishing dialects on the Moray Firth', *Scottish Language*, 2, pp. 42–8.

Duncan, A. A. M. (1975), *Scotland: The Making of the Kingdom*, The Edinburgh History of Scotland Vol.1, Edinburgh: Mercat Press.

Eagle, A. (2001), 'Wha Ye Writin For?', in Kirk and Ó Baoill (eds) (2001b), pp. 169–76.

Eagle, A. (2002), 'Stravaigin the Wab', *Lallans*, 60, pp. 110–12.

Eremeeva, V. (2002), 'A sociophonetic investigation of Glaswegian vowels', University of Glasgow: unpublished MPhil dissertation.

Erskine, J. G. W. (forthcoming), 'Annotated bibliography on Ulster Scots language and literature', in P. Robinson, A. Smyth and M. Montgomery (eds), *The Academic Study of Ulster Scots: Essays for and by Robert J. Gregg*.

European Journal of English Studies (2001), vol. 5, no. 2.

Fairclough, N. (1995), *Critical Discourse Analysis: The Critical Study of Language*, London: Longman.

Falconer, G. (2001), 'The Scots Leid in the New Poleitical Institutions', in Kirk and Ó Baoill (eds) (2001b), pp. 135–58.

Fellows-Jensen, G. (1990), 'Scandinavians in Southern Scotland?', *Nomina*, 13, pp. 41–60.

Fenton, A. (1972, 1985), 'A fuel of necessity: animal manure', in E. Ennen and G. Wiegelmann (eds), *Festschrift Matthias Zender. Studien zu Volkskultur, Sprache und Landesgeschichte*, Bonn: Ludwig Röhrscheid, pp. 722–734. Reprinted in A. Fenton, *The Shape of the Past. Essays in Scottish Ethnology*, Edinburgh: John Donald, pp. 96–111.

Fenton, J. (1995, 2000), *The Hamely Tongue. A Personal Record of Ulster-Scots in County Antrim*, 2nd edn, Ulster-Scots Academic Press.

Finkenstaedt, T., D. Wolff et al. (1973), *Ordered Profusion. Studies in Dictionaries and the English Lexicon*, Heidelberg: Carl Winter.

Firth, J. R. (1964), *Speech*, Oxford: Oxford University Press.

Fishman, J. A. (1980), 'Bilingual education, language planning and English', *English World Wide*, 1, pp. 11–24.

Fishman, J. A. (1991), *Reversing Language Shift: Theoretical and Empirical Foundations of Assistance to Threatened Languages*, Clevedon: Multilingual Matters.

Fishman, J. A. (2001), *Can Threatened Languages be Saved? Reversing Language Shift, Revisited: A 21st-Century Perspective*, Clevedon: Multilingual Matters.

Fleischman, S. (2000), 'Methodologies and Ideologies in Historical Linguistics: On Working with Older Languages', in S. C. Herring et al. (eds), pp. 33–58.

Forsyth, K. (1997), *Language in Pictland*, Utrecht: Keltische Draak.

Fox, D. (ed.) (1987), *Robert Henryson: The Poems*, Oxford: Clarendon Press.

Fransson, G. (1935), *Middle English Surnames of Occupation 1100–1350*, Lund: Gleerup.

Fraser, G. S. (1970), *Metre, Rhyme and Free Verse*, London: Methuen.

Fraser, I. (1999), *The Place-Names of Arran*, Glasgow: The Arran Society of Glasgow.

Foulkes, P. and G. Docherty (eds) (1999), *Urban Voices: Accent studies in the British Isles*, London: Arnold.

Foulkes, P. and G. Docherty (2000), 'Another chapter in the story of /r/: "labiodental" variants in British English', *Journal of Sociolinguistics*, 4, pp. 30–59.

Gelling, M., W. F. H. Nicolaisen and M. Richards (1970), *The Names of Towns and Cities in Britain*, London: Batsford.

Gifford, A. (1998), 'Scots language and teacher training: Viewpoint II', in Niven and Jackson (eds), pp. 105–14.

Gilmore, P. (ed.) (1999), *'Scots-Irish' words from the Pennsylvania mountains taken from the Shoemaker collection*, Bruceton Mills, WV: Scotpress.

Glauser, B. (1974), *The Scottish-English Linguistic Border. Lexical Aspects*, Bern: Francke.

Glenn, J. A. (1987), 'A New Edition of Sir Gilbert Haye's *Buke of the Ordre of Knychthede*', University of Notre Dame, Indiana: unpublished PhD dissertation.

Görlach, M. (ed.) (1985), *Focus on: Scotland*, Amsterdam: John Benjamins.

Görlach, M. (2000), 'Ulster Scots: A Language?' in Kirk and Ó Baoill (eds), pp. 13–32.

Görlach, M. and K. Lenz (2001), *A Textual History of Scots*, Heidelberg: Universitätsverlag C. Winter.

Graddol, D. (1996), 'Global English, Global Culture?', in D. Graddol and S. Goodman (eds), *Redesigning English: New Texts, New Identitites*, London and New York: Routledge.

Graham, I. C. C. (1956), *Colonist from Scotland: Emigration to North America 1707–1783*, Ithaca: Cornell University Press.

Grant, N. (2002), 'Educaetioun in the Unytit Kingrik', *Lallans*, 60, pp. 134–45.

Grant, W. (1931), 'Introduction' to *The Scottish National Dictionary*, vol. 1, Edinburgh: Scottish National Dictionary Association.

Grant, W. and A. Main-Dixon (1921), *Manual of Modern Scots*, Cambridge: Cambridge University Press.

Grant, W. and D. Murison (eds) (1931–76), *The Scottish National Dictionary*, 10 vols, Aberdeen: Aberdeen University Press.

Gregg, R. (1972), 'The Scotch-Irish dialect boundaries in Ulster', in Martyn Wakelin (ed.), *Patterns in the Folk Speech of the British Isles*, London: Athlone, pp. 109–39.

Gregg, R. (1973), 'The diphthongs /əɪ/ and /əʊ/ in Scottish, Scotch-Irish and Canadian English', *Canadian Journal of Linguistics*, 18, pp. 136–45.

Gregg, R. (1985), *The Scotch-Irish Dialect Boundaries in the Province of Ulster*, Canadian Federation for the Humanities.

Häcker, M. (1999), *Adverbial Clauses in Scots: A Semantic-Syntactic Study*, Berlin: Mouton de Gruyter.

Hagan, A. I. (2002), *Urban Scots Dialect Writing*, Oxford, etc.: Peter Lang.

Halliday, M. A. K. (1978), 'Antilanguages', *Language as Social Semiotic*, London: Edward Arnold, pp. 164–82.

Harris, J. (1985), *Phonological variation and change: Studies in Hiberno-English*, Cambridge: Cambridge University Press.

Hanks, P. (1992–3), 'The present-day distribution of surnames in the British Isles', *Nomina*, 16, pp. 79–98.

Hanks, P. and F. Hodges (1988), *A Dictionary of Surnames*, Oxford: Oxford University Press.

Haugen, E. (1966), 'Dialect, language, nation', *American Anthropologist*, 68, pp. 922–35.

Haugen, E., J. D. McClure and D. Thomson (eds) (1981), *Minority Languages Today*, Edinburgh: Edinburgh University Press.

Hamilton, A. M. (1998a), 'The endurance of Scots in the United States', *Scottish Language*, 17, pp. 108–18.

Hamilton, A. M. (1998b), 'Who speaks Scots in the United States: An analysis of social labels in *DARE*', unpublished typescript.

Harris, J. (1984), 'English in the north of Ireland', in P. Trudgill (ed.), *Language in the British Isles*, Cambridge: Cambridge University Press, pp. 115–34.

Harris, J. (1985), *Phonological Variation and Change. Studies in Hiberno-English*, Cambridge: Cambridge University Press.

Hayes-McCoy, G. (1937), *Scots Mercenary Forces in Ireland*, Dublin: Burns, Oates and Washbourn.

Hendry, I. (1997), 'Doric – An Investigation into its Use amongst Primary School Children in the North East of Scotland', University of Aberdeen: unpublished MLitt dissertation.

Herring, S. C., P. van Reenen and L. Schøsler (eds) (2000), *Textual Parameters in Older Languages*, Amsterdam and Philadelphia: John Benjamins.

Hershaw, W. (2002), *English: Teaching Scots Language: Staff Resources and Approaches [Advanced Higher]* National Qualifications Curriculum Support, Dundee and Glasgow: Learning and Teaching Scotland.

Hettinga, J. (1981), 'Standard and dialect in Anstruther and Cellardyke', *Scottish Literary Journal*, Supplement 14, pp. 37–48.

Hewitt, J. (1974), *The Rhyming Weavers and Other Country Poets of Antrim and Down*, Belfast: Blackstaff.

Hewlett, N., B. Matthews and J. Scobbie (1999), 'Vowel duration in Scottish English speaking children', *Proceedings of the International Congress of Phonetic Sciences*, San Francisco, pp. 2157–60.

Hey, D. (2000), *Family Names and Family History*, London: Hambledon and London.

Hill, G. (1873), *Historical Account of the Plantation in Ulster 1608–1620*, Belfast.

Hill, T. (1963), 'Phonemic and prosodic analysis in linguistic geography', *Orbis*, 12, pp. 449–55.

Hoad, T. F. (ed.) (1986), *The Concise Oxford Dictionary of English Etymology*, Oxford: Clarendon Press.

Hodgart, J. (1997), 'The Scots Language in the Schuil', in MacGillivray (ed.), pp. 84–9.

Hodgart, J. (1998), 'Scots language in the classroom: Viewpoint II', in Niven and Jackson (eds), pp. 77–92.

Hopper, P. J. and E. Closs Traugott (1993), *Grammaticalization* (Cambridge Textbooks in Linguistics), Cambridge: Cambridge University Press.

Horsbroch, D. (2001), 'A Hairst for a Bit Screive: Writin Historie in Scots', in Kirk and Ó Baoill (eds) (2001b), pp. 187–94.

Horsbroch, D. (2002), 'A Shot at the Baw: A Historie o the Gemm o Fitba in Scotland', *Lallans*, 60, pp. 11–37.

Horsburgh, D. (1997), 'Gaelic Language and Culture in North-East Scotland: A Diachronic Study', University of Aberdeen: unpublished PhD dissertation.

Horsburgh, D. and S. Murdoch (1997), *Daena Haud yer Wheisht, Haud yer Ain! Transcreives o the General Register Office (Scotland), Cognitive Research Programme Anent the Scots Leid, Summer, 1996*, Aberdeen: Aberdeen Scots Leid Quorum.

Hough, C. (1999), 'The trumpeters of Bemersyde: a Scottish placename reconsidered', *Names*, 47, pp. 257–68.

Hough, C. (2001a), 'The place-name Penninghame (Wigtownshire)', *Notes & Queries*, 48, pp. 99–102.

Hough, C. (2001b), 'P-Celtic *tref* in Scottish place-names', *Notes and Queries*, 48, pp. 213–15.

Houston, R.A. (1985), *Scottish Literacy and the Scottish Identity. Illiteracy and society in Scotland and northern England, 1600–1800*, Cambridge: Cambridge University Press.

Hudson, R. (1980), *Sociolinguistics*, Cambridge: Cambridge University Press.

Hume, A. (ed.), H. B. Wheatley (1865), *Of the Orthographie and Congruitie of the Britan Tongue*, Early English Text Society, original series, vol. 5.

Hutchinson, T. (ed.) (1969), *Wordsworth: Poetical Works*, revised by E. de Selincourt, Oxford: Oxford University Press.

Iacuaniello, F. (1992–3), 'Linguistic Awareness and Attitudes in a Sample of Scottish Speakers', *Scottish Language*, 11/12, pp. 62–71.

Ickringill, S. (1994–5), 'Not just a typographical error: The origin of Scotch-Irish', *Causeway*, 1, 5, pp. 32–5.

An Index by Region, Usage, and Etymology to the Dictionary of American Regional English, Volumes I and II (1993), Publication of the American Dialect Society, 77.

Insley, J. (1993), 'Recent trends in research into English bynames and surnames: some critical remarks', *Studia Neophilologica*, 65, pp. 57–71.

Jack, R. D. S. (1997), 'The Language of Literary Materials: Origins to 1700', in Jones (ed.), pp. 213–66.

Jack, R. D. S. and P. A. T. Rozendaal (eds) (1997), *The Mercat Anthology of Early Scottish Literature 1375–1707*, Edinburgh: Mercat Press.

Jackson, K. H. (1953), *Language and History in Early Britain*, Edinburgh: Edinburgh University Press.

Jackson, K. H. (1955), 'The Pictish Language', in F. T. Wainwright (ed.), *The Problem of the Picts*, Edinburgh: Nelson, pp.129–66.

Jakobsen, J. (1897, 1993), *The Dialect and Place Names of Shetland. Two Popular Lectures*, Lerwick: T. & J. Manson. Reprinted as *The Place Names of Shetland*, Orkney: The Orcadian.

Jakobsen, J. (1921, 1928), *Etymologisk Ordbog over det Norrøne Sprog på Shetland*. Translated as *An Etymological Dictionary of the Norn Language in Shetland*, 2 volumes, London: David Nutt. Reprinted New York: AMS Press, n.d.

Jamieson, J. (1808), *An Etymological Dictionary of the Scots Language*, 2 vols, Edinburgh.

Johnston, J. B. (1892), *Place-names of Scotland*, Edinburgh: Douglas; 3rd edn (1934), Edinburgh: Murray; repr. 1972, Wakefield: EP Publishers.

Johnston, P. A. (1983), 'Irregular style variation patterns in Edinburgh speech', *Scottish Language*, 2, pp. 1–19.

Johnston, P. A. (1997a), 'Older Scots Phonology and its Regional Variation', Jones (ed.), pp. 47–111.

Johnston, P. A. (1997b), 'Regional Variation', in Jones (ed.), pp. 443–513.

Johnston, P. A. (2000), 'Taming Volume III of the *Linguistic Atlas of Scotland*', *Scottish Language*, 19, pp. 45–65.

Johnstone, R. M. (2001), *Immersion in a second language at School: Evidence from international research*, Stirling: Scottish Centre for Information on Language Teaching.

Johnstone, R. M., W. Harlen, M. MacNeil, R. Stradling, and G. Thorpe (1999), *The Attainment of Pupils Receiving Gaelic-Medium Primary Education in Scotland: Final Report*, Stirling: Scottish Centre for Information on Language Teaching.

Jones, C. (1996), *A Language Suppressed: The Pronunciation of the Scots Language in the Eighteenth Century*, Edinburgh: John Donald.

Jones, C. (1997), 'Phonology', in Jones (ed.), pp. 267–334.

Jones, C. (ed.) (1997), *The Edinburgh History of the Scots Language*, Edinburgh: Edinburgh University Press.

Jones, C. (2002), *The English Language in Scotland: An Introduction to Scots*, Edinburgh: Tuckwell.

Joseph, J. (1987), *Eloquence and Power: The Rise of Language Standards and Standard Languages*, London: Pinter.

Joseph, J. (1999), 'Language and Culture in Scottish and Catalan Nationalism' (reply to Conversi 1999), ERSC Research Seminar on State and Civil Society in Scotland and Catalonia, University of Edinburgh, 101–11 December 1999.

Jucker, A. H. (ed.) (1995), *Historical Pragmatics: pragmatic developments in the history of English*, Amsterdam: Benjamins.

Kane, G. (1981), 'Music Neither Unpleasant nor Monotonous', in P. L. Heyworth (ed.), *Medieval Studies for J. A. W. Bennett*, Oxford: Clarendon Press, pp. 43–63.

Kennedy, A. L. (1994), *Looking For the Possible Dance*, London: Minerva.

Kiesling, S. (forthcoming), 'English input to Australia', in R. Hickey (ed.), *The Legacy of Colonial English: The Study of Transported Dialects*, Cambridge: Cambridge University Press.

King, A. (1997), 'The Inflectional Morphology of Older Scots', in C. Jones (ed.), pp. 156–81.

Kinloch, A. M. (1985), 'The English language in New Brunswick', in R. Gair (ed.), *Literary and Linguistic History of New Brunswick*, Fredericton: Fiddlehead, pp. 59–74.

Kinsley, J. (ed.) (1979), *The Poems of William Dunbar*, Oxford: Clarendon Press.

Kinsley, J. (1980), 'Review of Aitken et al. (eds), (1977),' *Modern Languages Review*, 75, pp. 356–7.

Kirk, J. M. and D. P. Ó Baoill (eds) (2000), *Language and Politics: Northern Ireland, the Republic of Ireland and Scotland*, Belfast Studies in Language, Culture and Politics, 1, Belfast: Queen's University of Belfast.

Kirk, J. M. and D. P. Ó Baoill (eds) (2001a), *Language Links: The Languages of Scotland and Ireland*, Belfast Studies in Language, Culture and Politics, 2, Belfast: Queen's University of Belfast.

Kirk, J. M. and D. P. Ó Baoill (eds) (2001b), *Linguistic Politics: Language Policies for*

Northern Ireland, the Republic of Ireland and Scotland, Belfast Studies in Language, Culture and Politics, 3, Belfast: Queen's University of Belfast.

Kitson, P. (1996), 'British and European river-names', *Transactions of the Philological Society*, 94: 2, pp. 73–118.

Klaeber, F. (ed.), (1950), *Beowulf*, revised edn, Lexington: Heath.

Kloss, H. (1967), ' "Abstand languages" and "ausbau languages" ', *Anthropological Linguistics*, 9: 7, pp. 29–41.

Kniezsa, V. (1989), 'The sources of the < i > digraphs: the place-name evidence', in McClure and Spiller (eds), pp. 442–50.

Kohler, K. J. (1966), 'A late eighteenth-century comparison of the "Provincial Dialect of Scotland" and the "Pure Dialect" ', *Linguistics*, 23, pp. 30–68.

Kolb, E. (1969), 'The Scandinavian Loanwords in English and the Date of the West Norse Change MP > PP, NT > TT, NK > KK', *English Studies*, 50, pp. 129–40.

Krapp, G. P. (1925), *The English Language in America*, 2 vols, New York: Ungar.

Kries, S. (1999), 'Lexikalische Reflexe skandinavischen Einflusses im älteren Schottisch und im Mittelschottischen', Free University of Berlin: PhD dissertation.

Kroch, A., A. Taylor and D. Ringe (2000), 'The Middle English Verb-Second Constraint: A Case Study in Language Contact and Language Change', in Herring et al. (eds), pp. 353–91.

Kuipers, C. (ed.) (1964), *Quintin Kennedy: Two Eucharistic Tracts*, University of Nijmegen: Dissertation.

Kurath, H., S. M. Kuhn, J. Reidy and R. E. Lewis (eds), (1952–2001), *Middle English Dictionary*, 12 vols and Plan and Bibliography, Ann Arbor, MI: University of Michigan Press.

Kurath, H. and R. I. McDavid Jr. (1961), *The Pronunciation of English in the Atlantic States*, Ann Arbor, MI: University of Michigan Press.

Kytö, M. (1996), *Manual to the Diachronic Part of the Helsinki Corpus of English Texts*, 3rd edn, Helsinki: Department of English, University of Helsinki.

Kytö, M. (2000), 'Robert Keayne's *Notebooks*: A Verbatim Record of Spoken English in Early Boston?', in Herring et al. (eds), pp. 273–308.

Labov, W. (1966), *The Social Stratification of English in New York City*, Washington: Center for Applied Linguistics.

Labov, W., S. Ash and C. Boberg (1997), 'A national map of regional dialects of American English', unpublished typescript.

Ladefoged, P. and I. Maddieson (1996), *Sounds of the World's Languages*, Oxford: Blackwell.

Laing, M. (1991), 'Anchor texts and literary manuscripts in early Middle English', in F. Riddy (ed.), *Regionalism in Late Medieval Manuscripts and Texts*, Cambridge: D. S. Brewer, pp. 27–52.

Laing, M. (1993), *Catalogue of Sources for a Linguistic Atlas of Early Medieval English*, Cambridge: D. S. Brewer.

Laing, M. (2000), '*Never the twain shall meet*. Early Middle English – the East-West divide', in Irma Taavitsainen et al. (eds), pp. 97–124.

Lamb, G. (1988), *Orkney Wordbook. A Dictionary of the Dialect of Orkney*, Birsay: Byrgisey.

Lass, R. (1987), *The Shape of English: Structure and History*, London: Dent.

Lass, R. (1990), 'Where do extraterritorial Englishes come from? Dialect input and recodification in transported Englishes', in S. Adamson (ed.), *Papers from the 5th International Conference on English Historical Linguistics*, Amsterdam and Philadelphia: Benjamins, pp. 245–80.

Lass, R. (1997), *Historical linguistics and language change*, Cambridge: Cambridge University Press.

Laver, J. (1994), *Principles of Phonetics*, Cambridge: Cambridge University Press.

Lawrie, A. C. (1905), *Early Scottish Charters Prior to A.D. 1153*, Glasgow: James MacLehose and Sons.

Lawrie, S. (1991), 'A linguistic survey of the use of Scottish dialect terms in North-East Fife', *Scottish Language*, 10, pp. 18–29.

Lawson, E. and J. Stuart-Smith (1999), 'A sociophonetic investigation of the "Scottish" consonants (/x/ and /hw/), in the speech of Glaswegian children', *Proceedings of the International Congress of Phonetic Sciences*, San Francisco, pp. 2541–4.

Leech, G. (1969), *A Linguistic Guide to English Poetry*, Harlow: Longman.

Lenz, K. (2000), 'The use of obsolete Scots vocabulary in Modern Scottish plays', *International Journal of Scottish Theatre*, 1:1 [www.arts.qmuc.ac.uk/ijost].

Leonard, T. (1984), *Intimate Voices 1965–1983*, Newcastle upon Tyne: Galloping Dog Press.

Leyburn, J. G. (1963), *The Scotch-Irish: A Social History*, Chapel Hill: University of North Carolina Press.

Lo Bianco, J. (2001), *Language and Literacy Policy in Scotland*, Stirling: Scottish C.I.L.T.

Lorimer, W. L. (1983), *The New Testament in Scots*, Edinburgh: Southside.

Lorvik, M. (1995), *The Scottis Lass Betrayed? Scots in English Classrooms*, Broughty Ferry: Scottish Consultative Council on the Curriculum.

Luick, K. (1903), *Studien zur englischen Lautgeschichte*, Wien and Leipzig: Braumüller.

Lustig, I. S. and F. A. Pottle (eds) (1986), *Boswell: The Applause of the Jury, 1782–1785*, London: Yale University.

Lynch, M. (1991), *Scotland: A New History*, London: Century; repr. (1995), London: Pimlico.

Macafee, C. I. (1983), *Varieties of English around the World: Glasgow*, Amsterdam: John Benjamins.

Macafee, C. I. (1988), 'Some Studies in the Glasgow Vernacular', University of Glasgow: PhD dissertation [revised as Macafee 1994].

Macafee, C. I. (1991/92), 'Acumsinery: Is it too late to collect traditional dialect?', *Folk Life*, 30, pp. 71–7.

Macafee, C. I. (1992/3), 'A Short Grammar of Older Scots', *Scottish Language*, 11/12, pp. 10–36.

Macafee, C. I. (1994), *Traditional Dialect in the Modern World: A Glasgow Case Study*, Frankfurt am Main: Peter Lang.

Macafee, C. I. (1996), 'The Case for Scots in the 2001 Census', unpublished paper submitted to the General Register Office (Scotland), and the Scottish Office [www.abdn.ac.uk/scots/whatson/case.htm].

Macafee, C. I. (ed.) (1996), *A Concise Ulster Dictionary*, Oxford: Oxford University Press.

Macafee, C. I. (1997a), 'Older Scots lexis' in Jones (ed.), pp. 182–212. [A revised version appears in the Preface of *A Dictionary of the Older Scottish Tongue*.]

Macafee, C. I. (1997b), 'Ongoing change in Modern Scots: the social dimension', in Jones (ed.), pp. 514–50.

Macafee, C. I. (1999), *A selected classified bibliography of the Scots language*. [www.unibg.it/anglistica/slin/scot-bib.htm].

Macafee, C. I. (2000a), 'The Demography of Scots', *Scottish Language*, 19, pp. 1–44.

Macafee, C. I. (2000b), 'Lea the Leid Alane', *Lallans*, 57, pp. 56–64.

Macafee, C. I. (2001a), 'Lowland sources of Ulster Scots: some comparisons between

Robert Gregg's data and *The Linguistic Atlas of Scotland* (vol. 3), in Kirk and Ó Baoill (eds) (2001a), pp. 119–68.

Macafee, C. I. (2001b), 'Scots: Hauf Empty or Hauf Fu?', in Kirk and Ó Baoill (eds) (2001b), pp. 159–68.

Macafee, C. I. (forthcoming a), 'Lowland sources of Ulster Scots: Gregg and *The Linguistic Atlas of Scotland* (vol. 3) compared', in P. Robinson, A. Smyth and M. Montgomery (eds), *The Academic Study of Ulster Scots: Essays for and by Robert J Gregg*.

Macafee, C. I. (forthcoming b), 'Scots and Scottish Standard English', in R. Hickey (ed.), *The Legacy of Colonial English: A Study of Transported Dialects*, Cambridge: Cambridge University Press.

Macafee, C. I and A. J. Aitken (2002), 'A History of Scots to 1700', *A Dictionary of the Older Scottish Tongue*, vol. XII, Oxford: Oxford University Press.

Macafee, C. I. and A. Anderson (1997), 'A random sample of Older Scots lexis', *Transactions of the Philological Society*, 95: 2, pp. 247–78.

Macafee, C. I. and B. McGarrity (1999), 'Scots language attitudes and language maintenance', in C. Upton and K. Wales (eds), *Dialectal Variation in English: Proceedings of the Harold Orton Centenary Conference 1998* (*Leeds Studies in English*, 30), pp. 165–79.

Macaulay, R. K. S. (1977), *Language, Social Class and Education: A Glasgow Study*, Edinburgh: Edinburgh University Press.

Macaulay, R. K. S. (1985), 'Linguistic maps: visual aid or abstract art?', J. Kirk et al. (eds), *Studies in Linguistic Geography*, London: Croom Helm, pp. 172–86.

Macaulay, R. K. S. (1991), *Locating Dialect in Discourse: The Language of Honest Men and Bonny Lasses in Ayr*, Oxford: Oxford University Press.

Macaulay, R. K. S. (1997), 'Ayrshire as a linguistic area', in E. Schneider (ed.), *Englishes Around the World*, vol. 1, *General Studies, British Isles, North America. Studies in Honour of Manfred Görlach*, Amsterdam and Philadelphia: John Benjamins, pp. 159–71.

Macaulay, R. K. S. and G. Trevelyan (1973), *Language, Education, and Employment in Glasgow*, Final Report to the SSRC.

MacDirmid, H. (1923), 'A Theory of Scots Letters II', *The Scottish Chapbook*, vol. 1, No. 8, pp. 210–14.

MacDiarmid, H. (1976), *Contemporary Scottish Studies*, A. McIntyre (ed.), Edinburgh: Scottish Educational Journal.

Macdonald, A. (1937), Typescript PhD dissertation, University of Edinburgh; pub. (1941) as *The Place-names of West Lothian*, Edinburgh: Oliver & Boyd.

MacDonald, J. R. (1993), 'Cultural retention and adaptation among the Highland Scots of North Carolina', University of Edinburgh: unpublished PhD thesis.

MacGillivray, A. (ed.) (1997), *Teaching Scottish Literature: Curriculum and Classroom Applications*, Edinburgh: Edinburgh University Press.

MacGregor, M. and A. Mackillop (2001), 'Clans of the Highlands and Islands', in M. Lynch (ed.), *The Oxford Companion to Scottish History*, Oxford: Oxford University Press, pp. 93–6.

MacKinnon, K. (2001), 'Fàs no Bàs (Prosper or Perish): Prospects of Survival for Scottish Gaelic', in Kirk and Ó Baoill (eds) (2001b), pp. 255–8.

Macleod, I., R. Martin and P. Cairns (eds) (1988), *The Pocket Scots Dictionary*, Aberdeen: Aberdeen University Press.

Macleod, I., with P. Cairns, C. Macafee and R. Martin (eds) (1990), *The Scots Thesaurus*, Aberdeen: Aberdeen University Press. Now published Edinburgh: Polygon.

Macleod, I., S. Rennie and P. Cairns (eds) (1998), *The Electronic Scots School Dictionary*, Edinburgh: Scottish National Dictionary Association.

MacPherson, J. A. (2000), *Revitalising Gaelic: A National Asset* (The Macpherson Task Force Report), Edinburgh: Scottish Executive.

MacQueen, J. (1990), *St Nynia*, Edinburgh: Polygon.

Marckwardt, A. L. (1948), '*Want* with ellipsis of verbs of motion', *American Speech* 23, pp. 3–9.

Marckwardt, A. L. (1958), *American English*, New York: Oxford University Press.

Marshall, W. (1936), *Ulster Speaks*, London: BBC.

Martin, B. and J. W. Oliver (eds) (1945), *The Works of Allan Ramsay, Vol. I*, Scottish Text Society, Third Series, 19, Edinburgh and London: Blackwood.

Marshall, R. K. (1983), *Virgins and Viragos. A History of Women in Scotland 1080 to 1980*, London: Collins.

Maté, I. (1996), *Scots Language GRO(S). A Report on the Scots Language Research carried out by the General Register Office for Scotland in 1996*, Edinburgh: General Register Office.

Mather, J. Y. and H. H. Spietel (1975, 1977, 1986), *The Linguistic Atlas of Scotland*, 3 vols, London: Croom Helm.

Maxwell, H. E. (1894), *Scottish Land-Names: Their Origin and Meaning*, Edinburgh: Blackwood.

McArthur, T. (ed.) (1992), *The Oxford Companion to the English Language*, Oxford: Oxford University Press.

McArthur, T. (1998), *The English Languages*, Cambridge: Cambridge University Press.

McCallum, N. R. and D. Purves (eds) (1995), *Mak it New: An Anthology of Twenty-One Years of Writing in 'Lallans'*, Edinburgh: Mercat Press.

McClure, J. D. (ed.) (1976), *The Scots Language in Education*, ASLS Occasional Papers, no. 3, Aberdeen: Association for Scottish Literary Studies.

McClure, J. D. (1980), 'Developing Scots as a National Language', in McClure, Aitken and Low (eds), pp. 11–44.

McClure, J. D. (1981a), 'Scottis, Inglis, Suddron: language labels and language attitudes', in R. J. Lyall and F. Riddy (eds), *Proceedings of the Third International Conference on Scottish Language and Literature, Medieval and Renaissance*, Stirling and Glasgow: Universities of Stirling and Glasgow, pp. 52–69.

McClure, J. D. (1981b), 'The Synthesisers of Scots', in Haugen, McClure and Thomson (eds), pp. 91–9.

McClure, J. D. (1985), 'The Debate on Scots Orthography', in Görlach (ed.), pp. 203–9.

McClure, J. D. (1994), 'English in Scotland', in R. Burchfield (ed.), *The Cambridge History of the English Language*, vol. V, Cambridge: Cambridge University Press, pp. 23–93.

McClure, J. D. (1997), *Why Scots Matters*, revised edn, Edinburgh: Saltire.

McClure, J. D., A. J. Aitken and J. T. Low (eds) (1980), *The Scots Language: Planning for Modern Usage*, Edinburgh: Ramsay Head.

McClure, J. D. and M. R. G. Spiller (eds) (1989), *Bryght Lanternis: Essays on the Language and Literature of Mediaeval and Renaissance Scotland*, Aberdeen: Aberdeen University Press.

McClure, P. (1998), 'The interpretation of hypocoristic forms of Middle English baptismal names', *Nomina*, 21 (1998), pp. 101–31.

McConnell, R. E. (1979), *Our Own Voice: Canadian English and How It Came to Be*, Toronto: Gage.

McDavid, R. I. Jr. (1978), Review of Linguistic Atlas of Scotland, *Journal of English Linguistics*, 12, pp. 76–82.

McDiarmid, M. and J. Stevenson (eds) (1980–5), *Barbour's Bruce*, 3 vols, Scottish Text Society.

McGarrity, B. (1998), 'A Sociolinguistic Study of Attitudes towards and Proficiency in the Doric Dialect in Aberdeen', University of Aberdeen: unpublished MPhil dissertation.

McHardy, S. (1998), 'The Scots Language Resource Centre', in Niven and Jackson (eds), pp. 121–4.

McIntosh, A., M. L. Samuels and M. Benskin, with M. Laing and K.Williamson (eds) (1986), *A Linguistic Atlas of Late Mediaeval English*, Aberdeen: Aberdeen University Press.

McIver, M. (1997), 'Modal verbs in Orkney English', University of Edinburgh: unpublished Honours dissertation.

McKinley, R. (1990), *A History of British Surnames*, London: Longman.

McPherson, D. (c.1710) [Letter from Maryland]. Printed in 1900 in J. L. McLean, *An Historical Account of Settlements of Scottish Highlanders in America Prior to the Peace of 1783*, Glasgow: John Mackay.

Meek, D. E. (1998), 'Place-names and literature: evidence from the Gaelic ballads', in S. Taylor (ed.), *The Uses of Place-Names*, Edinburgh: Scottish Cultural Press, pp. 147–168.

Menzies, J. (1991), 'An investigation of attitudes to Scots and Glasgow dialect among secondary school pupils', *Scottish Language*, 10, pp. 30–46.

Meurman-Solin, A. (1989), 'Variation Analysis and Diachronic Studies of Lexical Borrowing', in G. Caie et al. (eds), *Proceedings from the Fourth Nordic Conference for English Studies*, vol. 1, pp. 87–98, Copenhagen: Department of English, University of Copenhagen. Reprinted in Meurman-Solin (1993a).

Meurman-Solin, A. (1992), 'On the morphology of verbs in Middle Scots: present and present perfect indicative', in M. Rissanen, O. Ihalainen, T. Nevalainen and I. Taavitsainen (eds), *History of Englishes. New Methods and Interpretations in Historical Linguistics*, Berlin: Mouton de Gruyter, pp. 611–23. Reprinted in Meurman-Solin (1993a).

Meurman-Solin, A. (1993a), *Variation and change in early Scottish prose. Studies based on the Helsinki Corpus of Older Scots* (Annales Academiae Scientiarum Fennicae, Diss. Humanarum Litterarum, 65), Helsinki.

Meurman-Solin, A. (1993b), 'Periphrastic and auxiliary do in early Scottish prose genres', in M. Rissanen, M. Kytö and M. Palander-Collin (eds), *Early English in the computer age: explorations through the Helsinki Corpus* (Topics in English Linguistics, 11), pp. 235–51, Berlin: Mouton de Gruyter. Reprinted in Meurman-Solin (1993a).

Meurman-Solin, A. (1994), 'On the Evolution of Prose Genres in Older Scots', *Nowele*, vol. 23, pp. 91–138. Reprinted in Meurman-Solin (1993a).

Meurman-Solin, A. (1995a), The Helsinki Corpus of Older Scots (HCOS). Distributors: Oxford Text Archive, Norwegian Computing Centre for the Humanities. [www.hd.uib.no/corpora.htm].

Meurman-Solin, A. (1995b), 'A New Tool: The Helsinki Corpus of Older Scots (1450–1700)', *ICAME Journal*, vol. 19, pp. 49–62.

Meurman-Solin, A. (1995c), 'Marking of Stance in Early Modern English Imaginative Narration', in W. Görtschacher and H. Klein (eds), *Narrative Strategies in Early English Fiction*, Lewiston, New York and Salzburg: Edwin Mellen, pp. 25–52.

Meurman-Solin, A. (1997a), 'On Differentiation and Standardization in Early Scots', in C. Jones (ed.), pp. 3–23.

Meurman-Solin, A. (1997b), 'A Corpus-Based Study on *t*/*d* deletion and insertion in Late Medieval and Renaissance Scottish English', in T. Nevalainen and L. Kahlas-Tarkka (eds), *To Explain the Present. Studies in the Changing English Language in Honour of Matti Rissanen*, Helsinki: Société Néophilologique, pp. 111–24.

Meurman-Solin, A. (1997c), 'Text profiles in the study of language variation and change', in R. Hickey, M. Kytö, I. Lancashire and M. Rissanen (eds), *Tracing the trail of time. Proceedings from the Second Diachronic Corpora Workshop*, Amsterdam and Atlanta, GA: Rodopi, pp. 199–214.

Meurman-Solin, A. (1997d), 'Towards reconstructing a grammar of point of view: Textual roles of adjectives and open-class adverbs in Early Modern English', in M. Rissanen et al. (eds) (1997b), pp. 267–343.

Meurman-Solin, A. (1999a), 'Letters as a Source of Data for Reconstructing Early Spoken Scots, in I. Taavitsainen, G. Melchers and P. Pahta (eds), *Writing in Nonstandard English*, Amsterdam and Philadelphia: John Benjamins, pp. 305–22.

Meurman-Solin, A. (1999b), 'Point of View in Scottish and English Genre Styles', in N. McMillan and K. Stirling (eds), *Odd Alliances. Scottish Studies in European contexts*, Glasgow: Cruithne Press, pp. 25–51.

Meurman-Solin, A. (2000a), 'Change from above or from below? Mapping the *loci* of linguistic change in the history of Scottish English', in L. Wright (ed.), *The Development of Standard English, 1300–1800: theories, descriptions, conflicts*, Cambridge: Cambridge University Press, pp. 155–70.

Meurman-Solin, A. (2000b), 'On the conditioning of geographical and social distance in language variation and change in Renaissance Scots', in D. Kastovsky and A. Mettinger (eds), *The History of English in a Social Context. A Contribution to Historical Sociolinguistics* (Trends in Linguistics, Studies and Monographs 129), Berlin: Mouton de Gruyter, pp. 227–55.

Meurman-Solin, A. (2000c), 'Geographical, socio-spatial and systemic distance in the spread of the relative *who* in Scots', in R. Bermúdez-Otero et al. (eds), pp. 417–38.

Meurman-Solin, A. (2001a), 'Structured Text Corpora in the Study of Language Variation and Change', *Literary and Linguistic Computing*, vol. 16, no. 1, pp. 5–27.

Meurman-Solin, A. (2001b), 'Genre as a Variable in Sociohistorical Linguistics', in *European Journal of English Studies*, vol. 5, no. 2, pp. 241–56.

Meurman-Solin, A. (2001c), 'Women as Informants in the Reconstruction of Geographically and Socioculturally Conditioned Language Variation and Change in the 16th and 17th Century Scots', *Scottish Language*, vol. 20, pp. 20–46.

Meurman-Solin, A. (2002a), 'The progressive in early Scots', in T. Fanego, M. José López-Couso and J. Pérez-Guerra (eds), *English Historical Syntax and Morphology. Selected Papers from 11ICEHL*, Amsterdam: John Benjamins, pp. 203–29.

Meurman-Solin, A. (2002b), 'Simple and complex grammars: The Case of Temporal Subordinators in the History of Scots', in H. Raumolin-Brunberg, M. Nevala, A. Nurmi and M. Rissanen (eds), *Variation Past and Present. VARIENG Studies on English for Terttu Nevalainen* (Mémoires de la Société Néophilologique de Helsinki, 61), Helsinki: Société Néophilologique, pp. 187–210.

Meurman-Solin, A. (forthcoming a), CSC The Corpus of Scottish Correspondence, 1500–1800.

Meurman-Solin, A. (forthcoming b), CESWW The Corpus of Early Scottish Women's Writings.

Meurman-Solin, A. (forthcoming c), 'From inventory to typology in English historical dialectology', presented at the 12th International Conference and English Historical Linguistics, University of Glasgow, 2002.

Meurman-Solin, A. and K. Williamson (forthcoming), E/HCOS The Tagged Edinburgh-Helsinki Corpus of Older Scots, 1450–1650.

Middleton, S. B. (2001), 'A Study into the Knowledge and Use of Scots amongst Primary Pupils on Upper Deeside', University of Aberdeen: unpublished MLitt dissertation.

Millar, R. M. (1996), 'Gaelic-influenced Scots in pre-Revolutionary Maryland?', in P. S. Ureland and I. Clarkson (eds), *Language Contact across the North Atlantic*, Tübingen: Niemeyer, pp. 387–410.

Miller, J. (1993), 'The grammar of Scottish English', in J. Milroy and L. Milroy (eds), *Real English: The Grammar of English Dialects in the British Isles*, Harlow: Longman, pp. 99–138.

Miller, J. (2002), *Introduction to the Syntax of English*, Edinburgh: Edinburgh University Press.

Miller, J. and K. Brown (1982), 'Aspects of Scottish English syntax', *English World-Wide*, 3, pp. 3–17.

Miller, J. and R. Weinert (1995), 'The function of LIKE in spoken language', *Journal of Pragmatics*, 23, pp. 365–93.

Miller, J. and R. Weinert (1998), *Spontaneous Spoken Language: Syntax and Discourse*, Oxford: Clarendon Press.

Milroy, J. (1981), *Regional Accents of English: Belfast*, Belfast: Blackstaff.

Milroy, J. (1982), 'Probing under the tip of the iceberg: phonological normalisation and the shape of speech communities', in S. Romaine (ed.), *Sociolinguistic Variation in Speech Communities*, London: Arnold, pp. 35–47.

Milroy, J. (1992), *Linguistic variation and change: on the historical sociolinguistics of English*, Oxford: Blackwell.

Milroy, J. (1999), 'The consequences of standardization in descriptive linguistics', in T. Bex and R. J. Watts (eds), *Standard English. The Widening Debate*, London: Routledge, pp. 16–39.

Milroy, J. and L. Milroy (1991), *Authority in Language: Investigating Language Prescription and Standardisation*, 2nd cdn, London: Routledge.

Milroy, L. (1982), 'Social network and linguistic focussing', in S. Romaine (ed.), *Sociolinguistic Variation in Speech Communities*, London: Arnold, pp. 141–52.

Milroy, L. (1987), *Observing and analysing natural language*, Oxford: Blackwell.

Minugh, D. (1999), 'What aileth thee, to print so curiously? Archaic forms and contemporary newspaper language', in I. Taavitsainen et al. (eds), *Writing in Nonstandard English*, Amsterdam and Philadelphia: Benjamins, pp. 285–304.

Mishoe, M. and M. Montgomery (1994), 'The pragmatics of multiple modals in North and South Carolina', *American Speech*, 69, pp. 3–29.

Mittendorf, I. and E. Poppe (2000), 'Celtic Contacts of the English Progressive?', in H. L. C. Tristram (ed.), *The Celtic Englishes II*, Heidelberg: C. Winter, pp. 117–45.

Moessner, L. (1997), 'The Syntax of Older Scots', in C. Jones (ed.), pp. 112–55.

Montgomery, M. (1992a), 'The Anglicization of Scots in early seventeenth-century Ulster', in G. R. Roy and P. Scott, *The Language and Literature of Early Scotland: Studies in Scottish Literature*, 26, pp. 50–64.

Montgomery, M. (1992b), 'The etymology of *y'all*', in J. H. Hall et al. (eds), *Old English and New: Studies in Language and Linguistics in Honor of Frederic G. Cassidy*, New York: Garland Press, pp. 356–69.

Montgomery, M. (1994), 'The evolution of verb concord in Scots', in A. Fenton and D. A. MacDonald (eds), *Studies in Scots and Gaelic: Proceedings of the Third International Conference on the Languages of Scotland*, Edinburgh: Canongate Academic, pp. 81–95.

Montgomery, M. (1996), 'The future of southern American English', *SECOL Review*, 20, pp. 1–24.

Montgomery, M. (1997a), 'The language of Highland Scots emigrants: English or Scots or what?', Fifth International Conference on the Languages of Scotland and Ulster, Aberdeen, Scotland, August.

Montgomery, M. (1997b), 'Making the trans-Atlantic link between varieties of English: The case of plural verbal -*s*', *Journal of English Linguistics*, 25, pp. 122–41.

Montgomery, M. (1997c), 'The rediscovery of Ulster Scots', in E. W. Schneider (ed.), *Englishes around the World: Festschrift for Manfred Görlach. Volume 1*, Amsterdam and Philadelphia: Benjamins, pp. 211–26.

Montgomery, M. (1997d), 'The Scotch-Irish influence on Appalachian English: How broad? How deep?', in C. Wood and T. Blethen (eds), *Ulster and North America: Transatlantic Perspectives on the Scotch-Irish*, Tuscaloosa: University of Alabama Press, pp. 189–212.

Montgomery, M. (1997e), 'A tale of two Georges: The language of Irish Indian traders in colonial North America', in J. Kallen (ed.), *Focus on Ireland*, Amsterdam and Philadelphia: Benjamins, pp. 227–54.

Montgomery, M. (1999), 'The position of Ulster Scots', *Ulster Folklife*, 45, pp. 85–104.

Montgomery, M. (2000), 'The problem of persistence: Ulster-Scot-American missing links', *Journal of Scotch-Irish Studies*, 1, pp. 105–19.

Montgomery, M. (2001a), 'Eighteenth-century nomenclature for Ulster emigrants', *Journal of Scotch-Irish Studies*, 2, pp. 1–6.

Montgomery, M. (2001b), 'On the trail of Ulster emigrant letters', in S. Ickringill and P. Fitzgerald (eds), *Atlantic Crossroads: Historical Connections between Scotland, Ulster and North America*, Newtownards: Colourpoint, pp. 13–26, 133–7.

Montgomery, M. (forthcoming), 'Solving Kurath's puzzle: Establishing the antecedents of the American Midland dialect region', in R. Hickey (ed.), *The Legacy of Colonial English: The Study of Transported Dialects*, Cambridge: Cambridge University Press.

Montgomery, M., J. M. Fuller and S. DeMarse (1993), ' "The black men has wives and sweet harts [and third person plural -*s*] jest like the white men": Evidence for verbal -*s* from written documents on nineteenth-century African American speech.' *Language Variation and Change*, 5, pp. 335–54.

Montgomery, M. and R. J. Gregg (1997), 'The Scots Language in Ulster', in Jones (ed.), pp. 567–622.

Montgomery, M. and J. M. Kirk. (2001), ' "My mother, whenever she passed away, she had pneumonia": The history and function of punctual *whenever*', *Journal of English Linguistics*, 29, pp. 234–49.

Montgomery, M. and S. J. Nagle (1994), 'Double modals in Scotland and the Southern United States: Trans-Atlantic inheritance or independent development?', *Folia Linguistica Historica*, 14, pp. 91–107.

Montgomery, M. and P. Robinson (2000), 'Ulster: A linguistic bridge across the North Atlantic', *Journal of Scotch-Irish Studies*, 1, pp. 40–60.

Murdoch, S. (1995), *Language Politics in Scotland*, Aberdeen: Aberdeen Scots Leid Quorum [www.abdn.ac.uk/scots/steve/lip.htm].

Murison, D. (1979), 'The Historical Background', in Aitken and McArthur (eds), pp. 2–13.

Murray, J. A. H. (1873), *The Dialect of the Southern Counties of Scotland*, London: The Philological Society.

Murray, J. A. H. et al. (1989), *The Oxford English Dictionary* 2nd edn, 20 vols, Oxford: Oxford University Press.

Nässén, G. (1989), 'Norn weather words. 323 meteorological terms in Jakobsen's Dictionary and their extent in present-day Shetland dialect', Report no. 3, Norn: the Scandinavian element in Shetland dialect, Department of English, Stockholm University and Department of Linguistics, Trondheim University.

Nettle, D. and S. Romaine (2000), *Vanishing Voices: The Extinction of the World's Languages*, Oxford: Oxford University Press.

Nevala, M. (1998), 'By him that loves you: Address forms in letters written to 16th-century social aspirers', in Antoinette Renouf (ed.), *Explorations in Corpus Linguistics*, Amsterdam: Rodopi, pp. 147–58.

Nevala, M. (forthcoming), 'Family first: Address formulae in English family correspondence from the 15th to the 17th century', in I. Taavitsainen and A.H. Jucker (eds), *Diachronic Perspectives in Address Term Systems* (Pragmatics and Beyond New Series), Amsterdam: John Benjamins.

Nevalainen, T. (1991), *But, only, just: focusing adverbial change in modern English, 1500–1900* (Mémoires de la Société Néophilologique de Helsinki, 51), Helsinki: Société Néophilologique.

Nevalainen, T. (1999), 'Early Modern English Lexis and Semantics', in R. Lass (ed.), *The Cambridge History of the English Language*, vol. III (1476–1776), Cambridge: Cambridge University Press, pp. 332–458.

Nevalainen, T. (2000), 'Processes of Supralocalization and the Rise of Standard English in the Early Modern Period', in R. Bermúdez-Otero et al. (eds), pp. 329–72.

Nevalainen, T. and H. Raumolin-Brunberg (1989), 'A Corpus of Early Modern Standard English in a Socio-Historical Perspective', *Neuphilologische Mitteilungen*, vol. 90, no. 1, pp. 67–110.

Nevalainen, T. and H. Raumolin-Brunberg (eds) (1996), *Sociolinguistics and Language History. Studies based on the Corpus of Early English Correspondence*, Amsterdam and Atlanta, GA: Rodopi.

Newlin, C. (1928), 'Dialects on the western Pennsylvania frontier', *American Speech*, 4, pp. 104–10.

Nicolaisen, W. F. H. (1980), 'Tension and extension: thoughts on Scottish surnames and medieval popular culture', *Journal of Popular Culture*, 14, pp. 119–30.

Nicolaisen, W. F. H. (1991–2), 'Pictish place-names as Scottish surnames: origins, dissemination and current status', *Nomina*, 15, pp. 7–20.

Nicolaisen, W. F. H. (1993), 'Scottish Place Names as Evidence for Language Change', *Names*, 41.4, pp. 306–13.

Nicolaisen, W. F. H. (1996), *The Picts and their Place Names*, Rosemarkie: Groam House Museum.

Nicolaisen, W. F. H. (2001), *Scottish Place-Names: Their Study and Significance*, Edinburgh: John Donald.

Niven, L. (2002), *Scots: The Scots Language in Education*, AB Ljouwert/Leewarden: Mercator-Education [www.mercator-education.org].

Niven, L. and R. Jackson (eds) (1998), *The Scots Language: Its Place in Education*, Dundee: Northern College.

Norlin Airland Commeission o Fowkrichts (2001), *Makkin a Leit o Richts for Norlin Airland*, Belfast.

Nurmi, A. (1999), *A social history of periphrastic DO* (Mémoires de la Société Néophilologique de Helsinki, 56), Helsinki: Société Néophilologique.

Ó Maolalaigh, R. (1998), 'Place-names as a resource for the historical linguist', in S. Taylor (ed.), *The Uses of Place-Names*, Edinburgh: Scottish Cultural Press, pp. 12–53.

Onions, C. T. et al. (eds) (1966), *The Oxford Dictionary of English Etymology*, Oxford: Clarendon Press.

Orkin, M. (1973), *Canajun, eh?*, Don Mills: General.

O'Rourke, D. (ed.) (1994), *Dream State: The New Scottish Poets*, 2nd edn (2002), Edinburgh: Polygon.

Palander-Collin, M. (1999), *Grammaticalization and social embedding: 'I think' and 'methinks' in Middle and Early Modern English* (Mémoires de la Société néophilologique, 55), Helsinki: Société Néophilologique.

Parsley, I. (2001), 'Ulster-Scots: Politicisation or Survival?', in Kirk and Ó Baoill (eds) (2001b), pp. 177–80.

Parsons, D. and C. Hough, with T. Styles (1997–), *The Vocabulary of English Place-Names*, Nottingham: Centre for English Name Studies.

Partridge, E. (ed.) (1950), *Dictionary of the Underworld*, London: Routledge.

Partridge, E. (1966), *Origins: An Etymological Dictionary of Modern English*, 4th edn, London: Routledge.

Partridge, E. (ed.) (1984), *A Dictionary of Slang and Unconventional English*, 8th edn, rev. Paul Beale, London: Routledge.

Patterson, W. (1880), *A Glossary of Words in Use in the Counties of Antrim and Down*, London: English Dialect Society.

Perceval-Maxwell, M. (1973), *The Scottish Migration to Ulster in the Reign of James I*, London: Routledge and Kegan Paul. Reprinted 1990 by Ulster Historical Foundation, Belfast.

'Petition and Remonstrance to the President and Congress of the United States [Written by a North Carolina Planter]', (c.1794 [1927]), in W. K. Boyd, *Some Eighteenth-Century Tracts Concerning North Carolina, with introductions and notes*, Raleigh: Edwards and Broughton, pp. 489–503.

Philp, G. (1997), 'Introduction' to *Scorn, My Inheritance* by William Graham, Glasgow: Scotsoun.

Pollner, C. (1985a), *Englisch in Livingston. Ausgewälte sprachliche Erscheinungen in einer schottischen New Town*, Frankfurt: Peter Lang.

Pollner, C. (1985b), 'Old words in a young town', *Scottish Language*, 4, pp. 5–15.

Postles, D. (2001), 'Defining the "North": some linguistic evidence', *Northern History*, 38, pp. 27–46.

Pratt, T. K. (ed.) (1988), *Dictionary of Prince Edward Island English*, Toronto: University of Toronto Press.

Pringle, I. and E. Padolsky (1981), 'The Irish heritage of the English of the Ottawa Valley', *English Studies in Canada*, 7, pp. 338–53.

Pringle, I. and E. Padolsky (1983), 'The linguistic survey of the Ottawa Valley', *American Speech*, 58, pp. 325–44.

Purves, D. (1979), 'A Scots Orthography', *Scottish Literary Journal*, Supplement 9, pp. 61–76.

Purves, D. (1997a; revised and expanded 2002), *A Scots Grammar: Scots Grammar and Usage*, Edinburgh: Saltire Society.

Purves, D. (1997b), *The Way Forward for the Scots Language*, Forward Series: Paper no. 4. Peterhead: Scottish Centre for Economic and Social Research.

Reaney, P. H. (1997), *A Dictionary of English Surnames*, revised 3rd edn with corrections and additions by R. M. Wilson, Oxford: Oxford University Press.

Redmonds, G. (1997), *Surnames and Genealogy: A New Approach*, Boston: New England Historic Genealogical Society.

Reed, C. (1953), 'English archaisms in Pennsylvania German', *Publication of the American Dialect Society*, 19, pp. 3–7.

Registrar General for Scotland (1991), *Personal Names in Scotland*, Edinburgh: General Register Office [www.gro-scotland.gov.uk].

Rennie, S. and M. Fitt (2000), *Grammar Broonie*, Edinburgh: Polygon.

Riach, W. A. D. (1979–82), 'A dialect study of comparative areas in Galloway', *Scottish Literary Journal*, Supplement 9, pp. 1–16; Supplement 12, pp. 43–60; and *Scottish Language*, 1, pp. 13–22.

Riach, W. A. D. (1984), 'Galloway schools dialect survey', *Scottish Language*, 3, pp. 49–59.

Rissanen, M., M. Kytö and K. Heikkonen (eds) (1997a), *Grammaticalization at work: studies of long-term developments in English* (Topics in English Linguistics, 24), Berlin: Mouton de Gruyter.

Rissanen, M., M. Kytö and K. Heikkonen (eds) (1997b), *English in Transition: Corpus-based studies in linguistic variation and genre styles*, Berlin and New York: Mouton de Gruyter.

Robertson, R. et al. (1996a), *The Kist/A' Chiste*, Edinburgh: Scottish Consultative Council on the Curriculum/Nelson Blackie.

Robertson, R. et al. (1996b), *The Kist/A' Chiste: Teacher's Handbook (The Shottle)*, Edinburgh: Scottish Consultative Council on the Curriculum/Nelson Blackie.

Robertson, T. A. and J. J. Graham (1991), *Grammar and Usage of the Shetland Dialect* (reprint of 1952 edn with added introduction), Lerwick: The Shetland Times

Robinson, C. and C. A. Crawford (2001), *Scotspeak: A Guide to the Pronunciation of Modern Urban Scots*, Perth: Scots Language Resource Centre.

Robinson, M. (ed.-in-chief) (1985), *The Concise Scots Dictionary*, Aberdeen: Aberdeen University Press. Now published Edinburgh: Polygon.

Robinson, M. (1987), 'CSD as a tool for linguistic research', in C. I. Macafee and I. Macleod (eds), *The Nuttis Schell: Essays on the Scots Language presented to A. J. Aitken*, Aberdeen: Aberdeen University Press, pp. 59–72.

Robinson, P. (1984), *The Plantation of Ulster*, Dublin: Gill and Macmillan.

Robinson, P. (1989), 'The Scots language in seventeenth-century Ulster', *Ulster Folklife*, 35, pp. 86–99.

Robinson, P. (1997), *Ulster-Scots: A Grammar of the Traditional Written and Spoken Language*, Newtownards: The Ullans Press.

Robson, L. L. (1965), *The Convict Settlers of Australia*, Melbourne: Melbourne University Press.

Rogers, C. D. (1995), *The Surname Detective: Investigating Surname Distribution in England, 1086–Present Day*, Manchester: Manchester University Press.

Romaine, S. (1975), 'Linguistic variability in the speech of some Edinburgh schoolchildren', University of Edinburgh: unpublished MLitt dissertation.

Romaine, S. (1978), 'Postvocalic /r/ in Scottish English: Sound change in progress?', in P. Trudgill (ed.), *Sociolinguistic Patterns in British English*, London: Arnold, pp. 144–57.

Romaine, S. (1982), *Socio-Historical Linguistics, Its Status and Methodology* (Cambridge Studies in Linguistics, 34), Cambridge: Cambridge University Press.

Saadi, S. (2001), *The Burning Mirror*, Edinburgh: Polygon.

Scobbie, J., N. Hewlett and A. Turk (1999a), 'Standard English in Edinburgh and Glasgow: The Scottish Vowel Length Rule revealed', in Foulkes and Docherty (eds), pp. 230–45.

Scobbie, J., A. Turk and N. Hewlett (1999b), 'Morphemes, Phonetics, and Lexical Items:

The case of the Scottish Vowel Length Rule', *Proceedings of the International Congress of Phonetic Sciences*, San Francisco, pp. 1617–20.

Scottish Qualifications Authority (1999a), *English and Communication: National Course Specifications, Intermediate 1*, 3rd edn, Dalkeith and Glasgow: SQA [www.sqa.org.uk].

Scottish Qualifications Authority (1999b), *English and Communication: National Course Specifications, Intermediate 2*, 3rd edn, Dalkeith and Glasgow: SQA [www.sqa.org.uk].

Scottish Qualifications Authority (1999c), *English and Communication: National Course Specifications, Higher*, 4th edn, Dalkeith and Glasgow: SQA [www.sqa.org.uk].

Scottish Qualifications Authority (2000), *English and Communication: National Course Specifications, Advanced Higher*, 2nd edn, Dalkeith and Glasgow: SQA [www.sqa.org.uk].

Shaw, J. (1997), 'Gaelic and Cape Breton English', in H. L. C. Tristram (ed.), *The Celtic Englishes*, Heidelberg, pp. 308–19.

Shoemaker, H. (1930), *Thirteen Hundred Old Time Words of British, Continental or Aboriginal Origins, Still or Recently in Use among the Pennsylvania Mountain People*, Altoona: Times Tribune.

Simpson, J. A. and E. S. C. Weiner (eds) (1989), *Oxford English Dictionary*, 2nd edn, Oxford: Clarendon Press.

Smith, A. H. (1956), *English Place-Name Elements*, Parts I & II, English Place-Name Society, vols 25 and 26, Cambridge: Cambridge University Press.

Smith, J. J. (2000), 'Semantics and Metrical Form in *Sir Gawain and the Green Knight*', in S. Powell and J. J. Smith (eds), *New Perspectives on Middle English Texts*, Cambridge: Brewer, pp. 87–103.

Speitel, H. H. (1969), 'An areal typology of isoglosses near the Scottish-English Border', *Zeitschrift für Dialektologie und Linguistik*, 36, pp. 49–66.

Speitel, H. H. (1978), 'The word geography of the Borders', *Scottish Literary Journal*, Supplement 6, pp. 17–37.

Speitel, H. H. and P. A. Johnston, *Sociolinguistic investigation of Edinburgh speech*, Final Report to the ESRC (grant no. 000230023).

Spietel, H. H. and J. Y. Mather (1968), 'Schottische Dialektologie' in L. E. Schmidt (ed.), *Germanische Dialektologie: Festschrift für Walter Mitzka*, Wiesbaden: Franz Steiner, pp. 520–41.

Spittal, J. and J. Field (1990), *A Reader's Guide to the Place-Names of the United Kingdom*, Stamford: Paul Watkins.

Sprott, G. (1996), *Robert Burns: Pride and Passion: The Life, Times and Legacy*, Edinburgh: HMSO.

Stirling, A. (1994), 'On a Standardised Spelling for Scots', *Scottish Language*, 13, pp. 88–93.

Stuart-Smith, J. (1999a), 'Glasgow: Accent and voice quality', in Foulkes and Docherty (eds), pp. 203–22.

Stuart-Smith, J. (1999b), 'Glottals past and present: A study of T-glottalling in Glaswegian', *Leeds Studies in English*, 30, pp. 181–204.

Stuart-Smith, J. and F. Tweedie (2000), *Accent change in Glaswegian: A sociophonetic investigation*, Final Report to the Leverhulme Trust (Grant no. F/179/AX).

Taavitsainen, I. (1997a), 'Genres and text types in medieval and renaissance English', *Poetica: An International Journal of Linguistic and Literary Studies*, vol. 47, pp. 49–62.

Taavitsainen, I. (1997b), 'Genre conventions: Personal affect in fiction and non-fiction in Early Modern English', in Rissanen et al. (eds) (1997b), pp. 185–266.

Taavitsainen, I., T. Nevalainen, P. Pahta and M. Rissanen (eds) (2000), *Placing Middle*

English in Context (Topics in English Linguistics, 35), Berlin and New York: Mouton de Gruyter.

Taavitsainen, I. and P. Pahta (1997), 'The Corpus of Early English Medical Writing', *ICAME Journal*, vol. 21, pp. 71–8.

Tagliamonte, S. and J. Smith (2000), 'Old *was*, new ecology: Viewing English through the sociolinguistic filter', in S. Poplack (ed.), *The English History of African-American English*, Boston: Blackwell, pp. 141–71.

Taylor, S. (1994), 'Some early Scottish place-names and Queen Margaret', *Scottish Language*, 13, pp. 1–17.

Taylor, S. (1997), 'Generic-element variation, with special reference to eastern Scotland', *Nomina*, XX, pp. 5–22.

Taylor, S. (ed.) (1998), *The Uses of Place-Names*, Edinburgh: Scottish Cultural Press.

Thun, N. (1963), 'Reduplicative Words in English. A Study of Formations of the Types *Tick-tick, Hurly-burly* and *Shilly-shally*', University of Uppsala: unpublished PhD dissertation.

Tieken-Boon van Ostade, I. (1987), *The auxiliary* do *in eighteenth-century English: A sociohistorical-linguistic approach*, Dordrecht: Foris.

Tieken-Boon van Ostade, I. (1994), 'Standard and non-standard pronominal usage in English, with special reference to the eighteenth century', in D. Stein and I. Tieken-Boon van Ostade (eds), *Towards a Standard English, 1600–1800* (Topics in English Linguistics, 12), Berlin: Mouton de Gruyter, pp. 217–42.

Todd, L. (1971), 'Tyrone English', *Yorkshire Dialect Society Transactions*, 13, pp. 29–40.

Trask, R. L. (1997), *The History of Basque*, London: Routledge.

Traugott, E. C. and B. Heine (eds) (1991), *Approaches to Grammaticalization, vol. 1: Focus on theoretical and methodological issues* (Typological Studies in Language, 19), Amsterdam and Philadelphia: John Benjamins.

Trudgill P. (ed.) (1984), *Language in the British Isles*, Cambridge: Cambridge University Press.

Trudgill, P., M. Maclagan and G. Lewis (forthcoming), 'Linguistic archaeology: The Scottish input to New Zealand phonology', *Journal of English Linguistics*.

Tsiona, I. (1997), 'Linguistic Variation in the Speech of Greek Immigrants in Grampian, Scotland', University of Aberdeen: unpublished MLitt dissertation.

Tucker, R. W. (1934), 'Linguistic substrata in Pennsylvania and elsewhere', *Language*, 10, pp. 1–4.

Tulloch, G. (1989), *A History of The Scots Bible*, Aberdeen: Aberdeen University Press.

Tulloch, G. (1997a), 'Lexis', in C. Jones (ed.), pp. 378–432.

Tulloch, G. (1997b), 'The Scots language in Australia', in C. Jones (ed.), pp. 623–36.

Tulloch, G. (1997c), 'Scots as a literary language in Australia', in E. W. Schneider (ed.), *Englishes around the World: Studies in Honour of Manfred Görlach, volume 2: Carribean, Africa, Asia, Australasia*, Amsterdam and Philadelphia: John Benjamins, pp. 319–34.

van Buuren, C. (ed.) (1982), *The Buke of the Sevyne Sagis: A Middle Scots Version of the Seven Sages of Rome. Edited from the Asloan Manuscript (NLS Acc.4233), c.1515*, Leiden University Press.

van Buuren, C. (ed.) (1997), *The Buke of the Chess*, Edinburgh: Scottish Text Society.

Vennemann, T. (1994), 'Linguistic reconstruction in the context of European prehistory', *Transactions of the Philological Society*, 92: 2, pp. 215–284.

Watson, W. J. (1926), *The History of the Celtic Place-Names of Scotland*, Edinburgh: Blackwood; repr. (1993), Edinburgh: Birlinn.

Wells, J. (1982), *Accents of English*, 3 vols, Cambridge: Cambridge University Press.

Wentworth, H. (ed.) (1944), *American Dialect Dictionary*, New York: Crowell.

Weinert, R. and J. Miller (1995), 'Clefts in Spoken Discourse', *Journal of Pragmatics*, 25, pp. 173–202.

Weinreich, U. (1964), *Languages in Contact: findings and problems*, The Hague: Mouton.

Wettstein, P. (1942), *The Phonology of a Berwickshire Dialect*, Zurich: Bienne.

Wickens, B. (1980–1), 'Caithness speech', *Scottish Literary Journal*, Supplement 12, pp. 61–76 and Supplement 14, pp. 25–36.

Williamson, K. (1982/3), 'Lowland Scots in Education: An Historical Survey', *Scottish Language*, no. 1, pp. 54–77, and no. 2, pp. 52–87.

Williamson, K. (1992/93), 'A computer-aided method for making a Linguistic Atlas of Older Scots', *Scottish Language*, vol. 11/12, pp. 138–73.

Williamson, K. (2000), 'Changing spaces: Linguistic relationships and the dialect continuum', in I. Taavitsainen et al. (eds), pp. 141–79.

Williamson, K. (2002), 'The dialectology of "English" north of the Humber, c.1380–1500', in T. Fanego et al. (eds) *Sounds, Words, Texts and Change*, Amsterdam: John Benjamins, pp. 253–86.

Williamson, M. G. (1941), 'The Non-Celtic Place-Names of the Scottish Border Counties', University of Edinburgh: unpublished PhD dissertation.

Wilson, J. (1915), *Lowland Scotch, as Spoken in the Lower Strathearn District of Perthshire*, London: Oxford University Press.

Wilson, J. (1923), *The Dialect of Robert Burns as Spoken in Central Ayrshire*, Oxford: Oxford University Press.

Wilson, J. (1926), *The Dialects of Central Scotland*, Oxford: Oxford University Press.

Wokeck, M. S. (1999), *Trade in Strangers: The Beginnings of Mass Migration to North America*, University Park: Pennsylvania State University Press.

Wood, I. S. (1994), *Scotland and Ulster*, Edinburgh: Mercat.

Woods, A. (1986), *Statistics in language studies* (Cambridge Textbooks in Linguistics), Cambridge: Cambridge University Press.

Wright, J. (ed.) (1898–1905), *The English Dialect Dictionary*, 6 vols, Oxford: Oxford University Press.

Young, D. (1958), *'Plastic Scots' and the Scottish Literary Tradition*, Glasgow: William McLellan.

Youngson, M. (1992), 'A Plea for Respite from the "Aiblins" School', in *Chapman*, 69/70, pp. 91–2.

Index